'MATERIAL DELIGHT AND THE JOY OF LIVING'

'Material Delight and the Joy of Living'

Cultural Consumption in the Age of Enlightenment in Germany

MICHAEL NORTH

Ernst Moritz Arndt University Greifswald, Germany

Translated by Pamela Selwyn

ASHGATE

First published in German as *Genuss und Glück des Lebens: Kulturkonsum im Zeitalter der Aufklärung*.
German edition © Böhlau Verlag GmbH & Cie, Köln 2003

English edition © Ashgate Publishing Limited 2008

Published by
Ashgate Publishing Limited
Gower House
Croft Road
Aldershot
Hampshire GU11 3HR
England

Ashgate Publishing Company
Suite 420
101 Cherry Street
Burlington, VT 05401–4405
USA

Ashgate website: http://www.ashgate.com

British Library Cataloguing in Publication Data
North, Michael, 1954–
    Material delight and the joy of living : cultural consumption in the age of Enlightenment in
    Germany
    1. Consumption (Economics) – Germany – History – 18th century 2. Arts and society
    – Germany – History – 18th century 3. Enlightenment – Germany 4. Germany – Social life
    and customs – 18th century 5. Germany – Intellectual life – 18th century
    I. Title
    306.3'0943'09033

    ISBN 978–0–7546–5842–9

Library of Congress Cataloging-in-Publication Data
North, Michael, 1954–
    [Genuss und Glück des Lebens. English]
    Material delight and the joy of living : cultural consumption in the age of Enlightenment in
    Germany / Michael North ; translated by Pamela Selwyn.
        p. cm.
    Translation of: Genuss und Glück des Lebens.
    ISBN 978–0–7546–5842–9 (alk. paper)
    1. Consumption (Economics) – Germany – History – 18th century. 2. Germany – Social
    life and customs – 18th century. 3. Arts and society – Germany. 4. Germany – Intellectual
    life – 18th century. 5. Enlightenment – Germany.
    I. Title.

    HC290.5.C6N6713 2008
    306.3094'09033 –dc22   2007038992

Printed and bound in Great Britain by MPG Books Ltd, Bodmin, Cornwall.

Contents

List of Illustrations

Illustrations from the *Journal des Luxus und der Moden* and the frontispiece of
Die Vornehmsten Europäischen Reisen were supplied by the University Library of
Greifswald.

List of Tables

Foreword

The original impetus for this book came from a seminar on 'Culture and Consumption in the Age of Enlightenment' that I taught in the autumn/winter term of 1999/2000. Inspired by the lively discussions in the seminar, the students ultimately wrote a number of seminar papers and master's theses on the consumption of culture in the eighteenth century, which delved deeper into the themes of the seminar and at the same time complemented my own interests in 'art collecting and taste'. As a result, I also began to explore such areas as the history of reading, musical culture, theatre and opera with great profit and pleasure, and discovered how little attention German historians had paid thus far to the more entertaining side of the age of Enlightenment.

Because of the wide variety of themes, the book was a collective undertaking, which could not have been realised without the active assistance of a number of people. My fellow historians Georg Schmidt (Jena) and Wolfgang Weber (Augsburg) read and commented on the manuscript in detail, as did Carsten Zelle (Bochum) and Walter Werbeck (Greifswald) from the perspectives of literary studies and musicology, respectively. For that I offer my warmest thanks.

I am grateful to Ashgate, and especially to John Smedley, for their interest in the idea of an English edition, into which I was able to incorporate a number of inspirations drawn from British research on the history of consumption. I would particularly like to thank Frank Trentmann (London), who as director of the 'Cultures of Consumption' research programme brought me up to date on the latest research in the field.

If the book is as readable in English as it was in German, it is the work of my congenial translator Pamela E. Selwyn, and I would like to thank her here. A stay at the Netherlands Institute for Advanced Study (NIAS) in Wassenaar on the invitation of its rector Wim Blockmans allowed me the necessary time to revise my German manuscript for translation. The federal state of Mecklenburg-Vorpommern and the Faculty of Philosophy of the Ernst Moritz Arndt University of Greifswald generously covered the costs of the translation.

My greatest debts are to Doreen Wollbrecht, Robert Riemer, Matthias Müller, Christian Fricke and Kord-Henning Uber, who bore the brunt of work on the final production of the book with great commitment and stamina. They not only prepared the manuscript, illustrations, notes, tables and maps, but also checked quotations from eighteenth-century literature and compiled the index.

The book is dedicated to our little daughter Constanze. Her brothers had 'their books', and now she has one of her own.

Michael North, Greifswald, Autumn 2007

Note on Coins and Currency in Eighteenth-Century Germany

1 taler (reichstaler) = 24 groschen

1 guilder (fl) = 2/3 taler = 18 groschen = 60 kreuzer (kr)

1 mark banco (Hamburg) = c. 1 ½ mark courant = 1/3 taler

1 schilling banco = c. 1 ½ schilling courant = 1/16 mark banco

1 carolin (gold coin) = 8 ½ guilders

Introduction

The Eighteenth Century – An Age of Cultural Consumption

The eighteenth century has generally been considered the age of Enlightenment. According to this view, the inroads that reason made into the various areas of life and, with this, the advancement of education and scholarship in many European countries made the epoch what it was. Based on the analysis of texts, Enlightenment scholarship thus became the domain of theology, philosophy and literary studies. In addition to these approaches, sociologists have constructed a structural transformation of the public sphere, that is, a transformation of a bourgeois-literary sectoral public sphere into an emancipatory bourgeois-political general public sphere.[1]

In the light of such perspectives, which tend to reduce the public sphere to the arena of political discourse, it is not surprising that scholars of the Enlightenment have paid little attention to art and entertainment, and have thus largely ignored what Friedrich Justin Bertuch referred to as '[material] delight and the joy of living' (*Genuss und Glück des Lebens*).[2] Yet the active and passive enjoyment of culture reached a high point in the eighteenth century both at court and in the towns. No previous epoch could boast as many connoisseurs and amateurs in the various fields of art and music. Certain courts or court societies distinguished themselves by cultivating the Muses, giving precedence to the arts over other sociable activities such as hunts, military reviews, balls and gaming. Dabbling in poetry, music or drawing went hand in hand with support for court theatres, orchestras, art collections and landscape gardens. Although Duchess Anna Amalia's 'Court of the Muses' at Weimar appears to us a prime example of art connoisseurship, sociability and patronage, these phenomena were by no means limited to the courts of the Holy Roman Empire.[3]

Everywhere in Europe, people devoted themselves to the arts as both producers and consumers of the growing cultural offerings. Devotees of art, music or theatre profited from a commercialization of culture. The marketing of culture gradually became separated from its production. New cultural entrepreneurs conquered the field: theatre and opera impresarios, publishers, booksellers, art auctioneers, art print publishers, art dealers or lending libraries were just a few of these mediating figures, who came into their own in the eighteenth century, or even became protagonists of a new services sector.

Cultural supply expanded as a result of commercialization, and new opportunities for cultural consumption emerged. I would like to emphasize three aspects here:

1. The great breadth and diversity of cultural offerings: culture could be experienced directly, in theatres, concert venues or exhibitions, or indirectly through the press, in periodicals, books or prints, and it could even be ordered from a catalogue. In this way, the lines between 'high' and 'low' (popular) culture gradually blurred.

2. Relative ease of access: in the coffee house people could read the newspapers and magazines for the price of a drink, and a visit to an auction house or art dealer cost nothing. Paintings could be purchased for less than ten guilders. Entrance to pleasure gardens with musical entertainment, such as Vauxhall in London, cost only 1 shilling until 1792. Only operas and concerts were more expensive.

3. Identity formation through cultural consumption: the consumption of cultural goods transmitted social identity. Visits to the theatre, concerts or auctions served the purposes of self-presentation. Taste was a social affair, and the public became the cultural arbiters in matters of taste, or became part of a cosmopolitan elite of taste.[4]

At first, cultural consumption was concentrated in the large European centres of London, Paris, Naples, Amsterdam, Rome, Madrid, Lisbon, Vienna and Hamburg, which possessed theatres, concert halls, publishers and art dealers, and a sufficiently wealthy public. Even cities with fewer than 100,000 inhabitants, such as Edinburgh, Dublin, Stockholm, Copenhagen, Bordeaux, Barcelona, Cadiz, Seville, Frankfurt, Dresden and Leipzig, enjoyed a vibrant cultural life, however. Cultural consumption spread further over the course of the eighteenth century, reaching, for instance, the many princely residences and university towns in Germany, where a growing number of members of the functional elites *(Funktionseliten)* and educated middle classes *(Bildungsbürger)* met in coffee houses and at reading societies, attended the performances of theatre and opera companies, and played together in amateur orchestras.

All across Europe, a cultural identity emerged in which rank and nationality often receded, or various elements of different national cultures entered into a symbiosis. The desire of both enlightened aristocrats and bourgeois elites to participate in the new cultural developments was central here: 'Taste became one of the attributes of a new sort of person – the "sociable man" of Addison and Steele's *Spectator*, the *hônnete homme* of Voltaire's *Le Mondain* and the "Cosmopolitan" described by Wieland in *Der Teutsche Merkur* '.[5] The cultural consumer was educated, a connoisseur and lover of literature, music and art, and demonstrated this connoisseurship in society. As Kant put it: 'No one in complete solitude will decorate or clean his house; he will not even do it for his own people (wife and children), but only for strangers, to show himself to advantage.'[6]

Against this European backdrop, I try to analyse for the first time the elements of cultural consumption in Germany, which German historians have largely neglected until now, as well as the nascent market system for culture in the eighteenth century. Unlike John Brewer, whose *Pleasures of the Imagination* focuses on how English culture was shaped in the areas of 'print', 'paint' and 'performance',[7] I also treat such objects of consumption as travel, dress, interior decoration, gardens and stimulant beverages. I address the marketing and reception of art, music and literature too, of course, as well as the centres of cultural consumption. Processes of cultural transfer from Western Europe to the German territories also need to be reconstructed, since the new cultural commodities appeared in Germany not merely as material reality, but also as literary constructs in magazines, novels and letters. Thus, active participation in the arts was accompanied by the reception of journals and discourse among devotees of culture. For that reason, cultural historians are particularly interested in the questions of when, where and how these discourses became efficacious and influenced cultural consumption. In this context, we should also ask whether certain taste preferences can be ascribed to social groups, and whether middle-class cultural practices can be found in Germany that were distinct from those of the aristocracy, as suggested by the topos of the embourgeoisement (*Verbürgerlichung*) of art, literature and music, which is widespread in cultural studies. The role of cultural consumption in the framework of a German and European process of identity formation is one of the book's underlying concepts.

The study is also conceived as a Continental European contribution to the long-running Anglo-American debate about the emergence of consumer society and consumerism. This discussion was inspired by Neil McKendrick's thesis that a consumer revolution led to the birth of a consumer society in eighteenth-century England. McKendrick associated consumer society with nascent modernity, and at the same time with the Industrial Revolution. Its most salient characteristic was the explosion of new material goods, demanded by people (termed the 'middling sort' in recent literature) who aspired to emulate the aristocracy.[8] In the years that followed, some historians tried to shift the beginnings of consumer society geographically and temporally to the 13 American colonies, the Golden Age Netherlands or Renaissance Italy,[9] while others looked for the spread of 'modern consumerism' in the late nineteenth and twentieth centuries.[10] Here, they found themselves in the company of those neo-liberal economists of the 1960s who posited a connection between the western/American society of high mass consumption and western economic growth and industrialization.[11] This lent a rather teleological air to studies of the history of consumption.[12] This circumstance, and also the tendency to equate consumer society with modernity without thinking it through, has brought the notion of the consumer revolution under fire in recent years.[13] Scholars have begun to confront the results of research on north-western Europe with what we have learnt about non-European societies, such as China, which were characterized in the seventeenth and eighteenth centuries by a high consumption of material goods as well as sugar and tea among broad segments of the population.[14] Critics have also pointed to the absence of an analysis of the relationship between consumption and production, a challenge taken up by Maxine Berg in her book *Luxury and Pleasure in Eighteenth-Century Britain*, which focuses on new consumer products.[15] Frank Trentmann and the 'Cultures of Consumption' research programme, in particular, have asked when and how the consumer arose, and enquired into when consumer identity or even consumer self-awareness began to emerge.[16]

Even if self-aware consumers did not articulate themselves as such in either Germany or Britain, the present study shows, using a wealth of regional examples from the various spheres of cultural consumption, that both cultural consumption and its protagonists were socially constructed. The social, cultural, regional and national sites of consumption were also correspondingly diverse. Taking up demands that we contextualize the forms and functions of consumption, this insight may perhaps make a contribution to the debates of the twentieth and twenty-first centuries.[17]

Chapter 1

Books and Reading

I read … Swift and leafed through … the *Göttingische Anzeigen*. I would have liked to read more of Swift, but feared that I might become too accustomed to such reading matter.[1]

Today I had intended to work fiercely, but frittered away the morning again. I began reading Shandy early, and fell rather into lazing about once more.[2]

During my coiffure I read in Moore and felt rather merry, but afterwards was a bit downhearted, when I leafed through Whylt [sic]. Today I noticed once again, as I have so often before, although one might swear I had never noticed it at all, how greatly this sort of reading harms me.[3]

This was how the author Johann Anton Leisewitz, secretary to the Brunswick provincial diet (*Landschaftssekretär*), and one of the bookworms of the eighteenth century, commented on his own reading habits. Every day he documented not just what he read, but also his guilty conscience, since reading, much like watching television today, kept him from doing other things. Leisewitz read German and English philosophical and moral texts, but also Latin classics and above all the fashionable English literature of his day: Jonathan Swift, John Moore's travel accounts, Oliver Goldsmith's *Vicar of Wakefield*, Henry Fielding's *Tom Jones*, John Gay's *Beggars' Opera*, James Thomson's *The Seasons* and Laurence Sterne's *Life and Opinions of Tristram Shandy*. He also read John Locke's *On Civil Government*, David Hume's *History of England* and Robert Whytt's *Sämmtliche zur praktischen Arzneykunst gehör. Schriften* (The Works of Robert Whytt, MD, a translation from the English, published in Leipzig in 1771). He read Goethe's *Sorrows of Young Werther* together with his wife, who recited to him from the novel. According to the reading list he compiled, by 1779 Leisewitz had studied 40 books, leafed through another five works 'reading them almost completely', started to read nine books, and continually consulted eight larger compendia, copying out excerpts from them.[4]

Although the learned world may always have included encyclopaedic readers, the obsessive readers who devoured nearly everything they could get their hands on were a phenomenon of the eighteenth century. Rolf Engelsing coined the term 'reading revolution' to characterize the change from the traditional manner of reading, in which people largely read the same works intensively and repeatedly, to a modern form of extensive reading.[5] Although this style of reading now belongs to the past, and disparate reading practices coexisted even in the eighteenth century, with wide geographical and social variations, it was a time when reading attained a new importance for many people.[6] Reading became a leisure activity that, unlike the theatre, opera and concerts, one could pursue at home whenever one liked. A literary market developed that exploded the traditional forms of book production. New media, new modes of distribution and new reading institutions arose to meet the demands of readers and at the same time facilitated a genuine reading revolution. In what follows, we shall accordingly examine the media, book production and the book trade, book ownership and reading preferences.

Media

The increasing complexity of the media landscape was typical of the eighteenth century. Not only did the book open itself up to new topics and new strata of readers, but a wealth of new genres also emerged in the periodical press. In addition to calendars and almanacs, which for the first time reached those with little reading experience, journals were published in all fields of scholarship and knowledge. Travel, art, literature, fashion, music, theatre and theology were but a few of the topics to which the often short-lived magazines – frequently targeting a female readership – were dedicated. The intelligence gazette (*Intelligenzblatt*) was another particular genre.[7] Originally intended as an advertising paper, it developed into a medium for the economic-utilitarian enlightenment and even a forum for the discussion of the same moral and ethical questions that had been the focus of the moral weeklies in the first half of the eighteenth century. According to contemporary estimates, the most famous of these moral weeklies, the Hamburg *Patriot*, had already attained a circulation of up to 5,000 copies by the 1720s.[8]

In the second half of the century, few journals exceeded such print runs. Thus, Friedrich Schiller's *Historischer Calender für Damen* (Historical Calendar for Ladies) had up to 10,000 subscribers in some years, and Christian Martin Wieland's *Teutscher Merkur* (German Mercury) as well as Friedrich Nicolai's *Allgemeine Deutsche Bibliothek* (Universal German Library) had 2,500 subscribers each. The number of subscriptions to Friedrich Justin Bertuch's *Journal des Luxus und der Moden* (Journal of Luxury and Fashion) was comparably high (c. 1,500), while for the average periodical, a print run of between 500 and 750 may be considered substantial, since many were forced to make do with fewer than 300 paying readers. As a consequence, many new magazines did not survive their first year, and a few managed more than four years of publication, evidence of continuing demand by their readership. The long-lived journals accordingly surpassed their less successful rivals in the quality of printing and provision of copperplate illustrations.

We should also mention the incredible boom in the daily newspapers, which reached more than one million readers around 1750. Political events such as the Seven Years' War, the American independence movement or the French Revolution seemed to increase newspaper consumption to unheard-of proportions, so that top publications such as the *Hamburgische unpartheyische Correspondent* (Hamburg Impartial Correspondent) reached editions of up to 30,000 at the end of the eighteenth century. At this period, approximately 200 newspapers with an average print run of 300 reached some three million readers in Germany every week.[9]

Not only publishers profited from the expanding literary market; a growing number of authors benefited as well. It is estimated that the number of published writers increased from 2,000–3,000 in 1755 to c. 10,000 in 1800.[10] Even if the more prominent among them often held official positions – Gotthold Ephraim Lessing as ducal librarian, Friedrich Gottlieb Klopstock on a stipend from the Danish king, Wieland as a princely tutor, Goethe as a minister, Schiller as a professor of history – an increasing number of individuals took the risk of making a living as freelance writers.[11] Often, economic hardship drove them to sell their services in the literary marketplace. Thus Sophie von La Roche justified her editorship of the first German women's magazine, *Pomona* (1783), by explaining that she had to support her sons Carl and Wilhelm after her husband's dismissal from his post in Trier.[12]

Another example is Christian August Vulpius, brother of Goethe's future wife Christiane. While still at university, he had collaborated on Johann Friedrich Reichardt's *Bibliothek der Romane* (Library of Novels) in 1783 and the journal *Olla Potrida* (the name of a kind of Spanish soup) in 1784. At the same time he published his *Abenteuer des Ritters Palmendo* (Adventures of the Knight Palmendo), which might be seen as a rehearsal for his famous later novel *Rinaldo Rinaldini*. With the help of his future brother-in-law, Vulpius gradually began to make a living from his writing. From 1792, he worked on a freelance basis for Goethe's court theatre in Weimar, where he adapted plays and translated and wrote new dialogues for operas by Carl Ditters von Dittersdorf and Mozart. His earnings remained paltry, since an adaptation brought in only 1–3 taler and an opera text only 13 taler. Only when he gained a position as library registrar, and was later promoted to library secretary (in 1800) and librarian (in 1805) did his financial situation improve.[13] His tale of the brigand captain, *Rinaldo Rinaldini*, however, became one of the most widely read popular novels of the nineteenth century. Precisely because he did not fit into the aesthetic programme of Goethe and Schiller, Vulpius far surpassed the authors of Classicism in capturing the hearts of his readers. Literary history, however, has rarely paid much attention to authors of the reading revolution such as Vulpius.[14] Even the most important source of information about book production, the book fair catalogues, provides an incomplete picture of the publication of popular literature.

Book production

The book fair catalogues are a key source for the history of eighteenth-century book production. These lists of newly published works recorded the books traded at the Leipzig and Frankfurt fairs, and thus the greater portion of books produced in the German-speaking region. Even if the book fair catalogues have lacunae in that they do not record those works published between the fairs, scholars repeatedly cite them to estimate developments in book production and to reconstruct the shifting weight of different fields of literature as a percentage of production. Estimates of book production vary. Thus, the Leipzig book fair catalogue lists c. 980 titles for 1700 and 4,000 a century later. This would mean an annual production of 1,000 titles in the German-speaking region in the early decades of the eighteenth century. Other estimates arrive at 175,000 titles between 1700 and 1800, yielding an annual production of 1,750 titles. An analysis of the Leipzig book fair catalogues shows an increase in the number of new titles (see Table 1.1).[15]

Table 1.1   Number of new titles according to the Leipzig Book Fair Catalogue, 1700–1800

Year	Number of works
1700	978
1710	1,368
1720	979
1730	993
1740	1,326
1750	1,296
1760	1,198
1770	1,807
1780	2,642
1790	3,560
1800	4,012

The great expansion occurred in the years between 1760 and 1770; after that, book production would increase steadily. In the 1780s and 1790s, contemporaries spoke of 5,000 new titles a year. Such estimates are confirmed by the book trade journal *Magazin des Buch- und Kunsthandels* (Magazine for Booksellers and Art Dealers). According to book historian Reinhard Wittmann, announcements of new periodicals and books appearing in Germany between the Frankfurt and Leipzig fairs that did not make it into the book fair catalogues amounted to a total of 7,846 titles between 1780 and 1782, while the book fair catalogues list 8,354 titles for those years.[16] A total production of 15,000 titles during those three years, or an annual production of 5,000 titles, thus appears quite realistic.[17]

More significant than the absolute numbers of new titles is the information that the book fair catalogues provide about the subject matter of books and how it changed relatively over time. Rudolf Jentzsch's findings based on the

Leipzig Easter fair catalogues of 1740, 1770 and 1800 are still worth consulting here (see Table 1.2).[18]

Table 1.2   New titles by subject, 1740–1800

Subject area	Number of titles			Percentage of total production		
	1740	1770	1800	1740	1770	1800
Theology	291	280	348	38.5	24.5	13.6
Jurisprudence	97	61	129	12.9	5.3	5.0
History/ geography	85	110	272	11.3	9.6	10.6
Medicine	50	91	209	6.6	8.0	8.1
Philosophy	44	34	94	5.8	3.0	3.7
Fine arts and belles-lettres	44	188	551	5.8	16.4	21.5
General learning	40	52	37	5.3	4.5	1.4
Popular moral writings	25	39	119	3.3	3.4	4.6
Mathematics/ natural science	25	71	183	3.3	6.2	7.1
Classical philology	18	35	78	2.4	3.1	3.0
Political science	10	32	93	1.3	2.8	3.6
Agriculture, the trades, etc.	8	60	221	1.1	5.2	8.6
Practical manuals	7	16	53	0.9	1.4	2.1
Non-classical philology	5	16	28	0.7	1.4	1.1
Education and child-rearing	4	20	105	0.5	1.8	4.1
Popular periodicals	2	39	49	0.3	3.4	1.9
Total	**755**	**1,144**	**2,569**	**100**	**100**	**100**

In interpreting Jentzsch's data[19] and without going into detail here, let us note that in almost all subject areas, the number of books published increased markedly from one survey year to the next.[20] What changed were the relative proportions of the various areas as parts of the whole. The proportion of philology, philosophy and history/geography remained constant, while that of theology, jurisprudence and general learning (*allgemeine Gelehrsamkeit*) fell. The areas with dynamic but widely varying rates of growth were primarily the fine arts and belles-lettres as well, at some remove, as mathematics, natural sciences, agriculture, the trades, education and child-rearing and popular periodicals. In 1740, the book market was still largely orientated towards learned readers, whose demand was for works of theology, jurisprudence and general learning. After 1770, these areas were increasingly displaced by the fine arts and belles-lettres, and the natural and practical sciences. This shift was accompanied by a decline in literature written in Latin, which in 1740 had still represented 28 per cent of the registered titles. By 1770, only 14 per cent of titles appeared in Latin; that is, 86 per cent of newly published books were in German. In 1800, Latin made up only a scant 4 per cent of published titles.

If we examine the dynamic genre of 'fine arts and belles-lettres', its composition provides some interesting insights into developments on the literary market. Especially striking is the rise in the number of novels in the period in question, which together with the rubric 'literary works' (*Dichtung*) exhibits the strongest changes. Thus, in 1800, the Easter book fair catalogue records 300 new novels, 64 plays and 34 volumes of poetry. In 1740, it had listed only 20 novels, two plays and 10 volumes of verse. Novels were published mainly in northern Germany, including Leipzig, while southern Germany played a more important role in the publication of drama. This suggests that novel-reading was more widespread in the north, but may also have resulted from the more aggressive marketing strategies of north German booksellers and publishers, who succeeded in gaining a larger market share for their products.

The book trade

The book trade also underwent fundamental changes in the eighteenth century, most particularly the transition from a barter system (known as *Changehandel*) to cash exchange. The barter system meant that most booksellers (who at the time were generally publishers as well) paid for books in kind, that is, with other books. They also sold other products of the printing press such as pamphlets, calendars and prayer books (so-called *Kontant-Artikel*) for cash. The barter system offered a number of practical advantages for the sixteenth- and seventeenth-century book trade. It lowered the need for ready cash as well as for investment capital, and circumvented the financial losses and complications arising from currency exchange. At the same time, it allowed booksellers to settle their debts without money, by exchanging a few printed sheets. The printed word did not yet possess a material value of its own; all that counted was the printed sheet of paper, which was traded at the uniform price of 1 penny per sheet, no matter what its content. Given the high costs of printing and paper, authors' fees were still a negligible factor. As a consequence, the booksellers who went to the Leipzig and Frankfurt book fairs traded their printed sheets 1:1. As a rule, bookseller–publishers took four to six copies of their business partners' new products, and in some cases more, which they then traded with other booksellers. Two factors ensured that the system worked: tight networks among the many booksellers in university towns, capital cities and trading centres, and a relative homogeneity of the learned reading public.

As the demand for lighter reading matter grew over the eighteenth century, increasing disparities arose between the northern and southern German books traded at the book fairs, and the old barter system broke down. Philipp Erasmus Reich, co-owner of Weidmann's publishing house, set the process in motion. He had begun to pay many of his authors higher fees, which led him to insist that other booksellers order from him directly and settle their accounts semi-annually and in cash. Reich's model of fixed cash prices caught on. Because of their investments, bookseller–publishers who sold on this basis had to orientate themselves more towards the market, that is, public tastes. For this reason, Reich increasingly published translations of foreign authors and sought to bind attractive authors such as Wieland to his publishing company.[21]

In southern Germany, where members of the book trade were not yet ready to bow to the dictates of the new cash system, in addition to the persistence of barter, local bookseller–publishers also made use of Leipzig commissionaires to distribute their books. The system that still exists today, of receiving books on commission, also arose as a compromise between the direct cash trade and the use of Leipzig agents. In this case, publishers regularly sent their new titles to colleagues at a 30 per cent discount. If recipients could not sell the books within a certain period, they could return them. Only afterwards did they settle their accounts. This offered publishers a large distribution network for their new products, while booksellers now received a larger assortment of books from different publishers, without having to bind their capital immediately and for longer periods. Nevertheless, the division of labour between publishers and booksellers was not yet practised everywhere, and many transitional forms of both occupations existed well into the nineteenth century.

Thus publishers and authors profited differently from the growing book market, depending on their locations. A few examples will serve to illustrate this. Alongside Reich and his south German adversaries Franz Varrentrapp and Thomas Edler von Trattner, the Berliner Christoph Friedrich Nicolai was certainly the most important publisher of the Enlightenment. Well prepared by an apprenticeship in the book trade, Nicolai grasped the opinion-shaping opportunities of his time when the sudden death of his elder brother forced him to take over the family firm in 1758. Thus in the 12-volume account of his 1781 journey through Germany, the 'propagandist of the Enlightenment' offered an unrelenting critique of the conditions he observed everywhere. His reports, packed into the genre of the travel account, reflect the Protestant north German Enlightenment's feelings of superiority towards Catholic southern Germany, and have continued to influence scholars of the Enlightenment to this day.[22]

As a novelist, Nicolai deployed satire as a means of enlightenment. Thus, his three-volume novel, *The Life and Opinions of Magister Sebaldus Nothanker*, which reached an edition of 12,000 in four printings, also addressed the situation in the book trade:

> Not a few booksellers commission their authors to write whatever they believe will sell: history, novels, tales of murder, reliable accounts of things they have not seen, demonstrations of things they do not believe, and thoughts on matters they do not understand. For such books publishers do not need authors with a name, but rather those who work by the yard. I know of one who has ten or twelve authors sitting at a long table in his house, each paid a daily wage to write so many lines. I do not deny it – for why should I be ashamed of poverty? – I, too, have sat at that long table.[23]

Nicolai did not just criticize conditions, however, he also analysed the causes of this development:

> This learned tribe of teachers and learners, some 20,000 strong, so heartily disdain the other twenty million people who also speak German that they do not take the trouble to write for them … . The twenty million unlearned repay the disdain of the learned by ignoring them: They scarcely know that the learned exist. And because no learned man wishes to write for the unlearned, and yet the unlearned world has just as much need of reading matter as the learned one, the task of writing for the unlearned ultimately falls to the authors of *Inseln Felsenburg*, collections of homilies and the moral weeklies, whose abilities correspond more closely to those of the readers who have chosen them than the abilities of the greatest scholars do to those of their readers, and who are therefore far more widely read than the great geniuses, but who also do not raise their readers up even an inch, and indeed often contribute not a little to ensuring that the light of the truly learned does not spread to the unlearned. That is why some of our cities are so brightly illuminated, while entire lands remain in the deepest darkness.[24]

What was needed, in his view, was for the learned to disseminate their knowledge among the heretofore unlearned. Accordingly, his publishing programme as it was documented for 1787 focused more on pedagogical works and textbooks as well as scholarly literature than on belles-lettres. Of still greater importance, however, were the journals that Nicolai published, including the *Briefe, die neueste Literatur betreffend* (Letters on the Most Recent Literature, 1759–65), on which Lessing, Moses Mendelssohn and later Thomas Abbt collaborated. His best-known periodical, however, was his other review organ, the *Allgemeine Deutsche Bibliothek*. Conceived on the model of the English *Monthly Review*, this journal took on the task of introducing all new German titles to the learned world. In the 40 years of its existence (1765–1805), the journal is said to have printed reviews of 80,000 books. It reached a relatively large audience, and in its heyday sold 2,000 copies and more (2,548 in the peak year, 1777). In the 1790s, sales fell (much like the *Teutsche Merkur* (German Mercury), whose sales fell by half between 1774 and 1796, from 2,000 to 1,000 copies).[25] As long as it was selling more than 1,000 copies per issue, however, the *Allgemeine Deutsche Bibliothek* remained a profitable enterprise, earning Nicolai several thousand taler a year.

Not quite as successful financially was Georg Joachim Göschen, who went into business as manager and commissioning editor of the Gelehrtenbuchhandlung in Dessau and tried to position himself in the market as the publisher of the

Weimar authors. Thus, in the 1780s, his interests – mediated by Friedrich Justin Bertuch – coincided with Goethe's. Goethe was suffering at the time from the lack of an authorized complete edition of his works. Publishers at home and abroad were constantly reprinting (pirating) his work without his profiting in any way. He was furious at the prevalence of piracy, which Göschen was also battling. When Göschen offered to publish an eight-volume edition of his works in 1786, Goethe eagerly agreed. The prospects seemed promising. Goethe demanded 2,000 taler as his fee. Göschen planned an edition of 6,000 to be sold at 6 taler the set to 1,000 subscribers. The project did not proceed as anticipated, however. Because of his sojourn in Italy, Goethe did not prepare the volumes for the printer, nor did he read the proofs. When the first volumes appeared in 1787, Goethe was also disappointed by the appearance of the edition, noting that 'these volumes more closely resemble an ephemeral journal than a book intended to last for some time.'[26]

The volumes appeared slowly, and sales were halting. Although Göschen advertised several times in the *Journal des Luxus und der Moden* and the *Allgemeine Literatur-Zeitung* (General Literary Gazette), only 626 subscriptions materialized for an edition of 4,000.[27] Thus, in 1791, Goethe had to listen to Göschen telling him that his works were 'not as fashionable … as others that a large public finds to their liking'.[28] His earnings from the project were also correspondingly meagre. Göschen had more success with his complete edition of the works of Wieland, which appeared up to 1802 in 42 volumes. Wieland was nevertheless not fully satisfied with sales, despite the flat fee of 10,000 taler he received from Göschen, along with a loan of 3,000 taler to buy a country estate at Oßmannstedt.[29] Goethe, in contrast, made a profit only with the 1792 publication of Unger's Berlin edition of his collected works, for which he received 5,400 taler. Once he entered a business relationship with Johann Friedrich von Cotta, however, economic good fortune never deserted him again.

In 1787, Cotta had purchased the Tübingen publishing and bookselling enterprise that would later bear his name. Within a very short time, he had shifted his focus to contemporary literature, making his publishing house one of the leading addresses for journals and the works of Weimar Classicism. In 1794, Cotta launched the literary monthly *Die Horen* (The Horae) together with Schiller, who was hoping to improve his finances. Through Schiller, Goethe came into contact with the Tübingen publisher. First, Goethe published his short-lived journal *Propyläen* (Propylaea) there, and then his 12-volume collected works, beginning in 1805. The preceding negotiations had been fierce. Goethe earned 10,000 taler from the edition (1806–08), and another 2,000 from his novel *Elective Affinities*. The last, 40-volume edition of Goethe's works, which was also published by Cotta between 1826 and 1830, earned him a total of 60,000 taler. Thus, together with his other fees, Goethe reportedly gained 130,839 taler in all from his association with Cotta.[30]

That Cotta could offer such fees and attract and keep other authors such as Johann Gottfried Herder, Wieland, Friedrich Hölderlin, Jean Paul, F.W.J. von

Schelling, Johann Gottlieb Fichte, Ludwig Tieck and Johann Peter Hebel is an indicator of the financial resources and profit potential of his publishing empire. His journals and novel methods of author recruitment and text production through audience forums also contributed to this success. As an early industrial entrepreneur he also invested in other sectors, including steamships on the Rhine and Lake Constance, and linen manufacturing in Heilbronn.

He shared this strategy with the cultural entrepreneur Friedrich Justin Bertuch. Bertuch contributed to the cultural efflorescence of Saxony-Weimar not just as treasurer to Duke Carl August, but also by building a publishing enterprise based largely on periodicals, the Landes-Industrie-Comptoir, whose range he later expanded to include the manufacture of luxury goods.[31] Bertuch had started small as a writer and publisher. He worked first on Wieland's *Merkur*, where he was responsible for the business side of the journal. He also translated Cervantes's *Don Quixote* and self-published a Spanish-Portuguese literary magazine in Weimar from 1780–82. The *Allgemeine Literatur-Zeitung* followed in 1785, and in 1786 the *Journal des Luxus und der Moden*, which became a huge success.[32] Before that, Bertuch's wife had founded a silk flower factory in which Goethe's future companion and wife, Christiane Vulpius, would later work. Bertuch expanded his publishing activities in 1790 with the book series *Bilderbuch für Kinder* (Picture Book for Children), which illustrated the natural environment. Increasing numbers of publications such as the famous collections of travel accounts (*Bibliothek der Reisen*), the journals *London und Paris* and the *Allgemeine Geographische Ephemeriden* (General Geographical Ephemerides) followed.[33] Bertuch owed his success in large part to his unique combination of market orientation and literary politics. While not slavishly following contemporary taste, he did concentrate on journals and series with which he could simultaneously pursue his dedication to business and the Enlightenment. When it came to potentially risky literary enterprises such as the works of Weimar Classicism, however, he was rather cautious. The authors' fees he paid, as well as a glance at the profitability of his series, give us some idea of his entrepreneurial strategy and his success. To be sure, he did not pay astronomical fees such as the 100 taler per sheet that Goethe received from the Berlin publisher Johann Friedrich Vieweg for *Hermann und Dorothea*. The 10 taler per sheet he negotiated with Wieland for articles in the *Merkur* in 1782 was in the upper range of fees at the time. The *Allgemeine Literatur-Zeitung* paid 7 taler for reviews in 1786. By 1790, Bertuch was already offering a general reviewer's fee of 15 taler. He promised 3 taler a sheet even for articles in not particularly marketable scholarly journals such as the *Journal von und für Rußland* (Journal from and for Russia). Despite his advertising campaign this journal was never published.

The success of Bertuch's calculations is evident from the profits of his journals. In the case of the *Journal des Luxus und der Moden*, they constituted between 46 and 74 per cent of costs, which earned the two partners Bertuch and Kraus between 700 and 1,000 taler a year. Despite ample competition, this periodical, in particular, which did not aim for the centre of Enlightenment debate, was a big seller.

Figure 1   Friedrich Justin Bertuch. Stipple engraving by Carl August Schwerdgeburth, 1808

The map documenting the distribution of the *Journal* in 1791 already shows that it was read throughout Germany and beyond, although sales of the journal on to Russia, Britain, the Netherlands or Scandinavia are not indicated here.[34] Weimar, Berlin, Leipzig and Hamburg were clearly centres of distribution, but many other cities also had thirty or more recipients. The other journals, *London und Paris* and *Bilderbuch für Kinder*, also enjoyed market success. In 1807, for example, no fewer than 1,289 of the 1,325 printed copies of *London und Paris* were sold, far exceeding the 700 needed to cover expenses. With the exception of the *Handelsmagazin* (Commercial Magazine), all of Bertuch's periodicals covered their costs, so that, despite the Napoleonic occupation and restricted book distribution, his Industrie-Comptoir made a profit from nearly all of its publications.[35]

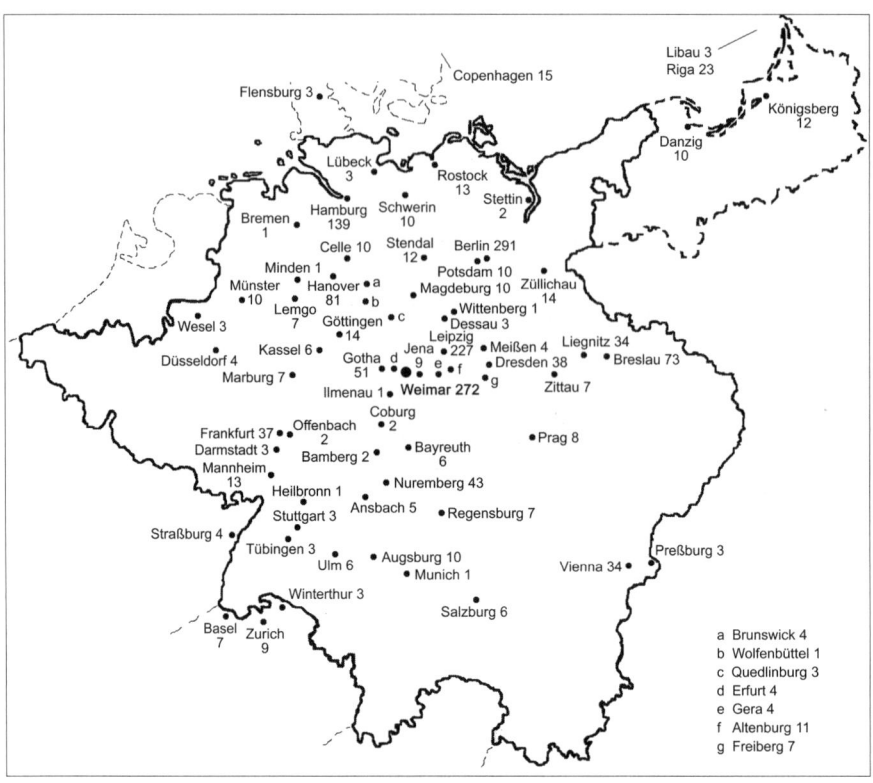

Libau 3
Riga 23
Copenhagen 15
Flensburg 3
Königsberg 12
Danzig 10
Lübeck 3
Rostock 13
Stettin 2
Hamburg 139   Schwerin 10
Bremen 1
Celle 10   Stendal 12
Berlin 291
Minden 1   Potsdam 10
Münster 10   Hanover 81 • a
Magdeburg 10   Züllichau 14
Lemgo • b
Wittenberg 1
Wesel 3   Göttingen 14 • c
Dessau 3
Leipzig
Düsseldorf 4   Kassel 6
Jena 227 • Meißen 4   Liegnitz 34
Marburg 7   Gotha d 51 • e • f
Dresden 38   Breslau 73
Ilmenau 1 • Weimar 272 g
Zittau 7
Coburg
Frankfurt 37 • Offenbach 2
Darmstadt 3   Bamberg 2 • Bayreuth 6
Prag 8
Mannheim 13
Heilbronn 1
Nuremberg 43
Straßburg 4   Stuttgart 3   Ansbach 5 • Regensburg 7
Tübingen 3   Ulm 6 • Augsburg 10
Winterthur 3   Munich 1
Vienna 34 •   Preßburg 3
Salzburg 6
Basel 7   Zurich 9

a Brunswick 4
b Wolfenbüttel 1
c Quedlinburg 3
d Erfurt 4
e Gera 4
f Altenburg 11
g Freiberg 7

Subscribers to the *Journal des Luxus und der Moden,* 1791

Book ownership

Up until now, we have examined periodical and book production from the perspective of marketing. How did potential readers respond to the new offerings, and what was demand for books like? With the exception of Rolf Engelsing's Bremen case study *Der Bürger als Leser* (The Citizen as Reader),[36] the history of German readership has not been investigated systematically, despite the availability of a wealth of potential source material. This includes public library catalogues, which recorded not just the books held, but in many cases also lending, and thus the borrowing behaviour of certain readers. The auction catalogues of private libraries and estate inventories document book ownership or non-ownership for a broader spectrum of the population.[37] Also impressive – albeit not representative – are the autobiographical accounts of reading experiences, while the membership lists of reading societies and the catalogues of lending libraries, for their part, encompass a broader group of readers. An examination of these sources provides some initial insights into readers and reading behaviour in the eighteenth century. The key question remains whether people actually read the books they owned, and whether they also had access to sources of reading matter other than their own books.

Let us begin with the example of a 'public' library, the Herzog-August-Bibliothek (Duke August Library) in Wolfenbüttel, whose lending records for the period 1714–99 have survived.[38] The library's character changed over the course of the eighteenth century. The Herzog-August-Bibliothek had always been a scholarly library, whose treasures attracted visitors from far and wide. It also served as library to the ducal court, from which courtiers and state officials could borrow for their work or personal edification. After the ducal residence moved to Brunswick in 1754, the library was opened to the citizens of Wolfenbüttel, which led to an upswing in borrowing. In the 1780s and 1790s, however, library director Ernst Theodor Langer, following the ever-current adage that 'the reader is the enemy of the librarian' tried to reverse this trend, keeping the broader public at bay with shorter opening hours and bans on borrowing. Despite such obstructive policies, over the eighteenth century 1,648 readers borrowed 21,848 titles (in 31,485 volumes) from the Herzog-August-Bibliothek, with nearly half of these reading books from the library during the period of more liberal opening hours between 1760 and 1780.[39]

If we break the titles down by subject areas, belles-lettres and historical works topped the list of books borrowed, ahead of theology, geography and works on classical antiquity (see Table 1.3).[40]

Table 1.3   Books borrowed from the Herzog-August-Bibliothek by subject area, 1714–99

Subject area	Number	Per cent
Belles-lettres	4,385	20.1
History	4,336	19.8
Theology	3,022	13.8
Classical antiquity	1,711	7.8
Geography	1,489	6.8
Philosophy	955	4.4
General	949	4.3
Law	872	4.0
State and politics	831	3.8
Natural sciences	544	2.5
Militaria	493	2.3
Language	488	2.2
Art history	443	2.0
Other	1,328	6.2
Total	**21,846**	**100**

Even court officials, who dominated the library's clientele, increasingly borrowed works of belles-lettres, alongside historical literature, while the female readership (13 per cent of borrowers) had always preferred this type of reading matter.[41]

For purposes of comparison, let us look at the private libraries of Hamburg citizens in the eighteenth and early nineteenth centuries, which have come down to us mainly in the form of auction catalogues. In the first half of the eighteenth century, in Hamburg – as in Bremen – the academic library[42] dominated among the scholars Fabricius, Richey and Reimarus. Only the library of the town councillor and poet Barthold Heinrich Brockes possessed substantial numbers of literary works, as well as books on art and music.[43]

In the second half of the eighteenth century, in contrast, the libraries for which we have information already had larger literary holdings. Thus, the mayor Jacob Albrecht von Sienen owned numerous works of literature and art as well as the classic travel accounts of his day. The syndic of the Senate Garlieb Sillem was also a significant book collector. Apart from works of jurisprudence, which he used professionally, he also owned titles by Klopstock, Bürger, Brockes, Gellert, Hagedorn, Gleim, Moritz, Wieland etc, as well as Rousseau's *Emile* and many works of 'Hamburgania'. Another local bookworm was Senator Johann Arnold Günther, who while still a boy had invested his first lottery winnings in books. He bequeathed his library of some 8,000 volumes to the Hamburg Patriotic Society, while leaving a smaller collection of literary works to his family. In his library, scholarly works and Hamburgania outnumbered literature and the arts. Particularly striking was his collection of works from the field of politics, which can be explained both by his professional activities and his engagement in the reforming activities of the Patriotic Society. Dominant here were studies of public administration and a collection of poor laws from a number of countries, cities and towns. Among the libraries of Hamburg merchants, Caspar Voght's particularly stands out. This library documents Voght's interest in agriculture, gardening and botany, which he also realized in the model farm he set up at Flottbek. For entertainment, he also read literature and travel accounts.[45]

On the whole, this overview shows that in late-eighteenth-century Hamburg, the scholarly library dominated by theology was a thing of the past and literary titles were on the rise among local officials and merchants, even though such works had already played an important role in the library of the poet Brockes. These figures tell us nothing, however, about the reading habits of merchants more generally, let alone of other strata of the population. In order to gain information on this, we need to look at the extent to which estate inventories document book ownership.

Walter Wittmann was the first scholar to analyse Frankfurt estate inventories for book ownership, and he arrived at the following conclusions: In 1700, of 50 merchant wills, only 36 (72 per cent) mention books. Twenty-seven (54 per cent) of the merchants owned only religious works and only seven (14 per cent) owned more than five books of secular content. In 1750, in contrast, of the 107 inventories studied only seventeen (16 per cent) contained no books, but

Table 1.4   Organization of Hamburg libraries by subject (books of different subject areas as a percentage of total holdings by collection)[44]

Collection Subject area	Fabricius (1738–41)	Brockes (1747)	Richey (1761–62)	Reimarus (1769–70)	v. Sienen (1804)	Sillem (1793)	Günther (1806)	Voght (1839)
Theology	35.11	12.36	17.32	25.37	7.67	4.27	3.26	4.70
Philosophy	4.79	7.39	2.41	4.90	–	–	1.90	See law
Law, politics, economics	6.98	16.31	11.38	8.73	3.55	25.60 (law only)	26.57	16.85
Medicine	2.80	1.78	2.00	–	–	2.22 (incl. chemistry and botany)		
Mathematics, natural science	6.30	7.64	3.87	8.41	14.15	5.87	3.57	7.45
Art, music	0.25	3.57	0.48	–	See belles-lettres	–	3.79	0.51
Geography, travel accounts, history	9.52	12.74	37.40	19.76	30.10	17.01	14.01	33.38
Ancient and modern philology	20.74	11.46	9.44	14.25	–	8.47 (incl. auxiliary sciences)	1.96	3.03
Belles-lettres	13.51	26.75	14.61	17.78	30.38 (incl. art)	15.33	6.37	31.10
Miscellaneous	–	–	–	–	–	–	35.47 (Hamburgania)	0.69 (Hamburgania)
Per cent of total	100	100	98.91	99.20	89.85	77.87	96.90	93.17

Note: In order to facilitate the comparison of collections, the subject areas marked with a dash (–) cannot be adequately represented.

over half (56 = 52.3 per cent) still contained no secular titles. Twenty-eight (26.2 per cent) of the merchants, however, listed more than five secular books. The figures for 1800 are unfortunately not useful for our purposes, since half of the 115 merchant inventories analysed contain no books. Nevertheless, the interest in books grew markedly among Frankfurt merchants as well in the course of the eighteenth century, and a division of readers into two groups becomes evident: a lower middle-class group, which still tended to favour religious literature passed down in the family, and another that preferred the new, secular subjects. This tendency clearly continued until 1800, if on a narrower basis. Now, alongside works of geography and history, we find the literary works of Gellert, Wieland, Klopstock and Lessing. Goethe and Schiller, in contrast, are represented only in exceptional cases. Of tradesmen's estate inventories from the period around 1750, 263 mention no secular books at all, 35 one or two such texts and 31 three or more.[46] Thus religious reading matter continued to dominate among artisans, a trend that persisted until 1800. In that year, 195 (65.2 per cent) of craftsmen's inventories contained no books and 264 (88.3 per cent) no books on secular themes. When people did read, they revisited over and over again the same works (intensive reading) that earlier generations had read in 1750 and before.[47] Let us try to breathe some life into these bare figures and look at the typical inventory of a tradesmen's estate. The Frankfurt blacksmith Augustin Geißemer's 1777 probate inventory offers an instructive snapshot. In addition to household furnishings of good quality, this artisan possessed the following books:

> Münsters Cosmographie in fol.
> Merianische Biebel
> Arnds Postillen
> Müllers Him[m]elskuß
> Arnoldts Postille
> Arndts wahres Christenthum
> Frankfurther groses Gesangbuch.[48]

With this list of titles, Geißemer found himself in good (tradesmen's) company. Among the townspeople of Tübingen and Speyer, too, Johann Arndt's *Vier Bücher vom wahren Christentum* (Four Books of True Christianity) enjoyed first place among the most read religious writers, while Heinrich Müller's *Himmlischer Liebeskuß* (Kiss of Heavenly Love) – alongside the Württemberg Pietists – can also be found among the most widely disseminated clerical authors.[49] Religious reading matter also dominated among the personnel of the Tübingen town council, merchants and artisans. In the mid-eighteenth century (1750–60), secular books represented only 18 per cent of books listed in estate inventories. Around 1800 (1800–10), the proportion had risen slightly to 22 per cent.[50] Etienne François found a similarly high proportion (80 per cent) of religious books for the city of Speyer (1780–86).[51]

Breaking down Tübingen book ownership along social lines, we arrive at the following results. While in the period 1750–60 the two mayors owned a total of 258 books, the four mayors of the period 1800–10 possessed an average of only 30 books each. Book ownership also fell among merchants, who now possessed only 163 books among the six of them (an average of 27 instead of 55 books each). Among artisans, there was also a slight decline, with shoemakers, bakers, tailors and butchers owning the most books.[52] A substantial number of inventories mention no books whatsoever, however: 11 per cent in 1750–60 and 22 per cent in 1800–10. Thus, the continuous rise in book production was not automatically reflected in book ownership. We can assume that the same is true of the subject matter of books and thus also the reception of the Enlightenment. Tübingen citizens – Hildegard Neumann makes an express exception for members of the university – read primarily for purposes of religious devotion (if they read the books they owned at all), and they read the books they had inherited. Accordingly, the authors of the Enlightenment, *Sturm und Drang* and Classicism appear only exceptionally in Tübingen inventories. The most frequently mentioned literary author is Gellert (15 times in 1800–10), followed by Schiller (five times), Schubart (once) and Goethe's poetry (once).[53]

The books owned by inhabitants of the proto-industrial manufacturing town of Laichingen (Schwäbische Alb region) were even more intensely dominated by religious themes. There, secular books made up only 1.5 per cent of reading matter in the inventories. Nearly every household possessed books, pointing to an exceptionally high rate of literacy stimulated by Pietism. A further observation is particularly surprising: while book ownership in Tübingen fell on average from ten to seven or eight, in Laichingen it rose from 11 (1748–51) to 13 or 14 (1781–91).[54] This increase possibly also owed something to the boom in the local linen-weaving industry and thus the general prosperity of the town. Enlightened middle-class literacy could also be found among the teachers, pastors, surgeons, merchants and officials, whose literary culture was marked by the reading of secular literature (for example, Gellert) and specialist texts as well as a bourgeois way of life.[55]

In addition to the above-mentioned books, a large quantity of smaller and less valuable forms of printed matter may also have existed in the Lutheran or Pietist regions cited here, which did not find their way into the inventories. They need to be included if we wish to supplement or round off the picture of their owners' reading behaviour.[56]

Reading societies and lending libraries

Where, then, can we look for significant quantities of the new works that turned intensive 'learned or devotional readers' into extensive readers? Some of these extensive readers could certainly be found in the new institutions of the reading societies and lending libraries. The reading societies, in particular, are consistently cited as central institutions of the bourgeois Enlightenment.[57]

Scholars point to English models, which were propagated on the Continent with the aid of the moral weeklies. Thus in the 1750s, several Bremen pastors pooled their resources and subscribed to a number of English weekly magazines in order to organize their 'leisure time' in a pleasant and useful manner.[58] The 'Private Society for the Study of the English Language and Literature' founded in 1750 in Stralsund could also be regarded as the first German reading society. Well over 400 such societies were established between 1770 and 1800.[59] The geographical focus lay in northern Germany, Saxony and Thuringia as well as the Rhine-Main region.

The reading society went through various developmental stages. Beginning with joint subscriptions and passing journals on from one member to the next, the societies then proceeded to acquire rooms where people could read and discuss and finally, as fully fledged reading societies, offered a range of services to their members.[60] Accordingly, these institutions ranged in size and structure from small, exclusive circles to large organizations with many members. The nobility, clergy and middle classes in the form of the liberal professions were frequently all represented in a single reading society, leading to a symbiosis of reading preferences. An example is the reading society of the electoral residence of Bonn, whose members included 49 noblemen, 25 theologians, 65 civil servants and 19 professors and secondary schoolmasters, all of whom were additionally linked by their affiliation with state service (functional elites).[61] The Ludwigsburg reading society also had a high proportion of aristocratic members between 1770 and 1796, as did its counterparts in Trier and the various reading societies that existed simultaneously in Detmold, the capital city of Lippe-Detmold.[62]

In Hamburg, educated people met for reading evenings in which, for example, they allocated roles and declaimed Lessing's *Nathan the Wise*. A number of other societies existed alongside it, of which the 'literary reading society' founded in 1790 tried to set itself apart by greater exclusivity.[63] Bremen experienced a veritable boom in the founding of reading societies, with 36 being established there by 1791. Membership numbers fluctuated between 20 and 100, while cities with fewer such societies reached higher figures. The Mainz society, for instance, boasted 300 members in 1788, which would grow to 452.

Far more interesting than the question of size is that of the literature circulating in the societies. Here we must distinguish according to both the literary tendency of the society and the availability of sources. Thus, the first type of society was that specializing in popular fiction, such as chivalric novels, which were often difficult to distinguish from lending libraries. This fact is substantiated by a remark in the Delmenhorst magazine *Der geheime Ausrufer* (The Secret Town Crier, 1808):

> But who nowadays still wishes to hear, let alone read, a sermon? To be sure, if it were a Rinaldo Rinaldini (by Vulpius) or such a monster, I would let it pass. One need only enter our lending libraries (which by the way are also probably called

1.*Hofrath R.Meyer* 2.*Frau v. Frilsch* 3.*v. Wolfskul.* 3.*§.R. v. Goethe.* 4.*G.R. v. Einsiedel.* 5.*Herzogin Anna Amalia.* 6.*Frl. Eliz. Gore.* 7.*Charles Gore.*
8.*Frl. Emilie Gore.* 9.*Frl. v. Jochhausen.* 10.*Frau v. Herder.*

Figure 2   An evening gathering hosted by Duchess Anna Amalia. Water-colour and pen and ink sketch by Georg Melchior Kraus, c. 1795

reading libraries) and enquire after such a highwayman, bandit or witch, and one will find that the book is either not at home or has had its spine and corners quite worn out from so much wandering from one [person] to the next … . Other, useful, books stand as if rooted to the spot and are covered in dust.[64]

A second group of societies favoured journals and foreign-language literature. Since the aims of reading here were 'general education, moral enlightenment and political information',[65] such a society ideally combined the useful with the pleasurable and, alongside the newest travel accounts, also offered its members journals such as Wieland's *Teutscher Merkur* or Reichardt's *Olla Potrida* (for more sentimental entertainment), poetry anthologies, plays and novels. Prominent among these novels were *Tom Jones* (Fielding), *Humphrey Clinker* (Smollett), *Der Roman meines Lebens* (The Novel of My Life; Knigge) and *Sebaldus Nothanker* (Nicolai). Did this correspond to actual reality on the ground? When the 177 volumes of Smidt's Reading Society in Bremen were sold there was at least some overlap in the journals, travel accounts and novels. The latter also included two novels by Jean Paul (Richter) that, it is worth noting, were absent in southern Germany (if we take Tübingen as an example). Typical was the large number of annuals and almanacs, including several ladies' calendars.[66]

This tendency is confirmed by the reading lists that have come down to us from Electoral Hanover for the 1790s. The reading societies had to submit these lists to the ministry in Hanover for approval, a measure intended to suppress the spread of ideas from France. Since smaller towns also obeyed Hanover's demands and the material has survived, we are informed about the reading habits of even Wunstorf an der Luthe or Jork in the Alte Land region. Thus, Wunstorf had two reading societies, whose periodical holdings included all of the major German journals – not just the *Teutsche Merkur*, Schlözer's *Staatsanzeigen* and the *Allgemeine Literatur-Zeitung*, but also the *Journal des Luxus und der Moden*, *Olla Potrida* and Nicolai's *Allgemeine Deutsche Bibliothek*. Among the books, the focus of interest was on entertainment and edification, as evidenced by the plays, novels, memoirs and gothic tales. The 'classics', in contrast, are completely absent, except for Bürger's poetry and Karl Philipp Moritz's novel *Anton Reiser*, which was partly set in Brunswick and Hanover.[67]

The analysis of book lists for a few other small reading societies in the Elbe-Weser region, however, shows that when it came to the quantity and quality of their holdings, no reading society was identical to the next. Their contents fluctuated between educational and entertainment value, which they emphasized to differing degrees. Thus, the reading society of Consistorial Councillor Watermeier in Stade offered 67 works from the various fields of learning and entertainment, with novels, plays and poetry making up about a quarter of the titles. North German writers such as Hölty, Moritz, Ebert and Büsch were well represented. A second smaller reading society (24 titles) was organized in Stade by F. Gerken, pastor of St. Wilhad's, with an emphasis on geography, history and natural history. Religion played only a minor role, and novels and other literary genres were wholly absent. In Verden, in contrast, schoolmaster Lüning's reading society devoted more than three-quarters of the 116 titles to popular literary genres.[68] Overall, educational considerations dominated among the people who ran reading societies – pastors, schoolmasters, sextons and postmasters – although some had financial interests as well. Only in Verden did the size and focus of holdings resemble those of a lending library.

It is not always easy to draw sharp lines between reading societies and lending libraries. The main difference was the profit motive, which was primary for lending libraries, but at most a side issue for reading societies. Accordingly, lending libraries always had their own premises, often containing thousands of titles. Such collections were founded in Frankfurt am Main and Karlsruhe as early as the 1750s. By the 1770s, Brunswick, Göttingen, Munich, Königsberg, Prague and Vienna had followed. At the end of the eighteenth century, one could find a lending library in nearly all small cities and market towns, while large cities such as Leipzig could boast nine such establishments. In 1811, Berlin had 27 lending libraries, of which Rudolf Werkmeister's 'Museum', with its 25,000 volumes, was the most important. Even in nearby Oranienburg, the postmaster made 12,000 volumes and some 100 newspapers available to the curious. Frankfurt had eighteen lending libraries in the late eighteenth century, some of which, like Fleischer's repository of fine art, evolved into cultural service centres. In his establishment, opened in 1795, Wilhelm Fleischer offered his customers three adjoining reading rooms, with a fourth room available for conversation. With time he set up a separate room for the entertainment of readers. The walls were adorned with paintings, while plaster casts of ancient originals contributed to the specific atmosphere. A year's subscription cost 1½ carolins (about 17 guilders). Later, monthly subscriptions were introduced for visitors to Frankfurt. Journals and newspapers were freely available, and new publications were integrated into the library after a short period on display and could be borrowed for a fee.[69]

'Culture vultures' also established literary sociability in the provinces. One of these enthusiastic amateurs was the Bremen physician Nicolaus Meyer, who had participated in literary teas in Jena and Weimar. He not only tried his hand at writing plays for amateur theatricals, but also founded several conversation circles in Bremen. Here, the members discussed modern art and delighted in the latest news from Weimar, which Meyer acquired from C.A. Vulpius or his correspondence with Goethe, whom he regularly supplied with wine from Bordeaux. Meyer also organized lectures on 'belles-lettres' for the 'Casino' literary society. In 1803, he made use of his connections as a spa doctor in Lilienthal near Bremen by making Lilienthal popular as a watering place for ladies by organizing 'private' sociable gatherings there.[70]

Thus, on the whole, people began to read more, as a way of using their leisure time wisely, and as a pastime more generally. Nevertheless, there continued to be large islands of non-reading or of literacy in a sea of non-reading, and even the islands of literacy did not automatically follow the Enlightenment or belles-lettres, let alone the classics. Jean Paul estimated that the literary public in Germany, including members of the reading societies and customers of the lending libraries, consisted of at most 300,000 persons, and he broke them down into the following categories:

> In Germany there are three publics: 1) the broad, almost uneducated and unlearned one of the lending libraries – 2) the learned one, made up of professors, [theological] candidates, students and reviewers – 3) the educated one, consisting of men of the world and women of breeding, artists and the upper classes, who are at least cultivated by contacts and travel (to be sure, the three groups often communicate).[71]

The commercialization of book production thus also continued to reach a slightly expanding literate minority and primarily satisfied the need for entertainment. Proponents of the Enlightenment, or even the authors of Classicism, remained on the margins, noticed only by 'men of the world and women of breeding'. Goethe was, accordingly, not particularly optimistic when he addressed the taste of readers in a letter to Johann Friedrich Reichardt:

> The Germans are, on average, honest, decent people, but they have not the slightest notion of the originality, invention, character, unity or execution of a work of art. In a word, they have no taste. On average, mind you. The interest of the cruder segment is kept alive by variety and exaggeration, and that of the more educated by a sort of honesty. Knights, highwaymen, benefactors, grateful folk, an honest, upright

tiers état, a disgraceful nobility etc and throughout a finely sustained mediocrity, from which [authors] dare take only a few steps down into the banal or up into nonsense. Those have been, for the past ten years, the ingredients and character of our novels and plays.[72]

Chapter 2

Travel and the Culture of Travel

> In no other age in the [history of the] world did people travel as much as they do in ours, where travel has become a sort of epidemic … . Indeed, even the learned man of slender means leaves his writing desk and undertakes journeys, not far, to be sure, but at least excursions, often with the intent of offering the world his hastily gathered remarks, and thereby recovering the costs incurred. Whether this frequent travel produces more advantages or disadvantages, whether it strengthens or weakens patriotism, increases or decreases the spread of true knowledge, I dare not judge.[1]

With these words, written in 1784, the *Teutsche Merkur* criticized the changing nature of travel and the culture of travel in the eighteenth century. People had, of course, travelled even before the age of Enlightenment. We need only think of pilgrims, the predecessors to modern mass tourism, of whom up to 500,000 populated the route to Santiago de Compostela in some years. Emperors and kings, reformers and humanists displayed a similar enthusiasm for travel. Merchants and artisans, artists and students also travelled, and not just to earn a living or to learn. In addition, the Grand Tour established itself in the sixteenth century as a form of educational journey for noblemen, which was intended to acquaint young aristocrats and patricians with the most important personalities and the political and cultural centres of contemporary Europe.

The eighteenth century witnessed a fundamental change in perceptions of travel, however. New groups of travellers adopted travel as an essential element of cultivation, adapting it to their own needs. This led to a re-evaluation of travel in the eighteenth century. No longer the privilege of certain groups, it now became something for 'everyone' who aspired to cultivation. Travel should not merely provide professional polish or pure pleasure, but also help to hone the intellect and increase knowledge, as well as educate the heart more generally. In a time of growing regional and national identity, it was also supposed to heighten or promote patriotism and the ability to place one's strength and capacities at the service of one's country.

The eighteenth century accordingly witnessed an intensification of travel for professional purposes. Officials travelled to take up a new post or to expand their professional knowledge. Professors, pastors and artists took journeys to cultivate contacts or make new acquaintances. The extensive travels of the princely *Kapellmeister* and municipal official (*Kantor* of the Thomasschule in Leipzig) Johann Sebastian Bach document in exemplary fashion this new range of professional journeys (see Table 2.1).

Table 2.1   Bach's official travels, 1703–50[2]

Place	Date (reason)
Sangerhausen	1702 (audition)
Arnstadt	1703 (organ inspection)
Lübeck	1704/05 (Buxtehude's 'Abendmusik', etc.)
Langewiesen	1706 (organ inspection)
Mühlhausen	1707 (audition), 1709, 1710 (guest performances: Council Election Cantatas)
Weimar	1708 (organ recital, Schloßkirche)
Traubach	1712 (organ inspection)
Weißenfels	1713 (guest performance at court: BWV 208), 1729 (guest performance), 1739 (occasion unknown, with Anna Magdalena)
Halle	1713 (audition), 1719 (failed attempt at a meeting with George Frideric Handel)
Erfurt	1716 (organ inspection)
Gotha	1717 (guest performance: 'Passion')
Leipzig	1717 (organ inspection, Paulinerkirche), 1723 (audition for position of Cantor)
Dresden	1717 (competition with Marchand), 1725, 1731 (organ recital, Sophienkirche), 1733 (delivery of the Missa BWV 232), 1736 (organ recital in the Liebfrauenkirche), 1738, 1741 (occasion unknown)
Karlsbad	1717, 1720 (with Prince Leopold and members of the Köthen court orchestra)
Berlin	1719 (harpsichord purchase), 1741, 1747 (guest performances at court: piano and organ recitals)
Hamburg	1720 (audition)
Schleiz	1721 (guest performance at court)
Zerbst	1722 (guest performance at court)
Gera	1724 (organ inspection)
Köthen	1724, 1725 (guest performance with Anna Magdalena), 1728 (guest performance), 1729 (guest performance at the funeral of Prince Leopold, with Anna Magdalena and Wilhelm Friedemann)
Unknown destination	1729 (absent from Leipzig for three weeks, before 20 March), 1736 (absent for two weeks after 17 July)
Kassel	1732 (organ inspection, accompanied by Anna Magdalena)
Altenburg	1739 (organ inspection)
Naumburg	1746 (organ inspection, Wenzelkirche)
Potsdam	1747 (guest performance at court: piano recital)

The purposes of Bach's journeys varied widely. They ranged from concerts and organ inspections as an invited expert to auditions and performances with the court orchestra, for instance in Karlsbad, or the purchase of a harpsichord in Berlin. Although Bach's travels were limited to northern and central Germany, they nevertheless expanded his musical, political, geographical and cultural horizons.[3]

Like Bach, many people travelled on personal or official business. They were joined by those who undertook journeys to spas for their health, as well as by the long-familiar figures of journeymen artisans and itinerant players. Long-distance pilgrimages, in contrast, became rare, and regional pilgrimages could not compensate for this loss of experience.

The noble Grand Tour changed fundamentally in the course of the eighteenth century. It no longer primarily served as a means of introducing young men to European court society and courtly manners, but now focused on training future rulers or officials. That is, it became an informational journey for political functionaries. Learned tutors chose the itinerary in such a way as to bring their pupils together with scholars, artists and entrepreneurs, as well, so that they might make useful connections. They also visited mines, ironworks, prisons, workhouses and political institutions. Thus in 1772, the young Karl-August von Hardenberg and his companion Lieutenant von Freytag stopped at the Imperial Chamber Court at Wetzlar, the Imperial Diet at Regensburg, the imperial court at Vienna and the courts at Berlin and Dresden, as well as most of the capitals of the imperial electors.[4]

If one travelled to the Netherlands, it was de rigueur to look in at the States General in The Hague (alongside a visit to the art collections). Participation in a session of the Conseil Général, the highest body of the Republic of Geneva, also provided future rulers such as the princes Ludwig Friedrich and Karl Günther of Schwarzburg-Rudolstadt, who made their journey in 1789–90, with insights into the political culture of old regime Europe.[5] On these educational journeys, the lines between noble and bourgeois models of travel, which have long been emphasized by scholarship on both the Enlightenment and the history of travel, became blurred.[6]

As people travelled more, modes of travel also changed. A new type of journey arose – travel within Germany, or to the German 'provinces'. It reflected not just an increasing awareness of the individuality of regional artificial landscapes – as expressed, for example, in Justus Möser's *Geschichte Osnabrücks* (History of Osnabrück) – but also a scholarly interest in the region and its most important sites, to which political functionaries also devoted attention. This led to the emergence of a large number of travel destinations, corresponding to the plurality of motivations for travel. Two examples will illustrate this more clearly.

One of the new breed of travellers was the cameralist Johann Beckmann, who undertook several journeys after completing his studies at Göttingen (1759–62). One of these, in late summer 1762, took him to the Brunswick region where, apart from visiting his uncle in Schöppenstedt, he also travelled to the cities of Helmstedt, Wolfenbüttel and Brunswick. In his journal, he not only pedantically noted the route of his journey, with times of arrival and departure, expenses and his meals, including the number of sandwiches consumed, but listed the libraries, museums, natural history collections, castles, churches and manufacturers he had viewed too. Furthermore, he recorded his impressions of the journey. That same year, Beckmann undertook another one-month journey, in which he visited Osnabrück, Utrecht, Narden, Rotterdam, Amsterdam, Leiden, Delft, The Hague, Groningen, Emden, Oldenburg and Bremen. The sights included coalmines and salt-works, as well as the classic industries of the Netherlands, such as clay pipe production in Gouda, the Leiden textile manufacturers and the Delft potteries. In 1763, Beckmann took up a position as Professor of Mathematics, Physics and Natural History at St Peter's Academy in St Petersburg, a post he left in 1765. From there, he travelled to Sweden and Denmark, staying for a time to study with Linnaeus at Uppsala. In 1766, he was appointed Professor of Economics at Göttingen, where he remained until his death in 1811. Here he made a name for himself with publications on technology and its history, for example his essays on the history of inventions. He also wrote reviews of travel literature and published a bibliography on the subject, in which he primarily presented foreign-language accounts of travels outside Europe.[7] His own travels thus served him well in his later career.

Johann Caspar Goethe was probably the more typical German educational traveller, however. On 30 December 1739, having recently finished his study of jurisprudence, he embarked on a voyage to Italy. Before that, he had spent six months each at the Imperial Diet in Regensburg and at the Imperial Aulic Council in Vienna. The future Councillor Goethe now completed the classic travel programme, for which he was able to use the infrastructure of the gentlemanly Grand Tour. He left wintry Vienna in time to make his way to Venice for Carnival. From there, he travelled via Bologna and Rimini to Ancona and over the Apennines to Rome. Naples was the southernmost destination on his itinerary. On his way home, he passed through Rome, Viterbo, Pisa and Lucca on his way to Florence, from where he travelled back to Venice. Further stations were Verona, Milan, Turin and Genoa and – by ship – Marseilles. It was not until a few years later that Goethe wrote up his notes, with the help of other travel accounts, producing a more than 1,000-page account of his journey under the title *Viaggio per Italia fatto nel anno MDCCXL* (Voyage through Italy Made in the Year MDCCXL). In this reflective stocktaking of his Italian journey, personal experiences and encounters play a particular role. One of the favourite themes of the good Lutheran and enlightened sceptic was mockery of the Italian belief in relics and miracles, for example in the spirit of Joseph trapped in a bottle. On the positive side, he emphasizes the relative openness of the Venetian ruling classes, which must have made a particular impression given the closed nature of the Frankfurt patriciate. He also mentions the Italians' pride in their own past, and presents it as a model for his contemporaries. On the whole, the father of the renowned Goethe viewed Italy from a critical and reflective distance, seeing the country's many curiosities with eyes schooled in Germany. Although we know nothing of how this travel account was received by the public, one thing is certain: for Johann Caspar Goethe, his educational journey to Italy was the adventure of a lifetime, an event that must also have stimulated his son's longing for Italy.[8]

The example of our protagonist also underlines how travel not merely served the ideal of forming the personality (as had been the case with the Grand Tour), but for educated middle-class men also represented a means of experiencing the world and acquiring knowledge of human nature and preparing for a career. After all, according to Franz Posselt's much-cited 1795 'Art of Travel', travel affords us the opportunity

> to compare the art of observation, the new impressions and ideas with the results of those one had previously, and to reflect upon them. In this way, understanding, judgement and reason are of necessity schooled, honed and perfected … . He who travels much and far thus also attains a broader purview and measure of things through the multifarious objects and comparisons that he has the opportunity to observe and make … .[9]

In addition, in a territorially fragmented Germany without a true political or intellectual centre, travel was supposed to help constitute a communicative structure – or structures – independent of the 'republic of letters'. Accordingly, for many travellers, travel represented the continuation or new beginning of a dialogue. Well-informed travellers were welcome conveyors of information, and an exchange of ideas with them was more authentic than travel literature, which focused on the publicity of information and had to follow the strictures of the genre. Once printed, the traveller's observations and information became public and took on a life of their own in the opinion-making process. Finally, travel and exchange with like-minded people also served the self-affirmation of the educated traveller, whether of middle-class or noble origin.

Working as a private or royal tutor offered even the less well heeled an opportunity to take part in the Grand Tour. In this way, Johann Georg Keyßler came to travel with the young Counts Carl Maximilian and Christian Carl von Giech through Germany, the Netherlands and France in 1713, and he used his time to visit libraries and meet scholars. His position as tutor to the Bernstorffs at Gartow, where he influenced the lives of the brothers Andreas Gottlieb and Johann Hartwig Ernst over a period of three decades, opened up whole new opportunities for travel. Keyßler taught his pupils history, statecraft and geography and travelled through Europe with them. He also supervised his pupils' studies in Tübingen and accompanied Johann Hartwig Ernst von Bernstorff, the future Danish foreign minister, to both Copenhagen and Regensburg, his first posting as ambassador from Holstein to the 'permanent' Imperial Diet.[10]

Carsten Niebuhr also owed his travel opportunities, which took him to Arabia and India, to royal Danish patronage. As part of a programme of support for research by King Frederick V and foreign minister Count Johann Hartwig Ernst von Bernstorff, Denmark equipped an expedition to the Orient in 1761, in which the Göttingen student Carsten Niebuhr, together with other scholars, took part as a cartographer. His 'Description of a Voyage to Arabia and Other Surrounding Lands'[11] is an impressive example of the attempt to report on experiences in foreign countries encyclopaedically and as objectively as possible, in the spirit of the Enlightenment. Unfortunately, this self-published work was not the bestseller Niebuhr had hoped for, which would seem to substantiate the theory that his exhaustively learned writing style was no longer in fashion.[12] The prolific author Johann Georg Forster, who greatly depended on the earnings of his pen, proved a good deal more successful. He had participated in Cook's second voyage around the world and caused a sensation in Europe with his literary account of the journey. Forster was also a diligent and acute traveller within Europe, who, like Keyßler, described the natural history collections, cabinets of curiosities and art galleries he visited in precise detail.[13]

The conditions of travel

Various factors contributed to the spread of educational travel in the eighteenth century. One of them was the growing safety of travel. The age of the great wars of religion in Europe had led not just to the deracination of soldiers and refugees but also to increased immobility. During the Thirty Years War, the fear of becoming embroiled in hostilities or falling into the hands of marauders or highwaymen had kept people at home. The territorial states of the eighteenth century, in contrast, took energetic measures against bands of robbers to make the roads safer, and managed to keep this danger within limits, so that travellers could bypass areas with bad reputation.[14] Religious prejudice against people of other confessions – which in the seventeenth century had still exposed travellers to Rome to suspicion in Protestant lands, because of the fear that they might return as (crypto-)converts – were on the wane. The spirit of Enlightenment brooked no such misgivings.

At least as important was the expansion of the stagecoach as a means of public transport. Regular schedules were slow to develop, however. To be sure, as early as the 1620s, a service had periodically been offered from Düsseldorf to the Netherlands, but the first regular stagecoach service in Germany was the fortnightly Imperial Post coach between Frankfurt and Kassel, beginning in 1649. This was followed in 1655 by a stagecoach between Brunswick, Celle and Hamburg, which, however, ran into resistance from the North German territories and was soon halted. In the 1660s, the Brandenburg post road between Cleve and Memel was converted into a stagecoach route. The Imperial Post and the Saxon Post offered an alternative route along the Aachen–Cologne–Frankfurt–Leipzig road and from thence by Polish Post to Russia via Warsaw. In the eighteenth century, the Imperial Post succeeded in establishing a regular stagecoach service by bringing suits before the imperial courts, purchasing privileges and signing bilateral agreements. Merchants and manufacturers in particular promoted the establishment of stagecoach services to replace the country coaches, which had travelled without changing horses.[15] The introduction of the more comfortable diligences and the transition to coaches that travelled everyday, known as *journaliers*, fundamentally changed the culture of travel.

The most important factors were the overcoming of technical problems, the improvement of routes and increased frequency of service. The stagecoaches served significant routes weekly, and the most important ones, such as the Paris–Frankfurt–Dresden route, daily, offering the first indications of a customer service orientation. Nevertheless, the deficiencies, which were also the result of topography and above all the state of the roads, remained virtually insurmountable. Thus in 1722, the average speed of the Electoral Saxon post coaches was 4.5 km/h, and of the Prussian 7.5 km/h, while the actual travel time of the Imperial Post can be reconstructed as 3–4 km/h. Road improvements, and above all the construction of highways, made for shorter travel times, but serious delays were a normal occurrence.[16] The merchants of many cities accordingly complained of the unreliability of the post conveyances. Contemporary travellers also often joined in the chorus of laments about the post coaches.

The poor condition of the roads, the discomforts of the post coaches and the excessive number of stops were just a few of the repeated complaints. Enlightened travellers were fond of mentioning the French highways and the English stagecoaches, which were light and equipped with spring suspension.[17] It was, accordingly, the system of light mail coaches that revolutionized the speed and comfort of travel in the early nineteenth century. Prussia, whose roads had still lagged behind the highways of the southern German states in the late eighteenth century, took the lead here. The motivation behind the Prussian reforms was to move people as quickly as letters. This aim was achieved for the first time in 1821 on the turnpike road between Koblenz, Cologne and Düsseldorf, with travel speeds of between 12 and 13 km/h. Another factor was the shortening of stops to 5 minutes to change horses and 30 minutes for meals. Daily stagecoach service between Paris and Berlin (with a connection on to St Petersburg) now became feasible.[18]

Thus it was only a Europe-wide network of post coaches that made possible the intensity of travel observable in the second half of the eighteenth century. Although travel remained costly, the conveyances were used with increasing frequency. How widespread stagecoach travel was is indicated indirectly by the warning of the enlightened traveller Friedrich Nicolai, who recommended to readers that they travel by post-chaise instead of the ordinary post in order to avoid 'bothersome' fellow travellers. Nicolai chose the most expensive form of travel, his own coach using the postal infrastructure, and explained his decision as follows: 'A comfortable conveyance is to a long journey what a comfortable home is to a human life.'[19] This naturally limited the opportunities for experiencing the alien environment. Contemporaries thus accused Nicolai

Figure 3   Englishmen travelling through Germany in a post-chaise. Etching, second half of the eighteenth century

of never really having left Berlin. While numerous writers, such as Herder on his Italian journey, remained within their own four walls in the form of a post-chaise, others, such as Johann Caspar Riesbeck, deliberately sought contact with other people 'in the ordinary public conveyances, which I greatly appreciate because of the company (even if it consists only of Jews, Capuchins and old women)'.[20] This is also confirmed by the historian Wolfgang Behringer, when he mentions, as an example of collective travel, the chance travelling companions of the theologian Abegg in the summer of 1798 as 'a man from Jena and a botanising scholar' (3 August 1798, from Gotha to Berka via Eisenach), and 'a Jew who called himself an optician, [and] two apprentice apothecaries, who introduced themselves as students'. En route from Berka to Hersfeld Abegg was then accompanied by an officer of the hussars with his wife and her maid. From Hersfeld to Alsfeld, he enjoyed conversing with a Hessian officer. In Alsfeld, they were joined by 'the cook from a nearby estate', and shortly thereafter by 'a finely dressed woman, who was the wife of the local forester and wished to make a visit in the next town. The woman and the cook chatted along incessantly, and I took great pleasure in the lieutenant's company.'[21] In such circumstances, other-perception became a truly intimate experience.

With changing travel habits and needs, the range of services offered by hostelries along the way also changed. Post stations and inns now expanded the number of rooms for guests. In addition, the number of German hostelries rose to about 80,000 in 1800.[22] Of these, August Ludwig Schlözer, writing in 1795, considered the majority to be 'cultivated' or 'semi-cultivated', while 'highly cultivated' inns were to be found only in large urban centres such as Frankfurt and Hamburg.[23] Nevertheless, English travellers in particular regularly complained of the desolate state of German inns. The travel literature also contains recommendations to travellers to observe the greatest possible cleanliness, which, given the notorious eighteenth-century aversion to washing, probably fell on deaf ears. Carrying one's own travel bed to avoid the vermin in the inns was also recommended, a suggestion that Johann Wolfgang von Goethe, for one, regularly followed.[24]

Travel was, naturally, also an economic factor. While it took money out of a territory when the inhabitants travelled, it also brought substantial sums back into the country with visitors. Innkeepers and hackney coachmen were not the only ones to profit from travellers; the growing hunger for travel also gave work and income to coach-makers, saddlers and blacksmiths. In addition, a culture of travel developed that benefited a range of trades. Trunks and boxes had to be made to carry luggage. Travellers needed sturdy and comfortable garments to wear, since finer town clothes often proved unsuitable. Compact travel utensils such as travel cutlery and writing cases were also useful. Printers and publishers, too, profited from the surge in travel, along with their authors and map engravers. Maps and travel literature of all kinds experienced a veritable boom in the eighteenth century. While book production as a whole doubled between 1770 and 1800, for example, the number of travel books jumped fivefold. This growing interest of an emerging educated middle class was served on the one hand by magazines that published travel accounts and briefer travel notes, and on the other by reading societies and lending libraries from which they could borrow travel literature.

Travel destinations

The choice of travel destinations was influenced not just by the latest reports in Bertuch's *Journal des Luxus und der Moden* or the *London und Paris* journal, but also by the oral accounts of travellers returned home as well as the written versions they published. A 'canon' of cities and sights that travellers simply had to visit in order to hold their heads up socially existed for both the Grand Tour and the educational journey.

Thus for the seventeenth-century Grand Tour, Paris, Madrid, Rome and also Venice and Vienna were musts. With France's rise to the position of culturally dominant European power in the seventeenth century, the maxim became: 'A German of noble blood/ if his deportment is otherwise to be approved of/ must first hasten to Paris.'[25] This esteem can be explained by the renown of the French noble academies, the spread of the French language in diplomacy, scholarship and literature, and the model of French absolutism under Louis XIV. France's cultural charisma as well as the increasingly tight stagecoach network attracted increasing numbers of educational travellers after the Seven

Years' War, until the French Revolution put an end to this form of cultivated tourism. Then came the hour of the 'Revolution tourist'. Apart from France, Italy, with Rome and Venice, continued to be propagated as a travel destination, while Madrid became less attractive.

Nevertheless, there were reservations regarding France. Cautious tutors even sought to keep their protégés away from the sinful city of Paris. Thus, Johann Georg Keyßler recommended and hoped 'that, should the Germans' excessive love of travel persist, Italy be chosen over France, and particularly Paris, as a destination for long sojourns by young men'.[26] Paris offered the temptations of vice, which were described in detail in special 'red light' guides.[27] Italy, in contrast, fascinated the traveller with antiquities, education or religion, although Italy also had vices on offer, along with its climate and medicinal springs. Travel to Italy received new impulses from Johann Joachim Winckelmann's *Sendschreiben von den herculanischen Entdeckungen* (Herculanæan Discoveries, 1762) and above all his *Anmerkungen über die Geschichte der Kunst des Alterthums* (Notes on the History of Ancient Art, 1767), which gave Naples, including Mount Vesuvius and Herculanæum, a firm place in the canon of travel destinations.[28] Thus, Italy too was perceived anew in the late eighteenth century, a process typified by Goethe's reports from Italy in 1786. Influenced by his father's accounts, books and pictures, he experienced a genuine culture shock upon his arrival in a 'new world', 'for, one might well say, a new life begins when one sees with [one's own] eyes the whole that one in part knew inside and out ...; everything is as I imagined, and yet everything is new.'[29] Thus a paradigm shift had occurred between the Italian journeys of the two Goethes. For the son, the focus was no longer on the acquisition of knowledge, as it had been in the case of Caspar Goethe, but on his personal impressions of nature, art and people. The recently abdicated Duchess Anna Amalia, whose 'journey of the Muses' (Herder) between 1788 and 1790 was dedicated to climate, art and music, could also not resist the 'therapeutic' effects of the south conveyed by Goethe. Apart from the obligatory programme of viewing art, Anna Amalia also sought self-fulfilment as an amateur artist. She took guitar lessons in Naples, and brought sheet music and at least one instrument back to Weimar, thus promoting the new fashion for guitars, as written about in the *Journal des Luxus und der Moden*, perhaps as a result of the duchess's enthusiasm.[30]

The Netherlands remained an important travel destination. To be sure, Leiden's textile manufactures and Delft faiences had lost their pre-eminent status in Europe, but they were still worth visiting. The legacy of the Golden Age of painting also beckoned, and princes such as Friedrich of Mecklenburg-Schwerin embarked on 'art tours' of the Netherlands, visiting painting galleries and artists' studios. This benefited princely collections throughout Europe. The Netherlands and its university towns were also attractive to scholars. Thus, in Utrecht, the above-mentioned Keyßler met the important archaeologist and Orientalist Hadrian Reland, who helped him gain access to additional scholars and libraries in Western Europe.[31]

Figure 4   The St Beatus Cave on Lake Thun with a group of travellers. Painting by Caspar Wolf, 1776, oil on canvas

There were new destinations as well, though. Anglophilia and the socio-political and emancipatory interests of middle-class Germans made England an important travel destination. The public nature of political life, the individuality of the British, the landscape gardens, the fascinating new world of commodities and the like attracted mainly politically interested members of the educated German middle class, but also scientists, technicians, agriculturalists and garden architects, while the weather and food kept the broader mass of tourists away from the island.[32]

Switzerland, in contrast, became the destination of choice for all those interested in nature. The scientific interest in a natural world full of perils was no longer central, but rather the enthusiasm for natural beauty and its romantic glorification. The literary discovery of mountain landscape through Albrecht von Haller's *Die Alpen* and Salomon Gessner's 'Idylls' inspired a mania for Switzerland. Rousseau's paean to the Valois or his enthusiasm for the landscape of Lake Geneva contributed to the emergence of 'Helvetism' – an enthusiasm for all things Swiss. To be sure, English travellers had visited Switzerland before, but it was only in the late eighteenth century that the country opened up more to tourism, when the Bernese highlands and Lake Lucerne joined Lake Geneva and the Rhône valley as travel destinations. Travellers spread word of the high quality of Swiss hostelries and the good condition of roads and footpaths, giving Switzerland the reputation as a travel destination that persists to this day.[33] Artists responded to this tourist interest by turning to landscape painting and prints of Swiss landscapes. The most famous in this respect was Caspar Wolf (1735–83), who produced not only seascapes and landscapes of rocks and trees for the Lucerne collector Joseph Anton Felix Balthasar, but also more than 200 depictions of the Alps, which were commissioned for graphic reproduction by the Berne printer–publisher Abraham Wagner. While Wagner exhibited the paintings publicly in his gallery without selling them, they served as the basis for the print series *Merkwuerdige Prospekte aus den Schweizer Gebuergen* (Remarkable Views of the Swiss Mountains, Berne 1777–78). In 1779, Wagner moved his gallery (*Kabinett Wagner*) to Paris and produced a French edition with coloured aquatints.[34]

Other painters such as Johann Ludwig Aberli (1723–86), Balthasar Anton Dunker (1746–1807), Heinrich Rieter (1751–1808), Johann Jacob Biedermann (1763–1830) and Sigmund Freudenberger (1745–1801) satisfied the growing tourist demand for Swiss landscape and genre souvenirs with *veduten* (views), coloured etchings, watercolours and panoramas. Aberli's prints became so popular that he had to develop large-scale production in a studio with the help of several assistants to do the colouring.[35]

Travel literature

Travel literature was among the bestselling genres consumed at the end of the eighteenth century. Once again, it was Goethe who confirmed this in a letter to Cotta, in which he offered his publisher Johann Christoph Sachse's *Autobiographie eines reisenden Bediensteten* (Autobiography of a Travelling Servant). 'One finds similar books in libraries and reading societies quite worn and well-used, and this little volume would doubtless also be worth the while of the book-lenders.'[36] It was not for nothing that the great collections of travel accounts arose around 1800.[37] Their considerable literary and thematic breadth corresponds to the wide social spectrum of their readership, since publishers had to respond to the highly diverse interests and knowledge of the various strata of readers. Descriptions of travels in European countries played an important role alongside accounts of early voyages of discovery and the many scientific expeditions of the eighteenth and nineteenth centuries, which, like Friedrich Justin Bertuch's 'New Library of the Most Important Travel Accounts', were reprinted again and again.[38] As these countries became better known, the travel accounts became more differentiated. The travel account with literary ambitions gained in importance, while factual information was relegated to separate texts. In this way, travel literature captured new audiences, since it no longer mainly served as information, but satisfied the entertainment needs of middle-class readers.

Magazines increasingly published travel accounts, targeting the 'armchair travellers' for whom reading replaced direct experience of foreign lands.[39] These accounts generally had an essayistic character and concentrated on a general theme or the depiction of episodes, while eschewing detail or extensive reflections.[40]

Practical travel literature occupied an especially important place. All travel guides trace their lineage back to Theodor Zwinger, who sought in his 1577 *Methodus apodemica* to make travel more methodical and bring order to the disorganized lives of itinerant students. Accordingly, even Johann David Köhler's later *Anweisung zur Reiseklugheit für junge Gelehrte, um Bibliotheken, Münzkabinette, Antiquitätenzimmer, Bildergalerien, Naturalienkabinette und Kunstkammern mit Nutzen zu besehen* (A Guide to Prudent Travel)[41] refers to Zwinger's *Methodus apodemica* and Heinrich von Rantzau's *Methodum apodemicum*.[42] With the travel boom of the eighteenth century, new travel guides were repeatedly compiled using old texts, and supplemented with new information. One example is Johann Peter Willebrandt's 'Historical Reports and Practical Notes on Journeys in Germany, the Low Countries, France, England, Denmark, Bohemia and Hungary' (1758).[43] This combination of travel account and handbook went through eight editions and reprints in 11 years. Willebrandt not only discusses forms of government, laws, currency and measures, but also offers observations on so-called national character and a good deal of practical advice, ranging from how much to tip the stagecoach driver to financing journeys with bills of exchange and the intellectual experience of travel:

37. Inform yourself precisely and as much as possible about the country's political system, trade, advantages and manufacturing; there is no better means to do so, however, than in the renowned coffee houses.
38. Do not stop at viewing the public buildings of towns from the outside only, as travelling journeymen often do, but enquire into the interiors, particularly the condition of workbenches and workshops, manufactories, poorhouses, pawn shops, orphanages and prisons.
39. In each place, seek out the acquaintance of the most skilful scholars and the best artisans. When possible, make an effort in each place to meet a member of the government, a scholar of the law and various merchants.
40. Frequent the bookshops as much as possible, as this is the easiest way to make the acquaintance of men of learning.
41. Should you find something advantageous in the customs and habits of this or that nation, do not forget to make note of it, so that you may make use of it in future in your homeland.
42. Never get angry with an Italian, gamble with a Frenchman or booze with a German.[44]

With his observations on national character, Willebrandt, like other authors of travel guides, also offers evidence of his perceptions of his own and foreign mentalities:

Just as the above-mentioned things differ from each other, so the temperaments and with them the manners and capacities of the Germans diverge. In respect to his nature and inclinations, a Mecklenburger, Holsteiner, Pomeranian, Brunswicker, Hanoverian, Hessian, Westphalian, Swabian or Austrian is nearly as different from a Brandenburger, Upper Saxon, Silesian or Franconian as the Frenchman is from

Figure 5   Frontispiece engraving and title page of the travel book *Die Vornehmsten Europäischen Reisen* by Peter Ambrosius Lehmann. Hamburg, 1729

the Englishman or Spaniard, the Italian from the Hungarian, the Pole from the Dutchman and the Greek from the Swiss in his nature and manner of thinking.[45]

Stereotypes and topoi played a significant role in this context. Thus, for example, Gottlieb Friedrich Krebel repeatedly reprinted another travel bestseller, Peter Ambrosius Lehmann's 'Foremost European Journeys' and embellished the work with delimiting statements calculated to bolster the reader's own identity and presumably also to increase sales; despite the dangers, he repeatedly stresses the value of contact with foreign people and places as something constructive and reinforcing:

To be sure, our opposite number objects that our travellers often bring nothing home with them from France, Italy and Spain but foreign vices, to wit, French frivolity, Italian voluptuousness and lechery, Spanish ambuscades, foolish manners, insufferable gestures, superfluous titles, ridiculous ceremonies, strange clothing, affected speech and the utter loss of German and paternal virtues. I must agree with him to some extent, for experience has often amply demonstrated that most people travel before they have acquired good morals at home, and are in a proper position to profit from visiting foreign lands. The possibility that a thing may be abused, however, is no reason to abolish its legitimate use.[46]

The aspect of education is a further focus of the travel guides. According to Franz Posselt, the purpose of his own book was

> none other than to provide guidelines for young people of the educated classes more generally, and budding scholars and artists in particular, concerning how they might benefit from travel. ... In itself, merely travelling to various countries, and thoughtlessly touring curiosities, teaches us nothing. If the traveller does not know what he should be looking and asking for, if he has not acquired the art of seeing and hearing, and reflecting upon what he has seen and heard, then he can travel through all the lands of the earth without becoming in any way wiser, better, more sensible, intelligent or useful to the world. To be sure, many young travellers, especially those who travel for fashion only, i.e., merely for the sake of travelling, believe that they have done everything if they have seen all the sights to be seen in a foreign land. Their only achievement is thus to be able to say: we saw that too.[47]

Not travel as such, but travelling the right way, contributed to the traveller's education. Many young travellers had to pay quite dearly for their travel experiences, since they were very ignorant in many areas, but above all in the art of travel.[48]

For Posselt, dealing with the world was a sort of 'self-education', which did not depend on the accidents of teaching by parents and schoolmasters. Self-education was free and corresponded to the 'human aspiration continually to educate one's understanding, one's heart and one's taste',[49] and thus to the educational ideals propagated by the Enlightenment and Classicism.

Travel also changed the traveller's identity; scholars of the Enlightenment have emphasized this shift of perspective or the altered ways in which people located themselves as something essentially new. This process stood in stark contrast, however, to the thorough preparations and gathering of necessary information recommended to every traveller, which minimized their spontaneous openness to the world. Nevertheless, 'insouciant' travellers did exist. Thus, for example, according to his 'Journey of a Livonian from Riga to Warsaw' (1795), Joachim Christoph Friedrich Schulz did not follow the advice of travel writers to acquaint himself with the Lithuanian language. For him, the word for 'horse' sufficed, together with a grasp of the currency system ('the proper counting of money'). This ignorance corresponded to his assessment of the local culture and his attitude towards the 'enserfed peoples' in Livonia, Courland, Lithuania and Russia, which transported numerous clichés. To be sure, he said, 'laziness and negligence' and a 'sluggish character' were widespread there, but he blamed this on the serfs' lords, who demanded more of them the more effort they expended. 'Thus his lord is to blame not just for his laziness, but also for his corrupt temperament, which, like all slavish character, expresses itself in treachery, malicious delight in the misfortune of others, cunning and deceit.'[50] Here Schulz's insouciance doubtless mingled with pre-existing stereotypes.

In no previous era did people reflect so often upon travel as in the second half of the eighteenth century. Travel was regarded as fundamentally positive: it expanded one's horizons and left one more cultivated and educated. Confronting the foreign was deemed beneficial for one's own culture and country. Contact with foreign peoples and cultures as well as the 'travel craze' were caricatured only when they appeared excessive. At least in the travel guides, which sought to anticipate as many experiences of the foreign as possible, the foreign lost its aura of danger. In addition, the standardization of travel behaviour – one could travel in one's own post-chaise as one might on a package tour to Italy – meant that one often saw only what one wanted (or was intended) to see. The foreign was exorcized, dissected and thereby domesticated. Thus the fascination of the foreign played a diminishing role in travel guides, and was relegated to the travel novel, and the occasional individual travel account.

The decline of travel literature also ushered in the demise of the traditional travel canon at the end of the eighteenth century. Freed from the strictures of encyclopaedic travel, young travellers no longer could or needed to explain why and where they were travelling. Self-reliant travellers could visit the wealth of destinations on offer as time and funds permitted.[51] Nothing illustrates this better, in closing, than Christian August Clodius's satirical poem of 1780.[52]

The Journey
So you're going to Paris, Rome and London? – 'Yes.'
Why? 'My late father,
Uncle and brother were there.'
The gentlemen returned more learned from their travels?
'Quite so, not a fine spread did they miss;
In all of Paris there was no witty coffee house,
Which they could not point out on the map.'
You wish to see Rome, and afterwards Naples,
To visit the tombs of Virgil, Horace and Catullus,
And understand the ancient poets? –
'No, poets are really not my concern.
The Clairon in Paris piques your curiosity? 'No'
So surely you're a connoisseur of antiquities? –
'Indeed not, 'tis a matter
On which I'm quite lost–' Allow me to guess,
Surely you're a friend of Nature?
'I – and Nature? – oh no!' – Is it the art of living
That attracts you then, the fine manners and worldly tone
Which gain one a name in Paris? –
'I have never paid the slightest attention to manners.'
Perhaps you are travelling on discreet affairs of state
For the advantage of our republic,
To make the acquaintance of Lord North and Saint Germain?

'Tis the first I've heard tell of those gentlemen.'
Your plan? 'Surely you jest, my friend' – who needs a plan,
When one can find one's way in the world travelling from post to post?
What am I trying to paint in this fable?
A German portrait of many a German journey.[53]

Chapter 3

Fashion and Luxury

I dread à la mode, as the Germans' downfall begins with the mania for the new. For in order to make an impression, a thing need only be à la mode.[1]

Around the middle of the seventeenth century the word *Mode* (fashion) entered the German language, taken from the French phrase 'à la mode'. The word evolved from its original use for clothing fashions to a more general reference to lifestyles and all they entailed. Thus, a body of writing emerged around the notion of 'à la mode' that was often quite critical of France.

In the early eighteenth century, the first 'Compendia of Gallant Fashion' appeared, with the aim of treating the manners and habits of fine ladies in an encyclopaedic manner. For other contemporaries, Zedler's 'Universal Lexicon' noted, fashion was:

more generally, and in its broadest meaning, the manner, mode, usage, custom, genre, form, shape or pattern, but more particularly the common or usual mode of dress, furnishings, coaches and rooms, buildings, manufactures, manners of speaking and writing, compliments, ceremonies and other pomp, feasts and other modes of living.[2]

Although other authors, such as Adelung in his 1798 dictionary, supported this view and understood fashion as 'the established manner of deportment in social life, customs, habits and in the narrower sense, the changeable mode of dress …,'[3] in general usage, the word came to be used above all to refer to clothing styles. Friedrich Justin Bertuch, editor of what was probably the most influential lifestyle magazine of the era, the *Journal des Luxus und der Moden*, also fought valiantly against this restriction of meaning. This effort is evident in a particularly drastic example of 1794, in which he published an article 'On the Invention and Antiquity of the Guillotine', and justified its inclusion as follows:

After all, we are not writing a Ladies' Journal or a work for the dressing-table, in which one seeks nought but nectar and ambrosia, and wishes to breathe only the sweet scents of Elysium. We leave that to others. Nay, we are writing the chronicle of the Spirit of our Age, to the degree that it is ruled, guided and shaped by Fashion; and from this standpoint one will easily see that our field of observations is very wide, and the manifestations therein highly diverse and rich in contrasts.[4]

Accordingly, the *Journal des Luxus und der Moden* intended to publish monthly reports:

> on each new fashion and invention as it appears in France, England, Germany and Italy, in whatever branch of luxury it may be … . The subjects of interest to us are, thus 1) female and male dress; 2) millinery; 3) jewellery; 4) knick-knacks; 5) furniture; 6) all manner of tableware and drinking vessels, for example silver, porcelain, glasses, etc; 7) equipage, both wagons and horse trappings and liveries; 8) house and room furnishings and decorations; 9) gardens and country houses.[5]

The journal also published accounts 'from social life' as well as on art and literature, which later came to be known as 'feuilletons'. Bertuch combined fashion with 'luxury' (*Luxus*), the definition of which also expanded in the eighteenth century. Thus, in the eighteenth century, it no longer had the solely negative connotations of excess, ostentation or display. Various scholarly disciplines also treated luxury from different perspectives.[6] No one expressed this ambiguity better than Friedrich Justin Bertuch himself in the introduction to his *Journal des Luxus und der Moden*:

> According to followers of the physiocratic system, Luxury is the Scourge of the State! It squanders the rich revenues on fruitless expenditures, prevents reproduction, enervates the physiocratic forces of the Nation, dissolves all sense of Morality and Honour, ruins the well-being of families and supplies the State with hordes of beggars!
>
> Luxury, says the financier and the technologist, is the richest source for the State; the almighty motive force of Industry, and the strongest mechanism of Circulation. It erases all traces of Barbarism in Manners, creates Arts, Sciences, Commerce and Trades, increases the Population and Forces of the State, and leads to Delight and Joy of Living! – Who of the two is wrong? – Both, we believe, when they make absolute claims about this important matter. The entire dispute rests upon an incorrect, or at least an insufficiently pure definition of Luxury.[7]

The discourse on fashion, which brought forth its own media, was new for the eighteenth century. As so often, the phenomenon originated in France. There, the new fashions were illustrated for the first time with the help of (life-sized) fashion dolls as well as woodcuts and copperplate engravings. These fashion plates were a new entertainment medium, which reached a highpoint in the *Gallerie des Modes* (1778–87), a series of some 420 colour engravings.[8]

The production of fashion books, in contrast, was initially quite modest. Only in the second half of the eighteenth century did corresponding bestsellers emerge, such as Rétif de la Bretonne's *Monuments du costume*, which went through 15 editions between 1774 and 1793.[9] Fashion almanacs, the first of which appeared in 1774, should also be mentioned here.[10] On this level, though, fashion had already played an important role in works such as the *Calendrier des*

Dames of 1750. The same is true of the magazines, which were usually quite short-lived.

The literary *Journal des Dames*, which examined Paris society critically and intensified the discussion among women, was the only one of these periodicals to attain greater significance. In 1761, this magazine reached 39 French and 41 foreign cities, from Cadiz to St Petersburg.[11] It brought in new circles of readers, and fashion played a central role. As a result, new journals sprouted up concentrating on fashion in the stricter sense, describing the latest styles on a monthly basis. Thus the *Courier de la Mode ou le Journal du Goût* appeared on the first of every month from May 1768 to 1770. In England, where well-to-do women had informed themselves about the late fashions by perusing almanacs such as *The Ladies Complete Pocket Book*, the *Macaroni and Theatrical Magazine or Monthly Register of the Fashions and Diversions of the Times* (London, 1772–73) and *The Lady's Magazine* (1770–1825/32) appeared nearly simultaneously.[12]

Ten years later the *Cabinet des Modes* – the first French fashion magazine (1785–93), 'which regards as its chief task the introduction of fashions, and regularly fulfils this task in word and image' – as well as Bertuch's *Journal des Luxus und der Moden* (1786) came onto the market.[13] All of these periodicals placed fashion and taste in the broader context of taste formation by linking art and fashion and thus reaffirming the cultural conditionality of fashion. Thus, for example, *The Lady's Magazine* of 1801 wrote:

> There have been at all times violent declaimers against an attention to dress, which has also had, from time immemorial, illustrious defenders. In fact, it is averred that the most polished and enlightened nations have been precisely those that have been most addicted to the cultivation of the arts of dress. There appears to be an immutable analogy between a taste for the arts and a taste for dress, in such a manner that the latter may almost be considered as a certain thermometer of the degree of the former.[14]

Although in the *Cabinet des Modes*, accounts of women's fashions outnumbered those of men's fashions and accessories (shoe buckles, belts and rings) as well as home furnishings, the needs of the female readership were also satisfied in a feuilleton section containing sensational stories, social critical observations, poems, and book and theatre reviews – not forgetting the advertisements of certain traders, which were commented upon by experts. Advice on self-presentation also occupied a special place, with recommendations to wear the latest fashions in the Tuileries, the gardens of the Palais Royal, the Bois de Boulogne or the Champs-Elysées.[15] This also included advice to gentlemen to keep their left hands in their waistcoats, which were unbuttoned halfway, a gesture adopted by Napoleon in particular, who made it his trademark. Although the *Cabinet* had to stop publication in 1793 under Jacobin rule, it embodied the rapid changes in fashions against the background of social and political transformation between the Rococo and the Empire.

New English magazines such as the *Fashionable Court Guide* and the *Gallery of Fashion* stepped in to fill the gap in the European market left by the *Cabinet*'s disappearance. They propagated English dress on the Continent and elevated London to the capital of fashion. This did not create a new trend, but merely bowed to a movement in taste that had been gaining momentum for some time. In the 1770s and 1780s, English men's fashion, in particular, achieved popularity on a par with tea drinking and riding in the new English coaches with spring suspension. In 1768, the author Peter Helferich reported on French Anglomania from Paris:

> We are, to some extent, avenged by the current Anglomania of the French. Everywhere one goes, one encounters walking Riding-Coats among whose folds there flaps a frail Creature … . It is strange how the Sons of Liberty submit slavishly to every Fashion, and that the subject Frenchman always adds some national ornament. He attaches a large bunch of flowers to the breast of his horse groom's costume, and behind his neck the little English cadogan swells to the size of a pudding. Where Miss sets a rose-adorned chip hat in the middle of her curly brown head, the chapeau à l'anglaise hangs crooked from the powdered Frenchwoman, and the rose becomes a garland.[16]

The material realities of London and Paris arrived in Germany as literary constructs. Particularly outside the large urban centres such as Hamburg or Frankfurt, it was magazines, novels and letters that helped to constitute Western European consumer culture. As in other cultural fields, the German territories lagged behind Western Europe in the area of fashion. The magazines accordingly illustrated the new fashions in word and image, which also made it possible to produce cheaper imitations. The coloured engravings brought the clothes alive, and formed the basis for their artisanal and technical reproduction. Germans were torn between the new English trends and old French influences. While the (north German) educated middle classes developed a yearning for the English way of life, Paris continued to be the model for aristocratic elegance. Even the new 'English style' spread and was marketed to the Continent by way of Paris. The cultural chasm could run through families. Thus the *Journal des Luxus und der Moden* noted:

> The inhabitants of Mecklenburg are like other Germans; they imitate both the English and the French, though with one important difference. The men arrange their clothes, their households, their carriages and gardens in the English style, while elegant ladies still follow the lead of Parisian fashion dealers, who send their outdated goods to the North.[17]

Thus gender roles were constructed and then cleverly supplemented with national stereotypes, such as the Anglo-French dualism, in order to keep readers interested. 'And yet it is not France alone whose magic wand we must fear. England and the perfected craft of her factories will and must necessarily become just as dangerous to us'.[18] It was, after all, the new English culture of

Figure 6 'Fashions of the Years 1701 and 1801', frontispiece engraving for the *Journal des Luxus und der Moden*, January 1801

commodities or consumption that was also becoming increasingly attractive on the Continent:

> The tasteful simplicity and solidity that England succeeded in bestowing upon all of her manufactured goods so recommends itself to and attracts us Germans that at present the word English [or] English goods already has such an irresistibly magical

allure for us, and has become nearly synonymous with perfection and beauty in works of craft.[19]

Bertuch accordingly reported monthly not just on new fashions and inventions from abroad, but also on social life, and art and literature. As time went on, these reviews of plays, concerts and books, which Bertuch had not originally planned, took up more and more space in the magazine, so that he eventually changed the title of his publication to reflect the new content. From 1813 it was known as *Journal für Luxus, Mode und Gegenstände der Kunst* (Luxury, Fashion and Art Objects) and from 1815 as *Journal für Literatur, Kunst, Luxus und Mode* (Literature, Art, Luxury and Fashion).

The *Journal* was accompanied by the so-called intelligence gazette (*Intelligenzblatt*) as an independent advertising supplement in which publishers, manufacturers and merchants could promote their wares. These ranged from English tea-urns and cucumber slicers to editions of prints from Rost Art Dealers in Leipzig, new sheet music, wallpaper, musical clocks and 'balloon' stoves. The range of luxury goods was quite comparable with that available in England. The luxury trades in the areas of silver, ceramics, glass, clocks and furniture maintained a leading position until technical innovations made it possible in the eighteenth century to put cheaper, mass-produced imitations on the market – tea caddies of silver-leaf or brass instead of solid silver and Wedgwood stoneware instead of porcelain – which soon asserted themselves in the fashion cycle.[20] The same can be said of Bertuch's offer, which promised 'the beautiful Wedgwood so-called Cameo Buttons, finished in the Stile of antique Gems'[21] as well as cheaper imitations made in Saxony-Weimar. These luxury products could be purchased from Bertuch's Landes-Industrie-Comptoir, which maintained a putting-out system with sample fairs. By perusing the *Journal* and ordering from Bertuch, one thus participated in the European world of commodities and consumer culture.

Reading was a decisive factor in the formation of consumer desires, and the literary discourse about them included particular aesthetic objects in personal lifestyles.[22] The *Journal* accordingly became an important voice in the cultural life of the emergent bourgeoisie, influencing both the traditionally Francophile aristocracy and, above all, the functional elites with their as yet uneducated tastes – making it an extraordinary source for historians.[23] For readers, the yearly subscription price of 4 talers for 12 issues was also affordable. That the magazine was also an economic success is evident not just from the subscription figures (1,488 in 1788 and 1,765 in 1799) – thanks to the reading societies and other forms of communal reading, the number of readers will have been ten times that – but also the longevity of this periodical, which appeared monthly for no fewer than 41 years.

Changing fashions and styles in the eighteenth century

What changes of fashions and styles did the above-mentioned magazines document in the course of the eighteenth century? These changes are nowhere as clearly illustrated as in the frontispiece engravings of the *Journal des Luxus und der Moden*, which in 1801 looked back on the year 1701. In the commentary on this print, the author notes a remarkably rapid transformation in fashions over the past century. Courtly conventions of taste were supplanted by new market conventions. One fashion replaced the other. This process began with the death of Louis XIV in 1715, when Philip II of Orléans took over the regency for the king, who was still a minor. In this fashion era, known accordingly as the *Régence*, the nobility left the court at Versailles, with its strict conventions, and turned their Parisian town palaces, particularly the salons, into their own miniature courts. They furnished them with a wealth of decorative items, including chinoiserie, for example wall hangings with Chinese motifs.[24] Even at home the ladies wore panniers, as documented by the famous *Shop Sign* of the art dealer Gersaint by Watteau.

Matters were no different in Hamburg. Thus the *Curieuse Antiquarius* reported in 1712: 'The lady wears skirts that are very wide at the bottom, as if they contained barrel hoops. Thus when two ladies meet in a narrow lane, as much confusion ensues as if two hay wagons were to drive side-by-side.'[25] The pannier persisted until the 1760s, but, much like French court ceremony, its influence on fashion waned. A simpler style of dress asserted itself, which was better adapted to female proportions and paid homage to the English model of privacy, comfort and functionality.

Men's fashions also became simpler in the eighteenth century. The traditional combination of *justaucorps*, waistcoat and breeches remained, but the *justaucorps* lost its flared skirts, acquired long sleeves, and came more closely to resemble an English frock coat. With time, the waistcoat shortened to waist length, while the knee breeches became ever tighter.

A closer examination of English fashion shows how strongly it influenced Continental styles. In England, the monochrome cloth frock coat had replaced the silk *justaucorps* as daytime clothing by the first half of the eighteenth century. In the 1750s, under the influence of military uniforms, the frock coat acquired its typical close-fitting form. Under this, men wore tight breeches of cloth or yellow suede. A waistcoat of the style known in England as a 'Newmarket', generally of white piqué, but sometimes of coloured silk, completed the ensemble. In Germany, young admirers of *Sturm und Drang* literature wore blue frock coats, yellow waistcoats and breeches as a so-called Werther costume to document their identification with the protagonist of Goethe's *Sorrows of Young Werther*. On their heads they wore a round black hat, which would eventually turn into the top hat. Men also demonstrated their emancipation from courtly manners by carrying a walking stick rather than a sword.

Englishwomen relinquished their panniers and Rococo headdresses. In the second half of the eighteenth century, they preferred the more figure-fitting gown that became widespread under the name 'robe à l'anglaise'. As a concession to taste, they wore bustle-pads in different shapes, over which the gowns fell in loose folds. They also adopted certain innovations from men's fashion, such as the *caraco*, a long jacket that recalled a frock coat. As outerwear, men and women alike wore *redingotes*, a corruption of the English term riding coat. Ladies' hairstyles became less formal and hair was worn loose to the shoulders in small curls, so that women could easily wear a large straw or felt hat.

This was the ideal that Bertuch's *Journal* also conveyed to German readers. The very first volume of the magazine featured colour plates showing the latest English fashions for men and women. The 'English ladies' costume' was described as follows:

> It is extremely flattering to a well-proportioned figure, shows a beautiful waist in all its grace thanks to the bodice, which is tight below and wide and somewhat loose above, and in general possesses the noble and unostentatious appearance of tasteful simplicity and decorum that so enhances the charms of the fair sex.[26]

In Germany, too, writers prepared the ground for the spread of English fashions. In his *Patriotische Phantasien* (Patriotic Fantasies), which originally appeared in the *Osnabrücker Intelligenzblätter*, Justus Möser addressed questions of dress and fashion on several occasions. Thus in a 'Letter to my Father-in-Law' (1767), he has a young husband recount how he convinced his wife to exchange her previous mode of dress for the new 'à la grecque' fashion. With a short gown that barely reached her feet and simple black shoes, she wore a rustic cap, thus approaching quite closely Möser's ideal of simple dress for noblewomen and peasants alike.[27] Goethe refined the idea by praising the aesthetic harmony between dress ('still emphasising the form, to a certain extent') and the body of the wearer. He had enjoyed just such a pleasing sight in Italy, when the future Lady Hamilton demonstrated Greek dress in the Naples home of her lover, Sir William Hamilton.

All this notwithstanding, the *Journal des Luxus und der Moden* demonstrably reported more frequently on French or Parisian fashion, although the editors' sympathies lay with English style and culture more generally. This circumstance is clear, for example, from Bertuch's plea for comfortable and suitable dress for children, the success of which the *Journal* noted in 1798. In the spirit of the Enlightenment, the *Journal* presented new clothing for children, for 'in his or her dress, too, a child should look like a child, and not a grown man or a little lady'.[28] English models were influential here, but also new ideals of childrearing. Accordingly, Bertuch also offered advice on raising children, suggestions for appropriate games and later a series of children's literature.[29]

Despite his sympathies for the British Isles, Bertuch was well aware of the competition raging between English functionality and French elegance, and thus of a cultural division that split Germany in two:

Figure 7   A young lady en *grande parure*. Illustration from the *Journal des Luxus und der Moden*, January 1804

The goods sold at the Frankfurt and Leipzig fairs have now been distributed to the storehouses of fashion everywhere, and provide an overview of new inventions and arrivals in this field. France offers us its left hand across the Rhine and the Main. The chief emporium of elegant sales is Frankfurt, Mainz etc. Leipzig, in contrast, and other northern cities such as Hamburg and Bremen enrich central Germany with English products. For that reason one can surely wager that the former part of Germany will be supplied with more tasteful, elegant, frivolous and graceful articles of fashion, and the latter with finer, daintier, more solid but not seldom also stiffer and more affected ones.[30]

Vienna was allegedly still wholly in French hands:

> In matters of fashion, Vienna still looks to Paris, by and large. There are ladies and modistes who regularly order mannequins and drawings from France. New fashions rarely grow in our native soil, and when they do, they do not rise to the reputation of Parisian ones.[31]

The *Journal*'s attitude towards Vienna was correspondingly critical, and the tone of reporting frequently sarcastic (for example, about an animal baiting there, which was announced as a charity event). However critical of France, writers were compelled to note that the success of English fashion also hindered the development of an independent German tradition:

> It is striking how England now sets the tone far more than France in all fancy goods, and fills the German market with them. I have good reason to doubt that Germany gains thereby, for English fancy goods, as fancy goods, are just as subject to the frivolous changes in fashion, but too solid and too dear. Germany can thus easily end up twice as indebted to England as it was to France.[32]

Germany also witnessed a certain Anglo-French symbiosis in matters of dress, which began even before the French Revolution. Thus informal, everyday clothes (*negligé*) tended to be 'English', while the more formal attire of *grande parure* (for example, at court) was 'French'. This changed little with the French Revolution. After courtly Rococo fashion fell out of favour, writers emphasized the informality of English style, now embellished with Revolutionary or military elements. In the *Journal*, the Phrygian cap became a ladies' hat, while buttons were described as 'à la Bastille', 'à la garde-bourgeoise', 'à la nation' or 'à la tiers-état'.[33] French gentlemen adopted military airs as Sansculottes; the *Journal* also introduced its German readers to the uniforms of the citizen militias and the National Guard. With time, however, antique attributes replaced the military ones. One of these accessories was the 'casque de Minerve', a helmet-like hat that ladies wore atop their new flatter, looser and unpowdered hairstyles.

The painter Jacques-Louis David, with his knowledge of classical dress, functioned as a sort of couturier, and helped give birth to the new republican women's costume. His portraits, particularly that of Madame Récamier – herself a fashion trendsetter – helped to spread the new style. Thus in the mid-1790s, the neo-classical gowns that would be known during the Napoleonic era as Empire gowns became all the rage. The high-waisted 'chemise anglo-grecque' became ever more daring. Women not only showed more and more bare skin – arms and décolleté – but also emphasized their figures with pads and flesh-coloured tricots. The *Journal* responded with caricatures and cutting comments on 'indecent French nudity'. Women neglected by nature helped themselves with artifice:

In a word, the ladies have applied the custom of lending their arms fullness and roundness with wax inserts to something more substantial, and, if Nature has cheated them of a bosom, they employ artificial surrogates of wax, which are so artfully adapted and shaped that Argus himself with his hundred eyes would not have noticed the innocent little ruse had it not been for an immodest chatterer who, having espied the invention at the bosom manufacturers, betrayed the secret by public announcement.[34]

Some, however, wrote positively of the new lighter garments. Caroline de la Motte Fouqué, for instance, while complaining of the degradation of old country-seats with such consumer goods as wallpaper, painted glass lanterns and horsehair sofas (instead of damask, crystal chandeliers and fauteuils), emphasized the mobility and bodily freedom that the new, lighter gowns offered.[35] Nevertheless, the *Journal* expressed relief in 1805 when the trend towards transparent materials gave way to heavier fabrics. The consecration of the Emperor Napoleon, and more particularly Empress Josephine's coronation regalia of velvet and satin, with references to numerous historical eras, had a lasting influence. Borrowings from the Renaissance (lace collar) as well as the Egyptomania that followed Napoleon's Egyptian campaign (puffed and gathered sleeves à la Mameluke) set new accents, which also spread to Germany.

Propagating a national taste

At the same time, efforts were also underway to distance Germans from the dictates of French taste. These efforts were nothing new. In the very first volume of the *Journal*, Bertuch had called for a promotion of native trade and industry and therefore also for increasing consumption among local German elites, particularly the functional elites.

Thus, in the first volume in 1786, Bertuch launched the test balloon of national dress and posed the question: 'Would it be useful and possible to introduce a German national costume?' In so doing, he took up old stereotypes and mercantilist ideas according to which the slavish emulation of the French was deleterious to morals, finances and the balance of trade, and deemed certain characteristics of national dress to be necessary:

Thus only two points are essential here:
    1) the choice of clothing, and
    2) the manner in which it would be agreed upon and introduced.
As to the first point, I believe we can accept the following principles. The clothing must be
    a) cheap;
    b) of colours that do not easily show dirt, durable, easy to wash and neither invented by nor dependent upon the whims of fashion;
    c) appropriate for all ages;
    d) easily acquired by the distinguished and the common, by rich and poor alike;

e) adapted to our climate;
f) not fantastical;
g) not deforming to the body;
h) bearing the mark of Germanness;
i) wearable in all seasons … .

There are, alas, some people who ridicule all things; there are others who see something dangerous or perfidious everywhere; finally, there are still others who find no good in anything unless it was discovered or proposed by themselves or some party to which they belong. That is sad, and from such as they I must surely expect no justice from any quarter for my recommendations, but this does not bother me. I am conscious of making these suggestions out of good, honest and patriotic German intent. I belong to no party, have devised these ideas on my own, and would be mightily pleased if the matter were to succeed, without any honour or even mention of my name … .[36]

When a woman reader announced a 'female rebellion', however, the idea was dropped. Although the following letter to the editor may well have been fictitious or commissioned in order to kindle enthusiasm for the *Journal* among its female audience or enter into dialogue with them, the arguments of this 'avid reader Friederike S*' are to be taken seriously:

I believe that the introduction of a German national costume would not merely fail to achieve the reasonable chief purpose of suppressing damaging luxury in dress (for national originality and German character are doubtless only secondary aims for the author), but would even entail great disadvantage for Germany. A large proportion of German manufactures, whose workers all earn their bread from the diversity of products and the choice and taste of customers, would lose their livelihoods through a national costume, which would permit only a few materials and colours, and many thousand tradesmen would be reduced to beggary at the stroke of the pen, or might even be forced to emigrate, for a velvet, taffeta or cotton weaver can no longer become a cloth-maker or a woollen weaver … . And finally, the fine gentleman who wishes to give Germany an eternal uniform seems not to reckon us poor women to be part of the nation, for he seeks so unlawfully to return us to the farthingales and ruffs of our great-great-grandmothers in the sixteenth century, dressing us in an eternal black, white and grey, like nuns, and to rob us of all salvation and comfort. For Heaven's sake, gentlemen, consider what topics of conversation we might have during a three or four hour coffee visit, at tea or on a promenade if there were no more new ribbons, bonnets, hats, gowns and sheath dresses [*fourreaux*]? The State and our husbands surely run two risks here: we shall either become learned and dispute new works and the mental faculties of our own and other women's men, or meddle in political affairs and rant about politics, both of which have previously been the undisputed privileges of men. So do what you can to keep the gentleman who assaults us so despotically from realising his awful plans; otherwise, I prophesy certain female rebellion in Germany. You can guess what I part I shall play in this.[37]

In his efforts on behalf of German national costume, Bertuch found himself in good company. Justus Möser had already called for the introduction of a national dress code, graduated by rank, which was intended to counteract the efforts of contemporaries to represent status through clothing, and thus to combat sartorial ostentation. Ultimately, this idea only bore fruit outside of Germany: in 1791, the Danish Academy of Sciences offered a prize for the best proposal concerning the introduction of national dress. The entrants referred to the Swedish law of 1778 as well as the sumptuary codes in St Petersburg and Russia's Baltic provinces.[38] Nevertheless, German fashions were propagated both overtly and covertly, which even had some effect in the area of male attire. Thus, for example, in the first volume of the *Journal*, a picture of a French horseman in the *Cabinet des Modes* is juxtaposed with the ideal of a German horseman, although the influence of English style on the latter is unmistakeable:

> The three-cornered hat with its rather military turned-up brim and black ribbon lends him a certain free and noble *air de tête*, just as the front corner, which turns straight up, adorns the upright, perpendicular position of the body on horseback. When the brim is turned down, the hat is large and perfectly round, completely shielding the shoulders from rain, and can, if the front corner is damaged, easily be turned up the other way, just as, worn the other way 'round, protects the eyes from the sun ... . The short, so-called Berlin frock coat, which overlaps a little at the breast, where it is fastened with a few buttons, and widens towards the bottom, lends the figure more chest, and conceals neither the thighs nor the form of the horse, protects the rider from spraying mud, and in general lends him an elegant, light and adroit appearance. The frock coat is lined in white because of the white underclothing. This and the black velvet collar give it something of a uniform, which is pleasing to the eye.[39]

With this description, the *Journal* picked up seamlessly where a previous fashion, namely the Werther costume, had left off. The cult of *The Sorrows of Young Werther* changed the manners, leisure activities, reading behaviour and clothing of the younger generation of the educated middle class. Werther fashion (a blue frock coat, yellow waistcoat and knee breeches) was thus the first trend in eighteenth-century German culture to be inspired by a literary discourse and not a court, although Carl-August of Saxony-Weimar made the costume (known as the *Werther-Anzug*) popular at his own court. Thus began – and this was central for all magazines – a culture of fashion in which literary fiction could easily set in motion trends in material culture. With the Werther costume, young men adopted an identity of their own, so that appearing in public in it was comparable to going out in jeans today. The success of the Werther outfit was not simply a product of reading, however; positive associations with the English gentry and the Prussian military also played a role.

> The young fashionable Berliner of the distinguished and largest class wears, from morning until night, boots, a round hat, a blue coat with a red collar, in a very military

style and very often with dirty linen. Dressed in this manner, he goes to lectures, under the Linden, to coffeehouses; a meal, again under the Linden, to the theatre, and very often into society. He enters polite society only when parents, a love affair, or some other convenience brings him there, and under no circumstances can he be bothered to change his attire.[40]

The propagation of national taste was a characteristic shared by many European fashion magazines, which often employed clichéd references to other European countries, especially England and France. By tracking down new trends and influencing taste, the magazines sought to fill the gap in the market between vendors, producers and traders.[41] By reading the *Journal des Luxus und der Moden*, for example, readers throughout the German territories participated in the new world of European commodities.

Wardrobe realities

As we have seen, the *Journal des Luxus und der Moden* affords interesting insights into the fashion discourse of the late eighteenth and early nineteenth century. To what extent was this discourse reflected in material reality? First, we need to ask how widely read the magazines were, and whether they succeeded in realizing the new trends in the European centres in a fashion cycle of five to seven months. We know that the *Journal des Luxus und der Moden* had several hundred subscribers in each of the large cities, and was disseminated in the smaller capitals at least through reading societies (cf. the map in Chapter 1 above). The material reality that we can reconstruct, for example using estate inventories, only partly confirms the evidence of the magazines. This finding may, of course, also be a result of the unfortunately rather sparse inventories that have come down to us for the decisive period of change (the modernization of dress) between 1770 and 1790.

Some inventories nevertheless confirm the development familiar to us from the fashion periodicals. Thus, in 1772, the Hamburg shopkeeper's widow Anna Plaehn left two *contuches* (a kind of overdress) of cotton in addition to two of silk.[42] The English clothes mentioned in Münster inventories of the late eighteenth century indicate even more clearly the gradual adaptation to English taste; the preference for cotton material or cotton dresses (perhaps even chemise gowns) is also in keeping with this orientation towards English fashion.[43] A willingness to make qualitative changes becomes evident along with the increase and differentiation in the clothing, gloves, hats, cloaks and other accessories mentioned by the inventories, which now appear in a wide variety of colours and fabrics.[44]

We also have evidence of the new men's fashions, at least in the estate inventory of the Jewish merchant Friedrich Maximilian Beer of Frankfurt, who died in 1795. He left a wide assortment of clothing, which included not just a 'cotton dressing gown', a silk dressing gown embroidered with yellow flowers

1791

Figure 8 A London buck, or beau, of the latest form, fashion and cut. Illustration from the *Journal des Luxus und der Moden*, November 1791

(lined in taffeta, with a matching waistcoat), 14 pairs of underpants, 37 shirts, as well as countless pairs of cotton and silk stockings, but also green woollen riding breeches, black jersey trousers, black cashmere trousers, black silk trousers, salt-and-pepper cloth trousers, grey cashmere trousers and striped 'Nanking' trousers of brown and yellow cotton after a Chinese model. Among his coats, a grey English cloth coat, a salt-and-pepper frock coat, a striped woollen frock coat and a blue coat with yellow buttons (in the Werther style) particularly stand out. His unique collection of 36 different waistcoats ranged from white muslin to white silk with a coloured border, and also included versions in red cashmere, yellow stripes, black stripes, green checks or half-silk flowered embroidery.[45] With these outfits he could easily approximate the ideal of a 'London buck' presented in the 1791 *Journal*, as well as the Werther fashion.

Beer's collection contradicts the prejudice stirred up by the magazines that only women succumbed to fashion mania. To what extent he was exceptional in this respect, or whether such sumptuous male wardrobes were common, is a question for further research, especially with respect to estate inventories of the early nineteenth century.

Bertuch's statement that 'fashion is indeed a cosmopolitan, who does not permit herself to be enclosed in a single country, and according to her innate penchant for contradiction prefers to rig herself out with contraband',[46] is therefore not without justification. Thus, on the one hand, a German fashion magazine such as the *Journal des Luxus und der Moden* addressed its readers as members of a purportedly backward German (fashion) nation, and on the other it measured German fashion trends against a Western European (fashion) identity, thereby paying homage to German progress. English and French developments were compared with trends in Hamburg, Mecklenburg, Berlin and Vienna, offering various potential identities to aristocratic functional elites and members of the educated middle classes. In this way, the *Journal des Luxus und der Moden*, like other periodicals, created a virtual marketplace for boundless cultural consumption.

Only against the background of the Napoleonic occupation, and above all in the political journalism of the Wars of Liberation, were high-necked dark dresses stylized as a 'German national costume', and also promoted in the pages of the *Journal* in 1814 in a mood of patriotic euphoria. A direct line was drawn here between the invasion of French customs along with French dress and the demise of the Holy Roman Empire, since the former had allegedly undermined German customs and with them 'the foundations of the throne and constitutions'.[47] For that reason, in 1814, a Munich woman suggested clothing reform, with the aim of 'the greatest possible simplification of garments' and the introduction of a 'formal dress code for all classes'. She recommended that the uniform of Bavaria's *Landwehr*, or reserve army, which was already considered as a national costume there, be adopted as national dress for all German men.[48] Bavarian dress – which has survived into the twenty-first century with loden jackets and dirndls – appears, however, to have had as little lasting influence as any of the other excessively patriotic fashion tips of the period around 1815.

Chapter 4

The Culture of Domestic Interiors

> I have three rooms next to each other, all of them for my own use. One is the so-called reception room [*Visitenzimmer*], the middle one a small drawing room [*Saal*] and then my sitting room [*Wohnstube*], with a bedchamber [*Schlafstube*] of moderate size. My husband lives on the other side of the reception room.[1]

This excerpt from a letter written by the newly-married Göttingen professor's wife Wilhelmine Heyne-Heeren in 1796 is indicative of the separation of female and male living space, which would prove typical of changes in domestic arrangements in the eighteenth century.[2] Wilhelmine Heyne-Heeren may have been influenced by Leonhard Christoph Sturm, whose 1721 *Vollständige Anweisung alle Arten von Bürgerlichen Wohn-Häusern wohl anzugeben* (Complete Instruction for the Suitable Arrangement of all Manner of Middle-class Dwelling-Houses) had already recommended:

> that in middle-class houses, especially the more distinguished ones, the rooms be arranged in such a way that the man can reach the woman's room from his own, without having to walk through the hallway, where anyone can walk freely to and fro ... . It is not, however, strictly necessary that the shared bedchamber lie between the two rooms, still less so that it be in the centre of the building, especially as this is often left by preference to the reception rooms. The best arrangement is when both the husband's and the wife's apartments have their own bedchamber, with a drawing room between the two.[3]

On the whole, the trend was from living patterns with large, undifferentiated rooms to ones with smaller, specialized rooms, with the parlour as the centrepiece of family life, which was also reflected in furnishings and domestic culture.[4] Although contemporaries often found the domestic architecture and living conditions in the small towns of southern Germany and the old commercial cities of northern Germany to be backward or old-fashioned, and travellers regarded only the capital cities and university towns as more modern, living arrangements were changing even in the traditional centres.

New, at least for the domestic architecture of the urban middle and upper classes, was the transition from a few large rooms to a number of smaller ones. This had already begun in the seventeenth century, to be sure, when the Low German hall or lobby houses with their simple spatial structure were partially subdivided, but it was only in the eighteenth century that attics previously used for storage were converted to living space and partitioned into rooms. In addition to the use of the principal floors in merchant houses, the fenestration of façades brought more light into the rooms. Moreover, the construction of specialized rooms altered the size and variety of uses of the old central hall. Accordingly, those who could afford it had more and more special-purpose rooms, for example, a drawing room in addition to the parlour, while poorer folk had to make do with one living room and a kitchen, or only a single room. Newly constructed multi-family dwellings and tenements with larger flats on one floor served the need for rented accommodation with specialized rooms.[5] In many towns, old houses underwent strikingly luxurious modernization, as occurred in 1797 in Stettin:

> the gentleman of the house, Madame, the young misses, the young gentleman, the menservants [and] the maids all want their own rooms now; the staff is no longer content with servants' quarters, they must be able to heat their rooms in winter, and then there are the parlours, reception rooms, dining rooms, entrance halls and whatever other names may be given to the rooms.[6]

Apart from travel accounts and autobiographies, important information on domestic culture also comes from the estate inventories that document the material possessions of the dead and that entered the record in cases where guardians had to be appointed, possessions distributed or inheritance disputes settled.[7] The abundance of these sources varies greatly across the German-speaking region, but the degree to which they have been studied is more uneven still. While Britain, the Netherlands and Spain have a long tradition of archiving and thus also reconstructing material culture,[8] we owe our information about Germany to a few ethnographers such as Ruth Mohrmann and Uwe Meiners and their detailed studies of the domestic culture of cities in Lower Saxony and Westphalia.[9] For southern Germany, we have only a few accounts of specific aspects, with no work thus far on the large urban centres. The source material on the eighteenth century is also extremely heterogeneous, since the surviving archived inventories are not evenly spread across the century or distributed representatively across a range of social strata. As a result, we must be content with the material we do have, supplemented by some newly archived inventories from Frankfurt and Hamburg, for both of which cities the material is quite sparse. Nevertheless, analyses of these Frankfurt and Hamburg inventories as well as recent studies on the Baltic cities of Copenhagen, Stralsund, Greifswald, Riga and Reval yield a variety of information.[10]

Particularly interesting are the inventories that record objects by room, thus making possible an initial reconstruction of how domestic spaces were used. According to these, in artisans' houses in Münster, the kitchen served as a living, working and cooking room, while the lobby houses on the main market square, despite their far higher standard, were still characterized in the seventeenth century by a multifunctional use of large rooms. In Lemgo (Westphalia), the transition to mono-functional rooms was completed only in the eighteenth century, with separate bedrooms and additional living rooms, while in Brunswick the parlour, which in the seventeenth century had already been equipped with furniture, textiles and other decorative elements as well as books and toys, was where the family spent most of their time.[11]

Nevertheless, here too a qualitative leap occurred in the eighteenth century with regard to both furnishings and use. Before we pursue in detail the new trends – such as the transition from trunks to cupboards and the differentiation of furnishings – we will first illustrate a few further examples of room use in the eighteenth century.[12] In Osnabrück, as in other Westphalian cities, the upper classes preserved the large saloon or drawing room (*Saal*) as the site of representation. Thus, at the home of the procurator and notary Cappel, this room was furnished in 1771 with the new chests of drawers, a walnut armoire, a pier table with a veneer of the same wood, chairs and armchairs upholstered in velvet, mirrors and pictures. In this room, the family cultivated a lavish lifestyle with dishes and drinking vessels of porcelain and silver. The carter Normann or the night watchman's widow Buschmann, in contrast, had only a multifunctional central room with simple furniture and dishes, although the Widow Buschmann could also retreat to a parlour furnished with a table, mirror and pictures. The master tailor Landwehr's house had two living rooms, a hall and two large 'chambers' (*Kammer*). One of the living rooms was also a workroom, while the other was furnished with pictures, tables, a wooden armoire (known in northern Germany as a *Schapp*) and a bed. The family probably lived mostly on the upper floor, where one of the rooms contained six leather chairs, a tea table, an armchair and several trunks. The presence of a Bible, a book of homilies, wine and beer glasses and plaster of Paris figures would also seem to confirm this supposition.

The house of the well-to-do wine merchant Knille, who ultimately went bankrupt, had still more specialized rooms. Here, the inventory marked the different rooms according to their functions, for example the gentleman's study, nursery, servants' quarters, entryway to the garden, drawing room and billiard room (with silk wallpaper). This luxury may have contributed to the wine merchant's financial decline. Without such bankruptcies, however, we would probably know as little of Knille's domestic interiors as we do of the tailor Landwehr's.[13]

A considerable differentiation of rooms (and houses) is also evident from the Frankfurt estate inventories, while the Hamburg inventories generally only list objects by material and function. The Frankfurt houses and flats, which were inhabited by both wealthy artisans and professionals and merchants, were characterized by numerous rooms. In 1777, the house of the blacksmith Augustin Geißemer situated in the Zeil, for example, had three lavishly furnished living rooms in addition to an attic and three bedrooms. Apart from an armchair (walnut), the first living room contained, among other furnishings, four armchairs, a coffee table, a telescope table, a walnut chest of drawers filled with a trousseau, a child's cupboard and a box of toys as well as a glass cabinet with a copper teapot, a china service and two long-stemmed glasses. The room on the first floor contained tableware, coffeepots, a teapot, cups for chocolate, the few books (see Chapter 1 above), oak and walnut armchairs, an upholstered armchair, paintings, a two-door walnut armoire (which mainly held clothing), and a pine cupboard for bed and table linens.[14]

According to an estate inventory of 1775, Margaretha Barbara Tanner, widow of Dr Ludwig Gottfried Tanner, lived even more luxuriously in her home, the 'De Groot House', on Horsemarket. The inventory mentions a total of 13 rooms in addition to the 'square' in front of the house. The most lavishly furnished were the ground-floor living room, the first-floor sitting room and the bedroom. The living room contained a mirror in a glass frame, a walnut chest of drawers, a walnut buffet cupboard (*Tresor*) and six cane chairs with blue cushions. Far more luxurious were the furnishings of the first-floor sitting room, which were graced by '1 walnut cabinet with 2 silver escutcheons and a porcelain pediment'. The cabinet contained a heavy silver coffee kettle, coffeepots, tea urns, a teapot and candelabra, sugar bowls and cups as well as solid silver cutlery (knives, spoons, forks), which had been absent in the Geißemer household, for example. Other items kept in this room included articles of clothing as well as books bound in silver, cuffs and other items in a chest of drawers, while a walnut chest with a glass cabinet held coloured porcelain plates and bowls with matching tea, chocolate and coffee cups with flowers painted on them. Valuables were kept in the bedroom, and the family's wealth was demonstrated by a silver bedside table with a mirror in a silver frame, candelabra, and a variety of fancy boxes.[15]

In Hanseatic cities such as Stralsund and Greifswald, in contrast, individual rooms only come to be mentioned rather later, which would seem to indicate that even in the eighteenth century, the home was still a mono-functional space. While in Stralsund we already have evidence of the differentiation of domestic space in the early eighteenth century – Hinrich Boldten's dwelling house was described as consisting of a 'front room' a 'large back room', a 'chamber', 'another small chamber', 'another small chamber', 'the upper room', the 'hall' and a kitchen ('Vorderstube …, grosse Hinterstube …, Kammer …, noch ein Caemmerchen …, noch ein Caemmerchen …, die Oberstube …, Hausdiele …, Kueche …') – in Greifswald it was not until 1799 that we find halls, rooms and chambers (*Dielen, Stuben, Kammern*) mentioned for the two storeys of Councilman Pritz's house there, for example.[16]

Furniture

Scholars of material culture organize the objects found in homes into groups. The focus of interest is on furniture, which is usually divided up into storage furniture, seating furniture and tables. From the Middle Ages on, trunks and chests were the most important forms of storage furniture. In the course of the early modern period, trunks, chests, boxes and coffers were gradually replaced as modes of storage by case furniture, a process that occurred at different rates in town and country and from region to region.[17] Although in many households

Figure 9   Chest of drawers, North German or Scandinavian, c. 1760

chests still dominated in the eighteenth century, with the exception of trunks, they gradually lost their importance as items of furniture and their place in sitting rooms and parlours, giving way to various forms of case furniture. In eighteenth-century inventories we find a wide range of different armoires (*Schapp*) and other types of cupboards, which were differentiated by wood, decoration and function. For the Brunswick towns of the eighteenth century Mohrmann encountered mainly 'pine' armoires and linen cupboards.[18] Despite the scant sources there were numerous oak, walnut and painted cabinets in Hamburg whilst the variations on case furniture in the wealthier Frankfurt households were extremely rich. The inventories record between nine and 18 different types of case furniture, differentiated not just by material (pine, oak, walnut, poplar), but also by function (clothes, bedding, book, kitchen, meat, victuals, milk, corner and hanging cupboards), the number of doors or the style (old-fashioned). We also find case furniture of a more decorative nature, such as cabinets, sideboards, buffet cupboards and numerous cupboards with porcelain pediments.

The modern item of furniture that reappeared in the eighteenth century was the chest of drawers or commode, which was not only suitable for storing silver and linens, but also became a decorative case when topped with a glass cabinet. Walnut chests of drawers of this kind are mentioned in Brunswick for the first time in the 1730s in court circles, in the inventories of the Wolfenbüttel privy councillor and vice-chancellor Alexander, the French cavalier Carl Ludwig Devaux, the sculptor Anton Detlef Jenner and the widow of the captain of the Wolfenbüttel municipal guard Bruns, and may have reflected courtly influence.[19] The same applies to the confiscated Frankfurt household goods of the former Württemberg court factor Joseph Süß Oppenheimer, who possessed one walnut, one pine and two black-stained chests of drawers.[20]

In most inventories, however, commodes appear only in the second half of the century, if at all.[21] In 1775, the household of Dr Tanner demonstrated its wealth and taste with four walnut chests of drawers, including one with a glass case, as well as an additional three commodes. At mid-century, though, the Frankfurt banker Gogel and the leather merchant Mergenbaum also each owned a chest of drawers, according to their inventories. In Hamburg, in contrast, of the two households documented for the 1770s, only the merchant Rötter's (1774) listed a secretary commode,[22] while in Münster the first mention of a commode is that belonging to the wealthy shopkeeper Jansen in 1784. They were apparently more common in the duchy of Brunswick.[23] Even in archaic Nürtingen, the bookseller Jenisch, whose wife had died in childbed in 1783, owned a new glass cabinet and a commode in addition to his old-fashioned buffet cupboard (*Trisur*), while that same year the merchant Fehleisen could call three chests of drawers and a secretary commode his own.[24] At the end of the eighteenth century, case furniture defined the hierarchy of value that in the seventeenth century had still been determined by beds. In the nineteenth century, sofas would become the most prestigious items of furniture.

Changes in seating furniture had already occurred in the eighteenth century, though. The trend was from hard chairs and benches to upholstered seating of various kinds. To be sure, the differences between unupholstered and upholstered chairs (*Stuhl* and *Sessel*) are not always clear in the inventories, for example when they simply use the word *Lehnstuhl* (armchair). In the second half of the eighteenth century, however, the number of upholstered chairs in the inventories rose sharply. At the same time, chairs increasingly appeared in sets of six. The inventory of the merchant Rötter in Hamburg (1774), for instance, lists 18 beechwood chairs, six each with green plush inlays, blue plush inlays and Russian leather.[25] Naturally, we also find mentions of walnut, oak and cane chairs, and, in the duchy of Brunswick, ten 'English' chairs (1732) and '12 ash-wood chairs in the English style'.[26] The variations in upholstered chairs were similarly wide. The household of Dr Tanner in Frankfurt, for example, enjoyed the luxury of two walnut armchairs covered in mockado, four armchairs upholstered in yellow linen, one armchair with a blue serge cover and two additional walnut armchairs. Six tabourets, low upholstered stools in different colours, were the *dernier cri* in elegant furnishings.

The end of the eighteenth century saw the advent of new forms of seating furniture for more than one person, such as canapés, sofas, chaises longues or ottomans, which gradually replaced leather settees. In Wolfenbüttel, a 'cane-bottomed walnut canapé' is documented for 1789, followed a year later by 'a sofa with 2 large mattresses and 2 cushions in green woollen stuff' as well as a 'sleeping sofa with a green silk mattress'.[27] These items of furniture only became standard in upper middle-class households in the early nineteenth century. This may explain their absence from the Frankfurt and Hamburg inventories, since these offer an extremely spotty record of the last decades of the eighteenth century, although the 'settee covered in green serge'[28] documented for Hamburg in 1776 may well have been an ottoman. In Greifswald, we find a canapé mentioned for the first time in 1776 as part of the dowry of Sophia Ulerica Harder, along with three sofas, a divan and two couches in the 1827 estate inventory of Mayor Odebrecht.[29] For Nürtingen, Meiners documents a sofa and six upholstered chairs belonging to the merchant Fink in 1796 and a canapé with 12 armchairs belonging to the town councillor and forestry official Preu in Weißenburg in 1798,[30] while Münster households only seem to have acquired sofas after 1810.[31] In Stralsund, the household of the lawyer Hercules already possessed a 'sofa with blue plush' and three canapés in 1775. These pieces were still rather isolated, for it was not until the end of the century or the beginning of the next that we find entire sets of seating furniture, such as those documented for 1817 for the household of Johann Arnold Joachim Pommeresche ('one sofa with eighteen chairs covered in black bombazine' and 'one sofa with twelve chairs covered in green bombazine and chintz').[32]

Tables also multiplied in the eighteenth century, with an extraordinary proliferation of forms. Apart from the trend from the traditional rectangular to the modern oval table,[33] a number of new types of tables reflected changes in domestic culture. These included not just new coffee and tea tables, card tables and one-legged *guéridon* tables designed to support a candelabrum, but also a variety of telescope tables, folding tables, gate-leg tables, bars, desks, and writing and glass tables, all of which could be produced with different finishes. Thus at mid-century, the Gogel house in Frankfurt boasted not just several of the tables with oilcloth covers that were becoming widespread in the eighteenth century, but also a table covered with a wool carpet, lacquered coffee tables (in addition to one with oilcloth), a painted bedside table, a lacquered Holland table, a leather-topped walnut card table for playing *L'ombre*, two *guéridons* and three walnut desks.[34]

In Greifswald, too, the number and varieties of tables increased over the eighteenth century, with the rich estate inventories documenting a large quantity of different tables. For instance, in 1777 Magister Zienssen owned 14 tables, including four tea tables and a space-saving folding table, which is mentioned here for the first time.[35] This underlines the fact that in the eighteenth century, the changes in interiors reached previously unheard-of dimensions, with the introduction of new items of furniture as well as variations on old forms. This was not simply the result of an increasingly differentiated vocabulary in the inventories. Although it is often too imprecise to attribute individual pieces to specific craftsmen, we can nevertheless pinpoint two phases of innovation in the eighteenth century: the 1730s and the 1770s. During both phases, new furniture appeared first in the households of court officials and later in those of merchants, artisans and professionals, expressing a new domestic culture, or establishing it in the first place.[36] To what extent other furnishings and home accessories also influenced this culture will interest us in the sections to follow.

Tableware and dinner services

Alongside prestige objects such as candelabra and mirrors, tableware and dinner services occupied an important place in domestic culture, and were also indicators of its social differentiation. The protagonists of new patterns of living also distinguished themselves from other households in matters of tableware. Looking at the Brunswick region, Mohrmann has located tableware and dinner services mainly among higher officials, whose proximity to the court may have provided initial impulses for their own homes. This recalls Norbert Elias's ideas about 'the civilization process', which he believed was recognizable above all in table manners and the use of spoons, forks or table napkins.[37] Thus, for example, the Wolfenbüttel privy councillor and vice-chancellor Alexander, whose ownership of two chests of drawers in 1735 we noted above, was also innovative in his silverware purchases. It was no longer silver tankards, cups and goblets, as in the seventeenth century, but candelabra, serving platters, coffee pots, terrines, soup plates, salt cellars, sugar bowls and a silver service for 12 consisting of knives, forks, table-, soup and coffee spoons that pointed the way to a new table culture.[38]

According to the 1742 inventory of his estate, however, the Gandersheim court clerk Johann Conrad Pini was also able to afford a substantial amount of silverware. To be sure, his cutlery included no silver knives or forks, but he did own seven silver bowls, in addition to corresponding table-, children's and soup spoons. He also used a large amount of pewter, since neither porcelain nor stoneware was available as an alternative in the requisite quantities. Matters were different at the end of the eighteenth century (1784) in the household of the judicial official von Alvensleben in Wolfenbüttel. He left behind a highly diverse assortment of coffee, tea and dinner services in Dresden, Zerbst and Japanese porcelain as well as faience and English stoneware. Other officials owned less porcelain, but made up for it with pewter and silver tableware.[39]

Among members of the liberal professions, only a few lawyers, such as Meiborn in Wolfenbüttel (1789), could compete with the Brunswick officials mentioned above. Meiborn owned not just a silver coffee service consisting of a coffee pot, cream jug and sugar bowl, but also a rich array of coffee and tea services of Dresden, Fürstenberg and Japanese porcelain, 'along with 4 chocolate cups'. The majority of Brunswick jurists did not achieve this standard even in the first half of the nineteenth century, and they lagged behind the households of officials when it came to knives and forks as well.[40]

In Frankfurt, too, table culture separated the wheat from the chaff. Only the households of Dr Tanner and Mergenbaum boasted elegant silverware and dinner services, while at mid-century Mr and Mrs Gogel were still making do with the same tableware they had received when they married. The assortment of silverware in the estate of Widow Tanner (1775) was very lavish, and included (among other items) 21 sugar spoons, one serving spoon, six soup spoons, fourteen knives, thirteen forks, one cake slice, seven salt cellars, one mustard pot, five teapots, two coffee pots, one cream jug, two sugar bowls, two slop bowls (*Schwenkkumbe*), four serving platters and two tea urns. She also left a variety of porcelain tea and coffee pots as well as cups, plates and bowls.[41] Less rich in terms of silver, but quite impressive nonetheless was the estate of Daniel Mergenbaum 15 years later. Thirteen knives, 12 forks, 13 spoons, a folding knife and fork, seven three-piece place settings, one pair of tongs, six gilded cups, one teapot, one coffee pot, one cream jug, one sugar bowl and one slop bowl (*Spühlkumbe*) were of silver, while the household met the rest of its tableware needs with objects made not only of pewter, but also brass and porcelain.[42] The Gogels, in contrast, sought to refine their table culture with 13 ivory-handled place settings, 15 spoons, two teaspoons, one serving spoon, one slotted spoon, one set of tongs, one sugar bowl and two serving platters (all of silver), as well as a large assortment of porcelain.[43] The fact that some 25 years later a large tradesman's household managed with a good deal less tableware, despite ownership of a walnut commode, is evident from the estate of the blacksmith Geißemer (1777). Here, most of the cutlery and tableware were of pewter: 15 spoons, three serving spoons, one teapot, one mustard pot, three coffee pots, two cream jugs, 23 bowls, eight soup bowls, two small teapots (*Teepötte*), 18 plates and 13 soup plates. Thirteen chocolate cups and 12 stem glasses are the only drinking vessels mentioned, while the household's other cultural needs, as indicated by book ownership, were probably modest.[44]

In Hamburg, too, only the inventories of Widow Plaehn and the merchant Rötter point to the beginnings of a more refined table culture as early as the 1770s. Even if the dishes, apart from those of pewter, already consisted to a significant extent of porcelain and stoneware pieces, the presence of six silver tablespoons, three pewter tablespoons, five silver teaspoons, and a silver sugar bowl and tongs suggests that the use of knives and forks was still unaccustomed in the Plaehn house, but that they already cultivated tea drinking – the inventory lists seven porcelain teacups as well as large stocks of tea.[45] Rötter, for his part, already boasted 22 porcelain teacups and 24 wine glasses, and, along with a basic set of dishes, 15 knives, including eight in black sheathes, 12 silver tablespoons, eight silver teaspoons, a few wooden spoons and one fork. Here, too, one cannot truly speak of refined dining culture.[46] Matters may have been different at the dinner parties held at Hamburg's country houses and more generally at the end of the eighteenth century, but we have no evidence one way or the other.

In smaller cities such as Lemgo or Greifswald, people also began using knives and forks in the 1760s and 1770s. Before that, they had eaten soup and porridge with spoons, and more solid food with their fingers, or with the tip of a knife. In Greifswald, at least, the number of knives and forks, which are mentioned together in equal numbers as sets, rose steadily beginning in this period. Even in the wealthier Greifswald homes, they were generally made of iron, although the same households frequently already owned a large assortment of silver spoons.[47]

Home decoration

Generally speaking, the second half of the eighteenth century witnessed a wave of innovation in wall and home decoration. Pictures, mirrors, clocks and also curtains, window shades, plaster figurines and furniture pediments suggest efforts to personalize the home atmosphere, which can also be interpreted as attempts to enhance the value of the private sphere and family life. Mirrors were the chief new element in the eighteenth century. Regarded as rarities in the seventeenth century, in the early eighteenth century they were still seldom encountered outside the courts and large cities. Thus, one mirror covered 'with a little green curtain' is mentioned in the Bavarian town of Weilheim in 1715. Mohrmann's study of the Brunswick region also yields only one larger collection of mirrors in the home of a merchant in 1736.[48] Not until the second half of the century does looking at oneself in the mirror appear to have become an everyday affair, facilitated, perhaps, by the sale of hand and wall mirrors by peddlers.[49] Thus, we find two mirrors with gilded and glass frames each in the Plaehn and Rötter households in Hamburg in the 1770s, together with a further walnut-framed mirror belonging to Anna Plaehn.[50] We encounter a far wider assortment of mirrors in Frankfurt. The house of Dr Tanner, for example, boasted nine mirrors (with gilded, silver, glass, black, brown and walnut frames) as evidence of tasteful interior decoration. The ten mirrors belonging to court factor Oppenheimer (1737) and the eight owned by Dr Caspar Sparr at the end of the seventeenth century represented the height of luxury.[51]

Walls were embellished with pictures as complements to the mirrors (or vice-versa). Such adornments could range from a few copper engravings to valuable collections of more than a hundred paintings.[52] Painting ownership was not a new phenomenon in the eighteenth century. In the late seventeenth century – in Hamburg even at mid-century – estate inventories mentioned substantial art collections. When his widow remarried in 1696, for instance, the late Dr Sparr's Frankfurt household contained some 60 paintings, of which, however, only two portraits and one religious history painting, 'Christ and the Samaritan Woman', were described.[53] Part of Oppenheimer's art collection, which consisted largely of portraits, is specified in greater detail:

1. portrait of Her Serene Highness the Duchess of Württemberg
1. ditto of the Bishop of Bamberg
1. ditto of the Elector of Cologne
1. ditto of the Elector Palatine
1. ditto of the Landgrave of Darmstadt

1. ditto of the Hereditary Prince of Darmstadt
1. ditto half-length of an old man
1. ditto of the wife
1. ditto of Süß
6. landscapes in gilded frames
1. painting of the story of Abraham and Isaac
1. nocturne
   P.N.: the other small paintings belonging here were already taken away in one of the little black commodes on the 15th ...
2. portraits, 1 old man and ditto woman, finely painted.[54]

The banker Gogel boasted a larger collection in all genres, divided among several rooms. The fact that we have documentation, for the first time in Frankfurt (and very rare for Germany more generally) of which pictures hung in which rooms, makes the Gogel inventory an extraordinarily valuable source for art and cultural historians. According to the inventory, the many mainly small-format landscapes and still lives hung above all in the lower rooms. The family portraits, allegories, religious history paintings, battle scenes and genre pictures (which we find in every room), in contrast, adorned the large parlour:

In the adjacent room [next to the small parlour]

Paintings

Which could not be easily taken down, but have been marked with numbers.
1.) 1 seascape
2.) St Francis with the Virgin Mary
3.) St John in the desert
4.) 1 landscape
5.) 1 old painting
6. 7. 8. et 9) 4 architectural vistas
10.) Doubting Thomas, large
11.) 1 kitchen scene, large
12.) 1 landscape
13.) 1 landscape
14.) 1 painting of farm animals
15.) 1 still life of fruit
17.) 1 still life of flowers
18.) 1 kitchen scene
19.) 1 nocturne
20.) 1 ditto
21.) 1 small landscape
22. 23. et 24.) 3 ditto
25.) Ruins representing the past
26.) 1 painting of farm animals
27.) 1 small landscape
28.) 1 landscape

29.) 1 ditto
30.) 1 seascape
31.) 1 old ruins
32.) 1 landscape with ditto
33.) 1 man with 1 flute
34.) Crucifixion of Christ
35.) 1 small picture of a dog
36. et 37.) 2 small landscapes
38.) 1 kitchen scene
39.) 1 peasant scene
40. et 41.) 2 plucking geese
42.) 1 peasant scene
43.) 1 ditto with a metallized frame
44. et 45.) 2 small landscapes
46.) 1 kitchen scene
47.) 1 small picture of farm animals
48.) the conversion of Paul
49.) 1 water scene
…

Downstairs in the counting house

large painting representing Adam and Eve
1 ditto painting of the nativity of Christ
1 ditto of Hagar
1 ditto of farm animals
…
In the above-noted back room …
1 large painting representing the golden rain
1 piece representing mortality
1 kitchen scene
1 nocturne
2 portraits, one of them depicting a painter
3 landscapes
1 kitchen scene with fruit
1 still life of flowers, 1 ditto small
1 water scene
1 landscape
1 head of an old man
1 head of an old woman
Another head of a man
1 ditto of a hermit
4 small pictures of trees
1 picture of the burning of Troy with 1 glass
1 small landscape with ditto
2 ditto somewhat larger
3 small poor ditto

1 old painting representing mortality

In the above-noted large parlour

9 family portraits, one of them life-size
1 painting depicting a peasant wedding
2 ditto depicting Dutch buildings
1 ditto of Cupid as Vulcan
2 battle scenes
1 picture of farm animals
1 ditto antique of the Crucifixion of Christ
3 still lives of fruit
1 small Brabant peasant scene
1 picture of the baptism of St John
1 night battle scene
1 storm at sea
1 Ovid. piece with Michas
2 pictures depicting Adam and Eve
1 party with music
6 small ditto.[55]

Unfortunately, the paintings are not attributed to specific artists. This would change at the 1782 auction of the collection, now numbering nearly 400 works, when the emphasis was on Dutch painters and the local masters Christian Georg Schütz (21 works) and Johann Conrad Seekatz (20 works). At this auction, Henriette Amalie of Anhalt-Dessau alone bought 43 items, including a *Ölberg* (Mount of Olives) by Johann Melchior Roos for 9 guilders, which is still in the Anhalt Gemäldegalerie in Dessau.[56]

In most cases, though, it was something of a miracle if those preparing the inventories bothered to examine the paintings more closely, and perhaps identify them. Accordingly, for most households we must be satisfied with mentions of 'diverse paintings', unless they were family portraits.[57]

Thus, in seventeenth-century Hamburg, the only collections for which we have more precise descriptions are those of Johann Outgertsen who lived at nearby Othmarschen and owned works by numerous painters, among them Rembrandt, Van Dyck, Van Goyen, Molijn and Ruysdael, or the 20 paintings belonging to the silk merchant Hans Heinrich Simons, who was also involved in trade with the Netherlands.[58]

The few surviving inventories from the duchy of Brunswick at least permit us to reconstruct the motifs of paintings in greater detail. While the sole larger seventeenth-century collection, that of a Brunswick mayor in 1686, was largely characterized by religious history paintings and Classical mythology along with a few landscapes, in two of the documented households of the 1730s the paintings mentioned were mainly landscapes. They also included alabaster and plaster figurines and framed calendars, which we also find in Frankfurt.[59] Homes in Frankfurt were also embellished with numerous engravings, plaster and porcelain figurines, and porcelain furniture pediments. Alabaster figurines were also mentioned in Hamburg, while the pediments there were generally of stoneware.

Besides mirrors and candelabra of varying qualities, the main prestige objects found in eighteenth-century households were different kinds of clocks. Apart from hourglasses, we find table or mantel clocks, longcase and wall clocks, frequently imported from France or England. A Wolfenbüttel inventory of 1784 mentions a wall clock with an enamelled dial made by Julien le Roy (1686–1759) in a finely worked tortoiseshell case (with gilded bronze engraving), and a Gandersheim list of 1787 features a gold clock by Simon Decharmes.[60] Both clockmakers, the latter of whom worked in London, were among the leading members of their trade. In Frankfurt, the Gogel family owned a walnut table clock, a wall clock, a house clock and a gilded clock, while the household of Dr Tanner had a table clock with a black case, a gold-enamelled clock and a clock with a gold case, although there is no mention of the makers.[61] Makers' names appear only to have established themselves in the second half of the eighteenth century, or at least to have become obvious enough to be recognized by inventory makers. In Hamburg, too – with the exception of a silver pocket watch – only an English hall clock by Joseph Herring (1767–1804, member of the Clockmakers' Company of London) belonging to Anna Plaehn is listed by maker.[62]

It was textile furnishings that created a comfortable and homely atmosphere. Apart from wallpaper, which is rarely mentioned in the estate inventories, these consisted mainly of curtains, carpets, tablecloths and pillows. To be sure, we hear of the silk wallpaper in the billiard room of the Osnabrück wine merchant Knille, as well as the damask walls in his saloon and the other rooms decorated with plaster mouldings and oilcloth wallpaper,[63] but as a rule, only the moveable curtains are mentioned, albeit in wide variety. The colours mentioned include yellow, white, green, blue and red, and the materials linen, taffeta, chintz, arras, serge, wool, velvet and muslin. The range of table linens was similarly broad. In Frankfurt, in addition to the large quantities of ordinary tablecloths, we also find table carpets of plush, arras, wool, silk and half-silk in various colours as well as chintz, damask and blue and white linen cloths for *guéridons*, children's tables and coffee tables. The Hamburg inventories indicate that tables were somewhat less lavishly adorned there. Here, too, though, the lists distinguish between 'table sheets' (*Tischlacken*) and 'tablecloths' (*Tischdecken*) as well as table napkins of linen, huckaback, damask, wool and half-silk in different colours. Table napkins were less numerous in Hamburg than Frankfurt, where the households of Dr Tanner, Gogel and Dr Schedel (1737) owned hundreds of them.

The details of textile decoration could be differentiated still further, but the information provided thus far doubtless suffices to suggest the bewildering array of possibilities that faced wealthy householders when choosing a carpet or a cloth to cover their tables. More tables meant more tablecloths, while the rise of upholstered furniture made it advisable to harmonize them with the colour and material of curtains. It is not quite clear who set the trends in the new culture of interior decoration. In the duchy of Brunswick, however, the court and its officials played a certain pioneering role. Whether this was also the case in larger cities is doubtful. Beginning in the eighteenth century, the trading centre of Frankfurt, with its fairs, developed into a market for luxury goods destined for the princely residences, and here it was probably the commercial classes that inspired the dissemination of new living patterns. We do not know to what extent this was also true of Hamburg, since the few surviving eighteenth-century inventories document a different social class from the Frankfurt records.

Did the magazines also provide models for the spread of new patterns of interior decoration? We cannot give a precise answer since it is difficult to demonstrate the influence of the periodicals in household reality. As a rule, the attributions of household items are too vague to permit us to recognize specific makers or objects. Thus, it is rare to find the new consumer goods propagated in the pages of the *Journal des Luxus und der Moden* reflected in the inventories, and when they are, it is only quite generally. Even if the first issue of the *Journal* in 1786 discusses an 'English' chair, canapé or fire-screen, and English chairs also appear in Wolfenbüttel inventories of the late eighteenth century, they were not necessarily the same pieces or actual imports from England, or even copies of English models. In this case, 'English' refers to a style, just as the descriptions 'French' or 'Turkish' were used to draw the public's attention to novelties. Thus, the inventories could indeed include such interesting entries as an 'English armchair for rooms decorated in the Chinese manner in summer- or country houses'.

Bertuch, however, presents this new 'English' furniture, built by 'the very clever English cabinetmaker Herr Holzhauer Jun. here in Weimar', using the example of the newly decorated green salon of Anna Amalie's Wittum Palace, clearly demonstrating both the duchess's openness to new decorative trends and the attractiveness of those trends. Holzhauer and his brother also worked on the interiors of Goethe's summerhouse, which may have attracted new customers. Nonetheless, even in Weimar's private households, English furniture inspired by the *Journal* remained the exception. One of these exceptions was an English chiffonier, a lingerie chest or sewing worktable, of which the *Journal* wrote in 1797:

> In the room of an elegant lady one finds small, dainty containers, which function at the same time as decorative furniture and can be easily moved, a very desirable and welcome affair … . The closed tabletop … can be lifted by hinges so that one may keep work things and other small objects one wishes to have close at hand in the green taffeta bag within.[64]

This piece of furniture stood in the house of the court officials Franz and Karl Kirms, who played a not insignificant role in Weimar's cultural life. Franz

Kirms's wife, Caroline Krackow, had been governess to the daughters of Grand Duchess Maria Pavlovna before her marriage. The influence of the court and the functional elites over the spread of new interior decorating fashions in the small princely capitals, even at the end of the eighteenth century, should not be underestimated. However, in cities such as Frankfurt, too, members of the nobility from surrounding territories were major purchasers of home furnishings. In this way, luxury goods came to the attention of urban households, although we may not find them reflected in the inventories. An example is the workshop of Abraham and David Roentgen at Neuwied. As cabinetmakers on the London model, they turned their carpentry workshop into a manufactory equipped to build furniture in series from prefabricated components in a variety of different qualities. While the early Roentgen pieces followed simple English patterns, by the 1760s they had come into their own and were producing writing desks and commodes with carved designs, parquetry or floral marquetry (ornamental veneers). For princely customers such as the Elector of Trier Johann Philipp von Walderdorff, they also built splendid marquetry desks featuring elaborate pictures in wood. David Roentgen significantly expanded the business and the range of products. After establishing themselves on the Hamburg market with a furniture lottery, they also opened branches in Paris, St Petersburg and Berlin. Although the market for luxury furniture of this type largely collapsed with the French Revolution, Roentgen's desks and ornamental cabinets, with their symbiosis of French, English, Dutch and German influences, are still considered to be 'models of perfection in cabinet-making'.[65] Even Goethe compares the fairy-tale castle described in his 1807 novella *Neue Melusine* (The New Melusina) to an 'artful writing table by Roentgen, where a single pull sets many springs in motion, and desk and writing-case, and pigeonholes for letters and money open all at once or one after the other'.[66] For contemporary domestic culture, however, Roentgen's furniture probably represented simply an episode, for the new trend was toward simplicity and comfort. We have already found some evidence of this development in the eighteenth-century estate inventories, but it would only come to full fruition in the Biedermeier period.

Chapter 5

Gardens and Country Houses

> Gardens are places where Man can enjoy all of the advantages of country life, all of the amenities of the seasons in comfort and tranquillity. All of the advantages and pleasures that Nature affords her sensible friend can be found within the precincts of an extensive and well laid out garden. Indeed, these advantages and delights are heightened and multiplied here to the degree that reason and taste endeavour to elevate a garden, through the charms of cultivation, above a place left to its own devices.[1]

In the course of the eighteenth century, changing sentiments towards nature led to a new attitude towards gardens and landscapes. This process is generally associated with the landscape garden, which replaced the geometrical precision of the baroque gardens. According to garden historians, it was only with the 'English garden' that the free-form landscape, with its natural beauties such as hills, valleys, meadows, brooks and trees, was able to establish itself. As evidence, historians cite the development of princely gardens since the late seventeenth century. The model for such gardens was Versailles and the domestication and rationalization of nature according to aesthetic principles that André Le Nôtre undertook there. Examples in Germany include the gardens of Max Emanuel of Bavaria at Munich-Schleißheim and Munich-Nymphenburg. The former was begun after the elector's return from the governorship in Brussels in the early eighteenth century, but only realized after 1715 because of entanglements in the War of the Spanish Succession. At almost the same time, a new garden plan was developed for Nymphenburg, which organized the park geometrically in the latest French taste. Here we find a typical baroque garden, divided into three principle zones: the grand parterre, a bosquet and a wooded area divided by radially spreading *allées*.

Further baroque gardens were established at Berlin-Charlottenburg, Kassel-Karlsberg (later Wilhelmshöhe), Hanover-Herrenhausen, Dresden and, by Max Emanuel's son Clemens August, at Augustusburg near Brühl.[2] In the age of the Rococo, the French garden schema declined. To be sure, even in the 1750s the French style of gardens, and especially the works of the garden theorist Dézallier d'Argenvilles, still attracted intense interest in Germany, but a longing for small and intimate garden spaces, together with the need for entertainment and amusement in nature, led to less severe forms. The layout of Rococo gardens was asymmetrical and segmented. Curved and serpentine paths replaced the baroque *allées*, making the gardens less easy to survey at a glance. Sanssouci near Potsdam, as a prime example of a Rococo garden, clearly demonstrates the less rigid layout. Fountains, springs and other water features – but also exotic pavilions and teahouses – were new elements in garden design, which sought to encompass a variety of worlds. Greenhouses, fruit trees and other plants as well as numerous flowerbeds, which were planted according to the seasons, rounded out the picture. Comparable Rococo gardens could be found at Veitshöchheim, Schwetzingen and Stuttgart-Solitude. Some of these gardens were redesigned soon after they were laid out to make them still less formal and more akin to 'natural' landscape.

Wörlitz near Dessau set new standards for German landscape gardening. In the 1760s, before succeeding to the throne, Prince Leopold III Friedrich Franz of Anhalt-Dessau had travelled to England twice with his architect Friedrich Wilhelm von Erdmannsdorff, visiting the island's most important landscape gardens. They made a virtue of necessity (the danger of the Elbe flooding) and completely redesigned the river and garden landscape. Inspired by English ideas and their own imaginations, they devised a new symbiosis between lakes, canals and woodlands, which were intended to awaken certain associations or emotions in those who strolled through the park landscape. At the same time, garden and agriculture, economic utility and landscape art were united in a terrain where cultivated plants, fruit trees, fields and pastures co-existed with numerous monuments and antique or historical structures. Thus the Gothic House with its collections recalled the history of the Holy Roman Empire, while cows and sheep grazed outside, symbolizing the model economy of the *hortus oeconomicus*, the union of the 'useful with the beautiful and edifying'.[3]

The great princely parks of Munich, Potsdam and Wörlitz have thus shaped our image of eighteenth-century garden design. This all but ignores private gardening, however, which had been flourishing since the late seventeenth century. People spent not just the summers in their gardens beyond the city walls, and town gardens also became objects of pleasure and investment, for which no expense was spared. Amateur gardeners bought, sold, traded and gave away flower seeds, and corresponded intensively with likeminded individuals. 'Art nurseries' on large plots of land produced seeds, plants and trees for sale to amateur gardeners.

Redesigning the landscape: Amateur gardeners and princely enthusiasts

Vegetable, fruit and herb gardens were common in medieval times. In Hamburg, for example, the fifteenth century witnessed a steady growth in demand for garden land, and the city profited from the rising rent revenues. In the second half of the sixteenth century, citizens began to plant gardens beyond the walls, so that they could escape the crowding and stench at least in summer. The circumvallation of Hamburg New Town in the seventeenth century offered new opportunities for the creation of many additional garden spaces. The tendency to lay out new gardens and country houses outside the city continued. The English and Dutch merchants who had settled on the Elbe were particularly active. This led to changes in the settlement and social structure of Hamburg's environs, for example, Billwerder, Hamm and Horn. During the summers in the eighteenth century, Hamburg citizens populated the 60 gardens in Horn and Hamm, which opened the kind of seasonal market for services (gardeners, coachmen, domestic servants) familiar to us from nineteenth-century watering places. All occupations were represented among garden owners, although according to the Hamburg garden almanac for 1792, merchants and town councillors dominated. They included wine and spice merchants, brokers, diplomats, sugar manufacturers, lawyers, bankers, pastors, professional gardeners and other craftsmen.[4]

Most of the surviving descriptions refer to the appearance of the gardens belonging to Hamburg's upper class, though. According to one account, the garden of the town councillor Caspar Anckelmann featured a summerhouse decorated with paintings and sculptures, as well as: 'The rarest plants and fruit trees in the world in large numbers, and of the plants that cannot survive our winters in the ground, some 400–500 were planted in boxes and pots so that nothing was lacking here that might delight the eye and the nose.'[5]

In an apothecary book of 1716, we already find prints of the gardens of the mayors Lucas von Bostel and Peter Lütkens. The first had divided his garden at Borgfelde into three rectangular sections, two of which were laid out with rectangular beds, trees and ponds, and the third, the pleasure garden, was divided into four squares with a tree in the middle of each.

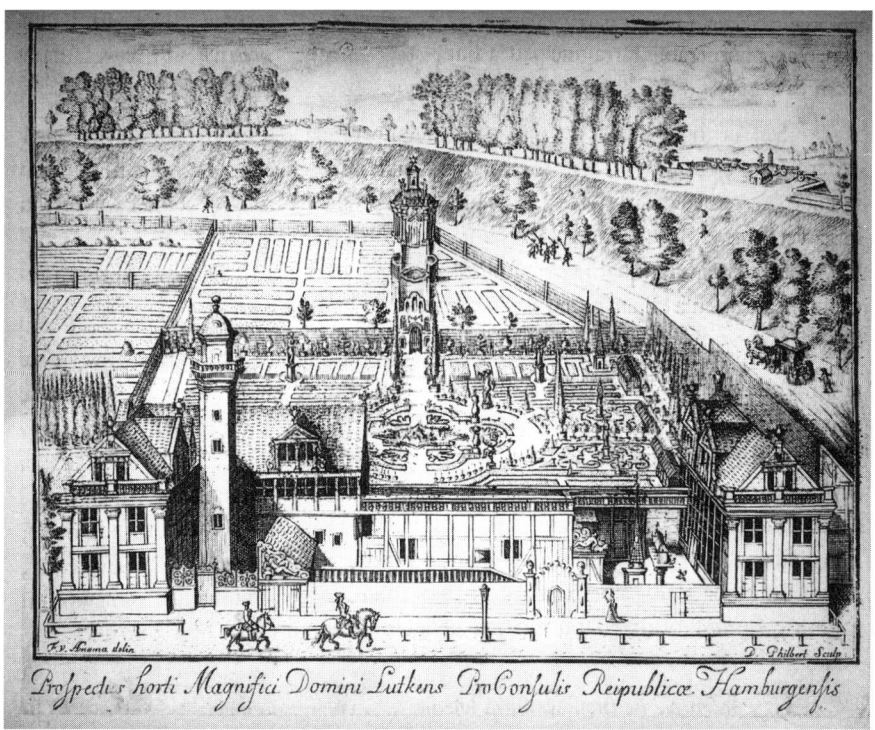

Figure 10   Mayor Peter Lütkens's house and garden near the Dammtor, etching by D. Philbert after F. v. Amama, 1716

Behind the buildings belonging to Peter Lütkens's property in Dammtor Strasse was a lavish garden dominated by a quatrefoil-shaped section with a fountain. Grouped around it were the mostly rectangular beds and further grounds adorned with statues and pyramids. The pleasure garden was adjoined by a simply structured kitchen garden. Such a layout combining pleasure and kitchen gardens was the ideal celebrated by Barthold Heinrich Brockes 1721 in his *Irdisches Vergnügen in Gott* (Earthly Pleasure in God):

> ... A bright gleam/ a more than golden sheen/
> Enchanting captured air and land/
> And moved me/ for wood and field so fine/
> To look upon the garden's gorgeous grace;
> In which Nature joins with Art/
> Where industry/ utility and pleasure are e'er allied
> Wherein we note in human works
> At once the hand of active Nature/
> And in the same the bright trace
> Of our Creator's power and presence.[6]

The baroque garden organized nature, whose great variety – as Brockes wrote in another passage – so bewilders the senses that 'they could combine nothing properly' (*nichts förmliches zusammenbrachten*).[7] The gardens of Hamburg's citizens were subject to diverse influences. Often, with their profusion of individual elements in a small space, they followed Dutch models, which they also imitated in situating country houses on the water, on the Alster and Bille. Most of these gardens were too small for an axial layout on the French baroque pattern. Corresponding gardens can be found, however, in the surrounding noble seats, such as Bendix von Ahlefeldt's estate at Jersbek, or the Wandsbek castle garden of Heinrich Carl Schimmelmann.

The widespread enthusiasm for flowers among amateur gardeners must also be mentioned. Communication about, and with the aid of, plants opened up new social contacts, an opportunity of which even well established citizens such as the Hamburg music director Georg Philipp Telemann availed themselves. Thus, on 27 August 1742, for example, he fell into conversation with Johann Friedrich Armand von Uffenbach about his 'insatiable hunger for hyacinths and tulips, and my avidity for buttercups and especially anemones', and offered him the following flowers:

Anemones
Amaranthus, chrystatus, tricolor globosus
Alcea theophrasti (hyacinth)
Astrantia nigra (masterwort)
Auricula muris etc. (mouse-ear)
Antirrhinum (snapdragon)
Aster atticus, autumnalis etc. (star wort)
Aster foemina. S. Conyza cerulea. (fleabane)

Amaranthus caudatus (love-lies-bleeding)
Panicum major & minor. (millet)
Aster chinensis
Balsamina (touch-me-not)
Bellis (daisy)
Campanula piramidalis, urticae folio, flore coeruleo (chimney bellflower)
Cariophillus, barbatus (sweet William)
Cyanus (cornflower)
Campanula urticae foli, flore albo
Calendula (marigold)
Chrysanthemum
Colchicum (autumn crocus)
Conv. Minor. S. Convolvus peregrinus (bindweed)
Campanula minima, fl. Coer.
Crocus
Corona imperialis (crown imperial fritillary)
Consolida regia (larkspur)
Flos Africanus major & minor, versicolor., S. tricolor.
Flos Adonis
Flos cardinalis
Flos poeticus
Fraxinella (gas plant)
Geranium pictum, atrum, flore coccineo
Galéga (goat's rue)
Geraneum magnum, maximo-flore
Hedisarum, clypeatum, rubr. Et alb. (French honeysuckle)
Hesperis odorata (sweet rocket).[8]

Telemann apparently knew Uffenbach from his years in Frankfurt. At that time, they had visited Castle Erbach in the Odenwald together, and the dilettante Uffenbach had written a cantata 'To Count Erbach's Castle Garden and the Orangery there during a Visit' to melodies by George Frideric Handel. Uffenbach was not the Hamburg composer's sole horticultural correspondent, however, just as the Dresden violinist, conductor and composer Johann Georg Pisendel was not the only friend to send Telemann the desired 'produce of the soil'; the Berlin composer and conductor Karl Heinrich Graun supplied him with flowers. Telemann also shared this enthusiasm with the Ludwigslust court composer and conductor Johann Wilhelm Hertel, who in 1787 published a *Kurze Geschichte der Nelken* (Brief History of the Carnation).[9]

In the late eighteenth century, 'landscape gardens' became popular among English merchants and Hamburg citizens alike. Not only did such parks spring up all along the banks of the Elbe between Altona and Blankenese; the traditional gardens in Horn and Hamm were also restructured and redesigned. Architects such as Johann August Arens and Joseph Jacques Ramée designed neo-Classical landscape gardens such as those belonging to Caspar Voght in Flottbek, Johannes Schuback in Billwerder, Georg Heinrich Sieveking's country house in Neumühlen or Baur's park in Blankenese. In the early nineteenth century, the Altona merchant Georg Friedrich Baur, for instance, had a garden laid out in the Romantic style complete with temples, a Chinese pagoda, the artificial ruins of a tower, grottoes, orangeries, palm houses and greenhouses.

Caspar Voght's model estate at Flottbek, mentioned above, represented a different type of garden – the 'ornamental farm', a deliberate symbiosis between agricultural land and the garden such as we also encountered at Wörlitz. Voght wrote to his successor Martin Johann Jenisch, who gave Jenisch Park its name:

> I seek to use the lovely trees, the pleasing alternation of hill and dale, the diverse groups of trees, the variations of land and river, views and vistas, in order to present, one after the other, to the eyes of those strolling along the paths that lead through the so diligently cultivated fields, a series of changing and distinct landscapes.[10]

The model farm and Jenisch Park were largely based on the plans of the Scotsman James Booth, whose tree nurseries would supply many landscape gardens in the period that followed. As we know from other cities and will see in more detail presently, gardening was a lucrative business or an expensive pleasure, depending on one's perspective. Thus, in other cities, it was mainly the wealthy who indulged in this luxury.

In 1680, the Nuremberg land register listed more than 350 gardens outside the city walls. Most of them had existed since the fifteenth century, but were redesigned on artistic principles in the seventeenth and eighteenth centuries. Above all, after the Thirty Years War, Nuremberg patricians rounded off their gardens by purchasing neighbouring plots. One of them, the garden of the Peller family, which they purchased in 1619 for the sum of 2,500 guilders, is even documented in a copper engraving by Jacob Sandrart. It shows a symmetrically arranged terrain divided into pleasure, fruit and vegetable gardens. The basic structure was defined by three axes, which were designed as arbours or pavilions. The Peller garden, like others in Nuremberg, revealed the signature of the city architect and garden theorist Joseph Furttenbach, to whom we shall return later. The owners of these properties were the patrician Imhoff, Haller, Kreß, Pömer or Tucher families, and also wealthier representatives of the liberal professions, who generally only visited the gardens in summer, but often lived there for part of the warm months. Servants and long- or short-term tenants looked after the gardens, which in the eighteenth century adopted the new French elements or forms of the baroque garden. To be sure, these innovations were only successfully introduced in the larger gardens outside the cities, although the 'inclination for gardening ... [had become] a ruling passion not just among the great and wealthy, but also among persons of all ranks and orders'.[11]

Eighteenth-century Leipzig underwent a construction boom, which did not stop at the city's fortifications. The city moat was drained, and the reclaimed land planted with trees and ornamental shrubs in 1702–03. Baroque gardens now replaced the suburban districts, which moved further beyond the city walls. Among the citizens' gardens, those of the Apels and Boses stood out. The two pleasure gardens of the Bose family, who maintained friendly neighbourly relations with the family of Johann Sebastian Bach, then *Kantor* of the Thomaskirche, followed the French style. The entire garden was oriented towards the summerhouse, whose upper storey offered views of a terrace-like parterre. An orangery is already mentioned in 1691 and depicted in an engraving.

The Bose gardens, like those of the Stieglitzs and the Krumbhaars, were surpassed only by the Apel estate. Andreas Dietrich Apel inherited this garden outside the Thomas Gate, whose existence is already documented in the seventeenth century, from his father-in-law and expanded it in 1701–02 by purchasing neighbouring plots of land. Apart from several dwelling houses and outbuildings, the garden consisted of a parterre divided into several sections with ornamental beds, *bosquets* and a fountain. Fan-shaped *allées* leading straight into the surrounding countryside established the expanse of the garden, which also featured canals with gondolas. Statues of Classical gods by the Dresden sculptor Bathasar Permoser lent the whole a courtly appearance, which was finally sealed by the actual presence of King August the Strong in 1714.[12] Some private individuals, too, like Anna Magdalena Bach, were also active 'gardening amateurs' who were overjoyed to receive a parcel of carnation plants.[13]

Frankfurt families cultivated the love of gardening, using both the southern bank of the River Main in Sachsenhausen and Bockenheim. Goethe's grandfather, Mayor Textor, had planted a pear tree in his garden near the Bockenheim Gate on the occasion of little Wolfgang's christening. Goethe's father, for instance, grew fruits and vegetables in the garden, as well as cultivating grapes and asparagus at his vineyard. In the early nineteenth century, the 'garden accounts' of Frau Aja, as Goethe's mother was known, show how intensively the garden was cultivated. In 1804, they harvested 'lovely asparagus, sour cherries, beans, pears, peaches, yellow, red and little white apples'. One year later, she mentions currants, mirabelle plums and apples, as well as pears and purple plums for preserves. In 1807, the garden, which had been fertilized the year before with 19 cartloads of manure, also produced strawberries, cucumbers and quince. Goethe's mother particularly enjoyed summer days in her friends' gardens. Leading Frankfurt families such as the d'Orvilles, Bethmanns, Stocks or Moritzs owned country houses with temples and grottoes on the model of English parks. In a letter of 21 June 1798, Catharina Elisabeth Goethe wrote to her future daughter-in-law Christiane:

> Everyone is either at their country houses or taking the waters. I also go to the country quite often to visit good friends … . All day Sunday I spend in Senator Stock's garden before the Bockenheim Gate, and during the week I am at Madam Fingerling's before All Saints' Gate, and then via Sachsenhausen to Herr Kellner's splendid estate, and in this way I have three or four places where I feel very comfortable. As you can see, Grandmother still enjoys life a good deal.[14]

An estimate from a dispute over a Frankfurt testament shows the kind of investments involved in these gardens. In 1738–41, Rebecca von Klettenberg fought with her stepbrother, Senator Heinrich Bernhard von Barckhaus, over the estate of their father, the cloth merchant and lay magistrate Heinrich Barckhaus. Apart from an extract from the account book, the parties to the dispute also documented purchases of property. Thus in 1686, their parents had bought '1 acre of vineyard on the Pfingstweide, 2 orchards before All Saints' Gate and 1 garden before All Saints' Gate on the Hanau Road'. The last was assessed, allowing us for the first time to judge the sums that citizens sank into their gardens. The total came to 59,075 guilders, and was broken down as shown in Table 5.1.[15]

Table 5.1   An inventory of the All Saints' Gate garden

66 orange trees	3,000
13 laurels	450
15 daisies	80
121 yew trees	5,445
10 ditto, globe-shaped	600
Indian plants	2,500
1 large aloe	500
6 smaller ditto à 100 fl	600
Bulbous plants, which are not to be assessed higher because they have ceased to bloom	4,000
Espalier and French fruit trees	7,000
The vineyard circa 1 acre	1,200
The maze	1,500
The 2 main paths with shrubberies	5,000
The circular allée	3,000
The ornamental beds	2,200
The forcing bed	1,100
The vegetable garden	8,000
The fish-pond with stone sides	3,000
The fountain	8,000
	fl. 59,075

The most expensive items were the 66 orange trees, the 121 yew trees and the fruit trees, but even these were surpassed by the cost of the fountain at 8,000 guilders.

Figure 11   Darmstadt *fête galante*. Painting by Johann Christian Fiedler and
Christian Georg Schütz the Elder, c. 1750, oil on canvas

In neighbouring Darmstadt in the 1770s, Landgravine Caroline assembled
a circle of 'sentimentalists' who devoted themselves to literature and music in
the open air. They included Matthias Claudius, Johann Heinrich Merck and
Herder's future wife Caroline Flachsland, among others. The garden pursuits of
this group may have resembled the scene captured by the court painter Johann
Christoph Fiedler, who depicted a group of ladies and gentlemen enjoying
music, clay pigeon shooting, card games and a picnic amidst a park landscape.
When Landgravine Caroline redesigned the Herrengarten in Darmstadt as an
English garden in 1766, only two local householders emulated her example:
Freiherr von Riedesel at his country estate and the Minister and political author
Karl Friedrich von Moser. Moser's garden, which was laid out in the 1770s, was
planted with imported trees and adorned with ruins, a hermitage and a pond.
The country house stood on an elevation, giving a view of the landscape that
Johann Heinrich Merck described as follows:

> From thence [the house] one strolls through serpentine avenues of foreign trees, of
> which there is a great variety … . Further downhill on the right one comes upon a
> pond of irregular shape. If one now continues down, one encounters the ruins of

a Gothic church. Behind the ruins is a plantation of all manner of fine evergreen trees. Further below is a small hermitage, built in the Russian fashion completely of logs and with a thatched roof.[16]

In 1780–81, Moser fell out of favour at court and was forced to sell his garden.[17] Today, Moser's garden is called the Prince Emil Garden after its purchaser, and the pond mentioned by Merck was replaced in 1987.

Around the court at Weimar, too, people sought to integrate natural country living into everyday life with the help of garden design. The model of the Wörlitz garden realm, which Carl August of Saxony-Weimar and Goethe visited in 1767, was a key influence. Work began turning the so-called cold kitchen, the steep banks of the Ilm and the baroque 'Star', a garden with a system of paths laid out on a star-shaped axis, into an English garden. In the 1780s, the Shooting-Box Garden (the garden of the Weimar riflemen), the Rothäuser garden (terrain on the right bank of the Ilm) and the Italian Garden, a former pleasure garden with arbours, a spring and an orangery, were added. Thus, out of a number of baroque gardens and newly purchased plots of land an English garden arose, with the aim of creating a coherent landscape. Since Goethe had withdrawn from the planning of the garden and Carl August, who wished to continue with the project, was constantly travelling, Friedrich Justin Bertuch assumed responsibility for its completion. Bertuch looked after the 'details in the park grounds' such as the erection of the 'three columns', the planting of domestic and so-called English trees, and the construction of the 'Roman House'.

In 1792, Goethe then took over above all as aesthetic advisor for the furnishings of the Roman House, while Bertuch designed the exterior space, but relinquished responsibility for the park in 1796. Bertuch clearly occupied a prominent position as a gardening author as well as publisher, and above all as the cultivator of his own large garden. Behind his house, which was built between 1780 and 1782 and looked like a town villa from the street side, he laid out an English garden, which lent the rear of the house the appearance of an English manor house. Passing through a garden hall, one traversed a terrace into the lower garden, which was structured according to the latest English patterns. Ornamental shrubs, a pond with a duck house as well as grottoes, statues and new garden furniture created a homely atmosphere, while orchards, greenhouses and vegetable patches served economic purposes. Bertuch's gardening activities were quite varied. They included collecting and cultivating new plants (including ones imported from England) in hothouses as well as selling and distributing bulbs, which he ordered from London, Haarlem or Dresden. He had the bulbs forced in greenhouses so that even in winter he could present flower arrangements in special jardinières. On the occasion of Grand Duchess Maria Pavlovna's birthday in 1817, he was able to provide a wide variety of irises, primroses, hyacinths, roses and other plants, earning a handsome sum in the process. Leases and the sale of fruits and vegetables contributed to the garden's economic success. Bertuch also experimented with new types of vegetables, such as broccoli, artichokes, cabbages, radishes and potatoes. He also maintained an orchard near Denstedt, where he grew apples, pears, plums, cherries, peaches and apricots.[18]

The Wörlitz garden realm influenced other prominent Weimar citizens as well. Goethe looked forward to having 'a sweet little garden outside the gates in a valley on the Ilm's lovely meadows', with 'a little old cottage, which I am having repaired'.[19] The duke had given Goethe the ramshackle house as a gift, and he refurbished it. Goethe's friends also felt the enchantment of the landscape on their evening visits, and were reminded of Dutch paintings:

> We dined in a quite charming little hermitage … . We drank a bottle of '60 Johannisberger to your health and that of Frau Aja and Friend Bölling, the corn merchant, and when we arose from table and opened the doors, lo and behold, through the secret machinations of the arch-magus, there spread out before us a sight more closely resembling a poetic vision come true than a scene of Nature. The entire shore of the Ilm illuminated, completely in the taste of Rembrandt – a marvellous enchanted chiaroscuro, which in its entirety created an effect beyond description. The duchess was as delighted as the rest of us. When we descended the little staircase of the hermitage and walked between crags and bushes along the Ilm towards the bridge, which connects this place with one of the points of the Star, the entire vision gradually disintegrated into a number of small Rembrandtian night pieces which one would have wished to gaze upon forever, and which now attained a life and a wonderful quality from the persons strolling about amongst them, which was quite splendid for my humble poetic self. I could have gobbled Goethe up for sheer affection.[20]

Wieland penned this description in a 1778 letter to his friend Johann Heinrich Merck. For his part, Wieland also aspired to country living. First he bought a garden outside the city, followed by a large house. In 1797, he added a country estate at Oßmannstedt, which included castle gardens, meadows and 40 hectares of fields. To be sure, the pleasure garden was neglected and Wieland failed to raise the money for its restoration, but he and his 11-member family enjoyed their life on the estate until 1803.

Goethe's friend Johann Friedrich Reichardt was able to pursue the ideal of rural life a few years longer. In 1792, at Giebichenstein near Halle, he laid out 'Reichardt's Garden' on around 2 hectares of land, following the model of Wörlitz. The property was divided into a valley and a hill garden. For Reichardt, too, a spacious garden hall with glass doors opening onto the garden served to let nature into the house, and helped make Giebichenstein a magnet for artists, scholars and politicians. In this way, he was able to compensate at least partly for the prestige he lost when he was dismissed as court *Kapellmeister* in Berlin (for supporting the French Revolution). Giebichenstein's renown continued to grow with Goethe's various stays there with Christiane Vulpius until 1806, when the property fell victim to the march-through of French troops.[21]

Berlin, too, experienced a veritable garden boom in the last third of the eighteenth century. While in the 1769 first edition of his 'Description of the

Royal Capitals of Berlin and Potsdam' Friedrich Nicolai mentions only the
Realschule botanical garden and the royal and Academy botanical garden,
and notes that the pleasure garden laid out under the Great Elector had been
destroyed by his grandson Frederick William I and transformed into a parade
ground, in the 1786 edition, he writes of numerous gardens and gardeners
specialized in growing flowers, vegetables (especially asparagus) and fruit trees.[22]
Nicolai organizes his description both topographically by district and street and
by the plants that grew in the gardens or by what the gardeners sold. Among
the garden owners, the names of well-known Berlin merchants and bankers, as
well as members of the functional elite, are particularly striking. A few of the
gardens mentioned include:

1. In Berlin proper.
    - Itzig's garden, containing various fountains
    - the garden of Councillor of War Beyer, containing a handsome array of
      blossoming carnations and buttercups
    - the garden of Consistorial Councillor Büsching. His first wife, née Dilthey,
      who died in 1777 is buried there. Her grave is covered by a flowerbed, in
      which forget-me-nots bloom all summer long. On the wall of the house
      above the flowerbed is a marble plaque bearing an inscription
    - Ephraim's Garden, the rear portion of which borders on Count Reuß's
      Garden; the most charming section of it is a meadow surrounded by shady
      walks. Here also stand six ten-to-twelve foot high statues after designs by
      Schlüter, which have been placed on the balustrades and roof of the palace.
      They represent Mercury, Juno, Bacchus, Flora, Leda and Venus. Amidst a
      shrubbery is a charming little pavilion shaded by a single plane tree, whose
      branches spread very wide
    - the garden of His Excellency the Minister of State Freiherr von Zedlitz.
      It has been newly laid out in the English taste. It contains an aviary with a
      fountain, as well as a large and handsomely designed orangery, and also a
      hothouse for pineapples etc.
    - the garden of the banker Herr Holzecker. It is splendidly maintained, and
      contains beautiful flowerbeds and excellent hothouses for grapes, peaches
      and other plants demanding special cultivation.[23]
2. In Kölln.
    - The large and beautiful Splittgerber Garden. It is somewhat narrow, but very
      long, reaching to the Köllnische Vorstadt. It has very charming parts; these
      particularly include an open summerhouse before the Wusterhausen Weir,
      where the rushing of the water has a pleasing effect, and an oval Chinese
      pavilion, on a little hill planted with high trees.
    - The quite large and beautiful garden of Daniel Itzig. The improvements
      and mostly new design were devised by the royal gardener Herr Heidert in
      Potsdam. Apart from hedges, arcades and shady plantations for pleasure,
      it contains several thousand fine fruit trees of the best sorts. It also has an
      open-air garden theatre. Similarly, there are a number of statues by Knöfler
      in Dresden.

4. In the Dorotheen- or Neustadt.
    - The Cesar Garden, because of splendid beds of buttercups, tulips, carnations and other kinds of flowers belonging to the royal singer Herr Concialini. The Gravius Garden. It contains a grotto hall, a round garden house built by Le Geay and a pleasing aviary with a section devoted solely to nightingales.

In the Friedrichstadt.
    - It is to the Court Preacher Reinhard at the Parochialkirche and his predecessor, the late Court Preacher Scharden, that flower-lovers in these parts owe the nurturing of beautiful tulips from seeds and instruction in how to propagate them with profit … and since then the following gardens have grown many exceedingly lovely tulips from local seeds … .[24]

These examples impressively document the richness of Berlin's gardening culture, which found expression not just in garden design, but also in the wide variety of plants. Thus, Nicolai's other lists of gardens reveal English auriculas, tulips, hyacinths, buttercups, carnations and roses, indicating the wide range of flowers that Berlin's nurseries could supply. Among the pot plants he also mentions as grown in the Berlin's nurseries were anemone, polyanthus, English and Persian iris and fritillary.[25]

It was not only the large cities and capitals that attracted attention with their many gardens and special landscaping. The small imperial city of Wetzlar, for example, also boasted numerous gardens, most of whose owners worked at the Imperial Chamber Court (*Reichskammergericht*). We have one of the court's assessors, Friedrich Wilhelm von Ulmenstein, to thank for a topographical description of Wetzlar including the gardens. The most significant of these was established by Judge Count Ambrosius Franz von Virmont. In the 1770s, Assessor Hermann Franz von Papius purchased the garden, expanded it and built an elegant country house. The ownership of gardens was not, however, restricted to officials of the *Reichskammergericht*. Thus, for example, the Italian-born merchant Gabriel Spinola laid out a pleasure garden before the Häuser Gate, and was followed by Johann Peter Schneider, a merchant and *Ratsschöffe* (assessor delegated by the town council to the court) and Johann Georg Langsdorff, scholaster of Wetzlar's college of canons.[26]

Garden theory and garden literature

Eighteenth-century readers wishing to inform themselves about gardening and garden design had a number of options. Only a century earlier, the selection had been a good deal narrower. The works of architectural theory by Joseph Furttenbach, with their many descriptions of gardens, accordingly played an important role in the seventeenth century. Furttenbach was town architect and councillor in Ulm, where he designed many public buildings. His books *Architectura civilis*, *Architectura universalis*, *Architectura recreationis* and *Architectura privata*[27] introduced Germans to Italian garden design, in particular, and set it on a par with architecture. He promoted not just large ornamental gardens with 'race-courses or riding schools' for the aristocracy outside the city, but also new walled gardens in the towns for the citizenry or the public. Furttenbach's designs are characterized by cruciform garden parterres, producing a systematic division of the space into four segments using paths, pergolas or a central pool. The bird's eye depiction of Furttenbach's own garden behind his Ulm home may show the only one he actually realized. It is striking for its lush flowerbeds, whose lavishness is confirmed by the published list of plants, which includes more than 100 tulips. His other recommendations of spring flowers included crown imperial fritillary, daffodil, hyacinth, iris, snake's head fritillary, anemone, crocus and Arabian star flower. In addition to these ornamental beds, each garden was supposed to have a vegetable garden and orchard as well, which in the case of smaller urban plots could also take the form of a kitchen garden or orange garden. Accordingly he also suggests fig, pomegranate, orange, lemon and lime trees. He also paid particular attention to grottoes and *coquillage* as well as water features, which must have fascinated him in Italian gardens.[28]

The French style, which in the eighteenth century would replace not only the Italian garden design propagated by Furttenbach, but also – in north-west Germany – Dutch influences, was disseminated through various channels. Designs for the formal gardens laid out by André Le Nôtre at Versailles were brought to Germany by his pupils. Simon Godeau, for example, designed Charlottenburg, while Dominique Girard planned the gardens at Schleißheim. French garden literature was similarly significant. Dézallier d'Argenville's *La théorie et la pratique du jardinage* (1709), for example, appeared in 1731 in a translation by the Salzburg landscape gardener Franz Anton Danreitter entitled *Die Gärtnerey, so wohl in ihrer Theorie oder Betrachtung als Praxi oder Übung: allwo von den schönen Gärten, welche man nur insgemein die Lust oder Zierd-Gärten zu nennen pflegt* ... (The Theory and Practice of Gardening, in which the Beautiful Gardens are Generally Known as Pleasure or Ornamental Gardens ...).[29] Le Nôtre and French garden design also attracted intense interest from Christian Cay Lorenz Hirschfeld, professor of philosophy and belles-lettres at the University of Kiel, who would open new paths for garden design in Germany, albeit also with frequent references to English authors such as William Chambers, Thomas Wathley, Joseph Addison and Henry Home. Hirschfeld's *Theorie der Gartenkunst* (Theory of Garden Design), which appeared in five volumes between 1779 and 1785, became a standard work, a must for any educated person who wanted to discuss gardens. Those who could not afford to buy the expensive volumes had to make do with the cheaper one-volume edition of 1775. They could also consult the article 'Garden' in Krünitz's *Oeconomische Encyclopädie* (Economic Encyclopaedia), which borrowed heavily from Hirschfeld,[30] or the periodical literature on gardening published by Bertuch.

Into the eighteenth century, gardens were deemed beautiful if they were laid out with regularity according to an architectural pattern. Hirschfeld represented a new generation for whom such artificial gardens had become obsolete and in need of replacement by new forms that opened onto, or were indistinguishable from, natural landscapes. The theory of garden design, which Hirschfeld understood as part of Johann Georg Sulzer's *Allgemeine Theorie der schönen Künste* (General Theory of the Fine Arts), provided the legitimation for such efforts. Sulzer had elevated garden design to a fine art with the argument that it derived directly from nature:

who is herself the consummate gardener. Thus just as the graphic arts imitate the beautiful forms created by Nature on behalf of Art, garden design imitates with taste and deliberation every beauty of inanimate Nature and combines what it finds individually with taste in a pleasure garden.[31]

In his theory, Hirschfeld is concerned with examining the effects of the natural beauty and variety of landscape systematically. Landscapes consisted of many 'connected areas', each with its own particular quality. Accordingly, 'pleasant', 'lively' and 'cheerful' country had a different effect from 'laughing' or 'alluring', 'romantic' or 'enchanting' landscapes.[32] Landscape was thus an aesthetic natural phenomenon created by 'the combination of several regions having different effects [on the beholder]'.[33] It does not matter whether these landscapes are laid out by nature or by human hands. Hills and babbling brooks produced a feeling of cheerfulness, while a forest could arouse a sense of solemn grandeur. In this way, Hirschfeld developed a method for capturing the aesthetic of a landscape and thus of garden design as well as other arts. Any gardener or artist familiar with the rules gained in this manner could apply them, and thus achieve certain aesthetic affects. Accordingly, garden designers should evoke as many aesthetic charms of the landscapes as possible:

The garden should positively affect the imagination and the perceptive faculties; and the garden designer should achieve this by means of the objects that properly belong to him … . He must thus first of all collect and choose those objects of beautiful Nature that have a superior power to bring forth the specified effects; he must form these objects, and combine and organize them in such a way as to heighten the impression.[34]

In order to provide model landscapes for garden designers, in the second volume Hirschfeld goes on to describe specific sites, such as Lake Keller in the North German region known as Holstein Switzerland:

This vista of such an expansive and open water surface between elevations and woodlands constitutes the principle part of this location. The clarity of the water, in which half the sky appears to be reflected, and the beauty of the surrounding woods … spread an uncommon jocundity on all sides.[35]

The experience of landscape was thus the ideal towards which every gardener and garden owner aspired. Hirschfeld was well aware that not only the owner's social standing, but also his purse and the personal atmosphere he intended to convey, could influence garden design. Nonetheless, Hirschfeld was accused, despite the initial enthusiasm for his work, of being too general and broad, and thus ill-suited to practical application. This criticism may have been as justified as that of his glorification of English gardens, but it is unjust to the extent that garden lovers also had a wide range of garden periodicals from which to choose.

Friedrich Justin Bertuch again offers a good example in the form of the *Allgemeine Teutsche Garten-Magazin* (Universal German Garden Magazine), the most important periodical in the field, which he began publishing in 1804. To be sure, in the first issue, Bertuch felt compelled to distance himself from Hirschfeld by shifting the origins of the landscape garden from England to China – for which he could cite French and English authorities – but he had already devoted space elsewhere to the reception of English authors or gardening writers. For example, Humphrey Repton's 1796 *Sketches and Hints on Landscape Gardening* had been reviewed in the *Journal des Luxus und der Moden* only two years after its publication in England. His 'recommendation of the golden willow for English gardens' in the *Garten-Magazin* for 1811 also shows the lasting effects of Hirschfeld's aesthetics:

> It is well known that the mourning, weeping or Babylonian willow (Salyx babylonica) is a very typical and virtually indispensable tree for landscape gardens in the English style, either to lend shade to a monument dedicated to the memory of a dear departed one, or to mark some other spot sacred to sweet melancholy and earnest reflection. On the edge of a lovely reflecting body of water, three weeping willows washing their long green hair in the silvery flood, its surface rippled by a gentle zephyr, often form a very beautiful and picturesque group. Or they conceal the figure of a bathing naiad, cloaking her as it were in a green mantle, and thus create a pleasant idyll.[36]

The *Garten-Magazin* also informed its readers not only about local Thuringian gardens, for example in descriptions of the Winter Garden or the Orangery at Meiningen or the Roman House in Weimar, but also kept them abreast, in words and pictures, of all the latest horticultural literature that the editors could get their hands on.[37] The books published by Bertuch himself had an even stronger practical orientation:

- Bartell, Ed. *Über die malerische Anlage und Verbesserung kleiner geschmackvoller Landhäuser oder sogenannter englischer Cottages* [On the Picturesque Design and Improvement of Small, Tasteful Country Houses or So-Called English Cottages], 1805
- Batsch, A.J.G.C. *Botanik für Frauenzimmer und Planzenliebhaber, welche keine Gelehrten sind* [Botany for Ladies and Non-Scholarly Plant Lovers], 1795, 2nd edn 1798, 3rd edn 1804, 4th edn 1818
- Butret, C. *Gründlicher Unterricht vom Schnitte der Fruchtbäume und anderen Verrichtungen, die Bezug auf ihre Pflege haben* [Thorough Instructions on the Pruning of Fruit Trees and other Activities Involved in their Maintenance]. From the French by J.V. Sickler, 1797

- *Garten-Memorandum für Liebhaber, welche ihren Gartenbau entweder selbst besorgen, oder doch richtig übersehen und leiten wollen* [Garden Memorandum for Amateurs, Who Either Garden in Their Own Right, or Aim to Supervise and Guide Properly], ed. F.J. Bertuch and J.V. Sickler, 1809, Hofbuchhandlung, Rudolstadt branch
- Reichert, Johann Friedrich, *Hortus Reichertianus, oder vollständiger Catalog für Handelsgärtner und Liebhaber der Gärtnerei* [Hortus Reichertianus, or Complete Catalogue for Commercial Nurseries and Amateur Gardeners], 1804, 2nd edn 1807
- Rudolphi, Johann Chr. Nelkentheorie oder eine in systematischer Ordnung nach der Natur gemalte Nelkentabelle [Theory of Carnations, or A Table of Carnations Painted from Nature in Systematic Order], Meißen, 1787, 2nd edn 1799

A further title was the pomological journal *Der Teutsche Obstgärtner* (The German Fruit Gardener), which merged with the new *Garten-Magazin* in 1804 and was intended to promote fruit growing in Germany. In order to increase the journal's didactic value, all of the fruits described in *Der Teutsche Obstgärtner* were modelled in wax and distributed, via Bertuch's Landes-Industrie-Comptoir, as a pomological collection packed for display in 26 wooden cases.[38]

Garden living – country houses

To close this chapter, let us turn our attention to life as it was lived 'in the garden', which we encountered earlier in a description by Goethe's mother in Frankfurt. We also find indications of such country house living in Berlin, where the first villas appeared on the southern fringe of the Tiergarten in the late eighteenth century. Thus, as we have already seen from the accounts of Berlin gardens, bankers and functional elites built 'garden' cottages and summerhouses where they lived during the summer months. Around 1800, some Berliners also began to live in their garden houses all year round. To this end, the young architect Friedrich Gilly built a country house for Privy Councillor of War and Inspector of Salt Mines for the Kurmark Johann Gottfried Mölter in 1799, while Carl Gotthard Langhans constructed a villa nearby for August Wilhelm Iffland, director of the National Theatre.[39]

Autobiographies, in particular, offer information about everyday life and leisure activities in the gardens and country houses. If we can take Hamburg canon Friedrich Johann Lorenz Meyer at his word, Hamburg occupied a special position here:

> I know of no other city so surrounded by suburbs with gardens and garden villages, in which each house contains a large family and domestic economy, and many buildings are constructed and furnished with taste, and most with more or less expenditure.[40]

What Meyer describes here is only the high point of a development that began in the seventeenth century and would end with the French occupation of the city. While the garden houses in the New Town were initially summerhouses offering temporary shelter from sun, rain or cold, it was only when people began to lay out gardens in Billwerder, Hamm and Horn that they erected solid country houses. Since the gardens were now farther from the city, people needed to be able to live there. Thus, Hamburg citizens could stay over the weekend, and in summer, wives and children could live at the garden house during the week as well, while husbands returned to the city to work. The structure of the summerhouse, with a large reception room on the first floor overlooking the gardens, was maintained at first and the utility rooms on the ground floor converted into bedrooms. A garden hall with a veranda or terrace was added, creating a transition between house and garden. Thus, festivities were gradually moved from the first to the ground floor, while the family increasingly lived on the first floor.[41]

Many country houses were converted farmhouses, such as the Newman House, which was torn down in the 1930s. Only towards the end of the eighteenth century did better-known architects such as Christian Friedrich Hansen, Johann August Arens and Axel Bundsen begin to attract attention with their designs for country houses. C.F. Hansen's first significant commission was for the merchant and ship owner Caesar Godeffroy IV built between 1789 and 1792. Like many other buildings by Hansen and his contemporaries, this villa in what is now the Hirschpark represents a variation on the old garden pavilion, but on a completely different scale. The park landscape and the situation on the sandy upland above the Elbe represented the perfect conditions for Hansen's designs and structures, of which the country houses for the English merchant John Blacker – chairman of the trading company known as the 'English Court' on the Krähenberg in Hamburg – and Peter Godeffroy (Caesar's younger brother) are just two examples. The construction of country houses was not, however, limited to the suburbs on the Elbe, as might be suggested by surviving examples.[42] Apart from Hansen's architectural activities in Schleswig-Holstein, J.A. Arens also designed country houses for numerous clients in Harvestehude and Hamm, almost all of which fell victim to the French occupation troops who cleared fields of fire for the artillery in 1813–14.[43]

Most accounts of life in country houses come from the period before the French occupation. They describe the leisurely pace and sociability of life in the gardens. The country house owner Georg Heinrich Sieveking, mentioned earlier, emphasized his stays in the country because they allowed him to 'tear himself away from the low mundane bustle and the daily round of trade and money-making, and remove himself to a more human region'. Time spent in the garden helped to compensate for the stresses of work and city life and thus reflects the emergence of leisure activities. Gardens also promised relaxation for wives and a healthy atmosphere for sickly relations. According to his journal, Ferdinand Beneke's family, for example, moved to the country in June 1823 for the health of his children and his ailing sister as well as his exhausted wife. Like many other Hamburg citizens, the Benekes rented a country house in Flottbek, and filled it with members of the extended family. The men generally only went out to the country at the weekend or on weekday evenings.[44]

Even as a bachelor, Ferdinand Beneke had spent a good deal of his free time in the gardens of Hamburg society. Particularly in June 1797, he either had friends collect him or rode by himself 'to Kirchenpaur's garden' in Hamm or other gardens. His sister Regina spent much time with the Amsincks in Moorfleeth. Thus, for the Beneke siblings and their friends, the summer passed with convivial gatherings in the gardens; sometimes they even missed the Sunday sermon as a consequence. The secularization of Sunday thus proceeded apace. At the same time, the country houses took on the character of salons when a hostess such as Johanna Margaretha Sieveking invited guests to come to breakfast or tea at Neumühlen.[45]

The fashion for garden living brought with it a growing informality in sociable relations. Where at mid-century people had attended country house parties in 'grand toilette', with panniers, swords and periwigs, etiquette was less strictly observed towards the end of the eighteenth century, as Senator Hudtwalcker recalled:

> Only eighteen years ago [in 1779], we had feasts in our gardens where we drove out in the blazing heat weighed down by our city finery, our chapeau-bas and swords, in order to sweat at the dining table for three hours and dry our sweat for another three at the gaming table. They have disappeared and now seem ridiculous – not by design, but merely through example, enlightenment, and improved taste.[46]

With the triumph of the English landscape garden English dress also came into fashion, and frock coats replaced the impractical *justaucorps*. Ladies left their panniers at home, preferring cotton fabrics and the loose flowing English skirts (see also Chapter 3 above). Country house and clothing fashions thus influenced each other, and even in the visual arts one finds connections between the English garden and the predilection for landscape painting as evident, for example, in Christian Ludwig von Hagedorn's essays on aesthetic theory.[47]

Chapter 6

Art and Taste

> My father's maxim, which he frequently and even passionately expressed, was that one should patronise living masters and spend less on dead ones, the appreciation of whom was mixed with a good deal of prejudice ... . In accord with these principles, he had kept all the artists in Frankfurt busy for several years: the painter Hirt, whose forte was painting oak and beech woods and other so-called rustic locales, complete with cattle; also Trautmann, who imitated Rembrandt and was so proficient at painting enclosed lights and reflections, as well as impressive fire scenes, that he was once commissioned to do a companion piece to a picture by Rembrandt; also Schütz, who followed Sachtleben's lead in diligently painting scenes of the Rhine region; and Juncker too, who, in the Dutch manner, very neatly executed flower and fruit pieces, still lifes, and scenes of persons quietly occupied.[1]

This quotation from Johann Wolfgang von Goethe nicely illustrates the reception of Dutch painting in the neighbouring countries. In Frankfurt, Hamburg, Paris and London, local painters adapted the 'Dutch manner' (*Holländermode*) and spread the taste for Dutch art among collectors. A decisive role was also played by imports of Dutch and Flemish paintings and the immigration of Dutch painters. The enthusiasm for Dutch art coincided with the emergence of an art market through which England, France and Germany inherited institutions of the Dutch Golden Age such as picture auctions and exhibitions.

When the Dutch art market diminished in the last decades of the seventeenth century, the rising English market formed one outlet for Dutch painters and paintings. An indigenous painting tradition hardly existed in seventeenth-century England. However, a number of Dutch and Flemish portrait painters and engravers had emigrated to England, and Dutch paintings were also imported in growing quantities. The market grew rapidly at the end of the century, when the auction, a method hitherto used primarily to sell off the household effects of the recently deceased or the bulk import commodities of the English East India Company, became recognized as a regular fixture in fashionable London social life. Thus, during a speculation boom, thousands of paintings changed hands. The 129 extant auction catalogues from the period between 1689 and 1692 mention 35,797 pictures, including Dutch genre paintings. After this explosion of interest in selling and buying paintings, the number of art sales per annum dropped substantially. By the early years of the eighteenth century, an entire generation of immigrant artists had substantially enlarged the stock of home-produced paintings, while Joseph van Aken and Pieter Angellis refined the low-genre Dutch droll into the English conversation piece. The number of picture auctions rose steadily from the 1720s on and by the 1730s, the auction had become the dominant method of buying and selling pictures in London. In this period, a number of virtuosi and artist-dealers such as Andrew Hay, Arthur Pond, Samuel Paris and Robert Bragge established themselves, purchasing works of art on commission abroad for clients or for resale at public auction. Dealing in antiquities, medals, manuscripts, prints, drawings and paintings, or combining portraiture, decorative painting and picture restoration with dealing, collecting and print selling, these men profited from a growing market for the decorative arts. In the 1740s, the emphasis shifted from imports to the recirculation of existing stocks, as prominent collections of high-quality paintings such as those of Lord Halifax, the painter Charles Jervas, the Earl of Oxford and the Duke of Chandos entered the market. At the same time, a circle of connoisseurs of Dutch art comprised of city merchants, gentry and artist-dealers formed in London. The second half of the eighteenth century saw the emergence of auction houses such as Cock's, Christie's and Sotheby's, and the struggle of British painters for appreciation.

While in England the foundation and success of the Royal Academy had elevated the position of artists and increased their independence from patrons, in France, Academy traditions and the Salon stifled the development of the art market and of taste for many years. Like other European countries – with the exception of the Netherlands – France and especially Paris were characterized by the absence of a specialized group of professional art dealers. The large number of public sales, which art dealers were not permitted to conduct, inhibited the rise of the professional dealer. Although in the seventeenth century dealers had occasionally held sales of important paintings, only in the early eighteenth century did they overcome sales restrictions by joining the merchands-merciers, who were permitted to sell a variety of goods. One of the pioneers of the Paris art market was Edmé-François Gersaint, who joined the mercers' guild in 1720 and contributed with his activities to the gradual erosion of the academic taste standards set by Colbert and Charles LeBrun on behalf of the Académie Royale de Peinture et de Sculpture. At first, Gersaint dealt in a wide range of luxury goods including Oriental porcelain, lacquered cabinets, marquetry, bronzes, mirrors, clocks, paintings, gems, shells and other 'naturalia'. Not until the 1740s did he begin to specialize in paintings and prints. He travelled frequently to Holland, buying paintings there that he then resold at auctions very different from earlier sales of paintings. Gersaint's auctions were characterized by viewing days prior to the auction and catalogues offering information and advice. Other dealers such as Pierre Remy, Jean-Baptiste-Pierre Lebrun and Alexander Paillet imitated Gersaint in this respect. Although Gersaint was more interested in the quality of paintings than in attributions, he shaped taste by promoting Netherlandish paintings and the immigrant Fleming Watteau. Gersaint's marketing efforts coincided with a growing interest in the Salon, which became not just a prominent diversion in Paris but also 'the first regularly repeated, open, and free display of contemporary art in Europe'.[2]

The commercialization of the visual arts continued in the second half of the eighteenth century. We know of more than 70 art dealers by name for the period 1740–80, while surviving catalogues document 581 auctions held between 1750 and 1770. The auction boom reached its climax in the years 1776 and 1777 with the sales of the famous collections of Blondel de Gagny, Randon de Boisset and Prince Conti. Paintings by Dou, Wouwerman, Metsu, Adriaen van de Velde and Potter brought the highest prices there, reflecting the success of the *écoles du Nord* on the Paris art market, which had become the major market for Dutch paintings after Amsterdam.

From the late seventeenth century onwards, German princely courts also bought Dutch paintings in larger quantities. While the collections in Berlin/ Potsdam, Dresden, Vienna, Düsseldorf or Bonn contained significant examples of Dutch painting in addition to Italian and French works, the newly established collections of the mid-eighteenth century at Kassel, Karlsruhe and Schwerin concentrated on Dutch and Flemish masterpieces. Duke Christian Ludwig II of Mecklenburg-Schwerin had become acquainted with Dutch art during his Grand Tour to Holland, and at Amsterdam and Hague auctions as well as on the Hamburg art market he purchased numerous cabinet paintings, which were catalogued for the first time in 1792. In his Kassel collection, however, Landgrave Wilhelm VIII concentrated on large formats. During his time as governor of the fortresses Maastricht and Breda, Wilhelm had already established a cabinet of paintings. In the 1730s, he bought several paintings by Rubens, including the *Flight to Egypt*, at Amsterdam auctions and his inventory of 1749 lists no fewer than 34 paintings by Rembrandt. In 1750, he succeeded in purchasing the Delft collection of Valerius Röver with 64 masterpieces, among them an additional eight Rembrandts. In 1759, Karoline Luise of Baden also began building up a cabinet of paintings. Having visited a number of collections and studied their catalogues and contemporary works of connoisseurship, she developed firm ideas about what she should have in her collection. Apart from the German painters Mignon, Roos, and Rottenhammer, her list contains only Dutch and Flemish painters.

As in England and France, the establishment of new collections of Dutch and Flemish art contributed to the erosion of classical standards of taste such as the hierarchy of genres. While history paintings had dominated the collections in Berlin, Potsdam, Dresden, Vienna, Düsseldorf, Mannheim, Salzdahlum and Schleißheim, in Kassel, history paintings made up only a quarter of the collection. In Schwerin and Karlsruhe, landscapes, genre paintings and portraits played a major role. This trend from history painting to landscapes and genre paintings is also typical of the bourgeois collections in Frankfurt and Hamburg. Unfortunately, we often lack probate inventories for German cities and must thus rely on auction catalogues and inventories drawn up by the collectors themselves.

Patterns of collecting

Our examination of Frankfurt collections yields the first data on the composition of representative collections for the 1760s, the 1780s and the period around 1800. The first Frankfurt collection that we can reconstruct is that of Baron Jacob von Häckel, who built up not only his own painting collection from the 1730s on, but also served as connoisseur and middleman for the collections founded in the mid-eighteenth century at Karlsruhe and Kassel by Karoline Luise of Baden and Wilhelm VIII of Hesse-Kassel.[3] According to the surviving auction catalogue of 1762 – the auction was only held two years later – the composition of Häckel's collection was as shown in Table 6.1. Landscapes and in particular genre paintings dominated, with histories and portraits and still lifes following at some distance. Another significant genre were animal portraits, so-called *Tier-Stücke*, which seem to have become more fashionable in the course of the eighteenth century along with animal and hunt still lifes.

Table 6.1   Percentages of paintings in Frankfurt collections by genres, 1762–1829[4]

Genres	Häckel 1762	Bernus 1780	Berberich 1784	Kaller and Michael 1790	Prehn 1829	Morgenstern undated
History	14	25	13	19	20	22
Landscape	23	35	26	42	44	35
Still life	9	12	13	6	2	1
Genre	26	11	28	17	9	22
Portrait	15	13	28	7	17	17
Animal	9	3	7	7	6	1
Other	4	1	3	2	2	2

The following years brought a significant increase in the number of landscapes in Frankfurt collections. Landscapes dominated, for example, in the collections of the banking family Bernus and the imperial aulic councillor (*Reichshofrat*) Berberich, auctioned in the 1780s, and in the dealer collections of Kaller and Michael, displayed in the same decade and auctioned in 1790.[5] In the Berberich collection, genre paintings were also quite important,[6] while in Kaller's collection, which had been acquired at various auctions, the percentage of landscapes exceeded 40 per cent for the first time.[7]

The last two decades of the eighteenth and the first two decades of the nineteenth century present us with a different kind of evidence in the collections of the confectioner Johann Valentin Prehn and the painter Johann Friedrich Morgenstern. These are not only documented in (auction) catalogues, but have

Figure 12   The cabinet of paintings of Johann Valentin Prehn. Watercolour
by Carl Morgenstern, 1829

also survived to a considerable extent *in natura* in the Historisches Museum in
Frankfurt. Prehn's is the only middle-class collection that we can reconstruct
for this period in Frankfurt. Prehn collected quantity rather than quality, and
bought originals as well as copies – influenced by printed collection catalogues
and fellow collectors – in the genres and subjects that he preferred and that
were considered de rigueur in his day. Landscapes significantly outnumbered
history paintings in his collection, followed by portraits and genre pictures.[8]

Even more interesting is the cabinet assembled by the painter Johann Friedrich
Morgenstern in the first two decades of the nineteenth century. Morgenstern, a
famous Frankfurt painter and restorer, constructed three triptychs, which he filled
with paintings he had copied from 'originals' in Frankfurt collections while they
were being restored in his workshop. The Morgenstern cabinet thus provides
a representative cross-section of the upper segment of Frankfurt collections
around 1800. Landscapes prevailed over genre and history paintings.[9]

Summarizing our inquiry into the genres represented in Frankfurt collections,
we can state that the closer we get to the end of the eighteenth century, and
the deeper we penetrate the middle segment of the art market and collections,
the more landscapes dominate, and the less important still lifes become. This
pattern is indeed consistent with evidence from Amsterdam and Delft. Prehn's
cabinet – apart from still lifes – quite closely resembles the situation in Delft
in the 1670s, although the proportion of histories was generally higher in
Frankfurt than in Holland.

The earliest Hamburg collection of Dutch paintings that we can trace was that of Johann Outgertsen (Outgers), who had moved from the Dutch Republic to Hamburg and had been active in the Amsterdam–Hamburg trade. His 1644 household inventory can be found in the records of the Reichskammergericht (Imperial Chamber Court). According to this inventory, Johann Outgertsen owned 68 paintings, including works by the best Dutch and Flemish painters and their special subjects: portraits by Rembrandt van Rijn, Jan Lievens and Claes Elliassen, seascapes by Jan Porcellis, landscapes by Ruisdael, Jan van Goyen, Van de Velde, Pieter Molijn and Kuyper, a religious painting by Antoni van Dyck, and a *vanitas* by David de Heem.[10]

More prominent than Outgertsen was Jacob de le Boe Sylvius, whose brother had been a patron of the Leiden *fijnschilders* (fine-painters) Gerrit Dou and Frans van Mieris. Jacob inherited his brother's collection and transferred it to Hamburg. In his book *Teutsche Academie der Bau-, Bild- und Mahlerey-Künste* (German Academy of the Arts of Architecture, Sculpture and Painting, 1675), Joachim von Sandrart praises him as a Hamburg collector and connoisseur. We have no information on the details of this collection, however. The same holds true for Anthon Verborcht, a Dutch physician living in Hamburg, whose collection was sold at auction in 1731. Unfortunately, the auction catalogue has not been preserved. We must therefore make do with surviving auction catalogues from the mid- and late-eighteenth century. Although Hamburg witnessed a number of auctions throughout the eighteenth century, evidence of Hamburg collections is not as abundant as one might expect.[11]

Most of the documented auctions were anonymous auctions with paintings collected in Hamburg, and sold there. Owing to the limited evidence and the lack of research, art historians have often relied on an article by Niels von Holst, who contends that Hamburg collections were dominated by genre paintings and by Dutch artists, with German, Italian and French paintings represented only in small numbers.[12] However, the few surviving catalogues of Hamburg collections present a different picture: in the small collection of the Ratsherr (councillor) and poet Barthold Heinrich Brockes (1747), the sales collection of the painter Balthasar Denner (1749) and an anonymous Hamburg collection, auctioned in 1793, landscapes dominated by far, while portraits and especially genres played a minor role. The more traditionally structured collections of Joachim Hinrich Thielcke and Pierre Laporterie, however, show a greater share of histories and notably genre paintings (see Table 6.2).[13]

To what extent were these collecting patterns influenced by imports of Dutch paintings? To answer this question, we must examine the above-mentioned collections with respect to Dutch paintings (see Table 6.3).

Table 6.2   Percentages of paintings in Hamburg collections by genres, 1747–93[14]

Genres	Brockes 1747	Denner 1749	Thielcke 1782	Laporterie 1793	Anonymous 1793
History	20	9	17	30	13
Landscape	30	45	27	33	42
Still life	18	13	5	4	8
Genre	7	9	23	20	13
Portrait	20	22	24	12	21
Animal	3	2	2	1	2
Other	2	0	2	0	1

Table 6.3   Percentages of nationalities of paintings in Frankfurt collections, 1762–1820[15]

Nationality of artist	Häckel 1762	Bernus 1780	Berberich 1784	Kaller and Michael 1790	Prehn 1829	Morgenstern undated
Dutch	13	17	15	27	13	54
Flemish	12	16	11	13	9	8
German	35	26	18	27	41	21
Italian	8	8	4	5	2	12
French	2	1	2	2	2	4
Others/ Unknown	30	32	50	26	33	1

Apart from Morgenstern's cabinet, which provides a cross-section of the upper segment of Frankfurt collections, Dutch (together with Flemish) paintings never constituted more than one-third of Frankfurt collections, while German, mostly Frankfurt, painters dominated and anonymous paintings also played an important role.

Imported Dutch collections were not transferred and integrated 'en bloc' into Frankfurt collections, but disseminated only gradually, painting by painting, competing with paintings by local artists and anonymous copies (in the Dutch style). The same pattern applies to the Hamburg collections (see Table 6.4).

Here, only the Denner sales collection shows a significant share of Dutch paintings, while his Hamburg fellow painters are underrepresented. Nonetheless, the influence of Dutch collecting patterns is clearly visible in the composition of Frankfurt and Hamburg collections.

Table 6.4   Percentages of nationalities of paintings in Hamburg collections, 1747–93[16]

Nationality of artist	Brockes 1747	Denner 1749	Thielcke 1782	Laporterie 1793	Anonymous 1793
Dutch	14	45	19	38	32
Flemish	6	7	10	10	12
German	35	31	24	19	35
Italian	3	8	2	13	4
French	1	1	1	7	1
Other/ Unknown	41	8	44	13	16

Art marketing and connoisseurship

In the eighteenth century, an art market emerged in Germany. This market arose regionally in territorially fragmented Germany, but it can be traced above all in the two major artistic and commercial centres of the Holy Roman Empire: Frankfurt and Hamburg. At some distance behind them, Leipzig and Cologne also played a minor role. Crucial for the gradual development of a German art market – for example in comparison with the Netherlands – were the small supply of paintings on the one hand and the modest demand, especially in the German cities, on the other. Imports of paintings and an increase in local art production were thus the preconditions for a growing art market. These conditions seem to have been present in the eighteenth century.

As in the seventeenth-century Netherlands,[17] the expanding eighteenth-century German art market generated the new profession of art dealers, mainly in the mid-eighteenth century, when painters and merchants began to specialize in the art trade. This new art trade developed its own areas of specialization. While 'international' art dealers sold to the courts and wealthy private collectors, the local art trade in cities such as Frankfurt and Hamburg expanded, supplying not just municipal collections but also the neighbouring courts. Art auctions – alongside patronage of local painters – became the key institutions for supplying art works on the local level.

Although auctions of paintings had already taken place in Germany in the seventeenth century – in 1690, for instance, the heirs of Duke Rudolf Friedrich von Holstein-Norburg sold his collection at Wolfenbüttel – it was only in the eighteenth century, and especially the latter half, that the number of art auctions rose significantly. The auction catalogues collected by the Getty Provenance Index in its project on the 'German Sales' clearly document this development (see Table 6.5).[18]

Table 6.5   Auction catalogues in Germany before 1800

	Total	Frankfurt	Cologne	Leipzig	Hamburg	Others
Total	298	40	9	27	140	82
before 1699	3	-	-	-	-	3
1700–59	32	2	1	3	16	10
1760–69	29	9	4	1	7	8
1770–79	62	7	-	-	40	15
1780–89	70	14	1	8	28	19
1790–1800	102	8	3	15	49	27

Out of a total of 298 recorded auctions 234 took place between 1770 and 1800. Before this period, auctions of paintings were isolated and irregular events, except in the case of Hamburg where a steady sequence of sales had already begun during the late seventeenth century, even if most of these primarily featured books. Twenty auctions took place in Hamburg before the end of the Seven Years' War in 1763.[19] Accordingly, Hamburg, with 140 auctions in all, was the leading art market in the Holy Roman Empire, followed by Frankfurt with 40 auctions, Leipzig with 27 and Cologne with 9. As to the number of paintings sold at auction, the difference between Frankfurt und Hamburg was less significant, because an average Hamburg auction contained fewer paintings than a Frankfurt auction. Thus the Hamburg catalogues register 17,895 paintings, whilst 10,153 paintings are recorded for Frankfurt.

Which factors influenced the importance of auction sites and thus the professionalization of the art trade? Hamburg, for example, benefited from its location, which was convenient for transit trade. Along with other foreign merchants, the city also attracted art dealers such as Gerhard Morell. He settled there in order to sell paintings of the highest quality from Dutch auctions to the German princely collections, such as Hesse-Kassel and Mecklenburg-Schwerin, but also to private collectors. Morell's correspondence with the Mecklenburg court, in which he carefully recorded the authenticity, quality and condition of works in Dutch private collections and occasionally recommended the purchase of a painting, is revealing in this regard:

> I must allow that the Weenix is good, however I invoke the experienced eyes of Your Serene Highness for evidence concerning the extent to which my v. Alst painting surpasses the Weenix as well as the v. Alst already in Your Serene Highness's possession with respect to diligence, beauty, composition, intelligence and good conservation. This piece has had the good fortune never to have been in the hands of such persons as render the master in the master[pieces] unrecognizable by cleaning, rubbing, correcting and retouching. This piece is without doubt by the most famous still life painter v. Alst, and is certainly his best offspring.[20]

Figure 13   Title page of a Hamburg auction catalogue, 6 October 1787

Morell was probably the first art dealer in Germany to gain a reputation as a connoisseur. Called to the Royal Danish court at Copenhagen in 1757, he purchased more than two hundred paintings for the collection in his capacity as *Garde des tableaux et autres Raretés de S. Majeste Danoise et Commissaire de la Cour*, including Rembrandt's *Christ at Emmaus*.[21]

Moreover, the art market in Hamburg profited from the city's liberal auction laws, products of the great tradition of auctioning import commodities. Like the commodity auctions, the art auctions were held at the exchange and organized by brokers. By 1785, more than 30 brokers were registered in the Hamburg art trade, most prominent among them Packischefsky, Bostelmann and Texier, who are mentioned on the title pages of several auction catalogues. Most of the collections were probably brought to Hamburg from outside, but Hamburg private collections, too, were 'recycled' with the help of auctions. Thus, they helped to satisfy the growing demand for paintings in urban households. After 1789, an increasing number of French collections was brought to Hamburg, often by Hamburg merchants, because of the favourable exchange rate and low prices in France.

As regards the Frankfurt art market, it mainly profited from the annual fair and the continuous flow of import commodities. That is why painters and art dealers such as Justus Juncker and Johann Christian Kaller held a series of auctions of imported paintings in Frankfurt between 1763 and 1765.[22] Another example is the collector and dealer Johann Baptist Ehrenreich, who carefully informed Karoline Luise of Baden of the forthcoming auction of 'a Collection of Dutch Masters' to be sold under the gavel of 'Messers Hl. Junkers and H. Kaller'. Ehrenreich, who like other dealers satisfied the private and princely demand for art, enclosed a letter with the catalogue and marked the paintings he recommended for purchase with asterisks, whereby one asterisk signified a 'good' picture, two a 'better' picture, and three asterisks an 'impeccable' piece. Unfortunately, only the letter has survived, and we do not know which paintings Ehrenreich marked. At another auction in Frankfurt, Ehrenreich bought paintings by Quiringh G. Brekelenkamp, Adriaen Brouwer and Herman Saftleven for the Countess of Baden for a sum of 375 reichstaler and 8 kreuzer. The Frankfurt modeller in wax and art dealer Christian Benjamin Rauschner also maintained connections to the court at Karlsruhe. It emerges from his catalogue of 1765 that he had purchased paintings in Holland expressly for auction in Frankfurt. Rauschner sent a list of paintings to Karlsruhe in the hope of selling some of them to the court. A large number of the pictures on this list had been auctioned from the holdings of Elector Clemens August in Bonn only the year before.[23] The most striking feature of the Frankfurt art market is the huge turnover of paintings from prominent collections. Even major collections were quickly dissolved by auction after the death of their owners. At these auctions, art dealers and collectors were the most important purchasers.[24]

The Leipzig art market, in contrast, was hampered by the city's rigid auction laws. The booksellers' and shopkeepers' guilds in particular were anxious to ensure that only the estates of local people were put on the auction block there. Accordingly, it was not until the 1780s that the art dealer Christian Heinrich Rost, who had begun his artistic career as a modeller of plaster figures, organized art auctions in Leipzig. He collaborated with the Proclamator of the University, Christoph Gottlob Weigel, and the auctions were held in a University auditorium. In 1782, Rost publicly solicited works of art to be sold at his first auction, which according to the catalogue took place on 1 August 1783. The items included engravings, drawings, paintings and books. This auction likewise marks the beginning of Rost's art trading enterprise, the Kunsthandlung, which was later succeeded by Weigel's Antiquariat- und Auktionsinstitut.[25]

Auction catalogues – often designed by artists or painters – played a crucial role in the promotion of the art trade and the spread of connoisseurship.[26] A good example is the *Catalogue d'un recueil d'un grand Seigneur de plusieurs superbes tableaux* of the 1765 Frankfurt auction organized by Chr. B. Rauschner. In his catalogue, Rauschner not only supplied the reader with careful descriptions, but also tried to place the paintings in the context of the master's oeuvre. Of a landscape by Paul Bril, for example, (no. 22), we read that:

> One knows that the colours of the landscapes by this master often tend to the green. This manner of painting, however, suits his paintbrush admirably and the two go well together. Tennier painted the staffage and placed it well. You will find few paintings by Paul Bril made with more care than this one.

Or consider the description of a still life by Jan Weenix (no. 102):

> A hare hangs from a nail, also a partridge; and on a marble table are placed a filet of hare, a hunting bag of green velvet and two blue woodpeckers; above hang a falcon crest, quail pipe and a hunting horn from a silken cord with tassels. I do not scorn any painter old or new; in view of this picture, however, I would frankly challenge any connoisseur to find another painting made with such assiduity, naturalness and all that may be derived from the human spirit, hand and paintbrush. Hamilton has a good deal to say, but he must not hang too close to this Weenix lest the connoisseur's eye overlook him [the Hamilton].[27]

We have numerous examples of similar contributions to connoisseurship because auction catalogues circulated among collectors, connoisseurs and dealers, and fairly soon became collectors' items in their own right. With the aid of auction catalogues, dealers and collectors kept informed of the market supply. As we know from the letters of Christian Ludwig Hagedorn, collectors received catalogues from dealers, corresponded about forthcoming auctions and the works to be sold, compiled lists of the desired paintings with respect to potential prices and issued written orders (so-called *commissionen*). In a letter of April 1741, Christian Ludwig Hagedorn wrote:

> I see from your written order that you have bid on a van der Velde and David Teniers without distinction up to the amount of 16 ducats. In my letter, however, I added the restriction 'animal painting or landscape'. These Adrian van der Velde has painted; thus if I get a Willem van der Velde, however worth the money it may be, I would get ships and seascapes, to which I have little inclination. If, however, I get one of those Petit Soldats of 6 or 4 inches by Tenier for 16 ducats, I would not have profited, for such a small piece has no further composition. Therefore I have restricted myself to animals and landscapes as my major field of collection, since I cannot hope to acquire a 'Sacrifice of Abraham' by D. Teniers. However, a very well painted, richly composed peasant piece would be no less pleasing to me than a landscape.[28]

Moreover, the auction catalogues allow us to trace the development of connoisseurship. For example, in the auction catalogue of the Hamburg Thielcke collection, the dealer differentiated between 'Unquestionably Rembrand' [sic],

'In the Manner of Rembrand', 'School of Rembrand' and 'As Beautiful as Rembrand'.[29] These distinctions can, however, also be interpreted as part of a marketing strategy, since the dealer was keen to meet collectors' growing demand for Rembrandts.

When it came to the promotion of paintings and taste, the painters themselves were as successful as the dealers. Painters organized auctions, mediated taste by selling paintings and copies of desired masters, and satisfied taste by painting in the esteemed style. In the case of Christian Ludwig Hagedorn, it was the Vienna painter Josef Orient who told him not only sell his own landscapes, but also landscapes by Pieter Mulier and a *Pigeon's Nest* by David König as a *compagnon* to a Jan Fyt. Orient also acted as advisor to the Hagedorn collection. That is why Hagedorn supplied him with a list of desired paintings.[30]

In the case of Frankfurt, we see painters active as dealers, such as Jacob Marell in the late seventeenth century and Justus Juncker in the eighteenth. The latter organized the above-mentioned auctions in 1763 together with Johann Christian Kaller.[31]

The situation was similar in Hamburg, where Balthasar Denner was the most successful painter-dealer. His workshop supplied different kinds of Dutch subjects, especially portraits and still lifes, and he earned his reputation with portrait commissions for the dukes of Holstein-Gottorp, the Danish king, the courts of Brunswick-Wolfenbüttel and Mecklenburg-Schwerin, not to mention his shorter sojourns in Amsterdam and London. What is more, he was quite successful in the auction and lottery business, as attested to by the catalogues of the 1749 auction and of a lottery, which are preserved in the Denner file in the Schwerin Archives.

By the end of the eighteenth century, a new type of business emerged in the German art trade, the so-called Kunsthandlung (art dealership). It combined the production, publication and sale of prints with auctions of paintings and sometimes also of antiquarian books. One example was the above-mentioned Rostsche Kunsthandlung in Leipzig. However, the prototype of the Kunsthandlung was probably the Prestel publishing enterprise in Frankfurt. In the 1780s, the painter and engraver Johann Gottlieb Prestel and his wife had specialized first in facsimile reproductions of drawings, and later of paintings in lavish portfolios that were promoted by Heinrich Sebastian Hüsgen, a Frankfurt collector and connoisseur. Reproductions of Dutch landscapes held a prominent position in this publishing enterprise, and satisfied as well as stimulated the *Holländermode* among the German public. In the nineteenth century, later generations made 'Prestel' into one of the leading German auction houses.[32]

Another Kunsthandlung belonged to Johann Friedrich Frauenholz in Nuremberg. Frauenholz had not only bought and sold the Praun cabinet – one of the famous sixteenth/seventeenth century Upper German art collections – but also regularly held auctions of prints and published the etchings produced by Ferdinand and Wilhelm Kobell after landscapes by Nicolaes Berchem, Philips Wouwerman, Jan Both, Adrian van de Velde, Jacob Ruysdael and others. These printed reproductions of paintings cannot be overestimated as a stimulus to collecting and taste among a growing public of collectors.[33]

The Kunsthandlung Dominik Artaria, founded in 1793 in Mannheim, offered an even wider range of items to potential collectors who visited their exhibition: paintings, engravings, etchings, sculptures, plaster copies of classical sculptures, portraits of princes and the like.[34] This assortment of products differed only slightly from the luxury goods publicized and offered for sale by the Weimar entrepreneur Friedrich Justin Bertuch in his *Journal des Luxus und der Moden*. He advertised replicas of antiquities, engravings, etchings and also contemporary sculptures. In addition, plaster busts of the Weimar heroes Goethe, Schiller, Wieland and members of the grand ducal family such as Anna Amalia and Carl August, as well as other cultural devotional items, met the demand of a growing number of tourists to Weimar.[35]

Connoisseurs played quite an important part in the stimulation of taste. On the one hand, as the example of Christian Ludwig Hagedorn illustrates, they visited prominent princely and private collections and informed broader circles about their contents. On the other hand, distinguished urban collectors such as Baron von Häckel acted as art experts, advising princes on the establishment of their collections. In 1759, for instance, Baron von Häckel distributed a selection of his paintings to Karoline Luise of Baden, from which she chose two still lifes by Rachel Ruysch. In exchange, she sent her portrait, while Häckel thanked her with a portrait by Mieris.[36] Häckel also stimulated taste through his commissions for Frankfurt painters. The auction of Häckel's collection was a major social event recorded by Goethe, who attended with his father. Goethe later told his readers that he himself had gained a reputation (at auctions in the company of connoisseurs) for being able immediately to recognize the subject of the painting at hand.

Less prominent than Häckel, but similarly influential, was Heinrich Sebastian Hüsgen, who not only frequently visited and bought at auctions, but also published on the subject of prominent Frankfurt collectors and collections. In his first publication, *Verrätherische Briefe von Historie und Kunst* (Revelatory Letters on History and Art) he wrote about Frankfurt and the Frankfurt area and the role that artists and scholars played in the general process of the refinement of society. In this context, he discusses Frankfurt collections as well as his own motivations for collecting. According to Hüsgen, collecting and connoisseurship contribute to the formation of the mind, the admiration of creation and the maintenance of a healthy body.[37]

More influential in stimulating taste was Hüsgen's second book, *Nachrichten von Frankfurter Künstlern und Kunstsachen* (Intelligence about Frankfurt Artists and Artistic Matters), a dictionary of artists that also provides a tour d'horizon of prominent Frankfurt collections. Emphasizing masterpieces by Dutch and German artists in Frankfurt collections, he set standards for future collectors.[38] Table 6.6 shows the composition of paintings in his personal collection (he also collected 'antiquities', drawings and prints), which was auctioned in 1808. It is characteristic of the late eighteenth century, although – as in the Morgenstern cabinet – Dutch painters dominated.

Table 6.6   Percentages of nationalities of paintings in the Hüsgen collection 1808[39]

Genre	%	Nationality	%
Histories	22	Dutch	34
Landscapes	38	Flemish	12
Still lifes	5	German	32
Genre	13	Italian	8
Portraits	20	French	5
Others	2	Others/Unknown	9

Hüsgen was successful as an adviser to and promoter of the Prestel publishing business in the 1780s as he was with his books.

Setting Trends in Eighteenth-Century Art Collecting

What was fashionable in eighteenth-century collections? One list of desired paintings was composed by Karoline Luise of Baden around 1759–60.[40] Having informed herself visiting galleries and perusing the catalogues of collections, reading contemporary works of connoisseurship such as *La vie des peintres flamands, allemands et hollandais* (1753–63) by Jean Baptiste Descamps and speaking with dealers, painters and connoisseurs, she developed clear notions about what she ought to have in her collection. Apart from the German painters Mignon, Roos and Rottenhammer, she was only interested in acquiring the works of Dutch and Flemish painters. Topping the list were Rubens, Van Dyck and Rembrandt. Then came the representative painters in the various genres: Brouwer, Van Ostade and Teniers for peasant genres; Bril, Van der Neer, Berchem and Saftleven for landscapes; Weenix, Potter, Wouwerman and A. van de Velde for animal portraits, wildlife and hunt landscapes; De Heem, Jan van Huysum and Rachel Ruysch for still lifes; Terborch, Metsu, Dou, F. and W. van Mieris, Netscher and Van der Werff for genre paintings. Later, Dujardin, Van der Heyden, Poelenburgh, Slingeland, Schalken were mentioned as well. In the years that followed, Karoline Luise succeeded in purchasing works by the desired painters and in the preferred genres for her collection, which she built up primarily for study purposes ('I regard my cabinet as a littérateur does his library, as a means of edification'),[41] and as a private academy, where she tried to unlock the secrets of paintings by copying the masterpieces. The latter seems to have been typical of several collectors. Christian Ludwig Hagedorn, for example, tried to prove his connoisseurship by making drawings and etchings of his own. His means and his collecting ambitions, however, were more modest than those of Karoline Luise von Baden, although the desired painters mentioned in his correspondence (as in Karoline von Baden's) include Teniers, Van de Velde, Wouwerman, Berchem, Mignon, Ostade, Van der Neer, Terborch, Mieris, Brueghel, Van der Werff, Dou, Rembrandt and Rubens. Of the above-mentioned artists, only paintings by Van de Velde, Berchem, Terborch, W. and F. Mieris, actually ended up in his collection, along with the works of other Dutch, Flemish and German painters.

These 'in' painters were even better represented in the collection of the Frankfurt connoisseur Heinrich Sebastian Hüsgen. He did not merely own two Mieris portraits, genres by Brouwer, a still life by De Heem, a history by Schalken and landscapes by Saftleven, Poelenburgh, Van der Neer and Van de Velde. Hüsgen's writings also emphasized paintings by these and other masters in Frankfurt collections – for example, the Gogel, Ettling or Chandelle collections, which also included works by Rembrandt, Rubens and Van Dyck.

The collectors of the emerging art centre, Berlin, followed this trend. Here, the first generation of collectors, merchant-bankers such as Johann Gottlieb Stein and Johann Georg Eimbke and the entrepreneur Johann Ernst Gotzkowsky, had lost their collections as a result of bankruptcies in the aftermath of the Seven Years' War, with the Gotzkowsky collection going to St Petersburg. According to Friedrich Nicolai, however, the number of new collections rose from 18 in 1769 to 41 in 1786. Among their owners we find the bankers – some of them of Jewish origin – Daum, Schickler, Schulze, Ephraim, Itzig and Meyer Warburg and members of the functional elites as well as the royal singer Concialini and the artist Daniel Chodowiecki. They collected paintings by Rubens, Poelenburgh, Rembrandt, Wouwerman, Berchem, Teniers and Mieris, in particular.[42]

The reality in Frankfurt, however, as documented by eighteenth-century auction catalogues, was that among the 'fashionable' painters, the only ones frequently represented in local collections were Melchior Roos with his pastoral landscapes, Rottenhammer with religious histories, and Brouwer, Ostade and Teniers with peasant genres. Equally distributed among the collections of Bernus, Berberich, Häckel and Kaller and Michael were also Van Dycks, Rubenses and Rembrandts, while landscapes by Berchem or Wouwerman appeared only in a few instances. They were replaced in Frankfurt collections by Schütz landscapes ('after Wouwerman'). In comparison, there was a considerable market demand for animal and hunt still lifes as well as for animal portraits by Jan Fyt and (as cheaper versions) by Hamilton, a demand that can be traced in all collections from Häckel to Hüsgen.

What of preferences on the national level? An examination of the auctions in all the German cities studied yields the figures shown in Table 6.7 for the top 12 painters.

Table 6.7   The top 12 painters at auctions in eighteenth-century Germany

Painter	'Original'	School[43]	Copy
Rubens	152	34	30
Rembrandt	133	17	19
J.M. Roos	101	1	0
David Teniers	87	13	4
Berchem	31	6	29
J.H. Roos	28	5	20
Van Dyck	22	2	2
J.D. de Heem	18	0	0
Van der Neer	12	0	0
C. de Heem	9	0	0
Brouwer	9	0	0
Netscher	8	0	0

Here Rubens is above Rembrandt, although Flemish and Dutch painters are nearly equally represented. Only two German painters, Johann Melchor and Johann Heinrich Roos with their Italian landscapes, are among the top group.

Whether the list of the top 12 was affected by relative prices is not yet clear. What we can say from the scattered evidence is that the importance of prices differed according to market segment. While in the upper market segment, in the realm of masterpieces, prices clearly counted – Hagedorn for example, rued the fact that he could not afford what he really wanted – in the middle segment of the market there were always alternatives available at reasonable prices: imitations by local masters or anonymous copies. At Frankfurt auctions, the majority of paintings sold for less than 10 guilders.[44] Henriette Amalie of Anhalt-Dessau, who purchased paintings to adorn her nearby palace, accordingly paid less than 20 guilders, and often less than 10 guilders, for the majority of her paintings. Even significant works such as Jan van Goyen's *Landscape with an Inn* and Samuel van den Hecken's *Four Elements in a Paradise Landscape* were sold in 1784 for 6 and 10 guilders, respectively. The most expensive picture was Balthasar Denner's *Old Woman with Kerchief*, which together with its companion piece cost 717 guilders. A 'pair of paintings with bathing nymphs' by Poelenburgh, at a price of 200 guilders, were about as expensive as the *Sleeping Organ Grinder* by the Leiden *fijnschilder* Willem van Mieris, which cost 108 guilders, and the *Young Woman Between Young and Old Suitors* by Caspar Netscher, which cost 131.[45]

The absence of differences of taste rooted in social origins, rank or geography is quite remarkable. By the second half of the eighteenth century, bourgeois and aristocratic collectors everywhere in Europe preferred Dutch painting either 'in the original' or in local versions. Information on the collections at Kassel, Karlsruhe or Schwerin, as well as Henriette Amalie's purchases on the Frankfurt art market, reveal that courtly conventions of taste no longer counted for much, and that aristocrats themselves were subject to the same market influences as bourgeois collectors. The nobility thus distinguished itself at best in the quality of the masterpieces they collected, or by demonstrating greater connoisseurship than bourgeois collectors or amateurs. Independent of such issues, a great demand for the artistic education of the public and the refinement of artistic skills existed in the German territories. These needs were addressed by state institutions such as the Berlin Academy of Arts, which regarded the 'education – that is the purification and broadening, the nourishment and cultivation – of public taste' as one of its chief tasks.[46] Reflections by Goethe and his painter friend Johann Heinrich Meyer in Weimar went in a similar direction: with the help of a competition, they sought to inspire artistic portrayals of themes from classical mythology.[47]

Chapter 7

Musical Culture

For many years now, so many virtuosi have flocked to Hamburg, so many have been lauded in the local newspapers, so many concerts advertised, one reads so much here of the passion for music that it would hardly be surprising if entire orchestras and opera companies were to pack their bags and move here in order to entertain such an audience of music-lovers, especially such a wealthy and lavish one.[1]

When music-lovers think of the eighteenth century nowadays, it is the cantatas and oratorios of Bach and Handel and the symphonies of Haydn and Mozart that come to mind. Those who listen more closely also become aware of a process of transition – from a preference for vocal music and opera in the age of Enlightenment to an increasing interest in instrumental music. This advance of instrumental music was associated with the changing significance of music within culture and society. Symphonies were used to open concerts and operatic productions and also, like instrumental concerts, as background music during theatre intervals. Sonatas for keyboard instruments as well as string trios and quartets were intended for domestic musical use, whether by aristocratic dilettantes or middle-class young ladies.

Music also became a topic of social discourse, however. It was not merely practised or more or less professionally performed, but also studied, analysed and critiqued. Along with reviews and accounts of performances, a musical public sphere emerged, which was promoted in the journals and gazettes. At the same time, musical production took on commercial characteristics. Composers, instrumentalists, publishers, editors, authors and reviewers all played a role, which was all the greater when a number of these functions were united in a single person.

The concert

The most important new phenomenon of eighteenth-century musical culture was the development of the concert into a separate type of event, accompanied by the growing professionalization of its protagonists. The forerunners of the public concert were, on the one hand, music for Vespers such as that played at St Mary's in Lübeck, and on the other, the performances of the *Collegia Musica*. The latter developed in the second half of the seventeenth century, alongside concerts at court, as private initiatives of musical amateurs or composers employed by the church or town. Thus Hamburg's *Collegium Musicum*, directors of which were Matthias Weckmann and Christoph Bernhard, received financial support from local merchants interested in hearing and playing contemporary Italian instrumental music. In the 1720s, these events were joined by public concerts under the direction of Georg Philipp Telemann. The Frankfurt musical tradition is also associated with Telemann, who before his departure for Hamburg had served as municipal music director and organized semi-public concerts with the city's professional and amateur musicians.

Aside from the *Stadtpfeifer Collegium* – town musicians who played at public occasions – Leipzig also boasted two *Collegia Musica* whose members played not just at dances, entertainments, serenades, birthdays and banquets, but also for services in the city's various churches. One *Collegium*, founded in 1701 by Telemann while he was still a student, played on a professional level after 1718 under the direction of Georg Balthasar Schott and Johann Sebastian Bach (from 1729). From 1723, the *Collegium* performed regularly at Gottfried Zimmermann's coffee house. The hall of the palace in Katharinen Strasse that housed Leipzig's largest and most famous coffee house could accommodate larger ensembles (with drums and trumpets) and up to 150 spectators. Here, Zimmermann organized weekly two-hour concerts, which during the summer moved outside to the coffee garden. The *Collegium* performed numerous vocal and instrumental works in these concerts, including *concerti grossi* by Handel and Locatelli and Italian solo cantatas by Porpora and Scarlatti. Bach himself provided 'moral' cantatas in addition to new overtures and instrumental concerti, of which the so-called coffee cantata poked fun not just at coffee drinking, but also at the concert venue. Special concerts were also held, for example, on the occasion of the coronation of Frederick August of Saxony as King August III of Poland. Bach was paid not just for his compositions, but also received money from the publication of the cantata texts. Thus, between 150 and 200 copies of the libretto were printed for performances in Zimmermann's coffee house and garden, which also gives some idea of the size of the audience. At open-air concerts on the Market Square attended by the king, between 600 and 700 copies might be sold.[2]

The second *Collegium*, composed largely of students, had been founded by Johann Friedrich Fasch, and performed during Bach's time under the direction of Johann Gottlieb Görner at Ennoch Richter's coffee house.[3] In 1743, 16 Leipzig noblemen and merchants established a new amateur ensemble, *Das Große Conzert*, which came to overshadow the *Collegia*. Membership cost 20 taler a year, which underscores the orchestra's exclusivity. The director was Carl Gotthelf Gerlach, Bach's successor as head of the above-mentioned *Collegium*. The concerts, held first in private homes, and later in the saloon of an inn, regularly drew an audience of 200–300. After Gerlach's death in 1761 (whose extensive music library was purchased by the printer Gottlob Immanuel Breitkopf) and the end of the Seven Years' War, the Kantor of St Thomas's, Johann Adam Hiller, revived this institution as a subscription concert series. The surviving concert programmes document the breadth of the musical offerings. Thus, for example, the following works were played at the concert of 17 December 1772:[4]

Concert.
Thursday, 17 December 1772.
(At the Three Swans)
Part. I
SINFONIA del Sgr. Vanmaldere.
ARIA del Sgr. Naumann, (Sgra. Schroeter).
CONCERTO per il Violino, (Sgr. Hertel).
Part. II
SINFONIA del Sgr. Sacchini, (Sgra. Schroeter).
PARTITA.

The composers included the court music directors (*Hofkapellmeister*) Johann Gottlieb Naumann (Dresden), Johann Wilhelm Hertel (Ludwigslust), Carl Ditters von Dittersdorf (Johannisburg, the court of the prince-bishop of Breslau) as well as the Brussels composer Pierre van Maldere and the Italian Antonio Sacchini. Berlin court *Kapellmeister* Johann Friedrich Reichardt's letter on a visit to Leipzig in 1774 also gives some indication of what such a concert might have been like.

1. Now another word on the famous *Große Concert*. This is true evidence of how little one may trust the judgement on works of art of those persons who possess no theoretical knowledge of art, and often not even fine senses and fortunate organs, and in any event, of how little one may trust general reputation. A fine and acute French author thus quite rightly remarks upon the extent to which those pleasures we so desire from afar lose infinitely in proximity.

2. In this concert, symphonies are played, arias sung – the finest adornment of the Concert, which Madem. Schröter provides – and concerti performed on various instruments. However well chosen and executed these may be, the accompaniment is always bad.

3. The symphonies, which are repeated often, are sometimes well executed. From this one sees that the other pieces would also be better performed if rehearsals were held more frequently, but the imagined perfection of these gentlemen presents a serious obstacle.

    …

7. That is the *Große Concert*, of which our Hiller is director. I wish this upright and worthy man better luck in a place where his merits will be better recognized and rewarded.[5]

The professional *Kapellmeister*, whose sympathies for the French Revolution would later cost him his position,[6] thus took a critical view of the musical collaboration between amateurs and professionals. Only the great singer Corona Schröter, whom he himself had previously accompanied, and his former teacher

Johann Adam Hiller met his approval, and he even expresses regret at their situation.[7]

In 1775 a new *Musiübende Gesellschaft* (Society for the Practice of Music) presented itself to the Leipzig public. Four years later, the Society would evolve into the *Interessante Concert für Musikliebhaber* (Interesting Concert for Music Lovers) in Leipzig. At a house on the Market Square they performed symphonies by Haydn, Dittersdorf and Stamitz, and instrumental concerts and vocal music by Hasse, Graun, Johann Christian Bach and others. In 1780, the city gave them the use of the cloth-makers' and wool-merchants' hall, the *Gewandhaus*, which had housed the municipal library for a time. After remodelling and the installation of seating, it opened as a concert hall in 1781. While the orchestra played standing at the top of the hall, the audience sat opposite each other in rows of seats running the length of the room. The orchestra consisted, apart from the musical director, of 27 persons, in the following order:

2 primi violini or principal players in the first and second violin

3 violini concertanti	1 violoncello rip.
1 violoncello	2 violini rip.
1 flauto	1 flauto rip.
1 oboe	1 oboe rip.
8 violini ripieni	2 corni rip.
2 violi rip.	2 fagotti rip.[8]

The following works were performed at the opening concert on 25 November: in the first part, a symphony by Joseph Schmitt, a hymn to music by Reichardt, a violin concerto and a string quartet; in the second part a symphony by Johann Christian Bach, an aria by Antonio Sacchini and a symphony by Ernst Wilhelm Wolff. Twenty-four concerts were planned for the annual subscription series. They took place Thursdays from 5 p.m. to 7 p.m., and included visiting artists – such as *Kapellmeister* Mozart in 1789 – who played their own compositions. The annual subscription cost 10 taler for male Leipzig citizens, and gave free entry for their families and tutors. Single tickets were available for visitors to the fair and other travellers, and cost 12 groschen. This made Leipzig the site of the kind of commercial music venue that existed otherwise only in English concert gardens and halls, with their orientation towards audience taste.

In comparison to England, the concert business was still rather underdeveloped in many German cities. The musicians at court might often have been more professional, to the extent that entire court orchestras did not fall victim to princely cost-cutting measures, or individual instrumentalists – like some members of Bach's Weimar ensemble – to rationalization. The urban audience appears to have differed little from the nobility in their need for entertainment, especially since the concerts brought together 'gentlemen and ladies, nobles, graduates and honest middle-class persons' in equal measure, as a 1787 account of a concert in Nordhausen put it.[9]

Figure 14   The Gewandhaus, outline engraving, early nineteenth century

At the same time, we should not underestimate the importance of impulses from court culture, even at the end of the eighteenth century. Not only were court concerts opened to a non-courtly public; the stimulation of the amateur sector also partially compensated for cultural losses, such as the removal of the Mannheim court, opera and orchestra to Munich in 1778 or the disbanding of the Kassel court orchestra in 1786.

From January 1786, Cramer's *Magazin der Musik* (Music Magazine) reported on conditions in Kassel, as well as most other centres of German musical life. According to the magazine's review of the winter concert season on 21 March 1787:

> In spite of the catastrophe that has befallen music here as a result of the abdication of the court orchestra, it continues to maintain itself in a quite unexpected manner, and the enthusiasm of amateurs even seems to have gained thereby. Throughout this winter, the Philharmonic Society has not merely continued its usual concerts to universal satisfaction, but also increased the number of its members threefold. It is a great comfort to local dilettantes that our excellent Herr Braun Junior has re-entered the official service of the landgrave, and that we may thus count upon keeping at least this virtuoso ... . The music performed this winter was generally by the best masters; the symphonies were largely by Haydn, often also by Pleyel, Ditters, Zimmermann, Rosetti and the like. The piano pieces [were] by Mozart, Kozeluch or Haydn; the arias by Sacchini, Paesiello, Naumann, Piccini and Grétry. Pergolesi's Stabat mater is on the programme for the coming Good Friday, and will be sung this time by the two Fräuleins d'Aubigny.[10]

As this demonstrates, in concert life, courtly-professional elements had already entered into a symbiosis with bourgeois-dilettante as well as aristocratic amateur elements. Thus, a commercial music scene by no means emerged fully fledged from a mature bourgeoisie, as Arnold Hauser claims in his *Sozialgeschichte der Kunst und Literatur* (Social History of Art and Literature),[11] or as Peter Schleuning has suggested more recently with the book title *Der Bürger erhebt sich* (The Bourgeois Stands Up).

Accounts from various German cities show how aristocrats, members of the functional elites and the professions as well as merchants played together in amateur orchestras just as they met in reading societies. Naturally, the amateur musicians in a princely residence such as Mannheim were far more likely to be aristocrats than in a small university city such as Greifswald. Thus, the musicians who played in Mannheim amateur concerts in 1778–79 included the following, most of them aristocrats and high princely officials:

> Violins: His Exc. Baron von Venningen, Baron v. Dalberg [the canon, brother of the theatre director], Baron v. Gemmingen, Herr v. Hetzendorff, Herr Goes and *Hofkammerregistrator* Heckmann, Concertmaster Fränzl as *Kapellmeister* and his son Ferdinand Fränzl. Viola: Herr Goetz, the music engraver and publisher [Johann Michael Götz, who engaged in extensive publishing activities]. Horn: Herr Ziwny. Violoncello: *Regierungsrat* v. Weiler, *Hofkammersekretär* Heckmann, *Hofkammerkanzlist* Baumann. Double bass: Secretary of the medical collegium Weber. Flute: Baron v. Gaugreben, Captain von Penzel [Benzel-Sternau], Abbé von Stengel [Franz Joseph von Stengel, *Co-adjutor* of Freising, Provost of St Andreas in Cologne], Sartori [the theatre cashier].[12]

In Greifswald, whose amateur concert series had been founded by 'the recently deceased academic *Amtshauptmann* Herr von Platen', the 'hobby musicians' met in 1786 at the home of the merchant and wine dealer Wilhelmi:

> In the house of the merchant and wine dealer Wilhelmi, a concert is to take place, with an orchestra consisting of 'pure amateurs'. Last winter, the players were, on the violin: Merchant Brunstein; [Theological] Candidate Quistorp; [Theological] Candidate Fischer the younger; second violin: Merchant Biel; Herr Wilcken and Herr Rehfeld, both students. On the viola: Advocate Brunstein; Magister Finelius. On the pianoforte: Director Rehfeld, Doctor von Aeminga, Advocate Graue. On the violoncello: Fencing master Willich, [Theological] Candidate Fischer the elder. On the double bass: Herr Hube. On the flute: Professor Otto, Registrar Dittmer, Secretary Rehfeld, Advocate Odenbrecht the younger.[13]

In Offenbach, in contrast, the amateur concerts even led to a professionalization of concert life. Here, the snuff manufacturer Peter Bernard, a virtuoso violinist and art lover, had founded two amateur orchestras, which regularly played at his manor house on the banks of the Main. No less a figure than Anton André, from the family of the Offenbach music publisher Johann André, composed for the ensemble, the high level of whose playing even gained them invitations to perform in neighbouring Frankfurt. They also acquired their own music director in 1795 in the person of the violinist Ferdinand Fränzl from Mannheim.[14]

Concerts were naturally a cost factor, since hall rental fees, sheet music and extra musicians all had to be paid for. For that reason, subscriptions for these events were generally advertised in the newspapers. Music lovers thus purchased subscriptions for a season, generally the winter season, either from the music society or a concert impresario, and paid between 4 and 12 talers. The price was a 'chapeau' for which the man paid and that entitled him to take along one or two women for free. Cities such as Oldenburg and Rostock were in the lower price category of 4 taler, while concertgoers in Halle had to pay 8 and those in Leipzig and Berlin between 10 and 12 taler. With more than 200 subscribers, and the sale of individual concert tickets, the Leipzig Gewandhaus concerts had a solid financial basis. Thus they already made a profit in the very first season of 1781–82, leaving room for the further development of concert life. In cities such as Oldenburg or Rostock, with only 50 or 60 subscribers, the possibilities were correspondingly more modest.[15]

In Leipzig too, however, with a population of 50,000, the number of concertgoers – even if we multiply the subscribers by three – was comparatively small. This may have been a result of the ticket prices. Nevertheless, we should take into account that the membership fees for the reading societies were on roughly the same level (between 3 and 12 taler), and that far more than 200 persons in Leipzig could have afforded a concert subscription after deducting the 100 to 150 taler a year required to secure their basic needs. Economic or material factors also played a role, but presumably not the decisive one. For example, in many cities, the subscription system lent and ensured a certain exclusivity. Visitors had to be introduced by a friend who was a member, and could not simply purchase concert tickets whenever they wished. Unlike in England, the market had not yet fully asserted itself, which also helps to explain the absence of important musical entrepreneurs such as Johann Christian Bach and Carl Friedrich Abel.[16] Even in large cities, musical demand was soon saturated by the extensive market production of 'composers and soloists', especially since concert life had to compete with other attractions among the new cultural offerings. This circumstance is underlined in a report from Hamburg, the cultural capital of northern Germany, which appeared in Cramer's *Magazin*:

> All of the virtuosi who come here believe that they will be welcomed with open arms, and straight away be offered concerts and, better yet, money and gifts, and that they will depart swathed in acclaim and rewards. That is the expectation fostered by the trumpeting newspaper articles, and the truth is quite the opposite of all that! We have not a single musical patron, not a single protector of the fine arts. Music lovers we have enough, but not amongst the rich portion of the population. Merchants have better things to do than to coddle starving artists. Scholars themselves generally live from the honour of their art. Ladies sing and play quite prettily in many cases (some of them very well), but none has come forward as a protectress of the arts,

and few could do so if they wished. We do have concerts here, but no public ones, and none of such significance as one finds at Berlin, Leipzig or Vienna. They also maintain themselves laboriously through subscriptions, which never rise to such a level as to keep even mediocre singers. The best, and best attended, concerts were once held by the great Bach, and after him by Herr M. Ebeling at the commercial academy, but these were abandoned when it was deemed harmful to the institute to entertain its pupils for a few hours every week with fine society and good music. Bach has retired, and has not performed in concert halls for some time. Moreover, in the summer, everyone who belongs to the beau monde lives in their gardens, and in the winter there are so many and such regular club meetings, assemblées, lotteries, picnics, balls and banquets that a concert has difficulty finding a few free hours into which it can insinuate itself. None may be held on Sundays, since it is against orthodoxy. Three or four days are post days, when no merchant or clerk has time even to think of concerts. Plays are given on the other days, so all that remains is Saturday, when everyone is recovering from the great banquets, gambling losses and business dealings, and preparing for new ones. What can poor music expect in this situation?[17]

Hamburg citizens, who had just discovered leisure, were torn between private entertainments in the home, the coffee house, club or larger societies and cultural consumption in the theatre and concerts.

In Bremen, too, the theatre and various concert events vied with each other, so that in 1791 cultural enthusiasts had only Thursday evenings free.

Mondays	Adolf Freiherr von Knigge's [highest Hanoverian official] society theatre
Tuesdays	Hesse's [commercial clerk] amateur concert at the cathedral school
Wednesdays	Dr Schutte's [lawyer] private concert, alternating with Dr Müller's [master at the Lycaeum, a private school he had founded] practice or family concert [*Übungskonzert*]
Thursdays	–
Fridays	Public winter concert in the stock exchange hall
Saturdays	Alternating house concerts at the homes of Knigge and Dr Iken [secretary] and so-called *Insurgenten* concerts of the [singing] musical 'ladies' [*Frauenzimmer*]
Sundays	Music in the church services.[18]

The situation was similar in Berlin, which boasted three public concert series. Apart from those run by the court orchestra musicians Georg Ludwig Bachmann and Johann Friedrich Ernst Benda, the sheet-music dealer and author Carl Friedrich Rellstab also organized a *Concert für Kenner und Liebhaber* (Concert for Connoisseurs and Amateurs) at the Hotel Stadt Paris beginning in 1787. Other musical events included concerts by visiting virtuosi as well as Reichardt's *Concerts Spirituels* during Lent, which always took place on Tuesdays. In all of these concerts, professional musicians played together with dilettantes. The latter had already gathered to play music in the *Musikausübende Gesellschaft* (Society for

Musical Performance), an example followed by the *Hörergesellschaft* (Society of Music Listeners) founded by members of the music-loving public.[19]

In Vienna, in contrast, musical life took place largely in the private salons, the so-called *Abendgesellschaften* (evening parties) given by the high and lower nobility as well as by merchants and court officials (functional elites), where they mingled with musicians and composers:

> Music works the miracle here that is normally ascribed only to love: it makes all classes equal. Aristocrats, bourgeois, princes and their vassals, superiors and their subordinates sit beside each other at one desk and forget the disharmony of their class in the harmony of the tones. All palaces and exchanges are open to the practicing artist, and the composer of any significance will be handled with all the distinction he could ever wish, which says a lot in the case of many of these gentlemen.[20]

Since Viennese cultural life was dominated by theatre and opera, there was little room for public concerts, which took place mainly during the summer and Lent, when the theatres were closed. At those times, artists such as Mozart or Georg Friedrich Richter rented the ballroom at the Mehlgrube, where they held piano concerts, for example. The concert impresario Philipp Jacob Martin also organized his first public concerts here, but he would soon move them to the Augarten, one of the largest pleasure gardens in Vienna. Concerts took place here in the off-season beginning in 1782, although Martin and his successor as organizer, Ignaz Schuppanzigh, did not always manage to find enough subscribers for the planned concerts.[21]

The musical market here was thus over-saturated, while elsewhere people stressed the exclusivity of the concert business. Thus, it not surprising that by the first decade of the nineteenth century, complaints had arisen about the dwindling audience for concerts. This stands in strange contrast to the boom in music journalism, which continued unabated in the early nineteenth century. The latter might be interpreted as an expression of the withdrawal of music consumption into the private sphere, and will be examined in the following section.

Sheet music and publishers

Naturally, sheet music represented the greater portion of musical publishing activities, with which composers and publishers alike reached a growing audience of connoisseurs and amateurs. Since the number of published pieces of music had grown to such an extent that it was impossible for one person to retain an overview, an extensive body of reviews and advertisements arose in the second half of the eighteenth century. Until specialized music journals came on the market, they appeared in the medium of the learned journal. At the end of the century, those interested in music could also read about the events of musical life and new publications in the fashion magazines and intelligence gazettes. 'Prenumeration' (prepaid subscription) and subscription played an important role in both sheet music publication and the journals.

Leipzig was the centre of German music publishing as it was in book publishing. Around the middle of the century, the printer Bernhard Christoph Breitkopf, who had already printed the texts of most of Bach's secular cantatas in the 1730s, refined the printing of musical notes, thereby facilitating the mass production of sheet music. His son Gottlob Immanuel, who had acquired Gerlach's music library in 1761, began to publish music catalogues regularly in 1762, providing the interested public with an overview of the current offerings in the sheet music market.

Productivity was further increased by Gottfried Christoph Härtel's entry into the firm as a partner and the introduction of lithography for printing scores. Other additions to the new market at the end of the century included the publication of the *Allgemeine Musikalische Zeitung* (General Musical Magazine) and editions of the complete works of famous composers. New music publishing companies founded in the second half of the eighteenth century were Schott in Mainz (1779), Simrock in Bonn (1793), André in Offenbach (1774), Götz in Mannheim (1773), Boßler in Speyer (1780), Amon in Heilbronn (1791), Nägeli in Zurich (1794), Gombart in Augsburg (1794, previously in Basel, 1789), Falter in Munich (1796), Leuckart in Breslau (1782), Günther & Böhme in Hamburg (1795, from 1799 Böhme only), Johann Peter Spehr in Brunswick (1791), Hummel in Berlin (1770) and Rellstab, also in Berlin (1784). Also noteworthy was the Leipzig Bureau de Musique founded by Franz Anton Hoffmeister and Ambrosius Kühnel, which competed not just with Breitkopf and Härtel, but also expanded its range to include popular music. Rudolph Werckmeister followed Hoffmeister's lead with his (short-lived) Bureau de Musique in Oranienburg (1802).[22]

Printed sheet music was sold with the help of the 'prenumeration' system. After the public announcement of the work and the call for 'prenumerations' or subscriptions, agents and book- and music shops distributed the scores to music lovers. Buyers paid a reduced price for the work in advance in the case of 'prenumeration', and after receipt of the score in the case of subscription. The publishers and composers usually carefully assessed demand on the sheet music market, launching new editions as a sort of test balloon.

Musicians and composers worked as agents for the publishers, and tried to win over as many subscribers and 'prenumerants' as they could. Agents took their fees either in free copies, which they could sell, or a certain percentage as a commission. Aside from letting and selling musical instruments, Johann Sebastian Bach also sold books and sheet music. The offerings included not just his own compositions, such as the volumes of his *Klavierübung* (Keyboard Exercise), but also the compositions and publications of his sons, pupils and colleagues. In 1729, newspaper advertisements announced that new musical publications such as Johann David Heinichen's treatise *Der General-Baß in der*

Composition (Figured Bass in Composition) and Johann Gottfried Werner's *Musicalisches Lexicon* (Musical Lexicon) were available from Johann Sebastian Bach in Leipzig as well as Johann Mattheson in Hamburg and Christoph Graupner in Darmstadt. The title pages of other works also contained the information that the editions could be purchased not only from the composer, but from Johann Sebastian Bach in Leipzig as well.[23]

Bach's son Carl Philipp Emanuel later blazed new trails in musical marketing. He was probably the most respected and successful composer of the late eighteenth century in Germany, and was always highly concerned with the saleability of his compositions. One example is his six collections of piano music 'for connoisseurs and amateurs', which he had printed by Breitkopf, but marketed personally between 1779 and 1787. His musical range addressed professionals and amateurs equally. For that reason, after the first collection, which contained only sonatas, the second and third collections also featured rondos to increase their appeal to amateurs.

A look at subscription ('prenumeration') figures reveals that after a good start of 519 ('my sonatas are selling like hot cakes'), they declined to 330 only a year later. Perhaps because of the rondos, professionals were stopping their orders, while amateurs may well have been purchasing this music in the shops. In order to counteract the falling numbers among connoisseurs, for the fourth collection C.P.E. Bach composed two fantasies, increasing the number of pieces to seven and of subscribers to 388. He was less successful at satisfying the taste of connoisseurs with the fifth and sixth collections, which combined sonatas, rondos and fantasies, and the number of subscribers levelled out at around 300.[24] Even these 300, though, assured the composer of a profit.

In the late eighteenth and early nineteenth century, it was mainly publishers who tested the market and increasingly paid attention to the wishes of amateur musicians. On the one hand, publishers made direct contact with amateurs, and on the other, they took to heart the information provided by their business partners, for example at the fairs. The desires of amateur musicians, which they expressed directly to publishers, provide an instructive glimpse of musical tastes. Thus in 1810, *Kantor* Weber of Sangerhausen wrote to the Bureau de Musique in Leipzig:

> As I place great store by new guitar sheet music for my entertainment, and am less interested in song than piano in particular, also with vocals and various string instruments, e.g. violin, viola, cello and also flute, and have not been sufficiently supplied by Herr Breitk[opf] and Härtel according to my wishes, I approach you with the query of whether you would be so good ... as to send me such things from time to time so that I may make a selection?[25]

The Leipzig Bureau solicited reports from professional musicians and trading partners throughout Germany, for example asking the composer Johann Franz Xaver Sterkel in Regensburg 'to note the regions and channels where your songs might best be distributed and sold ... .'[26] The information that the Bureau's

Vienna bookkeeper, Caspar Joseph Eberl, sent to Leipzig concerning Viennese musical taste was particularly important: 'Haydn, Mozart, Hoffmeister, Kreutzer, Frenzl, Gyrowetz etc ... for piano both with and without accompaniment, on the violin, flutes, guitar as well for other instruments ... .'[27] In this period, as the examples above show, the guitar became a fashionable instrument whose role in music was also addressed in Bertuch's *Journal des Luxus und der Moden*.[28]

The reputation of the composer (which could differ markedly from present-day assessments) was key to the successful sale of a work. A serenade by Leonhard von Call or piano variations by Joseph Gelinek and above all the piano compositions of Kozeluch and Pleyel could enjoy greater popularity among amateur musicians – particularly the ladies – than, for instance, a comparable edition of Beethoven.[29] Local preferences are also evident, as when the *Regensburger* Johann Franz Xaver Sterkel was forced to concede that 'not everything that pleases in southern Germany ... also had the good fortune to please in northern climes'.[30] The north Germans had always been prejudiced against 'south German tinkling'. Nevertheless, they could not halt the forward march of the south Germans.

Axel Beer's research allows us to reconstruct the following ranking for composers in Germany around 1800, based on their published works:

1. Wolfgang Amadeus Mozart
2. Ludwig van Beethoven
3. Joseph Haydn
4. Daniel Gottlieb Steibelts
5. Ignaz Pleyel
6. Franz Krommer
7. Leonhard von Call
8. Franz Anton Hoffmeister
9. Adalbert Gyrowetz
10. Johann Baptist Vanhal.[31]

Preferences had changed again by the second decade of the nineteenth century. While the *Journal für Literatur, Kunst, Luxus und Mode* (as it was now called) noted with resignation in 1823, 'for many years now, the Leipzig Musicalische Zeitung has neglected to review, or even to advertise, Beethoven's works',[32] an 1824 letter from the Viennese firm Artaria indicated the new trend in Vienna: 'The inclination towards Spohr, Weber, Onslow, Ries, Field and even Beethoven has diminished, and Rossini, Hummel, Mayseder, Moscheles and C. Czerny are now the musical heroes of the day in Vienna.'[33] Publishers had to take this into account, and catered 'more and more to the tastes of amateur musicians'.[34]

A reconstruction of publishing programmes broken down by genres and instruments must accept the fact of differing regional tendencies. Thus André, Breitkopf and Härtel published symphonies and instrumental music for amateur and subscription concerts while the princely court orchestras of southern Germany and Austria wrote their own repertoire. Nevertheless, publishers' catalogues reveal a strong decline of symphony scores in the nineteenth century, because they found fewer and fewer buyers. Chamber music still sold at the beginning of the nineteenth century, but was being displaced by increasingly dominant piano music. The latter's reception, too, showed regional variations, however. Thus between 1801 and 1810, music for piano made up nearly 40 per cent of the production of Leipzig publishers, while representing only 25 per cent of the output of André, Schott and Simrock. There was also a shift in taste away from piano sonatas and towards dances, fantasies, rondos and potpourris. The proportion of vocal music fluctuated between 10 per cent (André) and 40 per cent (Götz), with a preference for lieder and collections of lieder. In contrast, the collected works published by André, Breitkopf and Härtel, the Bureau de Musique and Simrock, which had been important for the reception of composers at least in professional circles, fell out of fashion. If the classics were to remain present in the nineteenth century, it would be above all in the guise of piano potpourris (from popular operas) and other arrangements, but naturally also on the operatic stage or in performances of oratorios.[35]

Music periodicals

The reception of music in the various periodicals also reflected changes in the audience. Apart from a few music journals such as the *Critischer Musicus*, music was initially discussed only in learned journals and political newspapers. Examples were the *Allgemeine Deutsche Bibliothek* (Universal German Library), the *Teutsche Merkur* (German Mercury), the *Altonaische gelehrte Mercurius* (Altona Learned Mercury), the *Göttingischen Anzeigen* (Göttingen Gazette) or the *Gelehrten Zeitungen* (Learned Journals) from Frankfurt, Jena, Leipzig, Kiel, etc., the *Berlinischen Nachrichten* (Berlin News), the *Berlinische privilegirte Zeitung* (Berlin Privileged Newpaper), the *Hamburgische Correspondent* (Hamburg Correspondent) and the *Hamburgische neue Zeitung* (New Hamburg Newspaper). In the 1780s, these were joined by a number of often short-lived music periodicals such as the *Musikalische Kunstmagazin* (Musical Art Magazine), the *Magazin der Musik* (Musical Magazine), the *Musikalische Almanach* (Musical Almanac), the *Musikalische Bibliothek* (Musical Library) and finally, as the first specialist music journal, the *Allgemeine Musikalische Zeitung* (1789). In the 1780s, fashion magazines such as the renowned *Journal des Luxus und der Moden* also began publishing accounts of musical events and advertisements for new musical publications. The many intelligence gazettes that sprang up at this time printed such advertisements on a large scale as well.

Let us begin with the learned and political journals, however. Here, it is striking that – as in the case of periodical production more generally – music reviews were published largely in northern and central Germany. As to the chronological development, according to Mary Sue Morrow's study of music criticism in Germany in the late eighteenth century, the newly founded music periodicals published 143 reviews in the 1760s, 331 in the 1770s and 501 in the

1780s. Between 1790 and 1798, they printed a further 387 reviews. In terms of genre, solo sonatas for piano or other keyboard instruments were at the top, before sonatas with piano accompaniment and piano concertos, while symphonies and string quartets were seldom reviewed. Although we now associate the late eighteenth century with string quartets and symphonies as typical musical forms, contemporaries apparently took a different view.[36]

Reviews both addressed the target readership of amateurs and their musical activities and set aesthetic standards for the literature under review. If we examine the contents of reviews, certain emphases emerge. One refers to the differing national musical styles, and attempts, by characterizing them, to create a German musical identity. German music emancipated itself only gradually from Italian and French models by adopting stylistic elements from both. For some reviewers, this process of disassociation did not proceed quickly enough. When the popularity and dissemination of Italian instrumental music and opera reached a high point in the middle of the eighteenth century, one reviewer of the piano version of the symphonies of Baldessare Galuppi pondered 'Why Herr Breitkopf does not publish such works by decent talented Germans, instead of forcing upon the world the monster births of shallow Italians?'[37] The *Hamburgische Correspondent*, in contrast, believed that the Germans could learn something in the field of melody, when it suggested to Johann Friedrich Reichardt in 1773 that 'if he learned a good melody from the Italians, without which all music is worthless and which we still find absent in some of his compositions … the journey will have been advantageous for him and for music.'[38]

Only Luigi Boccherini met the approval of the reviewers: 'You will find very few Italians so rich in serious, noble ideas and few who work out their pieces this well.'[39] At least among reviewers, a German musical identity emerged in opposition to the Italians, but all that they could initially say of it was that it differed from Italian music. Thus according to a review in 1767–68 of the sonatas for violin and cello of the 'notable' Johann Schwanberger – whom no one has heard of nowadays:

> Even now that he has been to Italy, we still recognize him as one of those Germans who, while willing to don any musical garb demanded of them, cannot deny the profundity of their knowledge … .[40] [The sonatas] are not as contrapuntal and fugue-like as the excellent trios of Kapellmeister Graun but also not as simple and empty as most Italian trios.[41]

The rivalry between Italian and German music played out in London as well. Here, the Italian violinist Felice Giardini commented polemically on Haydn's success in 1792 by circulating a satirical composition of two trios – one written in the German, and the other in the Italian style. The German organist Christopher Kollmann, who was active in London, responded with a 'sun of composers' (*Komponisten-Sonne*), at the centre of which he placed Johann Sebastian Bach, with Joseph Haydn, Carl Heinrich Graun and George

Figure 15 'Sun of composers' (*Komponisten-Sonne*), engraving after a drawing
by August Friedrich Christoph Kollmann, *Allgemeine Musikalische
Zeitung*, October 1799

Frideric Handel immediately surrounding him. The names of all significant
contemporary German composers radiate outwards in an inner and an
outer circle.[42]

Even when it came to defending the German musical heritage against
potential detractors, there was potent controversy within Germany. 'Good'
– north German-influenced – taste distanced itself from southern Germany.
Thus in the early 1780s, Carl Joseph Birnbach's *Concert pour le clavecin* was put in
its 'proper' place:

> Appears to come from the area along the Rhine or from southern Germany, and
> unfortunately that says it all. You can recognize all the jingle-jangle from down there
> instantly by the monotonous figures, the everyday modulations, the trite Alberti
> basses, the constant running up and down the scale, and similar little tricks … .[43]

The music of the Viennese composer Georg Christoph Wagenseil was also
attacked for its Italian influences, but the critics were already fighting a losing
battle. After the erection of a German musical 'monument' in the form of Carl
Philipp Emanuel Bach, against whom all contemporaries were measured, in the

1780s, north Germany, too, fell to the triumphal tones of the Viennese Leopold Kozeluch and Johann Baptist Vanhal. The audience's thirst for such music was so great that in Hamburg, a pseudo-Vanhal was able to cause quite a furore for a while. In the German provinces, in contrast, the old taste reigned supreme. When the solo flautist Friedrich Ludwig Dulon travelled through Pomerania at the same time, he noted:

> That in Greifswald, they prefer the old music above all else. Graun, Hasse, the Bachs, the Bendas, Quantz and several others of this type were all the rage there; symphonies by Vanhall or anything else in which the last movement merely resembled a rondo were deemed unbearable.[44]

This assessment, however, also reflects pride in the musical tradition of Germany, the 'fatherland of the piano'. Of contemporary composers, aside from the 'hero' Carl Philipp Emanuel Bach, critics also elevated Haydn to their musical Olympus. Reichardt observed in a 1782 review of the six Haydn symphonies (Opus 18) and the six string quartets (Opus 19): 'Even if we only had a Haydn and a C.P.E. Bach, we Germans could maintain that we have our own style, and that our instrumental music is the most interesting of all.'[45] Haydn and above all Bach were also held up to connoisseurs and amateurs as aids to the development of taste, whereby the noble enjoyment and pleasant diversion of listening to and playing music were also taken into consideration. A 1773 review of Bach's harpsichord concerti already remarks:

> In short, these concerti leave out nothing that would afford connoisseurs and amateurs alike noble enjoyment and pleasant diversion, thereby helping to maintain the respectable correctness of their taste, preventing them from falling into the swamps of musical triviality, and in fact further refining it.[46]

The discrepancy between connoisseurs and amateurs remained nonetheless, for the imitators of the Hamburg Bach, who put on the market 'all manner of pieces for connoisseurs and amateurs of the piano and song', failed to build a bridge between the two target groups:

> These pieces are quite good for amateurs, but may well not satisfy connoisseurs. Since Bach published his sonatas for connoisseurs and amateurs, a number of newer composers have used the same heading 'for connoisseurs', without perhaps considering or realizing that Bach meant something by this that only he could provide, and which another, consequently, who is not in a position to offer connoisseurs such excellent musical rarities, must not repeat.[47]

This was the view of one of the most influential music critics of the late eighteenth century, Johann Nicolaus Forkel, expressed in his *Musikalischer Almanach*. Forkel accordingly also continued to deem it his duty to help amateurs to become genuine connoisseurs. The ability to distinguish between works of art according to 'their rank' was an essential part of this.[48]

The female sex was believed essentially incapable of achieving connoisseurship. Instead, publishers and reviewers increasingly paid attention to their needs under the rubrics 'beginners', 'ladies' and 'amateurs'. Music journals and general periodicals and intelligence gazettes alike all came to recognize that this was the future of the market.

The end of the century saw a sharp decline in reviews in the learned journals. The growing production in popular genres rendered them less necessary. The new works were generally presented to music consumers in Hans Adolf Freiherr von Eschstruth's *Musikalische Bibliothek* or Carl Friedrich Cramer's *Magazin der Musik* in only a few reviews, and increasingly in brief notices, skilfully combined with a musical almanac, biographies, anecdotes and observations.[49] The *Allgemeine Musikalische Zeitung* took a similar tack after 1798, addressing connoisseurs with lengthy reviews and amateurs with brief annotations.

In the 1780s, the fashion journals such as the *Journal des Luxus und der Moden* discovered music lovers as an audience. Apart from general observations on such subjects as 'Fashion in Music, and the Newest Favourite Pieces in Individual German Provinces' or 'The Newest Favourite Music in Great Concerts, Especially in Regard to Ladies' Taste in Piano Playing',[50] the *Journal* regularly published accounts from Germany's stages. Correspondents sent news from Hamburg, Mannheim, Kassel, Zweibrücken, Berlin, Schwerin and Dresden as well as Vienna and Paris. The main focus, however, was on plays and above all opera. In the 1790s, accounts of concert life became more frequent, for example of the piano concerts of the Pixis brothers in Kassel (later in Weimar and Leipzig) or about the above-mentioned flautist Friedrich Ludwig Dulon as well as the concert of the Vienna Kapellmeister Joseph Wölfl in Leipzig. The Gewandhaus concerts were naturally present, but the *Journal* also took note of musical activities in the German provinces, for example in accounts of the winter season in Würzburg or Oldenburg. The *Journal*'s subscribers especially enjoyed reading about the concerts of the famous singer Gertrud Elisabeth Mara, for example her 1803 performances in Weimar, Dresden and Bad Lauchstädt. Her East Prussian concerts that same year were then written up in Leipzig's *Zeitung für die elegante Welt* (Journal for the Beau Monde).[51]

At least as important for the broader public were the 'recently published musical scores' that the *Journal* offered for the first time in 1795, and which could be purchased directly from the magazine's publisher. The particular advantage for subscribers was that they could order the sheet music to be delivered postage free to Leipzig, Frankfurt am Main or Nuremberg along with their magazine. The offerings included

1) Music for clavier or pianoforte
   - Bihler. Variations p. Clav. Oboe et Bass. Op. IV, Offenbach, Andree 3 fl.
   - Hoffmann, March from The Magic Flute with variations, Op. II. Ibid. 30 fl.
   - C. H. Kunze, VI Anglaises et VI Allemandes p. Clav. 4me Cahier, Heilbronn, Ammon. 30 kr.
   - Beczwarzowsky. Concert en Rondeau Op. II. Offenbach, Andree. 2 fl.

- Förster. Quartet. P. Clav. Viol. Alt. et. Bass. Op. VIII Livr. 1 Ibid. 1 fl 45 krz.

...

- B. de Dalberg. Sonate a 4 mains, in C major. Ibid. 1 fl 30 kr.
- Kuhn. Petite pieces. Op. VIII. Ibid. 1 fl. 30 kr.
- Kyrmayr. VI Airs varies. Mannheim, Götz, 20 kr. each, namely No. 7, Der Vogelfänger bin ich, etc. No. 8. Minuet from Don Giovanni. No. 9. Du feines Täubchen. No. 10. Bey Männern welchen Liebe fühlen. No. 11. Seyd uns zum zweyten Mal willkommen. No. 12. Dort vergiß etc. from Figaro.

2) Music for violin
- P. Wranitzky. VI Quart à 2. Viol. Alt et Bass. Op. XXX. Offenbach, Andrée. 6 fl.
- Gyrowez. III Quartet. Op. XIX. Ibid. 2 fl 45.
- Luchesi. VI Duos. à 2 Vio. Augsburg, Gombart. 3 fl 30 kr.
- Distler. VI Quartet à Viol. Alt. et Bass. Op. II. Ibid. 5 fl. 30 kr.

...

4) Music for flute
- Monzani. VI Trios à 2 Flutes et Bass. Augsburg, Gombart.
- Ditters. Hieronymus Knicker for 2 flutes and bass. Arranged by Ehrenfried. Mainz, Schott. 3 fl.

...

6) Symphonies
- P. Winter. Symph. in D. Livr. 1. Offenbach, Andree. 2 fl.

Interestingly, Bertuch combined these advertisements with reports and in some cases also reviews, making his mercantile interest quite evident.[52]

The intelligence gazettes, which apart from offering brief information – to differing degrees in different towns – served as advertising venues for buyers and sellers, took a different path. Josef Mančal recently analysed the *Augsburger Intelligenz-Zettel* (Augsburg Intelligencer) from the perspective of music and the music market, paying particular attention to two areas, advertisements for sheet music and instruments and 'notes on arriving and transit passengers'. The latter were intended to facilitate personal and business contacts and may be regarded as evidence of the professional mobility of musicians as well as the growth of travel on official business in the eighteenth century.[53] Between 1747 and 1799, more than 760 singers, musicians, virtuosi, concertmasters and *Kapellmeister*, music, orchestra, opera and theatre directors and composers both great and obscure travelled through Augsburg.[54]

A simple list of the places where *Kapellmeister* served – Berlin, Dresden, Eichstätt, Mannheim, Munich, Oettingen-Wallerstein, Regensburg, Salzburg, Stuttgart, Vienna, Copenhagen and St Petersburg – indicates the geographical dimensions of this artistic transfer, in which Augsburgers could participate directly or indirectly through their local intelligence gazette. The advertisements were mainly for sheet music, but also included concert announcements such as those of the Augsburg municipal trumpeter and impresario Gottfried Val[l]entin.[55]

Music lovers could scarcely escape the flood of musical advertisements. To be sure, eighteenth-century people were not actually bombarded with music the way we are today, but they were constantly confronted with it, at least journalistically. Because pieces of music were being composed or commissioned less and less for specific occasions and venues, their function changed from that of disposable products – which were recycled at most for parody works – to reusable ones, which had to survive in the anonymous musical marketplace. Composers no longer knew for which orchestras, soloists or dilettantes they were writing. Accordingly, they needed to satisfy audience or fashionable tastes on the one hand, and to turn their originality into a marketable product while at the same time hoping for a favourable reception 'in the press' on the other. Few composers were as successful in this as C.P.E. Bach, the 'first Classic in the musical arts'.[56] Nevertheless, the growing and increasingly complex market offered sufficient niches for other composers as well. It was mainly the still numerous German court *Kapellmeister* and *Kantoren* who, as surviving concert programmes show, found ample scope for outside activities in addition their official posts. Like the 'Sun of Composers' above (Figure 15), their works radiated beyond their territorial frontiers to reach other German, and often even European, states.

Chapter 8

Theatre and Opera

Apart from Schiller, Goethe and Lessing were the authors whose names inevitably ensured an empty house.[1]

This sarcastic comment by the actor and theatre director Friedrich Ludwig Schmidt memorably characterizes the situation of theatre in eighteenth- and early nineteenth-century Germany. The theatre was the most exciting entertainment medium of the era, comparable in its significance only to present-day cinema. The theatre entertained a growing audience not just with plays, but also with ballet and opera. Literary scholars and music historians often ignore this circumstance when they appropriate drama and opera as artistic genres and thus destroy the historical unity of this performance complex by breaking it down into separate disciplines. This chapter will, nonetheless, focus on spoken theatre.

A further topos of theatre historiography is the teleological interpretation of theatre history as one of linear progress from troupes of itinerant players to court and national theatres, and from simple entertainment to the education of humanity.[2] To be sure, the great density of the three branches of theatrical offerings in Germany should be viewed as progress, which is now seriously threatened by government spending cuts, but the public's need for entertainment and the commercialization of cultural offerings should not be underestimated as the humus in which the German theatrical landscape bloomed.

The commercialization of the theatre was accompanied by a professionalization and specialization of its protagonists, which affected actors, singers, authors, publishers and theatre directors in equal measure. By the late seventeenth century, a process of professionalization had already begun in the German theatrical world. Professional thespians, who both acted and sang, conquered the court and public stages and gradually replaced students and amateurs. What was initially absent were 'permanent' stages that permitted a settled and thus continuous theatrical life. The establishment of permanent playhouses by the courts and urban theatre managers created the preconditions for this development. Although this meant that the way was now open to bind actors and acting troupes to a specific location in the long term, it did not make guest performances or productions in other towns a thing of the past. Even after the founding of court theatres with permanent ensembles, quantitatively speaking, travelling troupes still dominated the German-speaking theatre. It was often more lucrative for a troupe to travel across the country with a limited repertoire than to compete with other troupes to keep the interest of a local audience by continually developing new productions. Thus, even ensembles with a permanent home often took their productions on tour to other court or urban playhouses.

At the same time, the court theatres expanded their cultural offerings. While theatre at court had long served only the prestige and diversion of sovereigns and courtiers, the public was now increasingly permitted to share in the cultural blessings. To this end, the courts subsidized their theatres, which were, however, run at the same time as private enterprises by those who managed them. Only the idea of a national theatre pursuing educational aims presupposed permanent funding by the authorities. Alongside these projects, actor-managers such as Konrad Ernst Ackermann founded playhouses at Königsberg (1754–55) and on the Gänsemarkt in Hamburg (1765), while private businessmen set up theatres in Leipzig (1766), Nuremberg (1800–01), Frankfurt and Würzburg (1803–04).

The repertoire and organization of theatres changed with the involvement of the courts and the admission of the public. In the place of temporary guest performances that pandered to princely tastes, runs and repertoires were significantly expanded. Berlin may serve as an example here. In the mid-eighteenth century, the city's cultural life was dominated by the Royal Opera House with the Italian operas of Graun and Hasse, and by the king's disdain for German pieces. Important Italian singers and dancers gave guest performances in Berlin, while German companies could not compete with French and Italian ensembles. In 1765, Franz Schuch opened a private theatre seating 700 in Behren Strasse. In the years that followed, the troupes of Carl Theophil Döbbelin and Gottfried Heinrich Koch also performed a broad German-speaking repertoire there. Döbbelin's company, in particular, consisted of nearly 80 actors, actor-singers and actor-dancers, who presented plays, operettas, music dramas (*Singspiel*), ballets and even operas. It became the core of the Royal National Theatre that opened on Gendarmenmarkt in 1786, which brought to the stage not just the dramas of Shakespeare, Schiller and Lessing, but above all the popular hits of Kotzebue and German opera. In 1802, the theatre moved to the new Royal Playhouse (Königliches Schauspielhaus) building designed by Carl Gotthard Langhans, also on Gendarmenmarkt, which seated 2,000. Its director August Wilhelm Iffland, who had been putting on plays in Berlin since 1796, made the Prussian capital a leading theatre metropolis.[3] Iffland had previously enjoyed successes with Konrad Ekhof's troupe at the Gotha Court Theatre (the first permanent, but short-lived, court theatre) and above all at the Mannheim National Theatre, and thus directly experienced and helped to shape the movement to revitalize German theatre.

The Mannheim National Theatre is often mentioned as a reform theatre in the same breath as the Weimar Court Theatre under Goethe. It owed its existence to the Elector and theatre enthusiast Karl Theodor, who had first revived the palace theatre with a French ensemble and then, after their dismissal in the 1770s, commissioned the architect Lorenzo Quaglio to remodel the Mannheim Arsenal as a theatre for German plays. When Karl Theodor inherited Electoral Bavaria in 1777 and took the troupe of German actors he had hired with him to

Munich, the National Theatre was founded as a compensatory or infrastructural measure for Mannheim, whose economy was threatened by the departure of the court. The actor Johann Christian Brandes had already pointed out the advantages of such a theatre in 1776: a good national theatre would educate a country's inhabitants about their language, customs and manner of thinking, reduce luxury in the middle classes, enrich citizens, create morally good human beings and would make sound economic sense for the state. The actor was also a citizen; the prince's contribution and those of well-off local inhabitants and foreigners passed through his hands into the hands of the poor; the money circulated and remained in the country.[4]

In the summer of 1778, Wolfgang Heribert von Dalberg, Palatine chamberlain and an amateur actor and playwright, transmitted these recommendations to the key political decision makers. A theatre would not merely bring the nobility and gentry from the country to the city during the winter months, but also help to realize plans to 'elevate the dramatic arts in Germany' which had long lain fallow.[5] The electoral administration thereupon approved start-up financing. The actors recruited included Karoline Schulze-Kummerfeld and Iffland from the dismantled Gotha Court Theatre, and Abel Seyler's troupe – which had already been through several bankruptcies – was engaged again. After opening with *Geschwind, eh jemand es erfährt* (Quick, before Somebody Finds Out), a comedy after Goldoni, the theatre's manager Dalberg tried to provide his new playhouse with a profile of its own, introducing a more naturalistic style of acting and a specific repertoire of premieres. Apart from Schiller's *Die Räuber* (The Robbers, 1782), *Fiesko* (1783), *Kabale und Liebe* (Love and Intrigue, 1784) and *Don Carlos* (1788), the company also performed Dalberg's adaptations of Shakespeare works. Iffland's successful plays *Verbrechen aus Ehrsucht* (Crimes of Ambition, 1784), *Die Mündel* (The Wards, 1784), *Die Jäger* (The Hunters, 1785) and *Die Hagestolzen* (The Confirmed Bachelors, 1791) were also performed regularly. Also part of the repertoire were Mozart's operas *The Abduction from the Seraglio* (1784), *Don Giovanni* (1789), *The Marriage of Figaro* (1790), *Così fan tutte* (1793) and *The Magic Flute* (1794).

Dalberg had high expectations of his theatre and particularly of the art of acting, which he sought to improve together with his actors in discussions on so-called committees. 'What is a national playhouse in the true sense of the term? How can a theatre become a national playhouse? And does such a German theatre worthy of being called a national stage actually exist?' were but a few of the questions examined in the effort to more closely approach the objective of 'the stage as a true school of manners'.[6]

By the 1790s, however, this optimism had given way to resignation, as subsidies from the elector and subscription and ticket sales no longer sufficed to finance the theatre. As no new funding sources were available and the electoral subventions became increasingly meagre and irregular, the end of the eighteenth century found the theatre languishing. Only the ceding of the portion of the Electoral Palatinate on the right bank of the Rhine to Baden in 1803 and the funding of the theatre by the Baden financial administration returned the Mannheim Theatre to a sounder basis in the nineteenth century.

Tight financing was symptomatic of attempts to found national theatres in late eighteenth-century Germany. The national theatre project in Hamburg had already failed. Hamburg assumed something approaching a pioneering role in the field of theatre and opera. The establishment of the theatre on Gänsemarkt in 1678 had made the city the home of Germany's first urban opera company. German-language operas by Reinhard Keiser and other composers with biblical, classical, mythological and historical themes had their premieres here. After the collapse of this Hamburg enterprise in 1738, no serious German-language opera was heard in Germany for several decades, because operas were put on only in the court theatres, where French and Italian reigned.

French influence, which Johann Christoph Gottsched and Friederike Caroline Neuber had deployed to reform drama and actors' training in Germany, persisted in acting styles via younger actors such as Gottfried Heinrich Koch, Carl Theophil Döbbelin and Johann Heinrich Schönemann. With their troupes' guest performances, both Schönemann and Koch had acquainted Hamburg audiences with a new style of acting. When Konrad Ernst Ackermann, who came from Schönemann's company, settled in Hamburg with his own troupe in 1764 and applied for a privilege to present German plays in Germany, a new era in the history of Hamburg theatre began. A new *Commoedienhaus* was built to replace the demolished opera house on Gänsemarkt, but it soon found itself in financial difficulties because of its very demanding programme. Thus in 1767, 12 Hamburg citizens took over the *Commoedienhaus* and Ackermann's Ensemble to form the Hamburgisches Nationaltheater (Hamburg National Theatre). Gotthold Ephraim Lessing was engaged as its dramaturge. Instead of entertainment, the theatre attempted an ambitious programme, which apart from original German works concentrated mainly on adaptations of French and English plays.[7] Soon, however, the National Theatre was faced with competition from a French troupe, and it had to be disbanded in 1769. Ackermann, whose contributions included the introduction of a new, less affected style, engaged the actors again.

In 1771, Friedrich Ludwig Schröder succeeded his recently deceased stepfather as manager of the Hamburg theatre. Schröder's first stint as director, which lasted until 1779, was characterized by his cultivation of Shakespeare and the production of new *Sturm und Drang* dramas. Schröder, who allied himself with the prominent Hamburg theatre critics, also addressed issues of theatre reform in his semi-official *Theatralisches Wochenblatt* (Theatrical Weekly). As a counterweight to Gottsched and Neuber, he propagated an orientation towards English models – particularly Shakespeare (as Goethe and Herder had also done, respectively, in the 1771 'Speech for Shakespeare Day' and the 1773 essay 'Shakespear'). Schröder, who had already made a name for himself both as an actor and a solo ballet dancer, gained in stature with his Shakespeare roles, whether as Lear, Falstaff or the ghost of Hamlet's father. In 1788, he also brought Jakob Michael Reinhold Lenz's *The Tutor* to the stage. Nevertheless, Schröder's era came to a temporary end in 1780. In the years that followed, he gave guest performances in many German theatres, particularly the Burgtheater in Vienna, before taking over the Altona Theatre in 1785 and then returning to the Theatre on Gänsemarkt from 1786–98. Now the programme featured Mozart's operas, such as *Don Giovanni* (1789), *The Abduction from the Seraglio*, *The Marriage of Figaro* (both staged in 1791) and *The Magic Flute* (1793), underlining once again the close relationship between drama and opera in the German theatrical repertoire at the end of the eighteenth century.[8]

This also applied to the Weimar Court Theatre, which gained national renown in the eighteenth century under Goethe's artistic directorship. The first companies to play there were those of Döbbelin, Gottfried Heinrich and Abel Seyler, the last of which put on Wieland's opera *Alceste* to music by Anton Schweitzer in 1773. Wieland took the opportunity to report in the March number of his *Teutscher Merkur* on the well-ordered theatrical life of Weimar, with its German theatre 'which anyone may visit three times a week at no cost'.[9] Only one year later, however, the palace, including the theatre, was destroyed by fire and theatrical life was again left to amateurs after Seyler's troupe departed for Gotha with its star Konrad Ekhof. Weimar personalities from court circles – above all Friedrich Justin Bertuch, who attracted attention as both a playwright and an actor – participated in the productions. Apart from plays by Voltaire, Destouches and Lessing, the theatre also staged music dramas.[10] Goethe wrote a number of pieces especially for this theatre, including *The Siblings* (1776), the fairy play with music, *Lila* (1776–77), or the comic opera *The Triumph of Sensibility* (1777) – the last two for the birthday of Duchess Louise.[11] Goethe appeared in productions of *The Siblings* (1776) and *The Accomplices* (1777), *Plundersweilern Fair* (1778), *Iphigenia in Tauris* or *The Lover's Whim* (1779), generally partnered with the singer Corona Schröter.

After Weimar's amateur theatre had faded away, perhaps because Goethe no longer had sufficient time and interest to devote to it, the *Teutsche Schauspieler Gesellschaft* (Society of German Players) under the management of Joseph Bellomo were engaged and remunerated with 320 taler a month. They were then replaced by the newly erected Weimar Court Theatre. Under Goethe's artistic direction, the directors for opera (Johann Friedrich Kranz) and drama (Franz Joseph Fischer) hired an ensemble that opened the theatre with Iffland's *The Hunters* on 7 May 1791.[12] The programme conceived by Goethe during his tenure from 1791 to 1817, which encompassed 601 productions, emphasized the plays of Kotzebue and Iffland (118 productions) as well as the international comedy repertoire (Molière, Marivaux, Beaumarchais, Goldoni, Gozzi and Holberg),[13] which served the duke's, the court's and the general public's desire for diversion. At some 500 spectators for each performance, a large proportion of them subscribers, the theatre had to put on a variety of plays to keep the theatrical enthusiasts interested. The ideas of Schiller (whose works were only performed 37 times) about the theatre as a 'moral institution' had as little chance

Figure 16   Backstage preparations for *The Magic Flute* at the Weimar Court
Theatre. Watercolour by Georg Melchior Kraus

of being realized as the high-flown ideal of a national theatre. Accordingly,
plays by Goethe, Schiller and Lessing comprised only 5 per cent of the total
repertoire in Weimar.

If Weimar nevertheless made a name for itself nationally, it owed much to
the style of playing that Goethe influenced over a number of years, in which
he stressed the training of actors and working through the language and metre
of the texts. That, at least, is the view of Goethe scholars, who may lend rather
too much credence to the self-presentation of the Classical authors.[14] Opera
and music drama played an important role in the programme. Thus Goethe's
productions of a number of operas were put on repeatedly, including *The Magic
Flute* (premiere 1794, 82 evenings), *Don Giovanni* (premiere 1792, 68 evenings), *The
Marriage of Figaro* (premiere 1793), *Così fan tutte* (premiere 1797), *Titus* (premiere
1799) and *The Abduction from the Seraglio* (premiere 1791, 49 evenings) – 'A truly
impressive Mozart cycle during the composer's lifetime and shortly after his
death!'[15] On 6 April 1799, Goethe's companion and future wife Christiane, an
avid theatregoer, attended her 30th performance of *The Magic Flute*.[16]

No survey of the German-speaking theatrical landscape would be complete
without a mention of theatrical culture in Vienna, which experienced an upswing
under Empress Maria Theresia. To the extent that they were interested in classic
and contemporary French drama, spectators from outside the court could now
visit the two court theatres, the Burgtheater and the Kärntnertortheater. The

court ballet and the opera were also expanded. Responsibility for the latter was in the hands of Christoph Willibald Gluck, artistic director since 1755 of the musical academy at the Burgtheater, who had already worked in Milan, London, Dresden, Copenhagen, Prague and Naples, and would enchant Paris with his 'reform' operas in the 1770s. Gluck developed his operatic style in reaction to the baroque virtuoso style of Pietro Metastasio, and emphasized simplicity, naturalness and less complicated plot structures.

As to drama, most of the works produced in Vienna were translations of French and English authors, although a small repertoire of original German plays was also performed. The plays were often adapted to Viennese comedies or harlequinades. For example, *The Merry Wives of Windsor* was transferred to Vienna as 'The Merry Adventures on the Wien River'. When Emperor Joseph II elevated the Burgtheater to a 'German national theatre', the issue was less programmatic educational goals than a preference for German-language theatre in the repertoire. A number of prominent German-speaking actors were engaged, including Johann Franz Hieronymus Brockmann, the 'Hamburg Hamlet'. He became director and manager at the Burgtheater in 1789, after Iffland turned down the position. Apart from plays, the Vienna Court Theatre's focus was on German music drama and opera, since the 'German national theatre' included spoken and musical theatre equally. In Vienna, German music drama met with such enthusiasm that new pieces were continually being staged. Mozart's *Abduction from the Seraglio*, which had its world premiere at the Burgtheater in 1782, also initially profited from the public's love for the genre.

Nevertheless, the trend at the Burgtheater soon returned to Italian opera, which was presented to Viennese audiences by a company under the direction of Antonio Salieri.[17] It is also against this background that we should view Mozart's Italian operas with libretti by Lorenzo da Ponte (*The Marriage of Figaro*, premiere on 1 May 1786; *Don Giovanni*, Viennese premiere on 7 May 1788 and *Cosi fan tutte*, premiere on 26 January 1790). They attained nothing approaching the success of Salieri's operas, however, since they demanded rather too much of Viennese audiences. Vienna naturally also lacked an artistic director such as Goethe, who staged *Don Giovanni* 68 times at the Weimar Court Theatre. It was only logical that Mozart, together with the impresario Emanuel Schikaneder, addressed *The Magic Flute* to the audience or market of Vienna's suburban theatres, providing them with the requisite 'comic figure' in the form of Papageno.[18]

The repertoire

Our sketch of developments in the theatre has noted repeatedly that the plays performed corresponded neither to today's repertoire nor to notions of a supposedly classic theatrical canon. Thus, the mayor of Hamburg who some time previously admonished that theatregoers in his city wanted to see recognizable (German) classics, and used this argument to topple the artistic director of the municipal theatre, would have felt quite out of place in Classical Weimar. All over eighteenth-century Germany, translations of French, English and Italian plays far outnumbered original German pieces on theatrical programmes. National theatre, therefore, did not mean German-speaking actors performing the works of German authors, but rather putting on plays in the German language. The plays were often adapted to suit the acting troupe and the audience, bowdlerizing the French or English original in the process. 'National theatre' thus began as a marketing slogan, which sparked a boom in German-language drama and music drama production in the last two decades of the eighteenth century. With the French Revolution, if not before, the adaptation and publication of French plays in Germany virtually collapsed.[19]

Theatre productions also focused largely on entertaining audiences. Theatrical impresarios, particularly the managers of the travelling troupes, relied on variety and, as in the nascent concert business, combined diverse elements: a comedy with fireworks or a tragedy with a pantomime ballet. At the same time, dramas, for example in Schröder's Hamburg Shakespeare adaptations, were provided with a happy end in the operatic mode, thus bowing to audience expectations. Comedies dominated the repertoire in any case. Thus four-fifths of the 250 performances by Ackermann's troupe in Hamburg consisted of comedies. The short-lived Gotha Court Theatre, too, put on 114 comedies, 13 tragedies and 44 dramas. Music drama also outweighed the spoken word. Gottsched's efforts at theatre reform accordingly achieved no far-reaching success. The Leipzig professor had not merely opposed the sumptuousness and lasciviousness of opera ('the most preposterous work ever invented by the human understanding'),[20] but also, with his demand for the unity of time, place and action and propagation of alexandrine verse as the standard metre, sought to remove scene changes and improvisation as elements of entertainment in the theatre. In the 1740s and 1750s, Johann Elias Schlegel, Christian Fürchtegott Gellert and Gotthold Ephraim Lessing further developed Gottsched's model dramas into the genres of 'sentimental comedy' (*rührendes Lustspiel*) and 'bourgeois (or domestic) tragedy' (*bürgerliches Trauerspiel*). Lessing's *Miss Sara Sampson* (1755), first performed by Ackermann's troupe in Frankfurt an der Oder, is a prime example of this new genre, which urged the audience to empathize with the fate of the characters on stage. Although skilful acting ensured that *Sara Sampson* moved audiences to tears,[21] *Emilia Galotti* was the only one of Lessing's works to gain a lasting place in the hearts of late eighteenth-century theatregoers, and to secure its rank among the 30 most performed plays.

Case studies of individual theatres confirm these observations. While the Gotha Court Theatre existed for only a few years and thus cannot document theatrical taste over a long period, we know which works were performed at the National Theatre in Mannheim during Dalberg's tenure (1779–1803). Here, too, German bourgeois drama represented the largest part of the repertoire. Otto von Gemmingen's *Der Deutsche Hausvater* (The German Paterfamilias, 1780) was the first such play to be integrated into the programme, but the genre would have its most successful protagonists in Schröder, Iffland and Kotzebue. To be sure, Dalberg included Shakespeare's tragedies and Schiller's dramas in the repertoire with programmatic intent, but only *Hamlet* and Schiller's *Robbers* made it onto the list of the 30 most performed plays. They were upstaged not merely by all of Kotzebue's plays, but also by Gemmingen's *Der deutsche Hausvater*, Rautenstrauch's *Der Jurist und der Bauer* (The Lawyer and the Peasant), Gotter's *Mariane*, Pilow's *Der taube Liebhaber* (The Deaf Lover) or Jünger's *Der Strich durch die Rechnung* (A Spanner in the Works).[22]

Table 8.1   Plays staged at the Mannheim National Theatre, 1779–1803

Author	Title	Genre	Number of performances	Year of premiere
Gotter, Friedrich Wilhelm	*The Suspicious Husband*	C	21	1779
Gozzi, Carlo	*Juliane von Lindorak*	D	20	1779
Rautenstrich, Johann	*Der Jurist und der Bauer*	C	40	1779
Shakespeare	*Hamlet*	T	27	1779
Bock, Johann Christian	*Die Holländer oder was vermag ein vernünftiges Frauenzimmer nicht?*	C	20	1780
Gemmingen, Otto Heinrich von	*Die Familie oder der deutsche Hausvater*	D	26	1780
Lessing, Gotthold Ephraim	*Emilia Galotti*	T	20	1780
Eckardt, Friedrich Samuel Lucas von	*Wer wird sie kriegen?*	C	20	1781
Gotter, Friedrich Wilhelm	*Mariane*	T	30	1781
Großmann, Gustav Friedrich Wilhelm	*Nicht mehr als sechs Schüsseln*	FD	21	1781
Shakespeare	*Taming of the Shrew*	C	23	1781
Gotter, Friedrich Wilhelm	*Zwei Onkel für einen*	C	23	1782
Pilow, trans. Friedrich Ludwig Ulrich Schröder	*Der taube Liebhaber*	C	33	1782
Richter, Joseph	*Der Gläubiger*	D	28	1782
Babo, Franz Marius	*Die Maler*	C	20	1783
Bretzner, Christoph Friedrich	*Die mißtrauischen Liebhaber*	C	28	1783
Murphy, Arthur	*All in the Wrong*	C	27	1783
Wall-Florian	*Die beiden Billetts*	C	32	1783

Author	Title	Genre	Number of performances	Year of premiere
Iffland, August Wilhelm	*Crimes of Ambition*	FD	21	1784
Schiller, Friedrich	*The Robbers*	D	20	1784
Brömel, Johann Friedrich	*Die buchstäbliche Auslegung der Gesetze*	C	25	1785
Iffland, August Wilhelm	*The Hunters*	SCL	23	1785
Jünger, Johann Friedrich	*Der Strich durch die Rechnung*	C	29	1785
Bretzner, Christoph Friedrich	*Das Räuschchen*	C	21	1786
Iffland, August Wilhelm	*Der Magnetismus*	C	24	1787
Dalberg, Wolfgang Heribert von	*Die eheliche Probe*	C	21	1788
Babo, Franz Marius	*Peter the Great, or the Russian Mother*	D	20	1789
Kotzebue, August von	*Misanthropy and Repentance*	D	29	1789
Kotzebue, August von	*The Indian Exiles*	C	22	1790
Kotzebue, August von	*The Virgin of the Sun*	D	25	1790
Kotzebue, August von	*Lovers' Vows*	D	20	1790
Jünger, Johann Friedrich	*Die Entführung*	C	21	1791
Spieß, Christian Heinrich	*Klara von Hohenreichen*	CD	27	1791
Ziegler, Friedrich Wilhelm	*Der König auf Reisen*	C	20	1793
Kotzebue, August von	*Indigence and Nobleness of Mind*	C	22	1794
Kotzebue, August von	*The Count of Burgundy*	D	25	1796

Abbreviations: T = tragedy, C = comedy, D = drama, FD = family drama, SCL = scenes of country life, CD = chivalric drama

That this repertoire was not specific to the Electoral Palatinate is evident from accounts in the contemporary periodical press. A 1795 report in the *Rheinische Musen* (Rhenish Muses) 'On the Taste for Music and Theatre in the North' highlights the same authors as those who were in vogue in Mannheim. Even if the article states that 'dramas originating in the imperial and Bavarian states rarely find easy acceptance in the North', it emphasizes Schröder, Jünger, Iffland, Babo etc., who were also box office hits in Mannheim, as well as Kotzebue or Gotter's *Mariane*.[23] Thus there was apparently no significant north–south divide in the theatrical repertoire. In his reconstruction of music drama and opera in the programmes of German playhouses, Reinhart Meyer also takes note of other genres, and remarks upon the absence of the oft-mentioned 'cultural chasm' between north and south. What differences did exist stemmed from the structure of the cities. When it came to opera and drama, the large commercial and fair towns showed similar preferences to the princely capitals. Only smaller towns as well as the residences of the prince-bishops displayed a stronger preference for spoken theatre. This was surely a function of the financial possibilities for realizing more elaborate theatrical productions. Where such productions were mounted, it illustrates the taste preferences familiar to us from larger cities.[24]

The reports on theatre in the various German territories that appeared regularly in the *Journal des Luxus und der Moden* point in a similar direction. According to these, programmes in Hamburg, Berlin, Dresden, Frankfurt am Main, Mainz, Mannheim, Munich or Graz featured Iffland, Schröder and Kotzebue in equal measure, with the addition of some local variations and music theatre.[25] Demand for the latter in particular grew increasingly towards the end of the eighteenth century. Thus the Mannheim artistic director Dalberg notes in a memorandum of 1790:

> With the appearance of the operetta *The Abduction from the Seraglio* and the like, the audience here as elsewhere began to parcel out its previous affection for drama, and all theatre directors now had to place operettas, which heretofore had been merely incidental, on the same footing as plays in order to make a change, and both to satisfy the wishes of the public and ensure better takings at the ticket office.[26]

The first season of the Dessau Theatre in 1794–95, in which Bossan's company put on 46 works, demonstrates how varied the repertoire of even a small court theatre could be. Here, too, the popular authors Iffland, Schröder, Kotzebue, Gotter and Babo made up the core of the programme, which was however supplemented and enriched by a range of music theatre, representing about one-third of the repertoire. Dittersdorf was on the programme with his hits (*The Doctor and the Apothecary*, *Little Red Riding-Hood*, and so on) along with Mozart's *Magic Flute* and the works of Paisiello, Benda, Wranitzky and Grétry.[27]

Table 8.2   Productions at the Dessau Court Theatre, 1794–95

Author	Title	Genre	Premiere
Dittersdorf, Carl Ditters von	*Little Red Riding-Hood*	CO	30 July 1794
Jünger, Johann Friedrich	*Er mengt sich in alles*	C	1 August 1794
Hagemeister, Johann Gottfried	*Das große Loos*	D	1 August 1794
Dittersdorf, Carl Ditters von	*Hieronimus Knicker*	CO	3 August 1794

Author	Title	Genre	Premiere
Hagemann, Friedrich Gustav	*Otto der Schütz, Prinz von Hessen*	D	5 August 1794
Salieri, Antonio	*Der Aufschluß*	CO	7 August 1794
Bossan, Friedrich-Wilhelm	*Der Vorabend*	P	9 August 1794
Mozart, Wolfgang Amadeus	*The Magic Flute*	O	11 August 1794
Kotzebue, August von	*The Indian Exiles*	C	15 August 1794
Dittersdorf, Carl Ditters von	*The Doctor and the Apothecary*	O	17 August 1794
Kotzebue, August von	*Misanthropy and Repentance*	FD	18 August 1794
d'Alayrac, Nicolas-Marie	*Die Beiden Savoyarden (Les deux pétits Savoyards)*	CO	20 August 1794
Gotter, Friedrich Wilhelm	*Der Spleensüchtige Engländer*	C	20 August 1794
Iffland, August Wilhelm	*Die Hagestolzen*	FD	22 August 1794
d'Alayrac, Nicolas-Marie	*Nina oder Wahnsinn aus Liebe (Nina ou la Folle par amour)*	O	26 August 1794
Schletter, Salomon Friedrich	*Getroffen! Getroffen!*	D	26 August 1794
Paisiello, Giovanni	*Die Schöne Müllerin (La molinara)*	CO	29 August 1794
d'Alayrac, Nicolas-Marie	*Die Wilden (Azémia ou les sauvages)*	O	5 September 1794
Hagemann, Friedrich Gustav	*Ludwig der Springer*	PD	7 September 1794
Ziegler, Friedrich Wilhelm	*Der seltene Onkel*	C	12 September 1794
Dittersdorf, Carl Ditters von	*Der Schiffspatron*	CO	14 September 1794
Desaides, Alexandre Nicolas	*Alexis und Justine*	CO	16 September 1794
Schröder, Friedrich Ludwig	*Heirath durch ein Wochenblatt*	C	16 September 1794
Goethe, Johann Wolfgang von	*Clavigo*	T	19 September 1794
Schubaur, Johann Lucas	*Die Dorfdeputirten*	CO	21 September 1794
Bossann, Friedrich-Wilhelm	*Tempel des Danks*	E	23 September 1794
Schröder, Friedrich Ludwig	*Der Fähndrich oder Der falsche Verdacht*	D	23 September 1794
Beck, Heinrich	*Die Quälgeister*	C	26 September 1794
Ziegler, Friedrich Wilhelm	*Der König auf Reisen*	C	30 September 1794
Iffland, August Wilhelm	*Scheinverdienst*	FD	2 October 1794
Nunez de Liam, Duarte	*Ignez de Castro*	T	5 October 1794

Author	Title	Genre	Premiere
d'Arien, Bernhard Christoph	*Das Landmädchen*	D	9 October 1794
Iffland, August Wilhelm	*The Hunters*	PM	12 October 1794
Babo, Franz Marius	*Bürgerglück*	FD	14 October 1794
Lafontaine, August Heinrich Julius	*Die Tochter der Natur*	D	19 October 1794
Bossann, Friedrich-Wilhelm	*Das Opfer der Schauspielkunst*	PE	19 October 1794
Wranitzky, Paul	*Oberon, König der Elfen*	O	19 July 1795
Iffland, August Wilhelm	*Alte Zeit und Neue Zeit*	D	21 July 1795
Kotzebue, August von	*Indigence and Nobleness*	C	23 July 1795
Iffland, August Wilhelm	*Dienstpflicht*	D	24 July 1795
d'Alayrac, Nicolas-Marie	*Rudolph von Creki (Raoul, sire de Créqui)*	O	26 July 1795
Benda, Georg	*Romeo und Julia*	O	28 July 1795
Iffland, August Wilhelm	*Magnetismus/ Macht die Augen auf und seht*	C	28 July 1795
Huber, Leopold	*Die Offene Fehde*	D	31 July 1795
Grétry, André Ernest Modeste	*Zemire und Azor*	O	31 July 1795

C = comedy; CO = comic opera; D = drama; E = epilogue in one act; FD= family drama; O = opera; P = prologue with song; PD = patriotic drama; PE = parting epilogue; PM = portrait of manners; T = tragedy

If we are to believe the accounts in the *Journal des Luxus und der Moden* this programme, too, was typical of theatrical life in the German territories. Even in distant Swedish Pomerania, travelling troupes brought the wider world to Stralsund and Greifswald audiences in the form of opera. Apart from Johann Adam Hiller's popular *Jagd* (The Hunt) and Benda's *Medea* (based on a play by Friedrich Wilhelm Gotter), here, as in Dessau, the programme of the 1780s and 1790s included Grétry's *Zémire et Azor*, Dittersdorf's *The Doctor and the Apothecary* and *Little Red Riding Hood*, Wranitzky's *Oberon* and Mozart's *Magic Flute* and *Don Giovanni*.[28] Popular works in this genre – *Die Jagd, Medea, The Doctor and the Apothecary* or *The Magic Flute* – were performed in nearly every theatre from Amsterdam in the west to St Petersburg in the east and Vienna, Graz or Trieste in the south.[29] They also reached the music-loving public through arrangements for piano, song and aria collections and published libretti, which were reprinted again and again. The most popular authors, such as Kotzebue or Gotter, who were also successful as librettists, published their plays and libretti in collected editions as well.[30]

Thrilling entertainment – if possible in words and music – thus best corresponded to the tastes of the listening and reading public. The genres mentioned above converged here, and the trend was towards an entertaining *genre mixte*. The lines between tragedy, which was performed increasingly rarely, drama and comedy became more permeable – and some successful authors deliberately blurred them, consciously playing with the emotions of their clientele. In both Kotzebue and Mozart, scenes that moved audiences to tears alternated in quick succession with light-hearted sequences. But that was certainly no guarantee of the lasting renown gained by Mozart, who was not so very successful in his own time. Had Kotzebue not been shot and killed by Ludwig Sand in 1819, a deed that triggered the Carlsbad Decrees and the so-called persecution of the demagogues, the most successful playwright of his day would probably have disappeared into obscurity.

The audience

We have referred several times to the desires and taste of the theatre audience, but who were they? All that one can say with certainty is that the audience was extremely heterogeneous, as the *Allgemeine Theaterlexikon* (General Theatrical Lexicon) of 1839 emphasized:

> What a distance exists between the student – who after the careful preparation of numerous readings of a classic work follows the performance from the pit, book in hand – and the fine gentleman, who sits yawning in his box in the first circle, digesting his splendid dinner; between the tradesman who saves all week to bring his family to the gallery on Sunday, and the connoisseur of music who, piano arrangement at the ready, judges the accomplishments of the orchestra and singers. The most highly cultivated mind alongside the crudest craving for pleasure, the pomp and comfort of the privileged classes alongside poverty and low inclinations![31]

In the eighteenth century, apart from court society, theatregoers came mainly from the moneyed and educated middle classes and the functional elites. The specific composition of the audience varied from place to place. Thus, those travelling companies that did not perform exclusively at court mainly sought out the urban commercial centres, which meant that in Hamburg, Leipzig or Frankfurt ('Monday is ball night, Fridays are for concerts, Tuesday, Thursday and Saturday for theatre')[32] they played to audiences with a largely mercantile orientation. This was still the case in the 1780s and 1790s, when a music-loving merchant such as Johann Heinrich Goßler attended the theatre regularly from September 1786 onwards with his wife Elisabeth, according to his household account books. Otherwise, the wives of Hamburg or Frankfurt merchants enjoyed the theatre without the 'gentleman of the house' and discussed what they had seen over punch at home.[33] The many guests passing through also took ample advantage of the cultural offerings of the large cities.[34]

In the princely capitals, in contrast, the audience changed fundamentally when court theatres became institutionalized and opened their doors to the paying general public. While in the major capitals such as Vienna or Munich court theatres and audiences retained their aristocratic character and thus (at least in Vienna), furthered the popularity of suburban theatres, audiences in the smaller princely residences were socially more diverse. Nevertheless, a certain social segregation was maintained with the help of theatrical architecture. The stage faced the central box of the first circle, in which the prince watched the performance with his courtiers (the latter, where necessary, in additional boxes). Wealthier citizens, members of the functional elites, scholars and artists sat in the second and third tiers, while military men, travellers and guests sat in the stalls, and the 'common folk' of tradesmen, journeymen and servants sat in the gallery or the separate 'commoners' or 'ordinary' benches in the pit.[35]

In Mannheim in 1779, an annual subscription for all 140 performances cost 16 guilders for the cheaper boxes in the second tier and 18 for those in the stalls, while those in the first circle were by far the most expensive at 28 guilders. They were accordingly usurped by government ministers and generals with their families, although the confectioner Schäfer could also afford a box in the first circle. Two bakers and a master butcher also had boxes in the third tier.[36]

When court theatres opened to the paying public, artistic directors had to satisfy their tastes along with those of the court elites. To be sure, aristocratic manners also rubbed off on middle-class theatregoers, but the master bakers or butchers who paid good money for their subscriptions expected varied entertainment and regular new productions in return, and they were not afraid to say so quite loudly. The fact that they had paid for the pleasure turned theatregoers into self-assured cultural consumers who were prepared to catcall and whistle along with the nobility – or without them.

The heterogeneity of audiences made for quite individual reception experiences. Thus, the higher nobility had a certain degree of expertise in artistic and aesthetic matters because of their own training in music and dance. Although some of them were amateur musicians, members of the middle classes and the functional elites, in contrast, tended to have less skill in this area.[37] Here, as among the 'simple spectators' who increasingly frequented the theatre at the end of the eighteenth century, the focus of interest was on how far what they saw on the stage corresponded to their own life experience or universal norms. Even among the connoisseurs, however, tastes varied. While some spectators – much like reviewers and journalists – tended to judge according to artistic and aesthetic criteria, others had a more emotional interest in identification. Some protagonists of the late Enlightenment criticized this 'mania' for the theatre or opera in similarly harsh terms as they had attacked the alleged offence of 'reading mania'. If the expectations of spectators were not met in this respect, they voted with their feet and chose other modes of entertainment instead. Thus attempts by the Mannheim Court Theatre's artistic director Heinrich Beck in 1801 to 'elevate the corrupt public again' with the dramas of Schiller and other authors failed because the audience preferred to go dancing instead.[38] The 'serving of wine, beer, liqueur, coffee, chocolate and tea and the provision of one or more billiard tables and permitted card games' in the theatre's refreshment rooms could not prevent this exodus.[39]

Attending the theatre was not the only way to take part in entertainment offerings and artistic achievements. Only those who read the magazines truly participated in German and even international theatrical life. The *Journal des Luxus und der Moden* regularly printed news and anecdotes of the theatre in London and Paris. In March 1786, for example, the rubric 'The Latest English Theatrical Luxury' contained a report on the pantomime play *Omai: Or the Trip Around the World*, which elaborately portrayed Cook's voyage on the stage of the Theatre Royal in Covent Garden.[40] An account of a 'papist cabal' intended to disrupt a performance of the anticlerical tragedy *Charles Neuf, ou la St.-Barthelemy* at the Théâtre de la Nation in Paris, but which only increased the play's success, also piqued the interest of magazine readers.[41] German theatre news, too, along with overviews of the repertoires of different theatres, openly discussed the causes of the success or failure of selected new productions. Particularly detailed attention was devoted to Berlin theatre, which was measured by its aspirations to the status of a national theatre. In December 1789, a reviewer reported from Berlin:

> The Indians in Exile have had rather good luck here. They were performed so often and in such quick succession on popular demand that they now appear to be lying at anchor with Sailor Jack and taking a rest … . Madame Unzelmann played the role of Burley with such naiveté and amiability that it is enough to make one forget the error of the improbability or rather the moral impossibility of such complete ignorance. Herr Fleck as Kaberdar was utterly in his element, and his tone, his eye and everything about him amply informed anyone who did not already know it of what he had been in India – a nabob … . When Musaffery, the loyal adherent of the religion of his fathers, broke out with a gratitude-filled and truly typical 'O Brama! Brama be praised!' at the wondrous turns of destiny towards the end, the audience laughed. Nota bene: they laughed! Renewed proof of the truth that Germany does not yet have a national pit to which one can appeal for good taste and fine and proper judgement.[42]

The Mannheim audience also took 'extraordinarily well to The Indians in Exile; especially to the inimitable performance of Mamsell Witthoft as an Indian woman'.[43]

Audiences found news about theatrical companies, their changing personnel ('Demoiselle Berwald has left the theatre here') and the performances of their favourites at least as important as the success and failure of the productions. 'On the 3rd of January Mad. Beck appeared on the stage for the first time since her delivery, as Therese in *Felix*. People received her as always, and called her before the curtain according to the custom.'[44] Just as the Mannheim audience celebrated the return of the wife of the local actor and later theatrical manager

Heinrich Beck, they stamped their feet or whistled at their favourites on other occasions, as when the Berlin actor Carl Czechtitzky missed his scene because he was sitting in a coffee house.[45]

Actors were iconic figures in the eighteenth century, with whom one could engage or identify. The members of no other occupational group penned as many memoirs as actors. Although German actors did not attain the national fame of such London greats as David Garrick, Sarah Siddons or Mary Robinson, thespians such as Konrad Ekhof, Johann Franz Brockmann, Friedrich Ludwig Schröder, August Wilhelm Iffland, Friedrich Fleck, Ludwig Devrient, Sophie Schröder, Karoline Jagemann or the Unzelmanns were known throughout Germany, and a singer such as Gertrud Elisabeth Mara was fêted as a prima donna in many European countries. Although being tied to a court theatre often restricted an actor's range of possible guest appearances, their mobility was probably comparable only to that of the *Kapellmeister*. The court theatres and princes vied with each for the favour of the top actors and actresses, and the fluctuation was considerable among even average members of the profession.[46]

The middle classes, too, basked in the reflected glory of actors. Goethe's mother, for instance, who supported the new Frankfurt *Commoedienhaus* under Gustav Friedrich Wilhelm Großmann with substantial patronage sums, invited the young Iffland, who was playing the lead in Schiller's *Kabale und Liebe*, to her home several times in 1784. That same year she fell in love with the young (but already famous) Carl Wilhelm Ferdinand Unzelmann, whom Großmann had engaged for his Frankfurt theatre. With his great talent for acting and improvisation, he shone not only in speaking roles but also as Figaro, Leporello or Papageno. Accordingly, the women of Frankfurt and Berlin succumbed to his charm not only in the theatre. His wife, the actress Friederike Auguste Caroline Unzelmann, who had to watch these affairs at close range, comforted herself after their 1803 divorce with the actor Bethmann, who was 14 years her junior.[47]

To a far greater extent than their male colleagues, actresses were subject to the interplay between art, eroticism and exploitation that made them particular objects of the audience's desire. Spectators often failed to distinguish between the actress as a person and the role she played.[48] An exemplary case is Karoline Jagemann, whom Iffland engaged for the Mannheim Court Theatre in 1792. Fifteen years old at the time, she had just completed one year of singing lessons, and was hired to play 'ingenues and peasant girls'. Her big break came with an engagement at Weimar as a concert singer (at a salary of 200 taler) and then as first singer at court (400 taler). Her unique position was enhanced by her official installation as the mistress of Grand Duke Carl August, with whom she had three children, and her elevation to the nobility. With this security – she could refuse any other offers – she was in a position to organize her artistic life according to her own lights, while other actresses had to walk the fine line between being a sex object and leading a 'profligate life'.[49] Naturally, theatregoers and readers were particularly fascinated by any hint of such scandal, which satisfied their thirst for entertainment, a thirst also served by actresses' memoirs. It was precisely the opportunities for identification with the characters as well as the actors who portrayed them that explains the boom in theatrical entertainment at the end of the eighteenth century, and not just in Germany.

Chapter 9

The New Stimulants and Sociability

> Around this time, an Englishman arrived in Hamburg and began to serve tea as well as coffee. A Dutchman followed him, and as a result tea and coffee drinking became quite common, so that anybody with the money to pay for it began to drink it, and it henceforth offered an occasion for many gatherings.[1]

In the sixteenth century, Europeans learnt the pleasures of coffee drinking from the Arab world. In the following century, coffee consumption spread to the European courts as well as noble circles, and gradually also to the large cities. It was not until the eighteenth century, however, that the drinking of coffee as well as tea and chocolate reached the middle classes. The enjoyment of coffee – institutionalized in the coffee house – became not merely a medium of the emerging public sphere, but also a middle-class leisure occupation indulged in with family and guests. Coffee and tea were, consequently, inextricably linked with the new consumer culture of the eighteenth century.

The various words for coffee in the European languages all derived from the Arabic *kahva*, since the stimulating brew of the seeds of a plant originating in the Ethiopian province of Kaffa had spread to the Arabian Peninsula beginning in the thirteenth and fourteenth centuries. The plant first came to the attention of Europeans in a 1582 book by the Oriental traveller Leonhard Rauwolf, as well as in Italian publications. Coffee spread to Europe from the Ottoman Empire and its Mediterranean harbours as well as from Mokka in present-day Yemen, which had been a regular port of call for ships of the English and Dutch East India Companies since 1609–10. It was only a matter of time, however, before the coffee monopoly of Yemen (the producer on the Red Sea) was broken. After coffee seeds were planted by Indian pilgrims to Mecca on the Ghats behind the Malabar Coast, the Dutch followed with coffee plantations in Java, Ceylon and Surinam. In the eighteenth century, the coffee tree then came to the Caribbean (Haiti, Santo Domingo and Martinique) as well as to Rio de Janeiro via Goa. In 1789, using slave labour, Haiti's plantations alone produced 60 million pounds of coffee a year, most of which was exported to France, from whence it was re-exported to Amsterdam and Hamburg.[2] The importation and distribution of coffee to Germany thus occurred both via Hamburg with its trading links with Amsterdam, London, Bordeaux and Nantes and via Venice and Vienna with their contacts in the Mediterranean and the Ottoman Empire.

It is not surprising that the first coffee house in Europe opened its doors in Venice in 1647. Others followed in the mid-seventeenth century in London, Oxford, Amsterdam, Paris and Marseilles, most of them founded by Armenian,

Jewish or Greek entrepreneurs. The most robust development was in England, where by 1700 London was positively littered with coffee houses. In 1739, the city already boasted 551 coffee houses alongside 207 inns and 447 taverns. Besides coffee, the coffee houses also offered their customers chocolate, wine, brandy and punch, which were served from a bar in the corner of the room. Apart from these pleasures, the coffee houses were also prized as centres of conversation and information. One came to chat with friends, but also to do business, exchanging money, goods and information. As the number of coffee houses grew, they became more specialized. The trade in stocks and funds was concentrated at Jonathan's Coffee House in Exchange Alley, for example. If one was looking for shipping and insurance services, Lloyd's Coffee House in Tower Street (later Lombard Street) was the place to go. It published a news sheet beginning in 1690 and a shipping list from 1734, and the company still has a name today in marine insurance. Lawyers met at Alice's and the Hell Coffee House, while Tory politicians frequented the Cocoa Tree, and Whigs gathered at Arthur's. Booksellers (the Chapter Coffee House), artists (Old Slaughter's Coffee House), writers (Will's), actors (Wright's in Covent Garden) and singers and dancers (the Orange in the Haymarket) all met in their own coffee houses.

Joseph Addison and Richard Steele, whose periodical *Tatler* influenced public opinion, accordingly classified the news they printed by sectors of society and the corresponding coffee houses.[3] The two men's association with Child's Coffee House in St Paul's Churchyard was so close that their admirers emulated them and went there as well.[4] The coffee houses were not merely centres of sociability, information exchange and business, however, but also institutions of cultural consumption, a circumstance that scholars who focus on the journalistic and political public sphere frequently fail to recognize. Thus customers also used the coffee houses as libraries, exhibition spaces, art auction houses, theatres and concert halls. Often viewed with suspicions by the authorities, Tories and royalists, the coffee house was idealized by Addison and Steele as a site of 'polite conversation'. For that reason, as coffee houses became increasingly popular among common folk, those who sought a more exclusive atmosphere increasingly withdrew to clubs and private associations.[5]

In the seventeenth century, coffee first made its way into the Holy Roman Empire, more specifically to Vienna, via aristocratic friends of the brew, since coffee houses only began to spread here towards the end of the century. Legend has it that the Viennese first acquired coffee during the Turkish siege of the city in 1683, when the routed Turks left their coffee stocks behind. In this case, however, it was again an Armenian who obtained the first imperial privilege to serve coffee in 1685. In 1697, Armenian entrepreneurs acquired privileges to open further coffee houses, the number of which was limited to four in 1700. The privilege encompassed the 'roasting and brewing of tea, coffee, chocolate and sherbets in public shops', thus incorporating the other new stimulants from the outset.[6] By 1737, despite the official restrictions, the number of coffee houses in Vienna had risen to 37, plus several in the surrounding suburbs. In

1770, the city already had 48 coffee houses, and in 1791 more than 80. Although Vienna could not compete with London or Paris in terms of numbers, it also developed a coffee house culture of its own. Magazines and newspapers played a role in this, along with the typical coffee house debates. Billiards, a fashionable game in the eighteenth century, also became one of the most profitable sources of income for coffee house owners. While in the early eighteenth century foreign visitors had marvelled at the free exchange of ideas in Vienna's coffee houses, by the end of the century they had lost some of their charm, and were now viewed by many Protestant north German intellectuals as refuges for layabouts. Friedrich Nicolai found it hard to enjoy the coffee houses of Vienna, for nowhere else in Germany did he see so many idlers. 'Whatever time of day one goes to the coffee house, or in summer to the coffee garden, one is sure to find a large number of persons doing nothing.' In 1804, Ernst Moritz Arndt complained in a similar vein that 'one can always find company in a Viennese coffee house, but only rarely conversation'.[7]

Differences thus existed from the English coffee house, but only if one follows Habermas in focusing on their emancipatory role in public discourse.[8] This did nothing to halt the popularity and proliferation of the coffee house in Austria, however. By 1800, Viennese-style coffee houses had spread to all of the capitals and regional centres of the monarchy. With the expansion of the coffee house, the modes of serving coffee also became more varied. By 1786, coffee with cream (4 kr), coffee with hot milk (3 kr), black coffee (3 kr) and double coffee with cream (12 kr) were already on the menu. Tea was more expensive than coffee, and chocolate dearer still. Those who could not afford such prices purchased their coffee at the many small coffee bars or from the street vendors who sold a cup of coffee and a crescent roll for 1 kr.[9]

In northern Germany, Cornelius Bontekoe, the Dutch personal physician to Frederick William of Brandenburg, encouraged the consumption of coffee and tea, which he believed promoted the circulation of the blood and prescribed in large quantities. He is said to have alleviated the Great Elector's gout symptoms with tea.[10] Dutch and above all English influences ultimately led to the establishment of coffee houses in the north. One must distinguish here between the large urban centres with numerous coffee houses and the smaller cities and princely capitals with one central, multifunctional coffee house.

An example of the latter is the Great Coffee House in Brunswick, for which Franz Heinrich Wegener received a privilege in 1714. Because of the economic success of this first Brunswick coffee house, the owner managed to have his privilege extended regularly, allowing, for example, for the (social) equality of all coffee house customers during their stay as well as the installation of a ballroom. Theatrical and musical performances and auctions also took place in this or another annex to the coffee house. Apart from the newspaper collection, billiard tables and a skittle alley provided diversion for customers. Around mid-century, the proprietor added a coffee garden with illumination and music. The first serious competition to the Great Coffee House arrived only in the 1770s, when the Hotel d'Angleterre, which was intended for persons of quality, was built next to the existing French Coffee House. In order to maintain its selection of newspapers and magazines, the owner of the Great Coffee House began to charge an admission fee (by yearly or monthly subscription). The next logical step was the establishment of a reading institute in the coffee house, membership of which cost four taler a year. As normal taverns were now also permitted to serve coffee, however, coffee houses had to offer extra incentives to attract clientele. Even the university town of Göttingen, where the establishment of a coffee house had been deemed essential in connection with the founding of the university in 1734, never acquired a Great Coffee House, let alone a literary café, because the Electoral Hanoverian administration deemed the existence of three or four coffee and billiard establishments to be sufficient.

The market-oriented Leipzig and Hamburg coffee houses stand out alongside these examples from territorial cities. Leipzig's coffee houses were frequented not just by members of the book trade and students, but also by intellectuals such as Johann Christoph Gottsched, who brought out a moral weekly, *Die Vernünftigen Tadlerinnen* (The Rational Female Tatlers) in imitation of *The Tatler*, and in his *Biedermann* used Lehmann's Coffee House in Leipzig as the *genius loci*.[11] The Leipzig coffee houses – especially Zimmermann's Coffee House – became famous as the sites of the concerts of the *Collegium Musicum*, directed first by Johann Gottlieb Görner and later (from 1729) by Johann Sebastian Bach. The concerts were held in the evening, and thus were not primarily intended as entertainment to accompany afternoon coffee, but rather as musical events in their own right. The connection to the coffee house, however, was created by performances such as that of Johann Sebastian Bach's coffee cantata, *Ach wie ist der Kaffee süße* ('Oh, How Sweet the Coffee Tastes').[12]

Hamburg, which acquired its first coffee house in 1677, numbered 6 in 1700, a figure that would increase fivefold over the century, rising to 32 in 1810. Typical of the Hamburg coffee houses was their openness to all, regardless of rank (*Freiheit des Besuchs*). At first, they were frequented mainly by burghers, scholars and merchants who sought to combine edification, pleasure and diversion. Certain coffee houses became the intellectual centres of Hamburg; the town councillor and poet Brockes, the poet von Hagedorn, the satirist Dreyer, the surgeon Carpser and pastors Zimmermann and Wilkens, for example, frequented Stuart's Coffee House (in the Neß). Business affairs were also settled in the coffee house.

At the same time, the coffee house facilitated the separation of work and leisure time. Since the coffee house was spatially separate from the workplace, the counting house, a visit represented an interruption in the work day, making the coffee house one of the first sites of leisure activity, in which the heretofore little practised lifestyle of leisure could develop. Sitting, sipping and conversing in the coffee house late into the night meant that people also stayed up later, so that the first signs of modern nightlife become evident in the coffee house.[13]

Figure 17   Family of the artist, painting by Johann Anton Tischbein, 1779, oil on canvas

The integration of leisure into the middle-class daily routine was probably more significant historically. People drank coffee and tea not just in the coffee house, but also at home with family and friends. As early as the 1720s, the *Patriot* poked fun at the garden activities indulged in by Hamburg citizens, which consisted solely of eating, drinking coffee and tea, and playing cards and dice.[14] The people of Hamburg, undaunted by such verdicts, integrated coffee into everyday family life, as we see in the self-portrait of the artist Johann Anton Tischbein with his wife and children (Figure 17).

Many Hamburg couples – for example, Ferdinand and Karoline Beneke – began the day by taking coffee together, while others such as Johanna Margaretha and Georg Heinrich Sieveking preferred to drink tea in the morning while reading the papers. In the afternoon, following the English model of five o'clock tea, the family gathered for tea or coffee, unless they went out to a coffee house instead. As luncheon came to be eaten in the afternoon because of the altered opening hours of the stock exchange, people drank coffee after the meal and then returned to work, doubtless grateful for its stimulating effects.[15] At least in Hamburg, coffee had a serious rival in tea. The cameralist Christian Ludwig von Griesheim observed that 'tea is so popular that no Hamburger can live without it.'[16] Johanna Schopenhauer may have brought the 'tea table' to early nineteenth-century Weimar from Hamburg, where she had lived for many years. While in Hamburg, the tea table of 'Doctor' Sophie Reimarus enjoyed renown well beyond the city's borders and Schopenhauer's tea table in Weimar became a centre of literary conversation, in which Goethe also regularly participated, and thus synonymous with the literary salon.

What was it about tea that made it so popular in north-west Europe, including Hamburg? Black tea, for whose existence in fourth-century AD China we have written evidence, reached Japan in the eighth century, where it was initially valued for its medical properties, until green tea became the preferred drink. In the late Middle Ages, Arab merchants brought word of the medical benefits of tea (in promoting digestion and alleviating the effects of intoxication) to Europe along with the first tea leaves. In the sixteenth century, however, travellers to China and Japan made tea truly famous in Europe. The Venetian Giovanni Battista Ramusio, for example, translated a Persian traveller's account of a Chinese tea ceremony, while the missionaries Gaspar de la Cruz and Matteo Ricci reported on Chinese tea consumption and Francesco Carletti on tea preparation in Japan. It was above all Dutch physicians, though, who propagated tea drinking for medicinal purposes in the seventeenth century.[17]

In the 1640s, smaller quantities of tea also reached London, where it was occasionally served in the coffee houses. The China trade of the Dutch and English East India Companies was still so limited and irregular that there was nothing approaching a constant supply of tea. Not until the 1690s did London grocers and tea merchants offer tea in larger quantities, and it was only then that urban and aristocratic customers demanded it. Tea soon became one of the pleasures of domestic and family life. Women could visit teashops unaccompanied without causing a scandal, and the ladies' tea party became so widespread an institution that satirists in England and the Netherlands began to mock it. Eighteenth-century London boasted several renowned tea gardens where couples and families went to enjoy themselves over tea and other refreshments, and to take leisurely walks and listen to music.

In the course of the eighteenth century, black tea became less expensive because of the growing European competition in the tea trade with China. While the Dutch East India Company in Batavia purchased tea indirectly through Chinese and Portuguese middlemen, English and French ships made regular ports of call in Canton in South China. Although the Dutch tea trade had at first corresponded to its English counterpart in terms of quantity, in time the English gained the upper hand. Falling tea prices and the reduction of the customs duty on tea during the 1780s allowed it to become a staple good in England and Scotland that, consumed with milk and sugar, also made a hot meal. Tea also attained great popularity in the Netherlands, while consumption in the rest of Europe lagged behind.[18]

In Germany, Hamburg, with its strong English and Dutch connections, stood out as a bastion of tea-drinking culture. By the early eighteenth century, local medical writers were promoting tea, along with coffee. An example is Stephanus Blancardus with his *Haustus polychresti: Oder Zuverlässige Gedancken vom Theé, Coffeé, Chocolate, u. Taback, mit welchen der grosse Nutze dieser ausländischen Wahren so wol in gesunden als krancken Tagen gründlich und umständlich gelehret wird* ('Haustus polychresti: Or reliable thoughts on tea, coffee, chocolate and tobacco, in which the great benefit of these foreign goods, in health and in sickness, is explained in depth and detail').[19]

One indicator of the spread of coffee and tea is their adoption as everyday drinks. Ethnographers have studied the role of coffee and tea in weekday meals.[20] They have discovered that around 1800, drinking coffee was also a widespread daily practice among farm servants in Westphalia, Hesse and Saxony, while in East Frisia porridge was gradually being replaced as a breakfast food by tea and bread. One must also distinguish socially between the wealthy marsh farmers (*Marschbauern*), who favoured imported products such as rice, raisins, sugar, coffee and tea, and the poorer *Geestbauern* (with less fertile soil) among whom at most the farm owner himself drank coffee or tea, while the labourers made do with butter and milk. In East Frisia, coffee and tea were at least served when farmers went visiting, and appear to have entered everyday use via the detour of Sunday consumption. The analogies to the urban 'coffee circle' (*Caffee-Cränzgen*) are unmistakeable. There were differences in coffee consumption within regions in both Schleswig-Holstein and West and East Prussia, where coffee and tea were far more widespread in the coastal marsh regions than in the less fertile areas of the uplands and hinterland, where beer frequently still dominated.

Outside of the large cities, coffee consumption was surprisingly low in southern Germany and Austria. This is indicated not just by the absence of prohibitions on coffee, which cannot be explained solely by the predilection for coffee of rulers such as Maria Theresia. Only towards the end of the eighteenth century, when coffee consumption rose substantially, were such prohibition measures discussed, and, during the period of the Continental blockade (1810–13), actually instituted. Although Josef Richter wrote in his 1800 *Das alte und das neue Wien* ('The Old and the New Vienna'), 'Then: coffee – the breakfast of ladies and the propertied classes; Now: coffee – the breakfast of fruit sellers and hucksters (*Obst- und Fratschelweiber*)',[21] in most rural areas coffee was served only in the houses of rich farmers and members of the middle classes, and then only on Sundays and holidays.

Rural manufacturing regions such as Vorarlberg, where cotton mill workers were already drinking coffee in the 1780s, were the exception. A similar situation was reported for the Berchtesgadener Land, where many local people were employed in cottage industry.[22]

Compared to coffee, tea remained a *quantité négligéable* in southern Germany. It was said even of Vienna that 'Very little tea is drunk here … . When one does get tea, it is ruined with lemon peel and cinnamon, and served in coffee cups.' Other travellers made fun of the uncultivated Viennese women who not only dressed in an antiquated fashion but also knew nothing about tea-drinking culture: 'The ladies of rank are still exclusively devoted to coffee and chocolate. Foreign teas they reject, and domestic ones they regard solely as medicine.'[23] Chocolate, which had to be imported from Spain, Portugal and France and was correspondingly expensive, was somewhat more popular here.[24]

Economic and social preconditions

In search of statistical material to estimate the relative role of coffee and tea consumption, we are dependent on figures on the importation and pricing of these products. For Hamburg, we have import figures in the form of the admiralty duties, which, given Hamburg's role as the main point of entry, provides the figures for Germany more generally. This source permits us to trace coffee and tea imports only indirectly via the goods on which duty was paid. The figures, as indicated in the bar graphs, nevertheless illustrate the development of imports for the two products.[25]

Coffee imports increased steadily over the eighteenth century, with the sharpest rise in the final decade. Tea imports, in contrast, remained constant at a far lower level, which, however, also rose in the 1790s. Apart from an increase in the amounts imported, higher prices may also have been responsible for this rise, since they were reflected in a higher value for goods on which duty was paid. With that in mind, let us look at the developments indicated by Figures 18 and 19, which are based on the Hamburg price lists.[26]

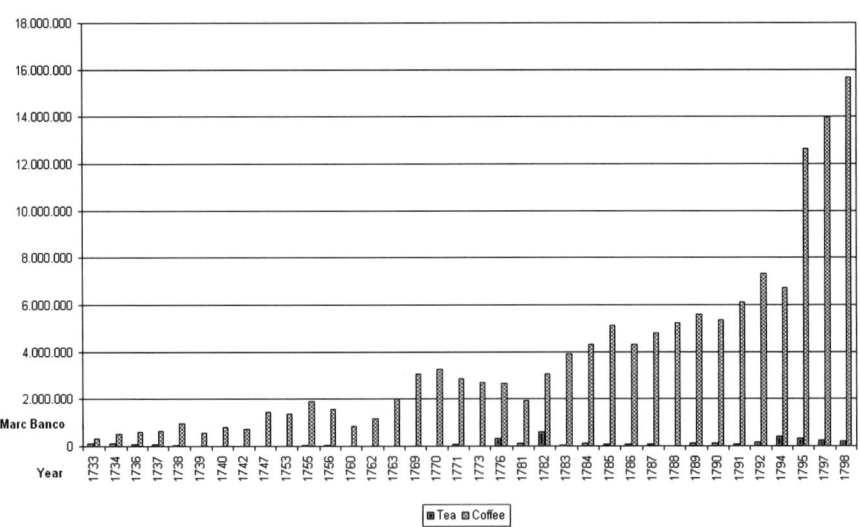

Figure 18   Tea and coffee imports into Hamburg (eighteenth century)

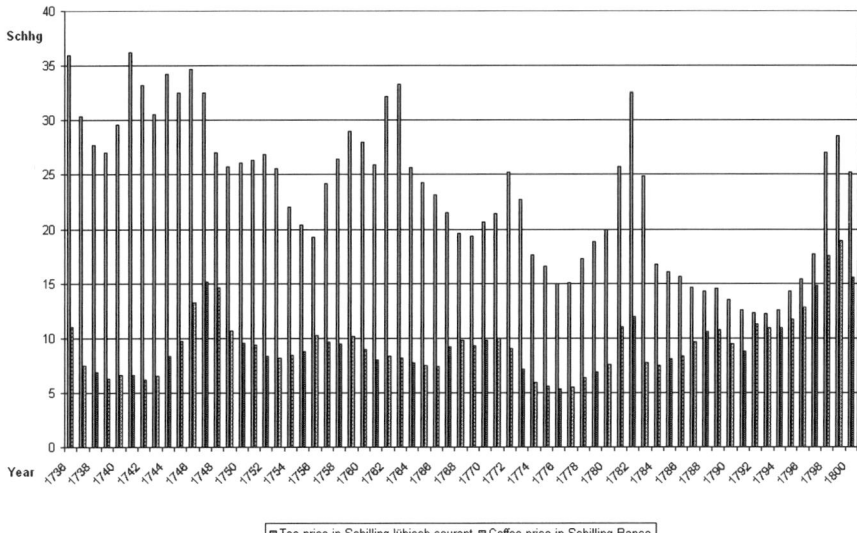

Figure 19   Tea and coffee prices in Hamburg (eighteenth century)

Tea was significantly more expensive than coffee during most years. Even if the prices for the two commodities are given in different currencies (coffee in 'bank' schilling and tea in 'lübisch courant' schilling, a local coinage used in Hamburg and Lübeck) and the coffee price had to be raised by approximately one-quarter to attain full comparability, when our records begin in 1736, one pound of Chinese brown tea cost three times as much as one pound of coffee from Martinique. Nevertheless, the price of tea fell markedly over the entire period in question, while coffee prices dropped only slightly in the 1770s. Accordingly, tea and coffee prices approached parity in the last decade of the eighteenth century, when tea prices reached their nadir and coffee became ever dearer. Among these long-term developments, several sharp jumps in prices stand out, particularly for tea, which can readily be connected with disturbances in intercontinental trade. These included the War of the Austrian Succession in the 1740s, the final phase of the Seven Years' War (1759–63), the Anglo-Dutch War of the 1780s and the latter phase of the American Revolution as well as the Napoleonic Wars at the end of the century, which caused a rise in prices for both commodities. Rises in grain prices may have had the opposite effect, to the extent that they limited the demand for coffee.[27] The fact that coffee prices fluctuated less than tea prices would seem to indicate that the coffee supply was less sensitive to crises than the tea supply. Although coffee imports fell in the years 1760–62 and 1781, the quantities of imports remained large enough, in comparison to tea, to keep the price stable.

At least as interesting as this observation of a long-term fall in tea prices and a stabilization of coffee prices on a low level is a comparison with the price structure or with general income developments. Only such a comparison allows us to assess how affordable these drinks were for the population. If we look at other prices, such as those for foodstuffs, there is a certain parallel development, at least with the price of coffee. Food prices also remained relatively stable in the second half of the century, although the Seven Years' War and crop failures in the early 1770s led to inflation and the general rise in price levels at the end of the century that affected all goods. If we go a step further and examine income development, local studies have found rising nominal incomes, for example for municipal employees in Göttingen, up to the end of the eighteenth century. If we take into account price developments in the early 1760s and 1770s, however, real incomes, which were also rising, lost in value as a result of inflation. Lower income groups, in particular, suffered a serious loss of real income. They will thus have profited little from the stable coffee price or the falling price of tea. For the rising middle- and higher-income groups, in contrast, coffee became ever cheaper and tea increasingly affordable. Moreover, there is evidence that in other European regions (such as England), people were consuming more, although statistically speaking real wages stagnated or even dropped. Did they refrain from satisfying other needs, or was consumption restricted to certain social strata?[28] The available sources do not permit us to answer this question.

Everyday culture and propaganda

Once again, it is estate inventories that provide information on the new 'paraphernalia' of home coffee and tea consumption. We owe many of our insights to the studies of Ruth Mohrmann on the Brunswick region, but in the meantime research has also been done on Frankfurt, Hamburg, the university town of Greifswald and other Baltic cities, such as Stralsund, Copenhagen, Danzig and Riga.[29] According to these sources, coffee as well as the equipment for serving coffee and tea is first mentioned in the late seventeenth century. In the duchy of Brunswick-Wolfenbüttel, for example, these mentions all refer to noble households or ducal officials. Thus, in 1678, the widow of the Abbot of Riddagshausen left 'a bag with Turkish beans', while in 1695, at his estate at Groß Twülpstedt, the judicial official *Hofgerichtsassessor* Conring already owned (among other things), 'a pewter teapot ... a coffee pot, a tea caddy, ... two old Hamburg tea mugs (*näpgen*), an earthenware teapot [and] a small tea table with two boxes'.[30] Wolfenbüttel Privy Legation Councillor Carl Heinrich von Bötticher, a high court official, had a more exquisite assortment of paraphernalia. In 1745, he owned:

> In silver – one coffee pot (*Kanne*), one milk jug, one little teapot, one sugar box, one tea caddy, one sugar caddy, 11 teaspoons, 1 coffee pot (*Topf*); in brass – 1 tea urn, one teapot with a pewter spirit lamp; in pewter – 1 chocolate pot, 1 small teapot; in tin – 1 small tea caddy, 2 tea canisters, 1 canister with tea; in porcelain – 5 ½ pair of cups in blue and white with real gold, 1 bowl in the same pattern, 1 sugar bowl

with a lid, 6 pairs of small multicoloured cups, 1 teapot, 1 white imitation porcelain milk pot, 1 sugar bowl with a lid, 1 chocolate mug, 6 brown coffee cups, 2 chocolate mugs, 1 teapot of terra sigillata [a kind of pottery], 1 paper bag filled with coffee beans.[31]

The Wolfenbüttel aulic councillor Alexander maintained similarly high standards in 1780:

> A coffee and tea service of Dresden porcelain, including: one coffee pot with a saucer, one cream jug, one teapot, one slop bowl, one sugar bowl, a dozen coffee cups, a half dozen tea cups, a half dozen chocolate cups – 15 rtl 14 gr, a small tea service of the same porcelain; one teapot with saucer, one milk jug with ditto, one slop bowl, five pair of teacups – 2 rtl, one dozen Sawan coffee cups – 1 rtl 10 gr, one small bowl with a plate of Sawan porcelain – 9 gr, five blue East Indian tea bowls [*Köpfgen*], one blue East Indian sugar bowl – 9 kr 6 dn, five ditto saucers, one little cup of the same porcelain, 2 gr 6 dn, one teapot with metal fittings of East Indian porcelain 9 gr 6 dn, one ditto of terra sigillata – 2 gr, one coffee pot, one teapot, one sugar bowl, one tea tin, one slop bowl, four saucers, two cups of blue and white Dresden porcelain, nearly all badly damaged – 12 gr.[32]

While the above-mentioned group was relatively homogeneous socially, Frankfurt and Hamburg reveal clear differences, both socially and chronologically, despite the limited number of inventories studied. The social spectrum ranged from the merchant and court Jew Joseph Süß Oppenheimer, whose property in Frankfurt was seized in 1737, to the blacksmith Augustin Geißemer. In addition to a 'packet of coffee beans' and a 'portion of chocolate', Joseph Süß possessed all of the necessary equipment to prepare coffee, tea and chocolate, a corresponding selection of services and a coffee table:

> 6 pairs of brown coffee cups and saucers, … 1 little brown teapot, 1 little Dresden teapot and 2 ditto bowls and 2 cups …, 4 linen coffee-table cloths …, 1 brass coffee pot, 1 ditto coffee kettle …, 3 large and small ditto [in copper] tea kettles, 1 ditto chocolate pot.[33]

Forty years later, the paraphernalia of coffee and tea consumption owned by the wealthy couple Dr and Mrs Tanner had become considerably more varied:

> 1 tea kettle with a coal pan, 2 teapots, 2 small ditto …, 2 copper tea kettles, 1 small coffee kettle …, 2 brass coffee kettles …, 1 ditto tea urn …, 2 old tea tables …, 1 coffee kettle with a wooden handle …, 1 ditto tea urn, 1 ditto coffee pot with a spigot, 1 ditto coffee [pot] …, 1 teapot with wooden handle [silver] …, 5 teapots [silver], one coffee tray [silver] …, 2 tea bottles …, 9 blue and white linen coffee-table cloths …, 3 small cotton coffee-table cloths …, 1 yellow coffee pot [porcelain] …, 1 ditto teapot …, 6 ditto chocolate mugs, 6 pair ditto teacups, 1 ditto tea bottle …, 6 pair brown coffee cups, painted inside with blue and red flowers, 8 coffee cups and 5 coffee bowls with blue flowers, 4 cups and 5 bowls with green and red flowers, 6 bowls and 6 brown coffee cups …, 6 blue and white chocolate mugs, 12 cups and

12 bowls white with coloured flowers …, 2 ditto teapots …, 6 pairs of grey and blue teacups …, 1 teapot with saucer …, 2 lacquer coffee tables, 1 coffee table with oilcloth …, 1 figured damask coffee-table cloth …, 2 coffee tables with oilcloth …, 1 pewter tea tray …, 3 lacquer coffee trays, 1 walnut ditto …, 5 teapots …, 2 coffee kettles …, 3 coffee pots …, 1 brass tea kettle.[34]

The blacksmith Geißemer, in contrast, left behind (in addition to cash and invested capital) only the necessities for preparing coffee (and tea):

1 coffee table with oilcloth …, 1 copper teapot; 1 coffee pot with a spigot [pewter] …, 2 coffee pots [pewter], 1 teapot [pewter], 1 small ditto …, 1 coffee pot [copper] …, 1 coffee kettle [brass] …, 12 chocolate cups in a basket …, 1 brass coffee pot …, 1 coffee pot [pewter], 1 teapot [pewter].[35]

Only the '12 chocolate cups in a basket' seem out of place here. Chocolate, the drink of the nobility and the rich, otherwise played only a minor role in ordinary households. The household possessions of Anna Plaehn of Hamburg confirm this. Despite her wealth – she left her heirs 12,000 marks in invested capital alone – she drank only coffee and tea. Apart from various sorts of tea (Bohea tea, green tea, Congou tea), in which she may have traded, the following items stand out:

One tea tray [silver], five teaspoons …, two coffee kettles and one ditto lid [copper] …, two tea kettles and one ditto lid [copper] …, one teapot with spirit lamp [copper] …, one coffee pot with three spigots [brass], one ditto with one spigot, one tea kettle with a spirit lamp [brass] …, one coffee burner with a foot [iron] …, one coffee pot [tin] …, one red tea table with gold lacquer–, one small tea table covered in oilcloth …, seven pairs of multicoloured porcelain teacups, six pair of ditto coffee cups, one teapot [porcelain] …, one tea caddy [porcelain] …, two metal teaspoons …, one wooden tea stand …, one old tea chest …, one flame-coloured [*feuern*] coffee chair …, several small old tea chests.[36]

In the provinces and small towns, the array of implements was far simpler. Even citizens of the university town of Greifswald generally only owned the utensils for preparing the new drinks, although some certainly could have afforded fine coffee and tea services. As early as 1749, the first tea table as well as teacups appear in the records for Greifswald, and in 1777 Magister Zienssen already owned four tea tables, and his household effects also included twelve teaspoons as well as two sugar spoons, one of them gilded.[37] Coffee consumption dominated here at any rate, which probably held true for the rural areas and the less well-off classes in Germany overall.

In Stralsund, too, the probate inventories give evidence of coffee- and tea-drinking. Diedrich Meyers Weyland's belongings, recorded in 1738, were particularly rich in this regard. Apart from the mention of a separate 'coffee room' (*Caffee-Stube*) we also find numerous utensils such as silver, pewter, brass or tin tea and coffee pots and kettles.[38]

Several different porcelain services, if possible from the Fürstenberg, Dresden or Meissen manufactures, together with a few elegant silver pots such as we find in the household of Dr Tanner were the height of table culture and thus limited to the aristocratic functional elites and wealthy bourgeois.[39] Nevertheless, English imports – whether of solid silver or more affordable stoneware – as well as numerous imitations increasingly found buyers. This is also evident in the rising numbers of tea urns and the extensive import collection offered by Friedrich Justin Bertuch. An example of Bertuch's clever marketing of the new fashion for tea appeared in the *Journal des Luxus und der Moden* in 1788. He first has an author rail against excessive tea consumption, then uses this attack to advertise the new tea style and the accompanying accessories, particularly the tea urn depicted in the article:

> Tea drinking, which has become so popular of late, is a harmful luxury that, like other comforts and pleasures, creeps over to us from England and, particularly in the higher class of the beau monde, has become practically universal. People visit each other towards evening for tea; the ladies love to gather at the tea table at six o'clock, to sit around familiarly, to chat and joke. This is the English custom, now, alas, transplanted to Germany. England is the first country in the world to consume huge quantities of tea annually, surely more than China herself, because nearly everyone in England drinks tea daily, without any of the strikingly devastating detriments to health noticed in other countries. In England, tea drinking is somewhat less damaging to the health because one eats luncheon quite late there, and often not at all in the evenings, and consumes many strong dishes and drinks, which are diluted and moderated by tea. In addition, one must mention the frequent and intense movement to which the English are given, and that in England little, if any, coffee is drunk. All of these are circumstances that differ from our own, particularly among the ladies. Our more distinguished beau monde mainly leads a sedentary, quiet, I might even say idle, life, drinks lighter wines and beers, but coffee twice a day, and eats softer but also fattier foods and pastries than the English – all of these circumstances that necessarily render the additional daily use of tea deleterious.[40] ... As gladly as we admit that the sparing use of tea, as a remedy that opens the pores and promotes transpiration, can be beneficial, and the tea table can contribute to the comforts of life, we must still agree with the author of the preceding article both that the excessive and daily enjoyment of tea is damaging given our general way of life, and that we have learnt this luxury mainly from England. The entire tasteful apparatus of an English tea table, and the handsome form and material of an English tea set, demonstrates this ... .[41]

While Bertuch promoted tea consumption and thereby propagated a new culture of drinking and sociability, the late absolutist states tried to contain the new stimulants with legislation, as coffee and tea consumption were held responsible for the outflow of money from the territories, thereby damaging domestic industry and impoverishing the inhabitants. We accordingly find such ordinances above all in those territories of northern and western Germany where the consumption of coffee was widespread. These included the Duchy

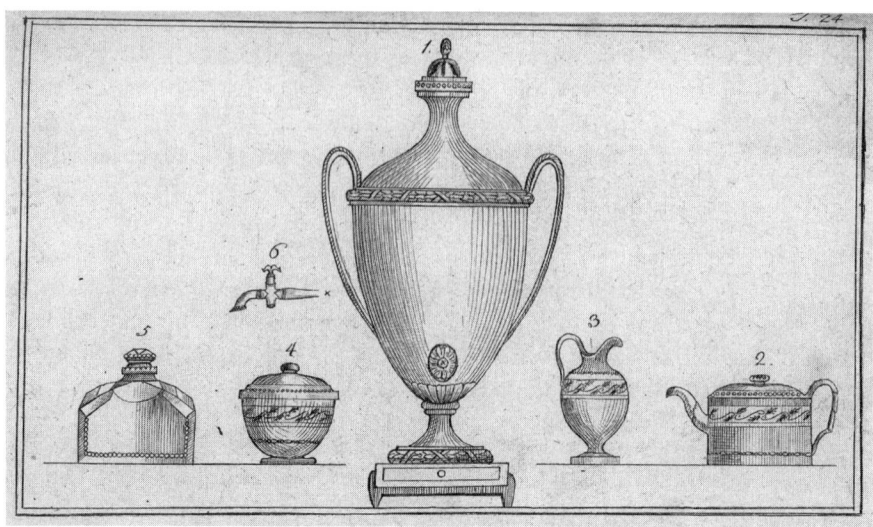

Figure 20 Tea urn and accessories from England. Illustration from the *Journal des Luxus und der Moden*, August 1788

of Braunschweig (1764), the bishoprics of Münster (1766), Hildesheim (1768) and Paderborn (1777), Hesse-Kassel (1766–73), Hesse-Darmstadt (1766–75), Electoral Hanover (1780), the County of Lippe (1781) and the regions of Ravensberg and Minden (1768–81), which belonged to Brandenburg-Prussia. Here, for example, an edict issued in 1768 by King Frederick II opposed 'the excessive drinking of coffee and tea among common citizens, tradesmen, day labourers and servants as well as farmers, tenants, cotters, millers and the like …'.[42]

Although warnings about daily or frequent coffee drinking appear exaggerated to us, the essay competitions organized by academies and societies illustrate the widespread concern about the economic and social consequences of coffee consumption. In 1777, the meeting of the *Königliche und Kurfürstliche Landwirtschaftsgesellschaft zu Celle* (Royal and Electoral Agricultural Society at Celle) addressed five questions on the subject, which archdeacon Johann Heinrich Reiß of Wolfenbüttel – himself presumably a great coffee and tea drinker – answered as follows under the rubric 'New Expenses':

> Some new expenses are occasioned by 1. The purchase of porcelain … . Fashion demands that one have cups not just for one's own daily use, but also special ones for visitors … . 2. The wholly novel expansion of household goods to include the other coffee utensils. One now needs burners, mills, pots and various small items that our forefathers did not require … . 3. The installation of reception rooms, which in most houses undoubtedly owe their origins to coffee, since all old people know that at the beginning of the century they existed in very few houses, because one did not need them until it became the done thing for the lady of the house, at

least, to receive visitors for coffee ... . 4. Finally, expenses for coffee and its actual accoutrements ... . In most places, the livelihood of brewers fell to the degree that the use of coffee increased ... .[43]

A new form of sociability entered German households along with coffee- and tea-drinking, permanently transforming domestic material culture and everyday life. All the prohibitions in the world were powerless against it. On the contrary, the legislation met with opposition and protests, for example in Hesse-Kassel, where merchants and the burghers of Marburg petitioned to be included in the group of privileged coffee consumers (*vornehmere Kaufleute und Fabricanten ... und sonsten Leute von gewissem Ansehen*).[44]

Coffee consumption rose steadily, and was even promoted by the cheaper coffee surrogates. The most important of these surrogates – propagated and privileged by the Prussian state and marketed in blue cylindrical packages under the name of 'Prussian coffee' – was chicory. It had already gained many adherents before the Continental blockade made it truly popular.[45]

Conclusion

Cultural Consumption and Identity

As this study has shown, eighteenth-century Germany participated in the European process of cultural commercialization and thus in the international community of cultural consumption. Although the German states were several days' journey from the great centres of cultural exchange such as London and Paris, German merchants and periodicals made pictures, books and objects of everyday use as well as fashion trends, theatrical performances and concerts accessible to a growing number of cultural consumers – whether materially or virtually. Art dealers and connoisseurs stimulated international artistic taste by encouraging rulers and citizens to collect Dutch landscape paintings. Impresarios and dilettantes – along with learned and music journals – helped create a market for German composers, whose work began to supplement the Italian and French traditions that had dominated concert programmes in Germany as well as Western Europe up to that point. In addition, French and English fashions vied with each other in the luxury journals for influence over the homes and gardens of German burghers and aristocratic functional elites.

Cultural consumption helped connoisseurs and amateurs to overcome the 'ennui of Reason'.[1] In the process, taste preferences became increasingly similar, for aristocrats and the middle classes participated equally in the new cultural offerings. At the 'courts of the Muses' at Weimar or Karlsruhe, rulers, particularly women, tried their hands at literature, painting, music or garden design, together with wealthy bourgeois with whom they communicated to an extent we should not underestimate. Without one estate explicitly emulating the other, taste emerged in the exchange between bourgeois and aristocratic collectors, amateur musicians and composers as the product of a process of social communication.

The need for entertainment also brought people together, for although nobles and commoners sat in separate parts of the theatre, they watched the same plays, often enough applauding and whistling together in the 'wrong places', read the same *Räuberromane* (novels about noble brigands) and devoured the monthly fashion news and gossip from the European capitals in the *Journal des Luxus und der Moden*. The cultural marketplace had made culture available to the paying public, a circumstance that neither aristocrats nor the middle classes regretted. The courts set their own standards of taste ever more rarely, although they took their role as patrons and mediators of culture quite seriously. Accordingly – contrary to frequent claims by scholars – we find no emancipatory bourgeois taste that distanced itself from the courts. It was not until the nineteenth century that the educated middle classes appropriated culture as their exclusive field of endeavour, transforming it into a sort of bourgeois substitute religion, from which they largely banished elements of entertainment, pleasure and variety.[2] The *Journal des Luxus und der Moden*, which is often cited in the literature as 'bourgeois',[3] also pursued the strategy of aristocratic–middle class rapprochement, for example when it postulated that 'the union of the learned with the circles of so-called fashionable society [*feine Welt*]' was a prerequisite for 'true enlightenment'.[4] Thus such findings as Maxine Berg's for England – that it was the middling classes who changed consumer practices by decorating their homes with the new objects[5] – do not apply to the German territories.

Here, eighteenth-century cultural consumers were recruited from the traditional urban burghers (*Stadtbürger*), out of which, according to Lothar Gall, the modern bourgeoisie later emerged.[6] It was the urban world of Hamburg, Frankfurt or Offenbach where the master confectioner Prehn could distinguish himself as an art connoisseur, or the snuff manufacturer Peter Bernard as an amateur violin virtuoso and orchestra founder, and where Dr Tanner and his wife attracted attention with their tasteful and elegant home furnishings. The new middle-class groups described by Hans-Ulrich Wehler also formed part of the audience for the new cultural offerings, however.[7] They included members of the economic bourgeoisie (*Wirtschaftsbürger*) such as the Berlin bankers Ephraim, Itzig, Daum or Splitgerber. In Berlin as well as the many princely residences in Germany, one should also mention the functional elites, officials closely associated with the court. These men, generally of aristocratic origins, made up a majority of both the garden owners and art collectors in Berlin. They also frequented the reading societies in capitals such as Bonn, Trier or Detmold, and played a pioneering role in innovative domestic interiors.

As to the regional distribution of cultural consumption, in many cases the absence of relevant studies permits only an impressionistic sketch. Nonetheless, if we take into account not just writing and the book trade but also art, music, theatre and material culture, we find ample evidence to qualify the (pre)conceptions concerning the dominance of the north German Protestant Enlightenment in Germany. To be sure, journal production and also art criticism were clearly dominated by northern Germans, but entertainment periodicals such as the *Journal des Luxus und der Moden* also had large numbers of subscribers in southern Germany. People's preferences in reading matter and their need for entertainment (if we think of the lending libraries) also did not differ significantly between north and south. Theatre programmes, with their strong emphasis on entertainment, even reveal substantial overlaps on the stages all over Germany. With the predilection for Dutch and Flemish masters, artistic tastes were also homogeneous. This was a pan-European trend which is also documented for England or France in the second half of the eighteenth century.

Such findings point to European cultural influences and their reception in Germany. These existed not just in art, but also in the fields of theatre, fashion, travel destinations and everyday culture. Chapter 3 above on fashion uncovers a certain north–south divide in respect of the influence of English and French models, but the cultural fault-lines could also run through families. In the long run, however, even southern Germans could not resist certain English influences, such as landscape gardening or tea parties.

These observations raise the question of whether identities were perhaps created in a manner rather different to that previously posited in the literature. Traditionally, historians have assumed that collective identities – or 'imagined communities' (Benedict Anderson) – could be linked above all to geopolitical units such as the state, the territory or the town. Only the nation or language as more abstract models of integration have been accorded a comparable function.[8]

Our examination of the eighteenth century has shown that consumption – including cultural consumption – also created identities. Thus, those who played music as amateurs, experienced art directly or consumed culture virtually through the magazines had a sense of belonging to the new European community of cultural consumers. Regardless of social or geographical location, one could be an art connoisseur, listen to or play pieces by the 'in' composers with other music lovers, tour ancient sites in Italy or enjoy the experience of landscape in Switzerland, dress in the Parisian or London style, and be as proud of German composers as one was of one's London-made 'cameo buttons'.

At the same time, devotees of culture also saw themselves as consumers, for instance in 1778 when the Munich theatre public claimed the right to whistle even in the presence of the elector – with the argument that they had, after all, paid admission.[9] This role of consumer was constructed in various ways in the journals and intelligence gazettes. The *Journal des Luxus und der Moden*, for example, created the role of the cultural consumer through systematic product information, overviews of the market and advertisements, and even addressed this clientele directly as 'ladies of taste' or 'connoisseurs of fine and beneficent luxury'.[10] After all, the articles, illustrations and advertisements demonstrated to readers which home furnishings were indispensable for an elegant way of life. References to the local production of luxury goods also created a further regional location and identity for consumption and taste. This also applied to the print editions sold by art dealers or the newest sheet music, which – although published in different parts of Germany – could be purchased through periodicals with local roots. The periodicals instructed their readers in matters of taste while confirming – as the journal *Charis* did in 1805 for the 'cultivated' ladies of Leipzig – their vast superiority 'in the culture of taste and manners' to the 'female world' of other cities.[11] In this way, they located (cultural) consumers, regardless of their regional or national roots, in a European culture of taste. Regional and national identities thus entered into dialogue with the 'entire cultivated world'.[12]

Notes

Introduction

1. Jürgen Habermas, *The Structural Transformation of the Public Sphere: An Inquiry into a Category of Bourgeois Society*, trans. Thomas Burger (Cambridge, MA, 1991). There is a vast literature on both the Enlightenment and Habermas. For an overview, see Roy Porter, *The Enlightenment* (2nd edn, Basingstoke, 2001), and Barbara Stollberg-Rilinger, *Europa im Jahrhundert der Aufklärung* (Stuttgart, 2000). For a critical appreciation of Habermas's notion of the public sphere, see James V.H. Melton, *The Rise of the Public in Enlightenment Europe* (Cambridge, 2001), pp. 1–15, and Tim C.W. Blanning, *The Culture of Power and the Power of Culture* (Oxford, 2002), pp. 5–14.
2. For an incisive account, see Carsten Zelle, 'Kunstmarkt, Kennerschaft und Geschmack. Zu Theorie und Praxis in der Zeit zwischen Barthold Heinrich Brockes und Christian Ludwig von Hagedorn', in Michael North (ed.), *Kunstsammeln und Geschmack im 18. Jahrhundert* (Berlin, 2002), pp. 217–38, here pp. 217–18. The quotation from Bertuch comes from the introduction to the first number of the *Journal des Luxus und der Moden* (January 1786), pp. 4–5. It is also reproduced in its entirety on p. 46 below.
3. Cf. Joachim Berger, 'Geselligkeit, Mäzenatentum und Kunstliebhaberei am "Musenhof" Anna Amalias – Neue Ergebnisse, neue Fragen', in Joachim Berger (ed.), *Der Musenhof Anna Amalias. Geselligkeit, Mäzenatentum und Kunstliebhaberei im klassischen Weimar* (Cologne, Weimar and Vienna, 2001), pp. 1–17. Ute Daniel, 'Höfe und Aufklärung in Deutschland – Plädoyer für eine Begegnung der dritten Art', in Marcus Ventzke (ed.), *Hofkultur und aufklärerische Reformen in Thüringen. Die Bedeutung des Hofes im späten 18. Jahrhundert* (Cologne, Weimar and Vienna, 2002), pp. 11–31.
4. John Brewer, '"The most polite age and the most vicious". Attitudes towards Culture as a Commodity, 1660–1800', in Ann Bermingham and John Brewer (eds), *The Consumption of Culture 1600–1800. Image, Object, Text* (London and New York, 1995), pp. 341–61, here pp. 348–9.
5. John Brewer, *The Pleasures of the Imagination: English Culture in the Eighteenth Century* (London, 1997), p. xviii.
6. Immanuel Kant, *Anthropology from a Pragmatic Point of View*, ed. Robert B. Louden (Cambridge, 2006), p. 137. Further down on the same page, Kant then concludes: 'Taste is, accordingly, a faculty of making social judgments of external objects within the power of imagination.'
7. Brewer, *Pleasures*.
8. Neil McKendrick, John Brewer, and J.H. Plumb, *The Birth of a Consumer Society: The Commercialization of Eighteenth-Century England* (London, 1982), pp. 9–33.
9. Carole Shammas, *The Pre-Industrial Consumer in England and America* (Oxford, 1990); Jan de Vries, 'The Industrial Revolution and the Industrious Revolution', *The Journal of Economic History*, 54/2 (1994): 249–70, and 'Between Purchasing Power and the

World of Goods', in John Brewer and Roy Porter (eds), *Consumption and the World of Goods* (London, 1993), pp. 85–132, Lisa Jardine, *Worldly Goods: A New History of the Renaissance* (London, 1996).

10. The literature on this period is immense. Important overviews are Susan Strasser, Charles McGovern and Matthias Judt (eds), *European and American Consumer Societies in the Twentieth Century* (Cambridge, 1998); Victoria de Grazia and Ellen Furlough (eds), *The Sex of Things: Gender and Consumption in Historical Perspective* (Berkeley, CA, 1996); Martin Daunton and Mathew Hilton (eds), *The Politics of Consumption: Material Culture and Citizenship in Europe and America* (Oxford, 2001); Erika Diane Rapaport, *Shopping for Pleasure: Women and the Making of London's West End* (Princeton, 2000); Michele Michelletti (ed.), *Political Virtue and Shopping: Individuals, Consumerism, and Collective Action* (Basingstoke, 2003); Don Slater, *Consumer Culture and Modernity* (Cambridge, 1997); Heinz-Gerhard Haupt, *Konsum und Handel: Europa im 19. und 20. Jahrhundert* (Göttingen, 2003); Lisbeth Cohen, *A Consumer's Republic: The Politics of Mass Consumption in Postwar America* (New York, 2003).

11. W.W. Rostow, *The Stages of Economic Growth: A Non-Communist Manifesto* (Cambridge, 1960).

12. This is particularly evident in the German responses to this scholarship in Michael Prinz (ed.), *Der lange Weg in den Überfluss. Anfänge und Entwicklung der Konsumgesellschaft seit der Vormoderne* (Paderborn, 2003).

13. The two volumes that emerged from the Cultures of Consumption programme (based at Birkbeck College, London) are fundamental here. Frank Trentmann (ed.), *The Making of the Consumer: Knowledge, Power and Identity in the Modern World* (Oxford and New York, 2006), and John Brewer and Frank Trentmann (eds), *Consuming Cultures, Global Perspectives: Historical Trajectories, Transnational Exchanges* (Oxford and New York, 2006).

14. Craig Clunas, *Superfluous Things: Material Culture and Social Status in Early Modern China* (Chicago, 1991). On the underestimation of China more generally, in this context as well, see Kenneth Pomeranz, *The Great Divergence: China, Europe and the Making of the Modern World Economy* (Princeton, 2000).

15. Maxine Berg, *Luxury and Pleasure in Eighteenth-Century Britain* (Oxford, 2005).

16. Frank Trentmann, 'The Modern Genealogy of the Consumer: Meanings, Identities and Political Synapses', in Brewer and Trentmann (eds), *Consuming Cultures*, pp. 19–69, and 'Knowing Consumers – Histories, Identities, Practices: An Introduction', in *Making of the Consumer*, pp. 1–27.

17. According to Frank Trentmann: 'Instead of working within a self-defined theory of mass consumer society, historians need to contextualize the different forms and functions of consumption, and the affiliated social visions and political systems competing with each other at the same time.' 'Beyond Consumerism: New Perspectives on Consumption', *Journal of Contemporary History*, 39(3) (2004): 373–401, quote on p. 398.

Chapter 1

1. 'Ich laß in Swift und blätterte … in den Göttingischen Anzeigen. Ich hätte gern noch im Swift gelesen, fürchtete mich aber mich zu sehr an diese Lecture zu

gewöhnen'. *Johann Anton Leisewitzens Tagebücher*, ed. Heinrich Mack and Johannes Lochner (2 vols, Weimar, 1920), vol. 2, p. 104.

2. 'Heute sollte nun gewaltig scharf gearbeitet werden, aber der Morgen ging wieder vor die Hunde. Früh laß ich im Shandy und kam wieder ziemlich ins Faullenzen … .' Ibid., vol. 1, p. 216.

3. 'Ich laß bey dem frisiren im Moore und ward dabey ziemlich munter, nachher aber wieder etwas niedergeschlagen, als ich im Whylt blätterte. Ich bemerkte heute wieder, was ich schon so oft bemerkt habe, ungeachtet man schwören sollte, daß ich es nie bemerkt hätte, wie sehr mir dergleichen Lecture schadet'. Ibid., vol. 1, p. 162.

4. Martina Graf, *Buch- und Lesekultur in der Residenzstadt Braunschweig zur Zeit der Spätaufklärung unter Herzog Karl Wilhelm Ferdinand (1770–1806)* (Frankfurt, 1994), pp. 228ff.

5. Rolf Engelsing, 'Die Perioden der Lesegeschichte in der Neuzeit. Das statistische Ausmaß und die soziokulturelle Bedeutung der Lektüre', *Archiv für Geschichte des Buchwesens*, 10 (1970): cols 945–1002. Cf. also Helmut Zedelmaier, 'Lesetechniken. Die Praktiken der Lektüre in der Neuzeit', in Helmut Zedelmaier and Martin Mulsow (eds), *Die Praktiken der Gelehrsamkeit in der Frühen Neuzeit* (Tübingen, 2001), pp. 11–30.

6. Rolf Engelsing, *Der Bürger als Leser. Lesegeschichte in Deutschland 1500–1800* (Stuttgart, 1974), p. 198. A more differentiated analysis of the reading practises than in Engelsing can be found in Roger Chartier, *The Cultural Uses of Print in Early Modern France*, trans. Lydia G. Cochrane (Princeton, 1987).

7. Holger Böning, *Das Intelligenzblatt. Dokumentation zu einer literarisch-publizistischen Gattung der deutschen Aufklärung* (Bremen, 1991), and 'Das Intelligenzblatt', in Ernst Tischer, Wilhelm Haefs and York-Gothart Mix (eds), *Von Almanach bis Zeitung. Ein Handbuch der Medien in Deutschland 1700–1800* (Munich, 1999), pp. 89–104. See also Sabine Doering-Manteuffel, Josef Mančal and Wolfgang Wüst (eds), *Pressewesen der Aufklärung. Periodische Schriften im Alten Reich* (Berlin, 2001).

8. Wolfgang Martens, *Die Botschaft der Tugend. Die Aufklärung im Spiegel der deutschen Moralischen Wochenschriften* (Stuttgart, 1968); Jörg Scheibe, *Der 'Patriot' (1724–1726) und sein Publikum. Untersuchungen über die Verfasserschaft und die Leserschaft einer Zeitschrift der frühen Aufklärung* (Göppingen, 1973); Martin Krieger, 'Patriotismus-Diskurs und die Konstruktion kollektiver Identitäten in Hamburg in der ersten Hälfte des 18. Jahrhunderts' (Habilitation thesis, University of Greifswald, 2001).

9. Martin Welke, 'Gemeinsame Lektüre und frühe Formen von Gruppenbildung im 17. und 18. Jahrhundert: Zeitungslesen in Deutschland', in Otto Dann (ed.), *Lesegesellschaften und bürgerliche Emanzipation – Ein europäischer Vergleich* (Munich, 1981), pp. 29–53, here p. 30. See also Holger Böning, 'Aufklärung und Presse im 18. Jahrhundert', in Hans-Wolf Jäger (ed.), *'Öffentlichkeit' im 18. Jahrhundert* (Göttingen, 1997), pp. 151–63.

10. Ernst Tischer, Wilhelm Haefs and York-Gothart Mix, 'Aufklärung, Öffentlichkeit und Medienkultur in Deutschland im 18. Jahrhundert', in Tischer, Haefs and Mix (eds), *Von Almanach bis Zeitung. Ein Handbuch der Medien in Deutschland 1700–1800* (Munich, 1999), pp. 18–21. Carsten Zelle proposes a similar estimate in 'Auf dem Spielfeld der Autorschaft. Der Schriftsteller des 18. Jahrhunderts im Kräftefeld von Rhetorik, Medienentwicklung und Literatursystem' in Klaus Städtke and Ralph Kray (eds), *Spielräume des auktorialen Diskurses* (Berlin, 2003), pp. 1–37, here p. 17. On

this basis, Siegfried J. Schmidt has constructed a new 'social system of literature'. See *Die Selbstorganisation des Sozialsystems Literatur im 18. Jahrhundert* (Frankfurt, 1989), pp. 254–72.

11. Zelle, *Auf dem Spielfeld der Autorschaft*, p. 18. Herbert Jaumann, in particular, has pointed to the 'intermediate position' of the author, even in the second half of the eighteenth century, between a corporatist-learned and official literary class and production for the market. See his 'Emanzipation als Positionsverlust. Ein sozialgeschichtlicher Versuch über die Situation des Autors im 18. Jahrhundert', *Zeitschrift für Literaturwissenschaft und Linguistik*, 11 (1981): 46–72.

12. 'Would you like to help me find female readers? You do a good deed for my sons, for I write "Pomona" for my Carl and my Wilhelm, to compensate in some way for what my husband's enemies have stolen from them. God bless you. Bless my enterprise and give me your helping hand.'
    'Wollen Sie beitragen, daß ich Leserinnen bekomme? Sie tun Gutes an meinen Söhnen, denn ich schreibe "Pomona" für meinen Carl und meinen Wilhelm, um in etwa zu ersetzen, was ihnen die Feinde ihres Vaters raubten. Gott segne Sie. Segnen Sie mein Vorhaben und bieten Sie mir die Hand dazu.' Sophie von La Roche to Johann Caspar Lavater, Speyer, 27 October 1782; quoted in Michael Maurer (ed.), *Ich bin mehr Herz als Kopf. Sophie von La Roche. Ein Lebensbild in Briefen* (Leipzig and Weimar, 1985), p. 245.

13. Sigrid Damm, *Christiane und Goethe. Eine Recherche* (Frankfurt, 2001), pp. 102, 174, 212–16.

14. Roberto Simanowski, *Die Verwaltung des Abenteuers. Massenkultur um 1800 am Beispiel Christian August Vulpius* (Göttingen, 1998).

15. Gustav Schwetschke, *Codex nundinarius Germaniae literatae bisecularis. Meß-Jahrbücher des Deutschen Buchhandels*, vol. 1: *Von dem Erscheinen des ersten Meß-Katalogs im Jahre 1564 bis zu der Gründung des ersten Buchhändlervereins im Jahre 1765* (Halle, 1850), pp. 178, 188, 198, 208, 218, 228, 238, 253, 273, 293, 313. The table was compiled from these sources by Maud Antonia Viehberg, *Vom Tauschhandel zum modernen Buchmarkt. Die Etappen des deutschen Buchhandels im 18. Jahrhundert*, MA thesis (University of Greifswald, 2001), p. 121.

16. Reinhard Wittmann, 'Die frühen Buchhändlerzeitschriften als Spiegel des literarischen Lebens', *Archiv für Geschichte des Buchwesens*, 13 (1973): cols 828–9.

17. Viehberg, *Vom Tauschhandel zum modernen Buchmarkt*, pp. 123–4.

18. Table compiled by Robert Riemer according to the figures in Rudolf Jentzsch, *Der deutsch-lateinische Büchermarkt nach den Leipziger Ostermeß-Katalogen von 1740, 1770 und 1800 in seiner Gliederung und Wandlung* (Leipzig, 1912), tables I–III.

19. Jentzsch, *Der deutsch-lateinische Büchermarkt*, p. 315–16. See also Helmuth Kiesel and Paul Münch, *Gesellschaft und Literatur im 18. Jahrhundert. Voraussetzungen und Entstehung des literarischen Marktes in Deutschland* (Munich, 1977), pp. 198–200. Johann Goldfriedrich, *Geschichte des deutschen Buchhandels*, vol. 2 (Leipzig, 1908), pp. 16–18.

20. The category 'general learning' is the only exception.

21. Reinhard Wittmann, *Geschichte des deutschen Buchhandels. Ein Überblick* (Munich, 1991), pp. 115–20; Helga Schultz, 'Der Verleger Friedrich Justin Bertuch als Kaufmann und Literaturpolitiker', in Gerhard R. Kaiser and Siegfried Seifert (eds), *Friedrich Justin Bertuch (1747–1822). Verleger, Schriftsteller und Unternehmer im klassischen Weimar* (Tübingen, 2000), pp. 331–50, here pp. 332–4. For Reich, see also Hazel

Rosenstrauch, *Buchhandelsmanufaktur und Aufklärung. Die Reformen des Buchhändlers und Verlegers Ph. E. Reich (1717–1787)* (Frankfurt, 1986).

22. Horst Möller, *Aufklärung in Preußen. Der Verleger, Publizist und Geschichtsschreiber Friedrich Nicolai* (Berlin, 1974), pp. 80, 99–114.

23. 'Da ist mehr als Ein Verleger, der seinen Autoren aufträgt, was er zu brauchen denkt: Geschichten, Romane, Mordgeschichten, zuverläßige Nachrichten, von Dingen, die man nicht gesehen hat, Beweise von Dingen, die man nicht glaubt, Gedanken, von Sachen, die man nicht versteht. Ich kenne einen, der in seinem Hause an einem langen Tische zehn bis zwölf Autoren sitzen hat, und jedem sein Pensum fürs Tagelohn abzuarbeiten giebt. Ich läugne es nicht, denn warum sollte ich Armuth für Schande halten? ich habe auch an diesem langen Tische gesessen'. Friedrich Nicolai, *Das Leben und die Meinungen des Herrn Magister Sebaldus Nothanker*, vol. 1 (Berlin and Stettin, 1774), p. 97.

24. 'Dieses gelehrte Völkchen von Lehrern und Lernenden, das etwa 20.000 Menschen stark ist, verachtet die übrigen 20 Millionen Menschen, die außer ihnen Deutsch reden, so herzlich, daß es sich nicht die Mühe nimmt, für sie zu schreiben; … . Die zwanzig Millionen Ungelehrte vergelten den 20.000 Gelehrten Verachtung mit Vergessenheit: Sie wissen kaum, daß die Gelehrten in der Welt sind. Weil nun kein Gelehrter für Ungelehrte schreiben will, und dennoch die ungelehrte Welt so gut ihr Bedürfnis zu lesen hat, als die gelehrte, so bleibt das Amt für Ungelehrte zu schreiben, endlich den Verfassern der Inseln Felsenburg, den Postillenschreibern, und der moralischen Wochenblätter, deren Fähigkeiten den Fähigkeiten der Leser, die sie sich gewählt haben, viel genauer entsprechen, als die Fähigkeiten der größten Gelehrten ihren Lesern: die daher weit mehr gelesen werden als die größten Genien, die aber auch ihre Leser nicht um einen Daumen breit höher hinaufheben, die vielmehr sehr oft nicht wenig beytragen, daß das Licht der wahren Gelehrten sich nicht auf die Ungelehrten ausbreitet. Daher sind einige Städte bey uns so helle, und ganze Länder sind in der größten Finsterniß'. Ibid., pp. 122–3. 'Insel Felsenburg' refers to the multi-volume novel by Johann Gottfried Schnabel, *Wunderliche Fata einiger See-Fahrer, absonderlich Alberti Julii, eines gebohrnen Sachsens, und seiner auf der Insel Felsenburg errichteten in vollkommenen Stand gebrachten Colonien* (Nordhausen, 1731–43).

25. Möller, *Aufklärung in Preußen*, pp. 198–208. See also Pamela E. Selwyn, *Everyday Life in the German Book Trade: Friedrich Nicolai as Bookseller and Publisher in the Age of Enlightenment 1750–1810* (University Park, Pennsylvania, 2000).

26. Goethe to Göschen, 27 October 1787; quoted in Karl Otto Conrady, *Goethe. Leben und Werk* (Düsseldorf and Zurich, 1999), p. 626.

27. Conrady, *Goethe*, p. 612. After the publication of six volumes, Göschen compiled an interim bill for Bertuch, which is analysed in Stephan Füssel, *Georg Joachim Göschen. Ein Verleger der Spätaufklärung und der deutschen Klassik*, vol. 1: *Studien zur Verlagsgeschichte und zur Verlegertypologie der Goethe-Zeit* (Berlin and New York, 1999), p. 114. On the complete Goethe edition, see Füssel, pp. 106–25.

28. Göschen to Goethe, 4 July 1791; quoted in Conrady, *Goethe*, p. 612; see Ibid. pp. 624–7 and also Nicholas Boyle, *Goethe. Der Dichter in seiner Zeit*, vol. 1: *1749–1790* (Munich, 1999), pp. 454–5. Siegfried Unseld's *Goethe und seine Verleger* (Frankfurt and Leipzig, 1993) remains inspiring.

29. Füssel, *Verlagsgeschichte*, pp. 91–104.

30. Conrady, *Goethe*, pp. 626–7.

31. For Bertuch's notions concerning a book publishing enterprise in Weimar, see Siegfried Seifert, '"Genie und Lumpen" – Programmatische Entwürfe Bertuchs zur Reform des deutschen Verlagsbuchhandels vor 1800. Überlegungen zu einem Forschungsansatz', in Gerhard R. Kaiser and Siegfried Seifert (eds), *Friedrich Justin Bertuch (1747–1822). Verleger, Schriftsteller und Unternehmer im klassischen Weimar* (Tübingen, 2000), pp. 291–9.

32. See also below, chapter 3.

33. Cf. Walter Steiner and Uta Kühn-Stillmark (eds), *Friedrich Justin Bertuch. Ein Leben im klassischen Weimar zwischen Kultur und Kommerz* (Cologne, Weimar and Vienna, 2001), pp. 42–120.

34. I thank Reiner Flik (Tübingen) for his friendly hint, as well as the data for the map conceived by Robert Riemer. See also Reiner Flik, 'Das Journal des Luxus und der Moden: Produktion, Vertrieb, Geschäftsergebnisse und Leserkreis', in Klaus Manger and Gerhard R. Kaiser (eds), *Das Journal des Luxus und der Moden. Kultur um 1800* (Heidelberg, 2004).

35. Schultz, ,Bertuch', pp. 336–47. On the mercantilist Bertuch, see also Reiner Flik, 'Statt Hofpoet Kulturunternehmer. Der Werdegang Friedrich Justin Bertuchs (1747–1822) und sein Beitrag zur Weimarer Klassik', in Marcus Ventzke (ed.), *Hofkultur und aufklärerische Reformen in Thüringen. Die Bedeutung des Hofes im späten 18. Jahrhundert* (Cologne,Weimar and Vienna 2002), pp. 197–222.

36. Engelsing, *Bürger als Leser.*

37. Reinhard Wittmann (ed.), *Bücherkataloge als buchgeschichtliche Quellen in der frühen Neuzeit* (Wiesbaden, 1984); Roland Folter, *Deutsche Dichter- und Germanistenbibliotheken. Eine kritische Bibliographie ihrer Kataloge* (Stuttgart, 1975).

38. Mechthild Raabe, *Leser und Lektüre im 18. Jahrhundert. Die Ausleihbücher der Herzog August Bibliothek Wolfenbüttel 1714–1799* (4 vols, Munich, London and New York, 1989).

39. Ibid., vol. 1, i–ixxx.

40. Ibid., vol. 4: *Systematisches Verzeichnis der entliehenen Bücher*, p. 577.

41. Ibid., vol. 1, ixxx–ixxxi.

42. Compiled by Martin Krieger and Robert Riemer. Krieger, 'Patriotismus-Diskurs', p. 125. Franklin Kopitzsch, *Grundzüge einer Sozialgeschichte der Aufklärung in Hamburg und Altona,* (2nd edn, Hamburg, 1990), p. 431–3.

43. Engelsing, *Bürger als Leser*, pp. 94–100.

44. Kopitzsch, *Sozialgeschichte*, pp. 428–45.

45. A fundamental work on Brockes is Hans-Georg Kemper, Uwe-K. Ketelsen and Carsten Zelle (eds), *Barthold Heinrich Brockes (1680–1747) im Spiegel seiner Bibliothek und Bildergalerie* (2 vols, Wiesbaden, 1998).

46. Walter Wittmann, *Beruf und Buch im 18. Jahrhundert. Ein Beitrag zur Erfassung und Gliederung der Leserschaft im 18. Jahrhundert, insbesondere unter Berücksichtigung des Einflusses auf die Buchproduktion (Nachlaßinventare 1695–1705, 1746–1755 und 1795–1805)* (Hanover, 1934), pp. 46–59, here p. 51. In eight cases, the type of book could not be reconstructed.

47. Wittmann, *Beruf und Buch*, pp. 68–83.

48. Institut für Stadtgeschichte, Frankfurt, records of the Imperial Chamber Court (ICC Frankfurt) 453, Quad. 15: 'Inventarium des Nachlasses von Augustin Geißemer, aufgenommen in seinem Haus auf der Zeil' (1777).

49. Hildegard Neumann, *Der Bücherbesitz der Tübinger Bürger von 1750–1850* (Munich, 1978), p. 36; Etienne François, 'Buch, Konfession und städtische Gesellschaft im 18. Jahrhundert. Das Beispiel Speyer', in *Mentalitäten und Lebensverhältnisse. Beispiele aus der Sozialgeschichte der Neuzeit. Rudolf Vierhaus zum 60. Geburtstag* (Göttingen, 1982), pp. 34–91, p. 45.

50. Neumann, *Der Bücherbesitz*, p. 35a.

51. François, 'Buch, Konfession und städtische Gesellschaft im 18. Jahrhundert', p. 37.

52. Neumann, *Der Bücherbesitz*, p. 6–10. The figures for craftsmen are as follows: shoemakers (1750–60 = 9.5; 1800–10 = 4), bakers (1750–60 = 7; 1800–10 = 7), tailors (1750–60 = 12; 1800–10 = 7) and butchers (1750–60 = 5; 1800–10 = 5).

53. Ibid., pp. 142–4.

54. Hans Medick, 'Ein Volk "mit" Büchern. Buchbesitz und Buchkultur auf dem Lande am Ende der Frühen Neuzeit: Laichingen 1748–1820', in Hans-Erich Bödeker (ed.), *Lesekulturen im 18. Jahrhundert* (Hamburg, 1992), pp. 59–94, here p. 68. A decline in book ownership is also noted by François for Speyer (pp. 39–42), with the number of religious books per estate inventory declining twice as much as that of secular books. This could speak in favour of changes in religious practise.

55. Medick, 'Ein Volk "mit" Büchern', pp. 90–93.

56. François, 'Buch, Konfession und städtische Gesellschaft im 18. Jahrhundert', pp. 53–4.

57. Otto Dann, 'Die Lesegesellschaften und die Herausbildung einer modernen bürgerlichen Gesellschaft in Europa', in Dann (ed.), *Lesegesellschaften und bürgerliche Emanzipation – Ein europäischer Vergleich* (Munich, 1981), pp. 9–28.

58. Engelsing, *Bürger als Leser*, p. 224.

59. Marlies Stützel-Prüsener, 'Die deutschen Lesegesellschaften im Zeitalter der Aufklärung', in Otto Dann (ed.), *Lesegesellschaften und bürgerliche Emanzipation – Ein europäischer Vergleich* (Munich, 1981), pp. 71–86, here p. 74.

60. Dann, 'Die deutschen Lesegesellschaften', p. 18.

61. Otto Dann, 'Eine höfische Gesellschaft als Lesegesellschaft', in Hans-Erich Bödeker (ed.), *Lesekulturen im 18. Jahrhundert* (Hamburg, 1992), pp. 43–57.

62. Rolf Engelsing, *Analphabetentum und Lektüre. Zur Sozialgeschichte des Lesens in Deutschland zwischen feudaler und industrieller Gesellschaft* (Stuttgart, 1973); Ute Daniel, 'How Bourgeois was the Public Sphere of the Eighteenth Century? or: Why it is Important to Historicize "Strukturwandel der Öffentlichkeit"', *Das Achtzehnte Jahrhundert*, 26 (2002): 9–17. Stefanie Kripsin, *'bei seinem Vergnügen in müßigen Stunden unterhalten seyn'. Lesegesellschaften in Detmold um 1800* (Bielefeld, 1999).

63. Kopitzsch, *Sozialgeschichte*, pp. 573–4.

64. 'Aber wer will heutigen Tags noch eine Predigt anhören, noch weniger lesen? Ja, wenn es ein Rinaldo Rinaldini (von Vulpius) oder solch ein Ungethüm wäre, so ließe ich es passiren. Man komme nur mal in unsre Leihbibliotheken (die man beyher gesagt auch wohl Lesebibliotheken nennt) und frage nach so einem Räuber, Banditen oder Hexe, und man wird finden, daß das Buch entweder nicht zu Hause oder von dem vielen Wandern von einem zum andern … an Rücken und Ecken durchgeschabt ist. Andere nützliche Bücher stehen wie angenagelt und sind mit Staub bedeckt'. *Der geheime Ausrufer* 11 (1808): 189; quoted in Engelsing, *Bürger als Leser*, pp. 235–7.

65. Stützel-Prüsener, *Lesegesellschaften*, p. 80.

66. Engelsing, *Bürger als Leser*, pp. 238–40.
67. Carl Haase, 'Der Bildungshorizont der norddeutschen Kleinstadt am Ende des 18. Jahrhunderts. Zwei Bücherverzeichnisse der Lesegesellschaften in Wunstorf aus dem Jahre 1794', in Otto Brunner, Hermann Kellenbenz, Erich Maschke and Wolfgang Zorn (eds), *Festschrift Hermann Aubin zum 80. Geburtstag* (2 vols, Wiesbaden, 1965), pp. 518–25.
68. Carl Haase, 'Die Buchbestände einiger Lesegesellschaften im Elbe-Weser-Winkel im Jahre 1794', *Stader Jahrbuch* (1977): 56–80, 65–73.
69. Wittmann, *Buchhandel*, pp. 193–7, and 'Gibt es eine Leserevolution am Ende des 18. Jahrhunderts?', in Roger Chartier and Guglielmo Cavallo (eds), *Die Welt des Lesens. Von der Schriftrolle zum Bildschirm* (Frankfurt, 1999), pp. 419–54.
70. Engelsing, *Bürger als Leser*, pp. 271–2.
71. 'In Deutschland gibt es drei Publikum oder Publika: 1) das breite, fast ungebildete und ungelehrte der Lesebibliotheken – 2) das gelehrte, aus Professoren, Kandidaten, Studenten, Rezensenten bestehend – 3) das gebildete, das sich aus Weltleuten und Weibern von Erziehung, Künstlern und aus den höhern Klassen formt, bei denen wenigstens Umgang und Reisen bildet (Freilich kommunizieren oft die drei Kollegien)'. Jean Paul, 'Brief und bevorstehender Lebenslauf. Konjektural-Biographie, sechste poetische Epistel', in Paul, *Werke*, ed. Norbert Miller, vol. 4 (Munich, 1962), p. 1070; quoted in Wittmann, *Buchhandel*, p. 199. Thomas Abbt was far more pessimistic, estimating the reading audience at 80,000 persons. 'Vom Verdienste des Schriftstellers, des Künstlers und des Predigers', in Thomas Abbt, *Vom Verdienste* (Frankfurt and Leipzig, 1783), p. 270.
72. 'Die Deutschen sind im Durchschnitt rechtliche, biedere Menschen aber von Originalität, Erfindung, Charackter, Einheit, und Ausführung eines Kunstwercks haben sie nicht den mindesten Begriff. Das heißt mit Einem Worte sie haben keinen Geschmack. Versteht sich auch im Durchschnitt. Den rohren Theil hat man durch Abwechslung und Übertreiben, den gebildetern durch eine Art Honettetät zum Besten. Ritter, Räuber, Wohlthätige, Danckbare, ein redlicher biederer Tiers Etat, ein infamer Adel pp. und durchaus eine wohlsoutinierte Mittelmäßigkeit, aus der man nur allenfalls abwärts ins Platte, aufwärts in den Unsinn einige Schritte wagt, das sind nun schon zehen Jahre die Ingredienzien und der Charackter unsrer Romane und Schauspiele'.
Goethe to Reichardt, Weimar, 28 February 1790, quoted in *J. F. Reichardt – J. W. Goethe. Briefwechsel*, ed. Volkmar Braunbehrens, Gabriele Busch-Salmen and Walter Salmen (Weimar, 2002), pp. 107–8.

Chapter 2

1. 'In keinem Zeitalter der Welt wurde so viel gereist, als in dem unsrigen, wo das Reisen zu einer Art von Epidemie geworden ist … ja selbst der unbemittelte Gelehrte entfernt sich von seinem Pult, und macht zwar nicht lange Reisen, doch wenigstens Excursionen, oft in der Absicht seine zusammengerafften Bemerkungen der Welt mitzutheilen, und sich dadurch für die aufgewandten Kosten schadlos zu halten. Ob dieses häufige Reisen mehr Vortheile oder mehr Nachtheile erzeugt, ob der Patriotismus dadurch mehr gestärkt oder geschwächt wird, die wahren Kenntnisse mehr verbreitet oder verringert werden, wag ich nicht zu entscheiden'. *Der Teutsche*

Merkur (November 1784): 151, quoted in Uli Kutter, *Reisen – Reisehandbücher – Wissenschaft: Materialien zur Reisekultur im 18. Jahrhundert* (Neuried, 1996), pp. 13–14.

2. Christoph Wolff, *Johann Sebastian Bach* (Frankfurt, 2000), pp. 227–8. The list contains only documented journeys; family tours and travel to the environs of Leipzig are not listed.

3. Ibid., pp. 227–32.

4. *Karl August von Hardenberg 1750-1822, Tagebücher und autobiographische Aufzeichnungen,* ed. Thomas Stamm-Kuhlmann (Munich, 2000), pp. 25–6, 109–12.

5. Joachim Rees, 'Vom Fürst und Bürgerfreund. Zum Funktionswandel der Prinzenreise in der zweiten Hälfte des 18. Jahrhunderts – ein Generationsvergleich aus Schwarzburg-Rudolstadt', in Marcus Ventzke (ed.), *Hofkultur und aufklärerische Reformen in Thüringen. Die Bedeutung des Hofes im späten 18. Jahrhundert* (Cologne, Weimar and Vienna, 2002), pp. 100–37.

6. See Joachim Rees, 'Winfried Siebers und Hilmar Tilgner, Reisen im Erfahrungsraum Europa. Forschungsperspektiven zur Reisetätigkeit politisch-sozialer Eliten des Alten Reiches (1750–1800)', *Das Achtzehnte Jahrhundert,* 26 (2002): 35–62.

7. Kutter, *Reisen,* pp. 274–83.

8. Albert Meier, 'Als Moralist durch Italien. Johann Caspar Goethes "Viaggio per l'Italia fatto nel anno MDCCXL"', in Hans-Wolf Jäger (ed.), *Europäisches Reisen im Zeitalter der Aufklärung* (Heidelberg, 1992), pp. 71–85.

9. 'die Kunst zu beobachten, die neuen Eindrücke und Vorstellungen mit dem Resultate der schon ehemals gehabten zu vergleichen, und darüber nachzudenken: so müssen Verstand, Urtheilskraft und Vernunft nothwendigerweise geübt, geschärft und vervollkommnet werden … . Wer viel und lange gereiset ist, bekömmt daher durch die mannichfaltigen Gegenstände und Vergleichungen, die er zu sehen und zu machen Gelegenheit hatte, einen größeren Gesichtskreis und Maaßstab der Dinge … .' Franz Posselt, *Apodemik oder die Kunst zu reisen. Ein systematischer Versuch zum Gebrauch junger Reisenden aus den Gebildeten Ständen überhaupt und angehender Gelehrten und Künstler* (2 vols, Leipzig, 1795), vol. 1, pp. 28–9.

10. Martin Krieger, 'Patriotismus-Diskurs und die Konstruktion kollektiver Identitäten in Hamburg in der ersten Hälfte des 18. Jahrhunderts' (Habilitation thesis, University of Greifswald, 2001), pp. 96–102.

11. Carsten Niebuhr, *Reisebeschreibung nach Arabien und andern umliegenden Ländern* (2 vols, Copenhagen, 1774–78).

12. Josef Wiesehöfer and Stephan Conermann (eds), *Carsten Niebuhr (1733–1815) und seine Zeit* (Stuttgart, 2002).

13. Gottfried Korff, 'Museumsreisen', in Hermann Bausinger, Klaus Beyrer and Gottfried Korff (eds), *Reisekultur. Von der Pilgerfahrt zum modernen Tourismus* (Munich, 1991), pp. 311–19.

14. Wilhelm Treue, 'Zum Thema der Auslandsreisen im 17. Jahrhundert', *Archiv für Kulturgeschichte,* 35 (1953): 199–212, and 'Zum Thema der Auslandsreisen im 18. und 19. Jahrhundert', in Ibid. 328–33.

15. Wolfgang Behringer, *Im Zeichen des Merkur. Reichspost und Kommunikationsrevolution in der Frühen Neuzeit* (Gottingen, 2003), pp. 240ff.

16. Ibid., pp. 512ff., 664ff.

17. *Zeit der Postkutschen. Drei Jahrhunderte Reisen 1600–1900,* ed. Klaus Beyrer (Karlsruhe, 1992), pp. 16–17.

18. Gottfried North, 'Eine Revolution im Reiseverkehr – Die Schnellpost', in Bausinger, Beyrer and Korff (eds), *Reisekultur,* pp. 291–7.

19. Friedrich Nicolai, *Beschreibung einer Reise durch Deutschland und die Schweiz, im Jahre 1781. Nebst Bemerkungen über Gelehrsamkeit, Industrie, Religion und Sitten,* vol. 1 (Berlin and Stettin, 1783), p. 6.

20. Johann Kaspar Riesbeck, *Briefe eines reisenden Franzosen über Deutschland. An seinen Bruder in Paris,* vol. 1 (n.p. [Zurich], 1783), pp. 2ff.; quoted according to Klaus Beyrer, 'Des Reisebeschreibers "Kutsche". Aufklärerisches Bewußtsein im Postreiseverkehr des 18. Jahrhunderts', in Wolfgang Griep und Hans-Wolf Jäger (eds), *Reisen im 18. Jahrhundert. Neue Untersuchungen* (Heidelberg, 1986), p. 50–90, here pp. 70ff.

21. Behringer, *Im Zeichen,* p. 480.

22. Cf. for this the fundamental publication providing a bulk of material: Friedrich Rauers, *Kulturgeschichte der Gaststätte,* 2 vols (Berlin, 1942).

23. August Ludwig Schlözer, *Vorlesungen über Land- und Seereisen (1795/96)* (Göttingen, 1962), pp. 40ff.

24. Walter Weber, 'Von Wirtshäusern, Reisenden und Literaten. Eine kleine Chronique scandaleuse des Wirtshauslebens', in Bausinger, Beyrer and Korff (eds), *Reisekultur,* pp. 82–90.

25. Theodor Berger, *Vor-Urtheile der Deutschen bey Antretung ihrer Reisen in auswärtige Lande, u. bes. nach Franckreich, nebst Anhang von Deutschlands Macht gegen angräntzende Königreiche u. Länder* (Frankfurt, 1734), p. 22; quoted in Thomas Grosser, 'Tour de France – Frankreich als Ziel deutscher Reisender', in Bausinger, Beyrer and Korff (eds), *Reisekultur,* pp. 229–35, here p. 230.

26. Quoted in Michael Maurer, 'Italienreisen – Kunst und Konfession', in Bausinger, Beyrer and Korff (eds), *Reisekultur,* p. 222.

27. Jeremy Black, *France and the Grand Tour* (Basingstoke, 2003), pp. 123–37.

28. For the English perspective on Rome and the South, see Jeremy Black, *Italy and the Grand Tour* (New Haven and London, 2003), pp. 46–67.

29. Quoted in Barbara Wolbring, 'Auch ich in Arkadien! Die bürgerliche Kunst- und Bildungsreise im 19. Jahrhundert', in Dieter Hein and Andreas Schulz (eds), *Bürgerkultur im 19. Jahrhundert. Bildung, Kunst und Lebenswelt* (Munich, 1996), pp. 82–101, p. 85.

30. Heide Hollmer, '"Ohne Künstler kann man nicht leben weder in Süden noch Norden" – Herzogin Anna Amalias Kunstwahrnehmung und Kunstförderung während der Italienreise (1788–1790)', in Joachim Berger (ed.), *Der Musenhof Anna Amalias. Geselligkeit, Mäzenatentum und Kunstliebhaberei im klassischen Weimar* (Cologne, Weimar and Vienna, 2001), pp. 107–24.

31. Everard Korthals-Altes, 'The Art Tour of Friedrich of Mecklenburg-Schwerin', in *Simiolus,* 31(3) (2004–05): 216–50; Martin Krieger, '"Ein scharfsinniger Gelehrter, und dabey ein redlicher Mann ...": Zur Biographie Johann Georg Keyßlers, Privatgelehrter und Erzieher bei den Grafen Bernstorff (1689–1743)', *Zeitschrift der Gesellschaft für Schleswig-Holsteinische Geschichte,* 125 (2000): 63–89.

32. Ingrid Kuczynski, 'Ins gelobte Land der Freiheit und des Wohlstands: Reisen nach England', in Bausinger, Beyrer and Korff (eds), *Reisekultur,* pp. 237–43. See also Michael Maurer, *Aufklärung und Anglophilie in Deutschland* (Göttingen, 1987).

33. Gert Robel, 'Reisen und Kulturbeziehungen im Zeitalter der Aufklärung, in B.I. Krasnobaev', Gert Robel and Herbert Zeman (eds), *Reisen und Reisebeschreibungen im 18. und 19. Jahrhundert als Quellen der Kulturbeziehungsforschung* (Essen, 1987), pp. 9–37,

here p. 18; Wolbring, 'Auch ich in Arkadien!', p. 89. Peter Faessler, 'Reiseziel Schweiz: Freiheit zwischen Idylle und "großer" Natur', in Bausinger, Beyrer and Korff (eds), *Reisekultur,* pp. 243–8. Fundamental for Switzerland in the eighteenth century is the publication Hellmut Thomke, Martin Bircher and Wolfgang Proß (eds), *Helvetien und Deutschland. Kulturelle Beziehungen zwischen der Schweiz und Deutschland in der Zeit von 1770–1830* (Amsterdam and Atlanta, 1994).

34. Willi Raeber, *Caspar Wolf 1735–1783. Sein Leben und sein Werk* (Munich, 1979), pp. 57–84; *Caspar Wolf (1735–1783). Landschaft im Vorfeld der Romantik,* exhibition catalogue (Basel, 1980); *Caspar Wolf. Ein Panorama der Schweizer Alpen* (Aarau, 2001).

35. Marie-Louise Schaller, *Annäherung an die Natur. Schweizer Kleinmeister in Bern 1750–1800* (Berne, 1990); Charlotte König-von Dach, *Johann Ludwig Aberli, 1723–1786* (Berne, 1987). See also Beat Trachsler, '1750–1790: Ludwig Aberli und Caspar Wolf' and '1790–1810: Die Kleinmeister und ihre Welt', in *Malerische Reisen durch die schöne alte Schweiz* (Zürich, 1982), pp. 88–185. See also Michael North, Art *and Commerce in the Dutch Golden Age* (New Haven–London, 1997), and Michael North, 'Republican Art? Dutch and Swiss Art and Art Production Compared', in André Holenstein, Thomas Maissen and Maarten Prak (eds), *The Republican Alternative. The Netherlands and Switzerland compared* (Amsterdam, 2008), pp. 193–210.

36. Johann Wolfgang von Goethe, 'Der deutsche Gil Blas', in Johann Cristoph Sachse, *Der deutsche Gil Blas* (Munich, 1964), pp. 5–6.

37. See, for example, Gottlieb Heinrich Stuck, *Verzeichnis von älteren und neueren Land- und Reisebeschreibungen* (vols 1 and 2, Halle, 1783 and 1787 – an addendum [Nachtrag] to vol. 1 was published at Halle in 1785); and Johann Beckmann, *Literatur der älteren Reisebeschreibungen. Nachrichten von ihren Verfassern, von ihrem Inhalte, von ihren Ausgaben* (2 vols, Göttingen, 1807–10).

38. *Neue Bibliothek der wichtigsten Reisebeschreibungen,* Friedrich Justin Bertuch (eds), (65 vols, Weimar, 1815–32).

39. Albert Meier, 'Textsorten-Dialektik. Überlegungen zur Gattungsgeschichte des Reiseberichts im späten 18. Jahrhundert', in Michael Maurer (ed.), *Neue Impulse der Reiseforschung* (Berlin, 1999), pp. 243–5.

40. Thomas Grosser, 'Der mediengeschichtliche Funktionswandel der Reiseliteratur in den Berichten deutscher Reisender aus dem Frankreich des 18. Jahrhunderts', in Hans-Wolf Jäger (ed.), *Europäisches Reisen im Zeitalter der Aufklärung* (Heidelberg, 1992), pp. 275–310.

41. Johann David Köhler, *Anweisung zur Reiseklugheit für junge Gelehrte, um Bibliotheken, Münzkabinette, Antiquitätenzimmer, Bildergalerien, Naturalienkabinette und Kunstkammern mit Nutzen zu besehen*, ed. Johann Friedrich August Kinderling (2 vols, Magdeburg, 1788).

42. Justin Stagl, 'Der wohl unterwiesene Passagier. Reisekunst und Gesellschaftsbeschreibung vom 16. bis zum 18. Jahrhundert', in B.I Krasnovaev, Gert Robel and Herbert Zeman (eds), *Reisen und Reisebeschreibungen im 18. und 19. Jahrhundert als Quellen der Kulturbeziehungsforschung* (Essen, 1987), pp. 353–84.

43. Johann Peter Willebrandt, *Historische Berichte und practische Anmerkungen auf Reisen in Deutschland, in die Niederlande, in Frankreich, England, Dännemark, Böhmen und Ungarn* (Hamburg, 1758), pp. 18–20, quoted in Uli Kutter, *Reisen – Reisehandbücher – Wissenschaft: Materialien zur Reisekultur im 18. Jahrhundert* (Neuried, 1996), p. 159.

44. '37) Unterrichtet euch genau, und so viel es möglich ist von den Landes Staatsverfassung, Handlung, Vortheilen und Fabriquen; solches aber kann nicht füglicher geschehen, als in den berühmtesten Coffeehäusem.

38) Lasset es nicht genug seyn, die öffentlichen Gebäude der Städte nur allein von aussen, wie reisende Handwerksburschen zu thun pflegen, anzusehen, sondern erkundiget euch auch nach den innerlichen Einrichtungen, insbesondere nach den Verfassungen der Werkstühle und Werkhäuser, Manufacturen, der Armen-, Leih-Waysen- und Zuchthäuser.

39) Suchet an jedem Ort die Bekanntschaft der geschicktesten Gelehrten und der besten Künstler. Wenn es möglich ist, so trachtet dahin, daß ihr an einem jeglichen Orte eine obrigkeitliche Person, einen Rechtsgelehrten, und verschiedene Kaufleute zu Bekannten erhaltet.

40) Besuchet so viel wie möglich, die Buchläden, weil man durch diesen Weg am leichtesten in die Bekanntschaft der Gelehrten kommet.

41) Findet ihr an den Sitten und Gewohnheiten dieser oder jener Völker etwas Vortheilhaftes: so vergeßet nicht, solches aufzuzeichnen, um künftig in eurem Vaterlande davon Gebrauch zu machen.

42) Zürnet mit keinem Wälschen, spielet mit keinem Franzosen, saufet mit keinem Deutschen.' Willebrandt, *Historische Berichte*, pp. 18–19.

45. 'So sehr nun obgenannte Sachen von einander unterschieden sind: so sehr wechseln auch die Gemüths-Arten und mit solchen die Sitten und die Fähigkeiten der Deutschen ab. Ein Mecklenburger, ein Hollsteiner, ein Pommer, ein Braunschweiger, Hannoveraner, ein Hesse, Westphälinger, Schwabe und Oesterreicher ist in Betracht der Natur, und der Neigung von einem Brandenburger, Obersachsen, Schlesier und Franken, fast so sehr unterschieden, als der Franzose von dem Engelländer und Spanier, der Italiäner von dem Ungarn, der Polack von den Holländern, und der Grieche von den Schweitzern in seiner Natur und Denkungs-Art entfernet ist.' Ibid., pp. 431–2.

46. 'Es wirft zwar unser Gegentheil ein, es brächten unsere Reisende aus Franckreich, Italien, Spanien u. öfters nichts anders wieder heim, als der Ausländer Laster z. B. der Frantzosen Leichtsinnigkeit, der Italiäner Ueppigkeit und Unzucht, der Spanier hinterlistige Nachstellungen u., närrische Sitten, unerträgliche Gebärden, überflüßige Titul, lächerliche Ceremonien, seltsame Kleidungen, eine affectirte Sprache, und den gäntzlichen Verlust der Teutschen und väterlichen Tugenden. Ich muß ihm hierinn zwar in etwas Recht geben, indem die Erfahrung oft mehr als zu viel bezeuget, daß die meisten reisen, ehe sie sich zu Hause mit einer guten Morale versehen, und recht geschickt sind, sich die Besichtigung fremder Lande zu Nutze zu machen: allein wegen des Mißbrauchs einer Sache ist nicht gleich derselben rechtmäßiger Gebrauch abzuschaffen.' 'Vorrede', Peter Ambrosius Lehmann, *Die vornehmsten Europäischen Reisen* (Hamburg, 1729).

47. 'Die Absicht des gegenwärtigen Werkes ist keine andere, als jungen Leuten aus den gebildeten Ständen überhaupt, und angehenden Gelehrten und Künstlern insbesondere eine Anleitung zu geben, wie sie mit Nutzen reisen sollen. ... Das bloße Reisen in verschiedene Länder, und das bloße gedankenlose Anschauen von Merkwürdigkeiten lehrt an und für sich nichts. Wenn der Reisende nicht weiß, worauf er sehen, und wornach er fragen soll; wenn er die Kunst zu sehen und zu hören, und über das Gesehene und Gehörte nachzudenken nicht besitzt: so kann er alle Länder der Erde durchreisen, ohne im geringsten weiser und besser,

verständiger, einsichtsvoller und brauchbarer für die Welt zu werden. Zwar glauben manche junge Reisende, zumal diejenigen, die bloß aus Mode reisen, d. h. die nur reisen, um zu reisen, schon alles gethan zu haben, wenn sie in fremden Ländern alles besehen, was sich besehen läßt. Ihr einziges Verdienst ist daher, sagen zu können: das haben wir auch gesehen.' Posselt, *Apodemik*, vol. 1 (Leipzig, 1795), pp. iv–v.

48. Ibid., pp. vff., quote on p. vi.

49. Ibid., p. 5.

50. 'So fällt auf seinen Herrn nicht bloß seine Faulheit zurück, sondern auch seine verderbte Gemüthsart, die sich, wie alle Sklavencharaktere, in Heimtücke, Schadenfreude, List und Betrug zeigt'.
Fr. Schulz, *Reise eines Liefländers von Riga nach Warschau, durch Südpreußen, über Breslau, Dresden, Karlsbad, Bayreuth, Nürnberg, Regensburg, München, Salzburg, Linz, Wien und Klagenfurt, nach Botzen in Tyrol*, vol. 1 (Berlin, 1795), pp. 60, 66–7, quoted in Rainer S. Elkar, 'Reisen bildet', in Krasnobaev, Robel and Zeman (eds), *Reisen und Reisebeschreibungen*, pp. 51–82, pp. 61–2.

51. Cf. Justin Stagl, *Eine Geschichte der Neugier. Die Kunst des Reisens 1550–1800* (Vienna, Cologne and Weimar, 2002), p. 317.

52. Winfried Siebers, 'Bildung auf Reisen. Bemerkungen zur Peregrinatio academica, Gelehrten- und Gebildetenreise', in Michael Maurer (ed.), *Neue Impulse der Reiseforschung* (Berlin, 1999), p. 177–88.

53. 'Die Reise
So gehn Sie nach Paris, nach Rom und London? – "Ja."
Warum? "Mein seliger Papa,
Mein Oheim und mein Bruder waren da".
Die Herren kamen wohl gelehrt von ihren Reisen?
"O, ganz gewiß, sie fehlten keinen Schmauß;
Es ist in ganz Paris kein witzig Caffeehaus,
Das sie nicht auf der Charte weisen".
Sie wollen wohl nach Rom, dann nach Neapel gehn,
Das Grabmahl des Virgils, Horaz, Catull zu sehn,
Und alte Dichter zu verstehn? –
"Nein, Dichter sind nicht eben meine Sache".
Die Clairon in Paris reizt Ihre Neugier? "Nein"
So werden Sie ein Freund der Alterthümer seyn? –
"Noch weniger; in diesem Fache
Bin ich versäumt" – Gestehn Sie mir es nur,
Sie sind gewiß ein Kenner der Natur?
"Ich – der Natur? – ach nein!" – Lockt Sie die Kunst zu leben,
Der feine Ton der Sitten und der Welt,
Durch die man in Paris gefällt? –
"Mit Sitten hab ich mich noch niemals abgegeben".
So reisen Sie vielleicht aus stiller Politik,
Zum Vortheil unsrer Republik,
Um Mylord North und Saint Germain zu kennen?
"Die Herrn hör ich zum ersten male nennen".
Ihr Plan? "Sie scherzen, Freund – Was braucht man einen Plan,
Da man von Post zu Post die Welt wohl finden kann?"

Was ich durch diese Fabel weise?
Ein deutsches Bild von mancher deutschen Reise.'
Christian August Clodius, *Neue vermischte Schriften*, vol. 3: *Dinokrates* (Leipzig, 1780), pp. 14–17; on Clodius (1737–84), see the article by Ernst Fischer 'Clodius, Christian August', in Walther Killy (ed.), *Literaturlexikon. Autoren und Werke deutscher Sprache*, 2 vols (Gütersloh and Munich, 1989), pp. 431–2.

Chapter 3

1. 'a la mode macht mir bang, weil der Teutschen undergang in der newen-sucht seinen anfang sucht. Dann, wasz haben will ein schein, musz nur a la mode sein'. Jacob und Wilhelm Grimm, *Deutsches Wörterbuch*, vol. 12 'L-Myth' (Munich, 1991).
2. 'überhaupt und nach seinem weitläufftigsten Verstande die Art, Weise, Gebrauch, Gewohnheit, Gattung, Gestalt, Manier, Façon oder Muster, besonders aber die gewöhnliche oder gebräuchliche Tracht und Manier in Kleidungen, Meublen, Kutschen und Zimmern, Gebäuden, Manufacturen, Schreib- und Red-Arten, Complimenten, Ceremonien und anderm Gepränge, Gastereyen und übrigen Lebens=Arten'. Johann Heinrich Zedler, *Großes Vollständiges Universal-Lexikon*, vol. 21 'Mi-Mt' (Leipzig and Halle, 1739, reprint, Graz, 1995), pp. 700–701.
3. Johann Christoph Adelung, *Grammatisch-kritisches Wörterbuch der Hochdeutschen Mundart, mit beständiger Vergleichung der übrigen Mundarten, besonders aber der Oberdeutschen* (2nd edn, vol. 3, Leipzig, 1798), cols 253–4, quoted according to Doris Kuhles, 'Das "Journal des Luxus und der Moden" (1786–1827). Zur Entstehung seines inhaltlichen Profils und seiner journalistischen Struktur', in Gerhard R. Kaiser and Siegfried Seifert (eds), *Friedrich Justin Bertuch (1747–1822). Verleger, Schriftsteller und Unternehmer im klassischen Weimar* (Tübingen, 2000), pp. 489–99, here p. 494, and *Journal des Luxus und der Moden 1786–1827. Analytische Bibliographie mit sämtlichen 517 schwarzweißen und 976 farbigen Abbildungen der Originalzeitschrift* (Munich, 2003). Still important is Ruth Wies, 'Das Journal des Luxus und der Moden (1786–1827), ein Spiegel kultureller Strömungen der Goethezeit' (PhD dissertation, University of Munich, 1953). For the aspect of fashion, see Gisela Jaacks, 'Modechronik, Modekritik oder Modediktat? Zu Funktion, Thematik und Berichtstil früher deutscher Modejournale am Beispiel des "Journal des Luxus und der Moden"', *Waffen- und Kostümkunde*, 24 (1982): 58–61.
4. 'Wir schreiben ja kein Damen-Journal oder ein Toilettenwerk, worinn man nichts als Nektar und Ambroisa sucht, und nur Wohlgerüche aus Elysium athmen will. Dieß sey Andern überlaßen. Nein, wir schreiben die Chronik des Geistes unser Zeit, in so fern er von der Mode beherrscht, geleitet und geformt wird; und aus diesem Standpuncte sieht man leicht, daß unser Feld der Beobachtungen sehr groß, und die Erscheinungen darauf höchst verschieden und abstechend sind'. *Journal des Luxus und der Moden* (April 1794): 193.
5. 'von jeder neuen Mode und Erfindung, so wie sie in Frankreich, England, Teutschland und Italien erscheint, in welchem Zweige von Luxus es auch sey, … . Unsere Gegenstände darinnen sind also 1) weibliche und männliche Kleidung; 2) Putz; 3) Schmuck; 4) Nippes; 5) Ammeublement, 6) alle Arten von Tisch- und Trinckgeschirre, als Silber, Porcellain, Gläser usw.; 7) Equipage, sowohl Wagen als Pferdezeug, und Livreen; 8) Häuser- und Zimmereinrichtung und Verzierung, 9)

Gärten und Landhäuser'. *Journal des Luxus und der Moden* (reprint, Leipzig, 1967), pp. 29–30.

6. See Maxine Berg and Helen Clifford (eds), *Consumers and Luxury: Consumer Culture in Europe 1650–1850* (Manchester, 1999), and Maxine Berg and Elizabeth Eger (eds), *Luxury in the Eighteenth Century: Debates, Desires and Delectable Goods* (London, 2003).

7. 'Luxus sagt der Anhänger des physiokratischen Systems, ist die Pest der Staaten! Er verschwendet den reichen Ertrag zu unfruchtbaren Ausgaben; hindert die Reproduction; entnervt die physiokratischen Kräfte der Nation; lößt alles Gefühl für Moralität und Ehre auf; zerrüttet den Wohlstand der Familien, und liefert dem Staate Schaaren Bettler!

Luxus, sagt der Finanzier und der Technolog, ist die reichste Quelle für den Staat; der allmächtige Hebel der Industrie, und das kräftigste Triebwerk der Circulation. Er verwischt alle Spuren der Barbarey in den Sitten; schafft Künste, Wissenschaften, Handel und Gewerbe; vermehrt die Population und die Kräfte des Staates, und bewürkt Genuß und Glück des Lebens! – Wer von Beyden hat Unrecht? – Beyde, däucht uns, wenn sie unbedingt über diese wichtige Materie deklamieren. Der ganze Streit ruht auf einem unrichtigen oder wenigstens nicht rein genug bestimmten Begriffe vom Luxus'. *Journal des Luxus und der Moden* (January 1786): 4–5.

8. Annemarie Kleinert, *Die frühen Modejournale in Frankreich. Studien zur Literatur der Mode von den Anfängen bis 1848* (Berlin, 1980), p. 37, and *Le 'Journal des Dames et des Modes' ou la conquête de l'europe féminine (1797–1839)* (Stuttgart, 2001).

9. Daniel Roche, *The Culture of Clothing. Dress and Fashion in the Ancien Regime* (Cambridge, 1994), pp. 13–15.

10. Kleinert, *Modejournale*, p. 45.

11. Kleinert, *Modejournale*, pp. 60–61.

12. On the importance of these fashion almanacs, see Rachel Kennedy, 'Fashion Magazines', in Michael Snodin and John Styles (eds), *Design and the Decorative Arts: Georgian Britain 1714–1838* (London, 2004), pp. 92–3; Amanda Vickery, *The Gentleman's Daughter: Women's Lives in Georgian England* (New Haven and London, 1998), pp. 161–94.

13. On fashion magazines see, recently, Astrid Ackermann, *Paris, London und die europäische Provinz. Die frühen europäischen Modejournale (1770–1830)* (Frankfurt, 2005).

14. 'Essay on Dress', *The Lady's Magazine or Entertaining Companion for the Fair Sex* (London, 1801): 635–8, esp. p. 635. I would like to thank Astrid Ackermann (Jena) for drawing my attention to this text. See her *Paris*.

15. Kleinert, *Modejournal*, p. 84.

16. 'Zum Theil sind wir durch die Anglomanie der heutigen Franzosen gerächt. Sie treffen überall auf wandelnde Riding-Coats, in deren Falten ein gebrechliches Wesen zappelt. ... Sonderbar ist es, daß die Söhne der Freyheit sich knechtisch unter jede Mode bequemen, und daß der unterthänige Franzos immer eine Nationalverzierung anbringt. Er steckt in seinem Reitknechtshabit einen großen Blumenstrauß an die Brust, und hinter seinem Nacken schwillt der kleine englische Kadogan zur Größe eines Puddings. Wenn Miss ihren mit einer Rose geschmückten Chip-Hat auf die Mitte ihres braunlockigen Kopfs setzt, so hängt der Chapeau à l'angloise schief auf der gepuderten Französin, und die Rose wird zur Girlande'. Quoted in Wiebke Koch-Mertens, *Der Mensch und seine Kleider*, vol. 1: *Die Kulturgeschichte der Mode bis 1900* (Düsseldorf, 2000), p. 339.

17. 'Die Meklenborger sind, den übrigen Teutschen gleich, Nachahmer der Engländer und Franzosen; doch mit dem Unterschiede, daß die Männer ihre Tracht, ihren Hausrath, ihre Equipagen und Gärten nach englischem Geschmack anordnen, hingegen die geputzte Dame sich noch nach dem Eigensinn einer Pariser Modehändlerin richtet, die ihre verlegene Waare nach Norden schickt.' *Journal des Luxus und der Moden* (September 1787): 301. English translation in Daniel L. Purdy, *The Tyranny of Elegance. Consumer Cosmopolitanism in the Era of Goethe* (Baltimore, 1998), p. 176.

18. 'Jedoch Frankreich ist es nicht allein, dessen Zauberstab wir zu fürchten haben. England und der vervollkommnete Kunstfleiß seiner Fabriken wird und muß uns nothwendig ebenso gefährlich werden'. *Journal des Luxus und der Moden* (August 1793): 410. Justus Möser also expressed similar ideas, recommending the introduction of a German fashion journal to reduce the expense of acquiring information from France. Furthermore, this fashion journal would enable domestic industries to compete with France. Wolfgang Cilleßen, 'Modezeitschriften', in Ernst Fischer, Wilhelm Haefs and York-Gothart Mix (eds), *Von Almanach bis Zeitung. Ein Handbuch der Medien in Deutschland 1700–1800* (Munich, 1999), pp. 207–24, pp. 219–20.

19. 'Die geschmackvolle Simplicität und Solidität, welche England allen seinen Fabrikwaaren zu geben gewußt hat, ist für uns Teutsche so ausserordentlich empfehlend und anlockend, daß das Wort Englisch, englische Waare, schon dermalen einen unwiderstehlichen Zauberreiz für uns hat, und beynahe ein Synonym der Vollkommenheit und Schönheit bey Werken des Kunstfleißes worden ist'. *Journal des Luxus und der Moden* (August 1793): 410.

20. Maxine Berg, 'French Fancy and Cool Britannia. The Fashion Markets of Early Modern Europe', in Simonetta Cavaciocchi (ed.), *Fiere e mercati nella integrazione delle economie Europe secc. XIII–XVIII* (Prato, 2001), pp. 519–56, here pp. 540–46, and *Luxury & Pleasure in Eighteenth-Century Britain* (Oxford, 2005), pp. 85–110.

21. *Journal des Luxus und der Moden* (August 1786): 295–6.

22. Ackermann, *Paris*, pp. 107–8.

23. Cf. Purdy, *Tyranny of Elegance*, pp. 1–21.

24. Koch-Mertens, *Der Mensch*, pp. 291–2.

25. 'Das Frauenzimmer trägt unten sehr weit abstehende Röcke / als wenn ein großes Tonnen=Band darinnen wäre / denn wenn ein paar Weiber einander in einer engen Strasse begegnen / so macht es ihnen soviel Verwirrung / als wenn zwey Wagen mit Heu gegen einander führen'. Paul Ludolf Berckenmeyer, *Vermehrter Curieuser Antiquarius, Das ist: Allerhand auserlesene Geographische und Historische Merckwürdigkeiten / So in denen Europæischen Ländern zu finden; Aus Berühmter Männer Reisen zusammengetragen / und mit einem zweyfachen Register versehen* (Hamburg, 1711), p. 63.

26. 'Sie ist einem wohlgewachsenen Körper überaus vortheilhaft, zeigt eine schöne Taille, durch das unten enge und oben weite und etwas lockere Corset, in ihrer ganzen Grazie und hat überhaupt das edle prunklose Ansehen einer geschmackvollen Simplicität, und Wohlanständigkeit, welches die Reize des schönen Geschlechts so sehr erhöhet.' *Journal des Luxus und der Moden* (April 1786): 141.

27. Martha Bringemeier, 'Wandel der Mode im Zeitalter der Aufklärung', *Rheinisch-Westfälische Zeitschrift für Volkskunde*, 13 (1966).

28. *Journal des Luxus und der Moden* (February 1787): 17ff.

29. Ulfhardt Stoewer, 'Der "Kulturunternehmer" Friedrich Justin Bertuch im Spiegel seines "Journals des Luxus und der Moden"' (dissertation as part of the state secondary school teachers' examination, University of Greifswald, 2001).

30. 'Die Frankfurter und Leipziger Meßwaren sind jetzt wieder allenthalben in den Magazinen der Mode vertheilt, und gewähren eine Uebersicht des neu Erfundenen und Angekommenen in diesem Gebiete. Frankreich reicht uns die Linke über den Rhein und Main. Sein Stapelplatz des eleganten Absatzes ist Frankfurt, Mainz u.s.w. Leipzig hingegen und andere nördliche Städte, wie Hamburg und Bremen, bereichern Mittel-Teutschland mit den englischen Produkten. Daher man auch sicher darauf rechnen kann, daß jener Theil Teutschlands geschmackvoller, eleganter, frivoler und anmutiger, dieser hingegen feiner, zierlicher, solider, aber auch nicht selten steifer und gezierter in seinen Modeartikeln besorgt ist'. *Journal des Luxus und der Moden* (June 1802): 353, quoted in *Frankfurter Modespiegel*, exhibition catalogue, Historical Museum of Frankfurt am Main, with an introduction by Bernward Deneke (Frankfurt, 1962).

31. *Journal des Luxus und der Moden* (December 1786): 439–40.

32. 'Es ist auffallend wie anjezt England weit mehr als Frankreich in allen Mode-Waaren den Ton angiebt, und in Teutschland den Markt damit füllt. Daß Teutschland dabey gewinnt, zweifle ich mit Recht; denn die Englischen Mode-Waaren, sind als Mode-Waaren, eben so dem frivolen Wechsel der Mode unterworfen, dafür aber zu solid und zu theuer. Teutschland kann also leicht an England doppelt so zinßbar werden, als es an Frankreich war.' *Journal des Luxus und der Moden* (December 1791): 687.

33. Annemarie Kleinert and Gretel Wagner, 'Mode und Politik. Die Vermarktung der französischen Revolution in Frankreich und Deutschland (1789–1793)', in *Waffen- und Kostümkunde* (1959), pp. 24–38.

34. 'Mit einem Worte, die Damen haben die Sitte, durch wächserne Anlagen ihren Armen Füllung und Rundung zu geben auf etwas noch Substantiellers angewandt, und sich statt der Busen, wenn die Natur die ihnen versagte, künstliche Stellvertreter von Wachs zugelegt, die so künstlich angepaßt und eingerichtet sind, daß Argus selbst mit allen seinen hundert Augen den kleinen, unschuldigen Betrug nicht erspäht haben würde, wenn nicht ein unbescheidener Plauderer, der die Erfindung bey den Busenfabrikanten ausgekundschaftet hatte, durch eine öffentlich Bekanntmachung zum Verräther geworden wäre.' *Journal des Luxus und der Moden* (March 1798): 204–5.

35. Caroline de la Motte Fouqué, *Geschichte der Moden 1785–1829* (reprint Hanau, 1988), p. 47.

36. 'Es käme also nur auf zwey Puncte an:
    1) Auf die Wahl der Kleidung, und
    2) auf die Art, über dieselbe einig zu werden und sie einzuführen.
    Was den ersten Punct betrifft, so glaube ich folgende Grundsätze annehmen zu dürfen: Die Kleidung muß seyn:
    a) wohlfeil;
    b) von Farben, die nicht leicht Schmutz annehmen, dauerhaft, leicht zu waschen, und von dem Eigensinne der Mode, weder erfunden, noch von demselben abhängig sind;
    c) für jedes Alter passend;
    d) vom Vornehmen wie vom Geringern, vom Reichen wie vom Armen, leicht anzuschaffen zu tragen;
    e) unserm Klima angemessen;

f) nicht phantastisch;

g) unseren Körper nicht entstellend;

h) das Gepräge von Teutschheit tragend;

i) in allen Jahreszeiten brauchbar ... .

Es giebt leider! Leute, welche alle Dinge in das Lächerliche ziehen; es giebt Andre, die in allem etwas Gefährliches oder Hinterlistiges sehen; Es giebt endlich noch Andre, welche nicht gut finden, als was sie, oder irgend eine von den Partheyen, zu welchen sie gehören, gefunden oder vorgeschlagen haben – Das ist traurig, und von Diesen muß ich freylich erwarten, daß sie meinem Vorschlage, von irgend einer Seite, keine Gerechtigkeit werden wiederfahren lassen; Allein das beunruhigt mich nicht. Ich bin mir bewußt, aus guter, ehrlicher, patriotischteutscher Absicht, diesen Vorschlag zu thun; Ich gehöre zu keiner Parthey, habe mir das Ding selbst so ausgedacht, und würde mich herzlich freuen, ohne weiter Ehre davon zu haben, auch je meinem Namen nennen zu wollen, wenn die Sache gelingen sollte ... .' *Journal des Luxus und der Moden* (February 1786): 72ff.

37. 'Ich glaube also bey einer einzuführenden teutschen National-Tracht würde nicht nur der vernünftige Hauptzweck, die Unterdrückung des schädlichen Kleider Luxus (denn die National-Originalität und das Teutsche Gepräge sind doch wohl nur Nebenzwecke des Hrn. Verfassers) nicht erreicht werden, sondern auch sogar viel Nachtheil für Teutschland daraus erwachsen. Ein großer Theil teutscher Fabriken, deren Arbeiter jetzt alle ihr Brod durch die Mannigfaltigkeit der Fabrikate, Wahl und Geschmack der Käufer haben, würden auf einmal durch eine National-Kleidung, die nur einige wenige bestimmte Zeuche und Farben zuließen, außer Nahrung gesetzt, und viele Tausend Fabrikanten würden mit einem Feder-Striche zu Bettlern gemacht, oder müßten sogleich aus ihrem Vaterlande auswandern; denn der Sammt-, Taft- oder Cotton-Weber kann kein Tuchmacher oder Wollen-Zeuch-Weber mehr werden. ... Und endlich rechnet uns denn der feine Herr, der Teutschland eine ewige Uniform geben will, für gar keinen Theil der Nation, daß er uns arme Weiber so ganz unbefugt, vielleicht wieder in die Wülste und Köllerchen unserer Urälter-Mütter aus dem XVIten Jahrhunderte stecken, in ein ewiges schwarz, weiß und grau, wie die Kloster-Schwestern einkleidern, und uns alles Heyl und Trost rauben will. Bedenken Sie doch ums Himmelswillen, meine Herren, wo sollen wir denn noch Stoff zu Plaudern bey einer drey bis vierstündigen Kaffee-Visite, beym Thee-Tische, oder auf einer Promenade hernehmen, wenn's keine neuen Bänder, Hauben, Hüthe, Roben, und Fourreaux mehr giebt? Zweyerley risquiren Staat und unsere Männer sicher dabey; entweder wir werden gelehrt und disputiren über neue Werke und Seelen-Fakultäten unserer und anderer Männer, oder wir mischen uns in politische Händel, und kannegiesern; welches doch beydes bisher noch ungestöhrte Vorrechte der Männer waren. Also thun Sie was Sie können jenen Herren, der uns so despotisch an den Kragen will, von seinem schlimmen Vorhaben abzumahnen, sonst prophezeyhe ich ihm sicher eine Weiber-Rebellion in Teutschland. Was ich dabey thun werde, können Sie rathen.' *Journal des Luxus und der Moden* (February 1786): 81ff.

38. Purdy, *Tyranny of Elegance*, pp. 180–85.

39. 'Der dreyeckigte etwas militärisch aufgekrämpte Huth mit der schwarzen Schleife giebt ihm ein gewißes freyes und edles Air de Tête, so wie die gerad aufsteigende Vorderspitze deßelben die gerade perpendikulare Richtung des Körpers zu Pferde verschönert. Der Huth ist, herabgekrämpt, vollkommen rund und groß, deckt bey

Regen die Schultern ganz für Näße, und kann, wenn vorn die Spitze beschädigt wird, leicht anders aufgesteift werden; so wie er auch, anders herumgesetzt, die Augen vor der Sonne schützt. [...] Der kurze, sogenannte Berliner Frack, der sich auf der Brust ein wenig übereinander schlägt, und da mit ein Paar Knöpfen zugeknöpft, unten aber etwas weit abgestochen ist, giebt der Figur mehr Brust, versteckt weder die Schenckel noch die Form des Pferdes, sichert vor dem Koth spritzen, und giebt überhaupt dem Reiter ein elegantes leichtes und adroites Ansehen. Der Frack ist wegen der weißen Unterkleider weiß gefüttert. Dieß und der schwarze Sammet-Kragen und dergleichen Aufschläge à la Marinière geben ihm etwas Uniformartiges, das dem Auge gefällt.' *Journal des Luxus und der Moden* (August 1786): 293–4. See also Martha Bringemeier, 'Wandel der Mode', p. 24.

40. 'Der junge Berliner nach der Mode von der feinen, und bey weiten der größeren Klasse, trägt vom Morgen bis zum Abend Stiefeln, runden Hut, blauen Rock mit rothen Kragen, in sehr militärischem Geschmacke, und sehr oft schmutzige Wäsche. So gekleidet geht er in die Kollegien, unter die Linden, aufs Koffeehaus, zu Tische, wieder unter die Linden, ins Schauspiel, und sehr oft in Gesellschaften, denn er geht nur in Gesellschaften, wenn Eltern, Liebschaften oder andere Konvenienzen ihn hinbringen, und kann sich doch darum unmöglich umkleiden ... .' *Journal des Luxus und der Moden* (April 1791): 178. Cf. Purdy, *Tyranny of Elegance*, pp. 147ff. The English translation is from Purdy, p. 166. On the 'Werther dicourse', see Walter Erhart, 'Beziehungsexperimente: Goethes "Werther" und Wielands "Musarion"', *Deutsche Vierteljahrschrift für Literaturwissenschaft und Geistesgeschichte*, 2 (1992): 333–60.

41. For a nicely observed study of the phenomenon, see Astrid Ackermann, 'Eine nationale Aufgabe – Mode und Kommerz', in Andreas Klinger and Gonthier-Louis Fink (eds), *Identitäten. Erfahrungen und Fiktionen um 1800* (Frankfurt, 2003), pp. 232–7.

42. Staatsarchiv Hamburg (StA Hamburg), Erbschaftsamt (Inheritance Office) D 71.

43. Uwe Meiners, 'Stufen des Wandels. Aspekte der Periodisierung der bürgerlichen und bäuerlichen Kultur im Münsterland (1500–1800)', in Günter Wiegelmann (ed.), *Wandel der Alltagskultur seit dem Mittelalter. Phasen – Epochen – Zäsuren* (Münster, 1987), pp. 275–308, here pp. 300–301.

44. Meiners, 'Stufen des Wandels', p. 302.

45. ICC Frankfurt 802, 'Auszug Inventariums über entseelten Bürgers und Handelsmannes Friedrich Maximilian Beer, Nachlaß vom 4. und 6. May 1795' (Extract from the inventory of the late citizen and merchant Friedrich Maximilian Beer, estate of 4 and 6 May 1795).

46. 'Die Mode wäre durchaus eine Weltbürgerin, [die] sich in kein Vaterland einschließen lasse und der ihr eingeborenen Neigung zum Widerspruch zu Folge, sich am liebsten mit Kontrebanden ausstaffire.' *Journal des Luxus und der Moden* (March 1802): 162.

47. *Journal des Luxus und der Moden* (June 1814): 388ff.

48. *Journal des Luxus und der Moden* (June 1814): 387ff. And Table 16. See also Wies, 'Journal', pp. 153–4.

Chapter 4

1. 'Ich habe drey Zimmer neben einander, die ich alle für mich brauche. Eines ist das sogenannte Visitenzimmer, das mittlere ein kleiner Saal und dem folgt

meine Wohnstube, wobei eine mittlere Schlafstube ist. Mein Mann wohnt an der anderen Seite des Visitenzimmers.' Quoted in Birgit Panke-Kochinke, *Göttinger Professorenfamilien. Strukturmerkmale weiblichen Lebenszusammenhangs im 18. und 19. Jahrhundert* (Pfaffenweiler, 1993), p. 90.

2. See also Adelheid von Saldern, 'Im Hause, zu Hause. Wohnen im Spannungsfeld von Gegebenheiten und Aneignungen', in Jürgen Reulecke (ed.), *Geschichte des Wohnens, 1800–1918*, vol 3: *Das bürgerliche Zeitalter* (Stuttgart, 1997), pp. 145–332, here pp. 155–6.

3. 'daß man die Austheilung der Zimmer auch in Bürger-Häusern / so vielmehr in vornehmen / also anstelle / daß der Mann aus seinen Zimmern in der Frauen Zimmer gelangen könne / ohne über die Theele [Diele] des Hauses zu gehen / da jedermann frey hin- und wieder gehet … . Daß aber eben das gemeine Schlaff-Gemach unmittelbar zwischen beyden Zimmern liege / ist eben so nöthig nicht / noch weniger aber / daß es eben an der Mitte des Gebäudes liege / sintemahl diese Stelle gerne und am besten den Sählen eingeraumet wird. Die beste Eintheilung ist / wenn so wohl des mannes als der Frauen Gemach sein eigenes Schlaff-Zimmer hat / und zwischen beyden ein Saal lieget.' Leonhard Christoph Sturm, *Vollständige Anweisung alle Arten von Bürgerlichen Wohn-Häusern wohl anzugeben* (Augspurg, 1721), fol. B 1a, fol. C 1b; quoted in Jens Friedhoff, '"Magnificence" und "Utilité". Bauen und Wohnen 1600–1800', in Ulf Dirlmeier (ed.), *Geschichte des Wohnens*, vol. 2: *500–1800, Hausen, Wohnen, Residieren* (Stuttgart, 1998), pp. 503–815, here pp. 646–7.

4. Uwe Meiners, 'Stufen des Wandels. Aspekte der Periodisierung der bürgerlichen und bäuerlichen Kultur im Münsterland (1550–1800)', in Günter Wiegelmann (ed.), *Wandel der Alltagskultur seit dem Mittelalter* (Münster, 1987), pp. 275–308, here p. 307.

5. Friedhoff, '"Magnificence" und "Utilité"', pp. 620–33.

6. 'der Herr, die Madame, die Demoiselles Töchter, der junge Herr, die Diener, die Mädchen, jeder will jetzt seine eigene Stube haben; mit Kammern ist die Dienerschaft nicht zufrieden, im Winter muß das Zimmer geheitzt werden können, dazu kommen dann noch Putzstuben, Visitenzimmer, Eßsäle, Entreezimmer, und was für Namen die Stuben noch mehr haben mögen.' Johann Jacob Sell, *Brief über Stettin und die umliegende Gegend auf einer Reise dahin im Sommer 1797 geschrieben* (Berlin, 1800) quoted in Volker Gläntzer, 'Nord-Süd-Unterschiede städtischen Wohnens um 1800 im Spiegel der zeitgenössischen Literatur', in Günter Wiegelmann (ed.), *Nord-Süd-Unterschiede in der städtischen und ländlichen Kultur Mitteleuropas* (Münster, 1985), pp. 73–88, here p. 83.

7. For estate inventories in cases where a guardian was appointed, see Uwe Meiners, 'Zur Wohnkultur der münsterschen Bevölkerung in der zweiten Hälfte des 18. Jahrhundert. Eine Fallstudie anhand von Nachlaßverzeichnissen', *Rheinisch-westfälische Zeitschrift für Volkskunde*, 25 (1979–80): 82–3. For those cities such as Frankfurt or Hamburg that provide few inventories, we are dependent on the inventories preserved in the records of cases brought before the Imperial Chamber Court.

8. Basic works are Lorna Weatherill, *Consumer Behaviour and Material Culture in Britain, 1660–1760* (London and New York, 1988); Ad van der Woude and Anton Schuurmann (eds), *Probate Inventories: A New Source for the Historical Stud of Wealth, Material Culture and Agricultural Development* (Utrecht, 1980); Jaume Torras and

Bartolomé Yun (eds), *Consumo, condiciones de vida y comercialización. Cataluña y Castilla, siglos XVII–XIX* (Valladolid, 1999).

9. Ruth-Elisabeth Mohrmann, *Alltagswelt im Land Braunschweig: Städtische und ländliche Wohnkultur vom 16. bis zum frühen 20. Jahrhundert* (2 vols, Münster, 1990), and 'Städtische Wohnkultur in Norddeutschland vom 17. bis zum 19. Jahrhundert (aufgrund von Inventaren)', in Günter Wiegelmann (ed.), *Nord-Süd-Unterschiede in der städtischen und ländlichen Kultur Mitteleuropas* (Münster, 1985), pp. 89–155, here pp. 90–96. See also Meiners, 'Zur Wohnkultur', pp. 80–103.

10. Jörg Driesner, 'Materielle Kultur in Greifswald im 17. und 18. Jahrhundert' (MA thesis, University of Greifswald, 2002), and 'Frühmoderne Alltagswelten im Ostseeraum: Materielle Kultur in Stralsund, Kopenhagen und Riga – Drei Regionen im Vergleich' (PhD dissertation, University of Greifswald, 2006); Corina Heß, 'Die materielle Wohnkultur Danzigs des 17. und 18. Jahrhunderts im Spiegel von Nachlassinventaren' (PhD dissertation, University of Greifswald, 2005), and *Danziger Wohnkultur in der Frühen Neuzeit* (Münster, 2007); Raimo Pullat, *Die Nachlassverzeichnisse der deutschen Kaufleute in Tallinn 1702–1750* (Tallinn, 1997).

11. Mohrmann, 'Städtische Wohnkultur', pp. 90–96.

12. Mohrmann, 'Städtische Wohnkultur', pp. 101ff.

13. Mohrmann, 'Städtische Wohnkultur', pp. 104–8.

14. ICC Frankfurt 453 (G16/736, 810–811, 1780–1788), Maria Catharina Geißemer, née Schmidt, married Damm, second wife, now widow, of the blacksmith Augustin Geißemer, ICC Frankfurt Quad. 15: Augustin Geißemer's estate inventory, recorded at his house in Zeil 1777.

15. ICC Frankfurt 37 (A36/1654, 76–78, [1585–] 1776–1781), Peter Aull, iron merchant, Frankfurt, reference number 77: Quad 44: Margaretha Barbara Tanner's estate inventory.

16. Driesner, 'Materielle Kultur in Greifswald', pp. 55–6, and 'Frühmoderne Alltagswelten im Ostseeraum', p. 288 (Stadtarchiv Stralsund [StA HST], Rep. 37, no. 199: Inventory of Hinrich Boldten, 1704). In the trading centres of Danzig and Riga, in contrast, the monofunctional use of space was already more advanced in the seventeenth century.

17. Mohrmann, *Alltagswelt*, vol. 1, p. 56.

18. Mohrmann, *Alltagswelt*, vol. 2, pp. 490ff.

19. Mohrmann, *Alltagswelt*, vol. 1, pp. 78–83.

20. ICC Frankfurt 756 (J 149/1832, 1200–1205, 1738–1766), 'Johann Georg and Johann Carl Wahler, merchants, and Beer Hertz Oppenheimer as representatives of the Frankfurt creditors of the Württemberg Court Jew Joseph Süß Oppenheimer, resident of Frankfurt from 1734, who was executed on 4 Febr. 1738 at Stuttgart', in diverse inventories etc. concerning Süß Oppenheimer's property left behind in Frankfurt, for example, the furnishings of the Posthaus, fols 34–40.

21. Driesner, 'Frühmoderne Alltagswelten im Ostseeraum', pp. 178ff.

22. ICC Frankfurt 578 (H 62/5202, 982–983, 1750–1766), 'Franz Adam Baron von Holbach, banker, Paris (born at Edesheim i. d. Pfalz)' therein: reference number 982: debenture 1720 (fol. 68), inventory of the estate of the married couple Gogel 1753 (fols 346–373), listing of the *Status massae* for Johann Noe Gogel (fols 381–384). ICC Frankfurt 455 (G 18/797, 814–816 [1749] 1762–1766) [Maria ?] Eva Gelhaar, née Mergenbaum, widow of the tanner Johann David Gelhaar, sister of Georg Daniel Mergenbaum, Frankfurt, reference number 816: inventory of the

property of Georg Daniel Mergenbaum in his house Am Rebstock (fols 36–73). StA Hamburg, Erbschaftsamt, D 74.

23. Meiners, 'Münster', p. 97; Mohrmann, *Alltagswelt*, vol. 2, p. 497.
24. Peter Höher, 'Konstanz und Wandel in Wohnausstattung und Hauswirtschaft (1630–1899). Das Beispiel Nürtingen am Neckar', in Günter Wiegelmann (ed.), *Wandel der Alltagskultur seit dem Mittelalter* (Münster, 1987), pp. 309–31, here pp. 318, 320.
25. Staatsarchiv Hamburg, Inheritance Office, D 74.
26. Mohrmann, *Alltagswelt*, vol. 2, p. 501.
27. Mohrmann, *Alltagswelt*, vol. 2, p. 503 and vol. 1, pp. 95–100.
28. StA Hamburg, Erbschaftsamt, D 71.
29. Driesner, 'Materielle Kultur', pp. 30–31.
30. Meiners, 'Wohnkultur in süddeutschen Kleinstädten vom 17. bis zum 19. Jahrhundert. Soziale Unterschiede und Wertstrukturen', in Günter Wiegelmann (ed.), *Nord-Süd-Unterschiede in der städtischen und ländlichen Kultur Mitteleuropas* (Münster, 1985), pp. 157–222, here pp. 179, 187.
31. Mohrmann, 'Städtische Wohnkultur', p. 103. Johann Baptist Meixner also possessed a sofa in Gobelsburg, Lower Austria, in 1797, while Schredl could admire his large picture collection from a canapé as early as 1761. Edith Eckhart, 'Die Verlassenschaften von Gobelsburg und Hadersdorf am Kamp als Quelle für die Kultur von Bürgern und Inwohnern im 18. Jahrhundert' (PhD dissertation, University of Vienna, 1977), p. 292.
32. Driesner, 'Materielle Kultur'. Heß, *Die Materielle Wohnkultur Danzigs*, p. 148 (StA HST, Rep. 3, Das Gerichtswesen der Stadt Stralsund, no. 5468: Inventory of the lawyer Hercules, 1775). In Riga, too, however, the trend towards seating groups is quite evident towards the end of the eighteenth century. After his death in 1797, Johann Georg Lehmann left behind 'one sofa covered in blue, two upholstered armchairs [*Fauteuils*] ditto, …, five large easy chairs [*Lehnstühle*] covered in black leather, one day-bed ditto, …, one brown-yellow sofa, three ditto upholstered armchairs '. The only mention we find of innovations in the area of furniture seating more than one person are references to canapés in the mid-eighteenth century. There is no mention of sofas, ottomans or other such pieces of furniture. Driesner, 'Frühmoderne Alltagswelten im Ostseeraum', p. 152 (Staatsarchiv Riga [StA Riga], Vogteigericht no. 1378-1-94: Inventory of Johann George Lehmann, 1797).
33. Meiners, 'Münster', p. 89.
34. ICC Frankfurt 578.
35. Driesner, 'Materielle Kultur', pp. 16–23.
36. Höher, 'Nürtingen', p. 322.
37. Norbert Elias, *Über den Prozeß der Zivilisation*, vol. 1, (2nd edn, Berne and Munich, 1969), p. 14.
38. Mohrmann, *Alltagswelt*, vol. 1, p. 201.
39. Mohrmann, *Alltagswelt*, vol. 1, pp. 203–6.
40. Mohrmann, *Alltagswelt*, pp. 222–3, vol. 2, p. 565. See also Chapter 9 below.
41. ICC Frankfurt 37.
42. ICC Frankfurt 455.
43. ICC Frankfurt 578.
44. ICC Frankfurt 453.
45. Staatsarchiv Hamburg, Inheritance Office, D 71.

46. Staatsarchiv Hamburg, Inheritance Office, D 74.
47. Driesner, 'Materielle Kultur', pp. 72–5; Thomas Spohn, 'Veränderungen der Tischsitten im Spiegel bürgerlicher Inventare des 17. und 18. Jahrhunderts', *Rheinisch-westfälische Zeitschrift für Volkskunde*, 30/31 (1954): 167–81.
48. Irmgard Gierl, 'Die Einrichtung der Weilheimer Bürgerhäuser von 1650–1724', in *Bayerisches Jahrbuch für Volkskunde* (1969): 120–24, here p. 122. Mohrmann, *Alltagswelt*, vol. 2, p. 545.
49. Meiners, *Süddeutschland*, pp. 169–70.
50. StA Hamburg, Erbschaftsamt, D 71, D 74.
51. ICC Frankfurt 37, 756, 1302 (S 18/1838, 1946, 1699–1732 (1777–1781) 'Johann Philipp Sparr, merchant, Frankfurt', Quad. 25: List of Dr. Caspar Sparr's estate with his grandmother's portion of inheritance, Quad. 127: 'Anna Margaretha's (widowed Sparr) inventory at the time of her marriage to Peter Petschmann in 1702.'
52. For the latter, see also Chapter 6 below.
53. ICC Frankfurt 1302.
54. '1. Portrait Ihrer Durchl. der Hertzogin zu Würtenberg
    1. dito des bischoffen von Bamberg
    1. dito des Churfürsten von Cölln
    1. dito der Churfürst von Pfaltz
    1. dito der Landgraf von Darmstadt
    1. dito der Erbprintz von Darmstadt
    1. dito eines alten Mannes brustbild
    1. dito die Frau vorstellende
    1. dito des Süßen Portrait
    6. Stück landschafften mit vergülten Rahmen
    1. stück die historie Abraham und Isaacs
    1. Nachtstück
    P.N: die übrige hierbey befindlich gewesene kleine Gemählde sind schon in einem der schwartzen Commodgen am 15. h. transportiret worden …
    2. Portraits, 1. alter Mann und dito Frau, fein gemahlt.' ICC Frankfurt 578.
55. 'In dem Zimmer daneben [neben der kleinen Wohnstube]
    An Gemälden
    So nicht woll abzunehmen gewesen, jedoch mit Nummer marquirt worden.
    1.) ein See Stück
    2.) S. Franciscus mit der H. Maria
    3.) S. Johannes in der Wüste
    4.) 1. Landschaft
    5.) 1. Alt Gemälde
    6. 7. 8. et 9.) 4 Rudera und Architectur Stücke
    10.) der unglaubige Thomas gros
    11.) 1. Küchen-Stück, gros
    12.) 1. Landschaft
    13.) 1. Landschaft
    14.) 1. Viehstück
    15.) 1. Küchenstück
    16.) 1. Obststück
    17.) 1. Blumenstück
    18.) 1. Küchenstück

19.) 1. d. Nachtstück

20.) 1. dito

21.) 1. Landschäftgen

22. 23. et 24.) 3. detti

25.) Ein Gemäuer die Vergangenheit Vorstellend

26.) 1. Viehstück

27.) 1. Landschäftgen

28.) 1. Landschaft

29.) 1. dito

30.) 1. Seestück

31.) 1. altes Gemäuer

32.) 1. Landschaft mit dito

33.) 1. Mann mit 1. Flöte

34.) Creuzigung Christi

35.) 1. Hundstückgen

36. 37.) 2. Landschäftgen

38.) 1. Küchenstück

39.) 1. Bauernstück

40. et 41.) 2. Gänsrupfen

42.) 1. Bauernstück

43.) 1. dito mit metallisirter Rahme

44. et 45.) 2. Landschäftgen

46.) 1. Küchenstück

47.) 1. klein Viehstück

48.) die Bekehrung Pauli

49.) 1. Wasserstück

…

Unten in der Contoir-Stube

1.   große Schilderey, Adams und Eva vorstellend

1.   dito Schilderey die Gebuhrt Christi

1.   d. die Hager

1.   d. Viehstück

…

In dem obsignirten hintern Camin …

1.   grose Schilderey, den guldenen Regen Vorstellend

1.   Stück, die Sterblichkeit Vorstellend

1.   Küchenstück

1.   Nachtstück

2.   Portraits, das eine einen Mahler Vorstellend

3.   Landschaften

1.   Küchen und Obststück

1.   Blumenstück. 1. d. Kleines

1.   d. Wasserstück

1.   Landschaft

1.   alter Manns Kopf

1.   d. Weiber Kopf

Noch 1. Manns Kopf

1.   d. Eremit

4. kleine Baumstückgen
1. d. den Brand Troja Vorstellend mit 1. Glas
1. Landschäftgen mit dito
2. d. etwas größer
3. kleine schlechte detti
1. altes Gemählde, die Sterblichkeit Vorstellend
[…]
In der obsignirten grosen Stube
9. Famillen-Portraits, worunter ein Lebens grös
1. Schilderey, eine Bauren-Hochzeit Vorstellend
2. d. Holländische Gebäude Vorstellend
1. d. Cupido als Vulcanus
2. Bataillen-Stücke
1. Viehstück
1. d. Antiques die Creuzigung Christi
3. Obststücke
1. Brabands Baurenstückgen
1. Stück die Taufe Johannis
1. Nacht-Bataille-Stück
1. See-Sturm
1. Ovid. Stück mit dem Michas
2. Stücke, Adam und Eva Vorstell.
1. Gesellschaft mit Music
2. Landschaften
6. kleine detti.'
ICC Frankfurt 578.

56. Thomas Ketelsen and Tilmann von Stockhausen, *Verzeichnis der verkauften Gemälde im deutschsprachigen Raum vor 1800*, vol. 1 'A–Hi' (Munich, 2002), pp. 107–8, no. 146 (1782/09/30). See also Chapter 6 below, p. 112.

57. Similar tendencies can be found in Stralsund and Riga. Those who prepared inventories only rarely took the time to record the motifs of art works, as in the case of Diedrich Meyer Weyland of Stralsund, who in 1738 could list as his own: '5 large paintings of fowl and other farm animals', among other pictures. It was deemed far more important to describe the picture frames in detail. In 1733, for example, the Riga household of Paul Wagler contained 'two mediocre portraits without frames, three small ditto with black stained frames, seven "Nürnberger Bilder" in gilt frames, three cut-out silhouettes with an oaken frame' (zwey mittelmäßige Contrefaits ohne Rahmen, Drey kleine dito mit schwartz gebeitzten Rahmen, Sieben 'Nürnberger Bilder' mit verguldeten Rahmen, Drei ausgeschnittener dito mit einem Rahmen von Eichen Holtz). Only in 1745 do we find a few more closely described pictures from the household of the Riga master artisan Martin Hayden, for example 'two landscapes, and three ditto, one picture with birds, one portrait of the late gentleman, one ditto, two paintings with silver frames in the Dutch manner, two small ditto with ditto, one landscape with a brown frame, [in the] Dutch [manner], one more a landscape without a frame, one still-life with a silver frame' ('2 Landschaften, noch 3 dito, …, 1 Bild mit Vögeln, …, 1 Conterfey des seel. Herrnn, 1 dito, …, 2 Schildereyen mitt silbern Ramenn holländisch Manier, 2 kleiner dito mit dito, …, 1 Landschaft mit braunenn Ramenn so holländisch, …,

1 noch eine Landschaft ohne Ramenn, …, 1 stilles Stück mit silbern Ramenn'). In Danzig and Reval, too, the subjects of pictures were mentioned seldom, and the artists' names not at all. Driesner, 'Frühmoderne Alltagswelten im Ostseeraum', pp. 239ff. (StA HST, Rep. 3, Das Gerichtswesen der Stadt Stralsund, no. 5384: Inventory of Diedrich Meyers Weyland, 1738; StA Riga, Vogteigericht no. 1378-1-936: Inventory of Paul Wagler, 1733), (StA Riga, Vogteigericht no. 1378-1-936: Inventory of Martin Hayden, 1745).

58. StA Hamburg, O17 and S116.
59. Mohrmann, *Alltagswelt*, vol. 2, pp. 539–40.
60. Mohrmann, *Alltagswelt*, vol. 2, pp. 539–40.
61. ICC Frankfurt 578, 37.
62. StA Hamburg, Erbschaftsamt, D 71. Data for the clockmakers can be found in Granville Hugh Baillie, *Watchmakers and Clockmakers of the World* (3rd edn, London, 1951, reprint London, 1972). I thank Dr Günther Oestmann of Bremen for kindly providing this reference.
63. Mohrmann, 'Städtische Wohnkultur', p. 108.
64. 'Im Zimmer einer eleganten Dame sind kleine niedliche Behältnisse, die zugleich als Ziermeubeln dienen und leicht fortbewegt werden können, eine sehr wünschenswerte und willkommene Sache … . Die verschlossene Tischplatte … hebt sich in Charnieren auf, um Arbeitssachen und andere Kleinigkeiten, die man schnell aus der Hand zu legen wünscht, in den darunter befindlichen Sack von grünem Taft verwahren zu können.' *Journal des Luxus und der Moden* (November 1797): 578–9, quoted in Angelika Emmerich and Susanne Schroeder, 'Weimarer historische Interieurs. Zum Ameublement im "Journal des Luxus und der Moden"', in Gerhard R. Kaiser and Siegfried Seifert (eds), *Friedrich Justin Bertuch (1747–1822), Verleger, Schriftsteller und Unternehmer im klassischen Weimar* (Tübingen, 2000), pp. 501–18, here p. 512.
65. For a good overview of Roentgen's workshops, see Friedhoff, '"Magnificence" und "Utilité"', pp. 723–35. Michael Stürmer's *Handwerk und höfische Kultur. Europäische Möbelkunst im 18. Jahrhundert* (Munich, 1982) remains a fundamental study for the eighteenth-century court context. See also Gloria Ehret, *Deutsche Möbel des 18. Jahrhunderts. Barock – Rokoko – Klassizismus* (Munich, 1986), p. 160.
66. Quoted in Rosemarie Schütz, 'David Roentgen (1743–1807). Der "Königliche Kabinettmacher" aus Neuwied', in *Möbel von Abraham und David Roentgen. Sammlung Kreismuseum Neuwied* (Neuwied, 1990), pp. 17–38, here p. 17.

Chapter 5

1. 'Gärten sind Plätze, auf welchen der Mensch alle Vorteile des Landlebens, alle Annehmlichkeiten der Jahreszeiten mit Bequemlichkeit, mit Ruhe genießen kann. Soviel Vorteile und Ergötzungen die Natur ihrem empfindsamen Freunde aufbewahret, soviel kann er in dem Umfang eines ausgebreiteten, wohl angelegten Gartens finden. Ja, diese Vorteile und Ergötzungen erhöhen und vervielfältigen sich hier in eben dem Grade, in welchem Vernunft und Geschmack bemühet sind, einen Garten durch die Reize der Cultur über eine sich selbst überlassene Gegend zu erheben.' Christian Cay Lorenz Hirschfeld, *Theorie der Gartenkunst*, 5 vols (Leipzig,

1779–85), here vol. 1, p. 154. Reprinted in part in *Garten und Wildnis. Landschaft im 18. Jahrhundert*, ed. Hansjörg and Ulf Küster (Munich, 1997), pp. 90–98.

2. Monique Mosser and Georges Teyssot, *Die Gartenkunst des Abendlandes. Von der Renaissance bis zur Gegenwart* (Stuttgart, 1993), pp. 105–98, 289–300; Mark Laird, *The Formal Garden: Traditions of Art and Nature* (London, 1992), pp. 41–72, 82–5. *Der formale Garten. Architektonische Landschaftskunst aus fünf Jahrhunderten* (Stuttgart, 1994), pp. 41–90, 123–30.

3. Erhard Hirsch, 'Hortus Oeconomicus: Nutzen, Schönheit, Bildung. Das Dessau-Wörlitzer Gartenreich als Landschaftsgestaltung der europäischen Aufklärung', in Heinke Wunderlich, *'Landschaft' und Landschaften im achtzehnten Jahrhundert* (Heidelberg, 1995), pp. 179–207; Adrian von Buttlar, *Der Landschaftsgarten* (Munich, 1980); Helmut Reinhardt, 'Gartenkunst in Deutschland im 18. Jahrhundert: Klassik, Rokoko und Neoklassizismus', in Monique Mosser and Georges Teyssot, *Die Gartenkunst des Abendlandes. Von der Renaissance bis zur Gegenwart* (Stuttgart, 1993), pp. 289–300. On allusions to the *Alte Reich* or German history, see Maiken Umbach, *Federalism and Enlightenment in Germany 1740–1806* (London and Rio Grande, Ohio, 2000), ch. 3 and ch. 5, as well as Michael Niedermeier, 'Germanen in den Gärten. "Altdeutsche Heldengräber", "gotische" Denkmäler und die patriotische Gedächtniskultur', in Jost Hermand and Michael Niedermeier, *Revolutio germanica. Die Sehnsucht nach der "alten Freiheit" der Germanen 1750–1820* (Frankfurt, 2002), pp. 21–116.

4. Peter Gabrielsson, 'Zur Entwicklung des bürgerlichen Garten- und Landhausbesitzes bis zum Beginn des 19. Jahrhunderts', in *Gärten, Landhäuser und Villen des hamburgischen Bürgertums: Kunst, Kultur und gesellschaftliches Leben in vier Jahrhunderten* (Hamburg, 1975), pp. 11–18.

5. 'Die rarsten Pflanzen und Fruchtbäume von der Welt in merklicher Anzahl und was hier zu Lande in der Erden nicht wohl überwintern mag, das stand in Kasten und Töpfen rund herum 400–500 Stücke, sodaß hier nichts fehlte, daran Aug' und Geruch sich ergözen mag.' Quoted in Gabrielsson, 'Zur Entwicklung', p. 16.

6. '… Ein heller Glanz / ein mehr als güld'ner Schein /
    Nam Luft und Land bezaubernd ein /
    Und reizte mich/ da Wald und Feld so schön/
    Der Gärten Pracht und Anmuth anzusehn;
    In welchen die Natur sich mit der Kunst verbindet/
    Wo Fleiß/ wo Nutz und Lust sich stets verschwistert findet;
    Woselbst wir in der Menschen Werken
    Zugleich die wirkende Natur/
    Und in derselbigen die helle Spur
    Von unsers Schöpfers Macht und, Gegenwart bemerken.'
    Barthold Heinrich Brockes, *Irdisches Vergnügen in Gott bestehend in verschiedenen aus der Natur und Sitten=Lehre hergenommenen Gedichten, nebst einem Anhange etlicher hieher gehörigen Uebersetzungen von des Hrn. de La Motte Französis. Fabeln mit Genehmhaltung des Herrn Verfassers nebst einer Vorrede herausgegeben von C. F. Weichmann* (Hamburg, 1721), p. 91.

7. Quoted in Wolfgang Kehn, 'Ästhetische Landschaftserfahrung und Landschaftsgestaltung in der Spätaufklärung: Der Beitrag von Christian Cay Lorenz Hirschfelds Gartentheorie', in Heinke Wunderlich (ed.), *'Landschaft' und Landschaften im achtzehnten Jahrhundert* (Heidelberg, 1995), pp. 1–23, here p. 4.

8. 'Anemone

Amaranthus, chrystatus, tricolor globosus. [Fuchsschwanz-Arten]

Alcea Theophrasti [Eibisch]

Astrantia nigra [Strenze]

Auricula muris etc. [Aurikel]

Antirrhinum [Löwenmäulchen]

Aster atticus, autumnalis etc.

Aster foemina. S. Conyza cerulea. [Berufkraut]

Amaranthus caudatus. [Fuchsschwanz]

Panicum major & minor. [Hirse]

Aster chinensis.

Balsamina. [Springkraut]

Bellis. [Maßliebchen]

Campanula piramidalis, utricae folio, flore coeruleo. [Glockenblumen]

Cariophillus, barbatus. [Bartnelke]

Cyanus. [Kornblume]

Campanula urticae foli, flore albo

Calendula. [Ringelblume]

Chrysantemum. [Margherite]

Colchicum. [Herbstzeitlose]

Conv. minor. S. Convolvulus peregrinus. [Winde]

Campanula minima, fl. Coer.

Crocus.

Corona imperialis. [Kaiserkrone]

Consolida regia. [Rittersporn]

Flos Africanus major & minor, versicolr, S. tricolor.

Flos Adonis. [Adonisröschen]

Flos cardinalis.

Flos poeticus.

Fraxinella. [Diptam]

Geranium pictum, atrum, flore coccineo. [Storchschnabel, Geranie oder Pelargonie]

Galéga. [Geißraute]

Geraneum magnum, maximo-flore.

Hedisarum, clypeatum, rubr. et. alb. [Süßklee]

Hesperis odorata. [Nachtviole].'

Quoted in Hansjörg and Küster, *Garten und Wildnis. Landschaft im 18. Jahrhundert*, pp. 66–7.

9. Ralph-Jürgen Reipsch, 'Telemanns "Bluhmen-Liebe"', in *Günter Fleischhauer zum 60. Geburtstag am 8 Juli 1988*, Telemann-Beiträge: Abhandlungen und Berichte, 2 (Magdeburg, 1989), pp. 34–46.

10. 'Die schönen Bäume, die liebliche Abwechslung von Hügel und Thal, die mannigfaltigen Baumgruppen, die so verschiedenen Land und Strom, An- und Aussichten suche ich zu benutzen, um auf denen, durch die mit solchem Fleiß bestellten Felder geführten Wege, eine Reihe wechselnder, in ihrem Charakter von einander verschiedener Landschaften dem Auge des Wandelnden der Reihe nach darzustellen.' Quoted in Ulrich Bauche, 'Von bürgerlicher Gartenkunst', in *Gärten, Landhäuser und Villen des hamburgischen Bürgertums* (1975), pp. 19–25, here p. 24.

11. '[Die] Neigung zur Gärtnerey … nicht nur bei Großen und Reichen, sondern auch bey anderen Personen von allen Ständen und Ordnungen zur herrschenden Leidenschaft.' Johann Prokop Mayer, *Pomona Franconia: Description des arbres fruitiers les plus connus et les plus éstimés en Europe, qui se cultivent maintenent au Jardin de La Cour de Wurzbourg*, vol. 1 (Nuremberg, 1776), p. xliv; quoted in Jens Friedhoff, '"Magnificence" und "Utilité". Bauen und Wohnen 1600–1800', in Ulf Dirlmeier (ed.), *Geschichte des Wohnens*, vol. 2: *500–1800: Hausen, Wohnen, Residieren* (Stuttgart, 1998), pp. 503–815, here p. 747.

12. For an overview, see Hugo Koch, *Sächsische Gartenkunst* (Berlin, 1910, reprint Beucha, 1999), pp. 71–84.

13. Christoph Wolff, *Johann Sebastian Bach* (Frankfurt, 2000), p. 429.

14. 'Alles ist in den Landhäusern oder in den Bädern – Ich bin auch sehr oft auf dem Land bey guten Freunden … den gantzen Sonntag bin ich vor dem Bockheimer Thor in Senator Stocks Garten – in der Woche vorm Allerheiligen Thor bey Madam Fingerling – dann über Sachsenhaußen auf einem prächtigen Gut bey Herrn Kellner, und so habe ich 3 bis 4 Orte, wo es mir sehr wohl behagt. Sie sehen hieraus, daß die Großmutter sich des Lebens noch immer freut.' Dagmar von Gersdorff, *Goethes Mutter. Eine Biographie* (Frankfurt and Leipzig, 2001), pp. 45, 75; subsequent quotes on pp. 375–6, 392.

15. *Inventar der Akten des Reichskammergerichts 1495–1806. Frankfurter Bestand*, ed. Inge Kaltwasser (Frankfurt, 2000), pp. 648–9, ICC Frankfurt 902, Quad. 23: 'Taxation des von Barckhaus'schen Gartens vor dem Allerheiligentor, am Hanauer Weg gelegen'.

16. 'Von da [Landhaus] wandelt man durch schlängelnde Gänge von ausländischen Hölzern, deren eine große Verschiedenheit ist. … Weiter abwärts rechter Hand trifft man auf einen Teich in unregelmäßiger Form. Wendet man sich nun abwärts, so stößt man auf die Ruinen einer gotischen Kirche. Hinter den Ruinen ist eine Pflanzung von allerley Arten feiner Nadelhölzer angelegt. Niedriger liegt ein kleines Eremitenhäuschen, das auf russische Art aus ganzen Stämmen erbauet und mit Stroh gedeckt ist.' Quoted in E. Merck, *Johann Heinrich Merck (1741–1791). Ein Leben für Freiheit und Toleranz – Zeitdokumente* (Darmstadt, 1991), p. 108.

17. Niedermeier, 'Germanen in den Gärten', pp. 99–100.

18. Angelika Schneider, 'Friedrich Justin Bertuch – ein Beförderer der Gartenkunst', in Gerhard R. Kaiser und Siegfried Seifert (eds), *Friedrich Justin Bertuch (1747–1822). Verleger, Schriftsteller und Unternehmer im klassischen Weimar* (Tübingen, 2000), pp. 629–57, here pp. 632–3.

19. Goethe to Auguste Stolberg, Weimar, 17–24 May 1776, in *Johann Wolfgang von Goethe, Briefe an Auguste Gräfin zu Stolberg*, ed. Jürgen Behrens (Frankfurt, 1982), p. 43; quoted in Gabriele Busch-Salmen, Walter Salmen and Christoph Michel, *Der Weimarer Musenhof. Dichtung, Musik und Tanz, Gartenkunst, Geselligkeit, Malerei* (Stuttgart and Weimar, 1998), p. 33.

20. 'Wir speiseten in einer gar holden kleinen Einsideley … Wir tranken auf deine und Frau Aja's und Freund Bölling, des Kornhändlers, Gesundheit eine Flasche Johannisberger 60er aus, und wie wir nun aufgestanden waren und die Thüre öfneten, siehe, da stellte sich uns, durch geheime Anstalt des Archi-Magus, ein Anblik dar, der mehr einer realisierten dichterischen vision als einer Naturscene ähnlich sah. Das ganze Ufer der Ilm, ganz in Rembrands Geschmack, beleuchtet – ein wunderbares Zaubergemisch von Hell und Dunkel, das im Ganzen einen

Effect machte der über allen Ausdruk geht. Die Herzogin war davon entzükt wie wir alle. Als wir die kleine Treppe der Einsiedley herabstiegen und zwischen Felsenstücken und Buschwerken längs der Ilm gegen die Brücke, die diesen Platz mit einer Ecke des Sterns verbindet, hingiengen, zerfiel die ganz vision nach und nach in eine Menge kleiner Rembrandtischen Nachtstücke die man ewig hätte vor sich sehnen mögen, und die nun durch die dazwischen herumwandelnden Personen ein Leben und ein Wunderbares bekamen, das für meine Poetische Wenigkeit gar was herrliches war. Ich hätte Göthen vor Liebe fressen mögen.' Wieland to Merck, 27 August 1778, *Wielands Briefwechsel,* ed. Waltraud Hagen, vol. 7 (January 1778– June 1782), (Berlin, 1992), pp. 113–14.

21. Busch-Salmen, Salmen und Michel, *Weimarer Musenhof,* pp. 34ff.

22. Friedrich Nicolai, *Beschreibung der Königlichen Residenzstädte Berlin und Potsdam* (Berlin, 1769; reprint Hildesheim, Zurich and New York, 1988), pp. 50–51, 119, and *Beschreibung der Königlichen Residenzstädte Berlin und Potsdam, aller daselbst befindlicher Merkwürdigkeiten, und der umliegenden Gegend,* (13 vols, Berlin, 1786), vol. 2, pp. 569–70, 929–35, 937ff.

23. 'I. In Berlin an sich selbst.
Der Itzigsche Garten, worinn verschiedene Springbrunnen befindlich sind,
Der Garten des Hrn. Kriegsrath Beyer, worinn eine schöne Flor von Nelken und Ranunkeln befindlich ist,
Der Garten des Hrn. O. K. R. Büsching. In demselben ist dessen erste 1777 verstorbene Gattin, geb. Dilthey begraben. Auf der Grabstelle derselben ist ein Blumenbeet, worauf den ganzen Sommer Blümlein Vergiß mein nicht blühen. An der Wand des Wohnhauses über dem Blumenbeete, ist auf einer marmornen Tafel eine Inschrift,
Der Ephraimsche Garten, dessen Hintertheil gränzt an den gräflich Reußischen Garten, die reizendste Partie desselben ist eine von den schattigten Spaziergängen umgebene Wiese. Hier stehen auch sechs, zehn bis zwölf Fuß hohe Statuen nach Schlüters Erfindung, welche auf die Brustgeländer, auf dem Dache des Schlosses, haben sollen gesetzt werden. Es sind: Merkur, Juno, Bacchus, Flora, Leda und Venus. Noch ist in einem Gebüsche ein artiges Kabinet, welches von einem einzigen Plàtanusbaum, dessen Zweige sich sehr weit ausbreiten, beschattet wird,
Der Garten Sr. Excellenz des Staatsministers Freyherrn von Zedlitz. Er ist nach engländischem Geschmacke neuangelegt. In demselben ist ein Vogelhaus, mit einem Springbrunnen, auch ein großes und schön angelegtes Orangeriehaus, ferner ein Treibhaus für Ananas u.s.w.,
Der Garten des Bankiers Hrn. Holzeckers. Er ist treflich unterhalten. Es sind darinn schöne Blumenfloren, und trefliche Treibhäuser zu Wein, Pfirsichen und andern Gewächsen die besondere Kultur erfordern.'
Nicolai, *Beschreibung* (1786), vol. 2, pp. 929–33.

24. 'II. In Kölln.
Der große und schöne Splittgerbersche Garten. Er ist etwas schmal, aber sehr lang, da er bis in die Köllnische Vorstadt geht. Er hat sehr reizende Partien; dazu gehört besonders ein offnes Lusthaus, vor dem Wusterhausischen Wehr, wo das Rauschen des Wassers eine angenehme Wirkung macht, und ein ovales chinesisches Lusthaus, auf einer kleinen und hohen Bäumen bewachsenen Anhöhe,
Der überaus schöne und große Daniel Itzigsche Garten. Die Verbesserungen und meist ganz neue Anlage sind von dem Königl. Gärtner Herrn Heidert

in Potsdam angegeben worden. Er enthält ausser Hecken, Bogengängen und schattigten Plantagen zum Vergnügen, auch einige tausend schöne Fruchtbäume von den besten Sorten. In demselben ist ein Gartentheater unter freyem Himmel. Desgleichen stehen darinn verschiedene Statuen von Knöfler in Dresden,
IV. Auf der Dorotheen= oder Neustadt.
Der Cesarsche Garten, wegen einer dem Königl. Sänger Herrn Concialini gehörigen vortreflichen Blumenflor von Ranunkeln, Tulpen, Nelken und anderen Arten von Blumen. Der Graviussche Garten. In demselben ist ein grottirter Saal, ein von Le Geay gebautes rundes Gartenhaus, und ein angenehmes Vogelhaus, worinn eine Abtheilung blos für Nachtigallen ist,
V. Auf der Friedrichsstadt.
Der Herr Hofprediger Reinhard an der Parochialkirche und sein Vorgänger, der verstorbene Hofprediger Scharden, waren diejenigen, welchen die Blumenfreunde die Erzeugung schöner Tulpen aus Saamen, und die Anweisung wie ihre Fortpflanzung mit Nutzen anwendbar sey, in hiesigen Gegenden zu verdanken haben … und seitdem sind in folgenden Gärten viele und ausnehmend schöne Tulpen aus hiesigen Saamen gezogen worden … .'
Nicolai, *Beschreibung* (1786), vol. 2, pp. 934–8.
25. Nicolai, *Beschreibung* (1786), vol. 2, pp. 940–41.
26. Friedhoff, 'Magnificence', pp. 751–2.
27. Joseph Furttenbach, *Architectura civilis* (Ulm, 1628), *Architectura universalis* (Ulm, 1635), *Architectura recreationis* (Ulm, 1640), and *Architectura private* (Ulm, 1641).
28. Dorothee Nehring, 'Die Gartenentwürfe Joseph Furttenbachs d. Ä.', in Monique Mosser and Georges Teyssot (eds), *Die Gartenkunst des Abendlandes. Von der Renaissance bis zur Gegenwart* (Stuttgart, 1993), pp. 156ff. See also Dieter Hennebo and Alfred Hoffmann, *Geschichte der deutschen Gartenkunst*, vol. 2: *Der Architektonische Garten. Renaissance und Barock* (Hamburg, 1965), pp. 96–103; Friedhoff, 'Magnificence', pp. 740–46.
29. Frantz Antoni Danreitter, *Die Gärtnerey, so wohl in ihrer Theorie oder Betrachtung als Praxi oder Übung: allwo von denen schönen Gärten, welche man nur insgemein die Lust- und Zierd-Gärten zu nennen pflegt ...* (Augsburg, 1731).
30. Christian Cay Lorenz Hirschfeld, *Theorie der Gartenkunst*, vol. 1 (Leipzig, 1775). Johann Georg Krünitz, *Oeconomische Encyclopädie* (16 vols, Berlin, 1779).
31. 'die selbst vollkommenste Gärtnerin ist. So wie also die zeichnenden Künste die von der Natur gebildeten schönen Formen zum Behuf der Kunst nachahmen, so macht es auch die Gartenkunst, die mit Geschmack und Überlegung jede Schönheit der leblosen Natur nachahmt und das, was sie einzeln findet, mit Geschmack in einem Lustgarten vereinigt.' Johann Georg Sulzer, *Allgemeine Theorie der schönen Künste* (2 vols, Leipzig, 1771, 1774), vol. 1, p. 421, quoted in Dieter Hennebo and Alfred Hoffmann, *Geschichte der deutschen Gartenkunst in drei Bänden* (3 vols, Hamburg, 1962–65, vol. 3: *Der Landschaftsgarten* (Hamburg, 1963, reprint, 1981), pp. 111–12.
32. *Theorie der Gartenkunst*, vol. I, pp. 209ff. For an interpretation, see Kehn, 'Ästhetische Landschaftserfahrung', p. 6.
33. Kehn, 'Ästhetische Landschaftserfahrung', p. 8.
34. 'Der Garten soll also auf die Einbildungskraft und auf das Empfindungsvermögen vortheilhaft einwürken; und dieses soll der Gartenkünstler mittelst der Gegenstände veranstalten, die ihm eigenthümlich zugehören. … Er muß daher zuförderst solche Gegenstände der schönen Natur sammeln und auswählen, die eine vorzügliche

Kraft haben, die angegebenen Wirkungen hervorzubringen; er muß diesen Gegenständen eine solche Ausbildung geben, und sie in eine solche Verbindung und Anordnung bringen, daß dadurch der Eindruck verstärket werde.' *Theorie der Gartenkunst,*vol. 1, pp. 83–4, quoted in Kehn, 'Ästhetische Landschaftserfahrung', p. 11.

35. 'Diese Aussicht auf eine so ausgebreitete und freye Wasserfläche zwischen Anhöhen und Waldungen macht das Hauptstück dieser Lage aus. Die Klarheit des Wassers, worin sich der halbe Himmel zu spiegeln scheint, und die Schönheit der Wälder umher ... verbreiten von allen Seiten eine ungemeine Heiterkeit.' Hirschfeld, *Theorie der Gartenkunst*, vol. 2, p. 154.

36. 'Die Trauerweide, Thränenweide, Babylonische Weide (Salix babylonica) ist bekanntlich ein sehr characteristischer und beinahe unentbehrlicher Baum für Landschaftsgärten im Englischen Stile, um entweder ein Monument, dem Andenken eines geliebten Todten geweiht, damit zu beschatten; oder sonst irgend einen der süßen Melancholie und dem ernsten Nachdenken heiligen Platz damit zu bezeichnen. Am Rande eines schönen Wasserspiegels bilden oft drei Trauerweiden, welche ihre langen grünen Haare in der Silberfluth, die ein sanfter Zephyr kräuselt, waschen, eine sehr schöne malerische Gruppe. Oder sie verstecken gleichsam, in einen grünen Mantel gehüllt, die Figur einer badenden Najade, und bilden so eine liebliche Idylle.' Quoted in Ulrich Müller, 'Friedrich Justin Bertuch und die landschaftliche Gartenkunst', in Gerhard R. Kaiser and Siegfried Seifert (eds), *Friedrich Justin Bertuch (1747–1822). Verleger, Schriftsteller und Unternehmer im klassischen Weimar* (Tübingen, 2000), pp. 607–27, here p. 613.

37. Müller, 'Bertuch', pp. 622f.

38. Schneider, 'Bertuch', p. 643.

39. Helmut Engel, *Villen und Landhäuser* (Berlin, 2001), pp. 7–16.

40. 'Ich kenne keine andere Stadt, die mit Vorstädten von Gärten und Gartendörfern so rings umgeben ist, worin jedes Haus eine große Familie und Stadthaushaltung faßt, manche Gebäude mit Geschmack, die meisten mit mehr oder weniger Aufwand errichtet und möbliert sind.' Friedrich Johann Lorenz Meyer, *Skizzen zu einem Gemälde von Hamburg* (Hamburg, 1802), pp. 59–60.

41. Gisela Jaacks, 'Landhausleben', in Gisela Jaacks (ed.) *Gärten, Landhäuser und Villen des hamburgischen Bürgertums. Kunst, Kultur und gesellschaftliches Leben in vier Jahrhunderten* (Hamburg, 1975), pp. 45–52, here p. 46.

42. Bärbel Hedinger, *C. F. Hansen in Hamburg, Altona und den Elbvororten. Ein dänischer Architekt des Klassizismus* (Munich and Berlin, 2000); Gerhard Wietek, *C. F. Hansen 1756–1845 und seine Bauten in Schleswig-Holstein* (Neumünster, 1982).

43. Kai Mathieu and Manfred F. Fischer, 'Baukunst und Architekten', in Jaacks (ed.) *Gärten, Landhäuser und Villen des hamburgischen Bürgertums. Kunst, Kultur und gesellschaftliches Leben in vier Jahrhunderten* (Hamburg, 1975), pp. 26–44, here pp. 38–41.

44. Anne-Charlott Trepp, *Sanfte Männlichkeit und selbständige Weiblichkeit. Frauen und Männer im Hamburger Bürgertum zwischen 1770 und 1840* (Göttingen, 1996), pp. 203–8.

45. Trepp, *Sanfte Männlichkeit*, pp. 235ff., 388–9.

46. 'Noch vor 18 Jahren [i.e. 1779] hatten wir Schmausereien auf unseren Gärten, wo wir in brennender Hitze mit städtischem Prunk beladen, Chapeaubas und Degen hinfuhren, um drei Stunden am Tisch zu schwitzen und drei Stunden nachher am Spieltisch den Schweiß abzutrocknen. Sie sind verschwunden und lächerlich

geworden – ohne irgendeine Verabredung, bloß durch befolgtes Beispiel, durch Aufklärung, durch besseren Geschmack.' Quoted in Jaacks, 'Landhausleben', p. 47. After Percy Ernst Schramm, *Neun Generationen. Dreihundert Jahre deutscher 'Kulturgeschichte' im Lichte der Schicksale einer Hamburger Bürgerfamilie (1648–1948)* (2 vols, Hamburg, 1963–64), vol. 1, p. 344.

47. Jaacks, 'Landhausleben', p. 48. See also Claudia Susannah Cremer, 'Hagedorns Geschmack. Studien zur Kunstkennerschaft in Deutschland im 18. Jahrhundert' (PhD dissertation, University of Bonn, 1989), pp. 273ff.

Chapter 6

1. Johann Wolfgang von Goethe, *From My Life: Poetry and Truth*, vol. I, trans. Robert R. Heitner, *Goethe's Collected Works*, vol. 4 (New York, 1987), p. 34.

2. Thomas Crow, *Painters and Public Life in Eighteenth-Century Paris* (New Haven and London, 1985), p. 3.

3. Ulrich Schmidt, 'Die privaten Kunstsammlungen in Frankfurt am Main von ihren Anfängen bis zur Ausbildung der reinen Kunstsammlung' (PhD dissertaion, University of Göttingen, 1960), Appendix. Jan Lauts, *Karoline Luise von Baden. Ein Lebensbild aus der Zeit der Aufklärung* (Karlsruhe, 1980, 2nd edn, 1990), p. 165.

4. *Catalogue d'un fameux Cabinet de tableaux des meilleurs maîtres, recueilli, avec beaucoup de choix et d'exactitude pendant plusieurs années et délaisse par feu monsieur le baron de Haeckel dont la vente se fera publiquement a Francfort sur le Mein, dans un terme qu'on annoncera par les Gazettes* (Frankfurt, 1762). Städelsches Kunstinstitut, Frankfurt.

5. *Verzeichnis einer betraechtlichen Sammlung von Gemaelden der besten und beruehmesten Teutschen, Italiaenischen und Niederlaendischen Meister, nebst einem Anhang von einigen Kupferstichen. Welche die Jacob Bernusische Beneficial-Erben in hrem Haus zum großen Saalhof allhier in Frankfurt am Mayn, gleich nach hiesiger Ostermeß, Montag den May 1781 und die folgende Tage, durch oeffentliche Versteigerung zu den Meistbietenden zu überlassen gesonnen sind* (Frankfurt, 1780). Städelsches Kunstinstitut, Frankfurt.

6. *Verzeichnis von Gemaelden der beruehmtesten Niederlaendischen, Franzoesischen, Italiaenischen und Deutschen Meister, welche von den Freyherrl. Von Berberichschen Erben zu Frankfurt am Mayn in dem Senkenbergischen Stiftungs-Hause nach der naechstbevorstehenden Herbst-Messe, Montags, den 27. September und die darauf folgenden Tage, oeffentlich an den Meistbietenden gegen baare Bezahlung ueberlassen werden sollen* (Frankfurt, 1784). Städelsches Kunstinstitut, Frankfurt.

7. *Verzeichnis einer betraechtlichen Gemaeldesammlung von den beruehmtesten Italiaenischen, Deutschen und Niederlaendischen Meistern, welche von den Eigenthümern Kaller und Michael in dem allhiesigen Bildersaal im Creuzgange, Mittwochs den 25ten August durch die Geschwornen Herrn Ausruefer an die Meistbietende gegen baare Bezahlung im 24 fl. Fuß losgeschlagen und ueberlassen werden sollen* (Frankfurt, 1790). Städelsches Kunstinstitut, Frankfurt.

8. *Verzeichniss der Gemälde, Handzeichnungen, Kupferstiche und Bücher, welche zur Hinterlassenschaft von Herrn Johann Valentin Prehn gehören, und zu Ende nächster Herbstmesse versteigert werden sollen* (Frankfurt, 1829). Reprint in Viktoria Schmidt-Linsenhoff and Kurt Wettengl, *Bürgerliche Sammlungen in Frankfurt 1700–1830* (Frankfurt, 1988), pp. 45–107.

9. Reconstructed in Schmidt-Linsenhoff and Wettengl, *Bürgerliche Sammlungen*, pp. 123–42.

10. 'Johann Outgersen in Othmarschen, für sich und als Bevollmächtigter des Johann Simons, Bürger zu Glückstadt, und des Johann van de Wouwer in Othmarschen.' StA Hamburg, O 17, pp. 785–7.

11. Michael North, 'Kunstsammeln in Hamburg im 18. Jahrhundert', in Olaf Matthes and Arne Steinert (eds), *Museum – Musen – Meer. Jörgen Bracker zum 65. Geburtstag* (Hamburg, 2001), pp. 53–65.

12. Niels v. Holst, 'Beiträge zur Geschichte des Sammlertums und des Kunsthandels in Hamburg von 1700 bis 1840', *Zeitschrift des Vereins für hamburgische Geschichte*, 38 (1939): 253–88, here p. 256. See also Claudia Susannah Cremer, 'Hagedorns Geschmack, Studien zur Kunstkennerschaft in Deutschland im 18. Jahrhundert' (PhD dissertation, University of Bonn, 1989), p. 131.

13. Another traditional collection containing histories, landscapes and genres was auctioned anonymously. See *Catalogus einer schönen Sammlung auserlesener Cabinet=Mahlereyen und Portraits, welche in einem bekannten Sterbehause in der Neustädter Fuhlentwiete, an der Ecke der Neustraße, den 12ten April 1775 an die Meistbietenden verkauft werden sollen.* Hamburger Kunsthalle, Hamburg. The graph below shows the paintings by genre.

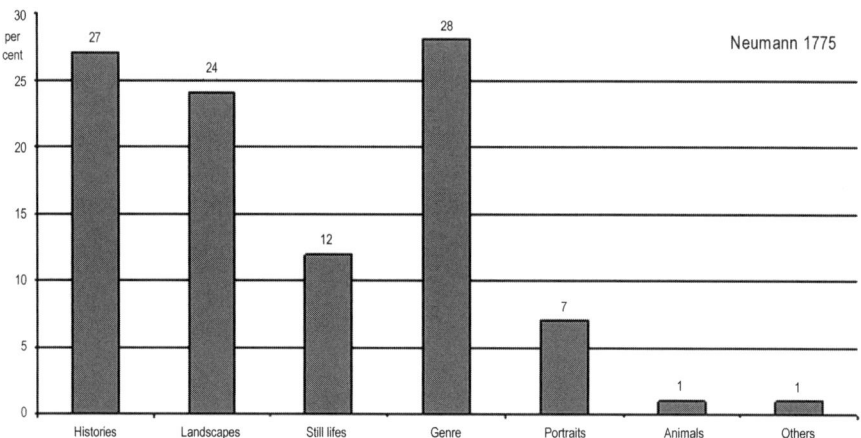

14. *Verzeichnis einiger Schildereyen und auserlesener Zeichnungen von den beruehmtesten Meistern, so von dem seel. Herrn Raths-Herrn Brockes gesammelt worden, und allhier im April dieses Jahres oeffentlich an den Meistbietenden verkaufet werden sollen* (Hamburg, 1747) Schleswig-Holsteinisches Landesarchiv, Schleswig; reprinted in Hans-Georg Kemper, Uwe-K. Ketelsen and Carsten Zelle (eds), *Barthold Heinrich Brockes (1680–1747) im Spiegel seiner Bibliothek und Bildergalerie* (Wiesbaden, 1998), pp. 309–15. *Catalogus einer Sammlung auserlesener Kunst-Mahlereyen, welche am Donnerstage, den 31 Julii, vormittags um 10 Uhr, im Dennerischen Hause am Gaensemarkt oeffentlich an die Meistbietende verkauft werden sollen* (Hamburg, 1749). Landeshauptarchiv Schwerin. *Verzeichnis einer schoenen Gemaelde-Sammlung von Italienischen, hollaendischen und Deutschen Meistern, groeßtenteils in sehr saubern Raehmen, aus einer hiesigen bekannten Verlassenschaft entstehend, welche den 7ten Juny 1793 auf dem Boersen-Saal oeffentlich an den Meistbietenden verkauft werden soll, durch die Mackler: Bostelmann & Pakischefski* (Hamburg, 1793). Hamburger Kunsthalle, Hamburg.

15. Inventories from Frankfurt (Häckel, 1762; Bernus, 1780; Berberich, 1784; Kaller, 1790; Prehn, 1829; and Morgenstern), reprinted in Schmidt-Linsenhoff and Wettengl, *Bürgerliche Sammlungen*, pp. 45–107; see also pp. 123–42.

16. See n. 14 above.

17. Michael North, *Art and Commerce in the Dutch Golden Age* (London and New Haven, 1997) pp. 93–8. Marten Jan Bok, *Vraag en aanbod op de Nederlandse kunstmarkt, 1580–1700* (Utrecht 1994).

18. Tilmann von Stockhausen, 'Kunstauktionen im 18. Jahrhundert. Ein Überblick über das Verzeichnis der verkauften Gemälde im deutschsprachigen Raum', *Das Achtzehnte Jahrhundert. Mitteilungen der Deutschen Gesellschaft für die Erforschung des achtzehnten Jahrhunderts*, 26 (2002): 63–78.

19. Thomas Ketelsen, 'Art Auctions in Germany during the Eighteenth Century', in Michael North and David Ormrod (eds), *Art Markets in Europe 1500–1800* (Aldershot, 1998), pp. 143–52, here p. 144, and 'Barthold Heinrich Brockes "irdisches Vergnügen" in Gemälden und Zeichnungen. Ein Beitrag zum Sammlungs- und Auktionswesen im frühen 18. Jahrhundert', *Das Achtzehnte Jahrhundert,* 21 (1997): 153–77, here 172–3.

20. 'Ich muß gestehen der Weenix ist gut allein ich ruhfe Ehrw. Hochfürstl. Durchl. erfahrene Augen zu Zeugen wie weit mein v. Alst dieses so wohl als den v: Alst welchen Ehrw. Hochfürstl. Durchl. schon besitzen, in Fleiß, Schönheit, Composition Verstand und guter Conservirung übertrifft, dieses Stück hat das Glück gehabt, nie in den Kunst Händen solcher Leute zu gerathen, die durch putzen, reiben, corrigiren und retouchiren den Meister in den Meistern selbst unkentlich machen, dieses stück ist kein Zweifels=Knoten, es bedeutet nicht, sondern ist von dem berühmtesten Stilleben Mahler v Alst, und zwar seine beste Geburth … .' Staatsarchiv Schwerin, 'Hofstaatssachen – Kunstsammlungen – Angebote und Erwerbungen': 101, 'Gemäldehändler Morell 1745', f. 14v–15.

21. Ketelsen, 'Art Auctions', pp. 144–5.

22. Lauts, *Karoline Luise von Baden*, pp. 174–5.

23. Ibid., pp. 145ff.

24. Schmidt-Linsenhoff and Wettengl, *Bürgerliche Sammlungen*; Michael North, 'Kunstsammeln und Geschmack im ausgehenden 18. Jahrhundert: Frankfurt und Hamburg im Vergleich', in Michael North (ed.), *Kunstsammeln und Geschmack im 18. Jahrhundert* (Berlin, 2002), pp. 85–103; Schmidt, 'Die privaten Kunstsammlungen in Frankfurt am Main'.

25. Karl Wilhelm, *Wirtschafts- und Sozialgeschichte des Kunstauktionswesens in Deutschland vom 18. Jahrhundert bis 1945* (Munich, 1990), pp. 193–202.

26. See Ketelsen, 'Barthold Heinrich Brockes', pp. 169–70.

27. Translated from the French originals. No. 22: 'On sait, que le coloris des paisages de ce maître tombe beaucoup dans le verd; Mais cette façon de peindre convient bien à son pinceau & s'accordent bien ensemble. Tennier en a fait l'étalage & l'a bien placé; On trouvera peu de paisages de Paul Brille qui soient faits avec plus d'attention, que celui-ci' ; and no. 102: 'C'est un lièvre pendant à un clou, de même qu'une perdrix, une table de marbre, sur la quelle est posé un filet de lièvre, une gibecière de velour verd & deux pies bleu; Il y a aussi une couverture de faucon, un siflet de caille, & un cor de chasseur de corne pendu à un cordon de soie avec une hupe. Sans mépriser aucun peintre ni moderne, ni ancien, je demande en considerant ce tableau, à chaque connoisseur, si on pouroit trouver un tableau fait

avec tant d'assiduité, si au naturel, & où il y eut tout ce qui dépend de l'esprit de l'homme, de fa main & de son pinceau. Hamilton vent beaucoup dire, mais il ne faut pas, qu'il soit posé trop près de ce Weeninx, sans quoi l'oeil d'un connoisseur ne fait point attention à lui.' *Catalogue d'un recueil d'un grand Seigneur de plusieurs superbes tableaux des plus Peintres, Italiens, François, Flamands, Hollandais & Allemands, qui ont été amenés des Pays-Bas ici à Francfort sur le Mayn avec beaucoup d'autres pièces précieuses en yvoire, en porcelaine & en ambre, de même que six pièces de paisages à la mosaïque avec des pierres orientales* (Frankfurt, 1765), pp. 15, 35. Bibliothèque d'Art et d'Archéologie de l'Université, Paris.

28. 'Aus deinem Commissions-Billet ersehe ich, daß du auf einen van der Velde und David Teniers indistincte Commission bis auf 16 Duc. gegeben. In meinem Pompilio aber hatte ich restrictive: Vieh-Stück und Landschafft zu beyden hinzugesetzt. Dergleichen hat Adrian van der Velde gemahlt; wenn ich also einen Willem van der Velde bekäme, so zwar auch wohl das Geld werth, so bekäme ich Schiffs- und See-Stücke, wohin ich eben nicht inclinire. Hingegen, wenn ich für 16 Ducaten so einen Tenierschen 6- und 4-zolligten Petit Soldat bekäme, würde ich nicht profitiret haben, weil solch' ein klein Stück keine weitere Composition hat. Also habe ich mich auf Landschafften und Vieh-Stücke als meine HauptCollection eingeschränckt, denn auf ein Sacrifice d'Abraham von D. Teniers darf mir wohl keine Rechnung machen. Doch wäre mir ein sehr gutgemahltes reich componirtes BauernStück ... nicht weniger angenehm als eine Landschafft.' Cited in Cremer, 'Hagedorns Geschmack', p. 28.

29. The original German terms were 'Ohnfehlbar Rembrand' (no. 318), 'Im Gusto von Rembrand' (no. 156), 'Aus der Schule von Rembrand' (no. 147), and 'So schön wie Rembrand' (no. 52). *Catalogus eines vortrefflichen Sammlung Cabinet=Mahlereyen, welche vor funfzig und mehreren Jahren mit vielem Gusto und Kenntniß gesammelt worden und sich unter dem Nachlaß des seel. Herrn Joachim Hinrich Thielcke befinden, in dessen Sterbehaufe auf den großen Bleichen selbige auch den 18 Merz, 1782, und folgende Tage durch Mackler Peter Texier an den Meistbiethenden, gegen baare Bezahlung, grob Courant, öffentlich verkauft werden sollen.* Kunsthalle Hamburg, Hamburg.

30. Cremer, 'Hagedorns Geschmack', pp. 20–25.

31. Schmidt, 'Die privaten Kunstsammlungen', Appendix.

32. Ernst Rebel, *Faksimile und Mimesis. Studien zur deutschen Reproduktionsgrafik des 18. Jahrhunderts* (Mittenwald, 1981), pp. 83–113; Schmidt-Linsenhoff and Wettengl, *Bürgerliche Sammlungen*, pp. 115ff.; Wilhelm, *Wirtschafts- und Sozialgeschichte*, pp. 150–60.

33. Edith Luther, *Johann Friedrich Frauenholz (1758–1822). Kunsthändler und Verleger in Nürnburg* (Nuremberg, 1988). For a good overview, see *In Rembrandts Manier. Kopie, Nachahmung und Aneignung in den graphischen Künsten des 18. Jahrhunderts*, exhibition catalogue (Bremen and Lübeck, 1986–87).

34. Hans Peter Thurn, *Der Kunsthändler. Wandlungen eines Berufes* (Munich, 1994), pp. 91–3; Tenner, *Mannheimer Kunstsammler und Kunsthändler bis zur Mitte des 19. Jahrhunderts* (Heidelberg, 1966).

35. A recent overview of Bertuch's multifarious activities can be found in Gerhard R. Kaiser and Siegfried Seifert (eds), *Friedrich Justin Bertuch (1747–1822). Verleger, Schriftsteller und Unternehmer im klassischen Weimar* (Tübingen, 2000).

36. Lauts, *Karoline Luise von Baden*, p. 165.

37. Heinrich Sebastian Hüsgen, *Verrätherische Briefe von Historie und Kunst* (Frankfurt, 1776).

38. Heinrich Sebastian Hüsgen, *Nachrichten von Frankfurter Künstlern und Kunst-Sachen enthaltend das Leben und die Werke aller hiesigen Mahler* (Frankfurt, 1780).

39. *Verzeichnis einer Sammlung von Gemaelden, Handzeichnungen, Kupferstichen, Alterthuemern, geschnittenen- und ungeschnitten Steinen, Kunstsachen von Holz und Elfenbein, nebst Kupferwerken, Buechern etc., welche der verstorbene Herr Hofrath H. G. Huesgen hinterlassen und am 9ten May dieses Jahrs und folgende Tage, dahier oeffentlich versteigert werden sollen* (Frankfurt, 1808).

40. Lauts, *Karoline Luise von Baden*, p. 158.

41. 'Ich betrachte mein Kabinett nur wie ein Literat seine Bibliothek, nämlich als Mittel zur Belehrung'. Ibid., p. 157.

42. Christoph Frank, 'Die Gemäldesammlungen Gotzkowsky, Eimbke, und Stein: Zur Berliner Sammlungsgeschichte während des Siebenjährigen Kriege', in Michael North (ed.), *Kunstsammeln und Geschmack im 18. Jahrhundert* (Berlin, 2002), pp. 117–94.

43. In the catalogues, *Schule, Manier, Gusto*.

44. In comparison, the salary of a Frankfurt dairymaid amounted to 20–30 guilders a year.

45. Gerhard Kölsch, 'Die Gemäldesammlung der Prinzessin Henriette Amalie von Anhalt-Dessau sowie ihre weitern Sammlungen im Überblick', in Manfred Großkinsky and Norbert Michels (eds), *Die verstoßene Prinzessin. Kunst, Karriere und Vermächtnis der Henriette Amalie von Anhalt-Dessau* (Frankfurt, 2002), pp. 71–90, here p. 79.

46. Sybille Badstübner-Gröger, 'Einige Bemerkungen zur geschmacksbildenden Rolle der Berliner Akademie-Ausstellungen im späten 18. Jahrhundert', in Michael North (ed.), *Kunstsammeln und Geschmack im 18. Jahrhundert* (Berlin, 2002), pp. 195–215.

47. Karl-Otto Conrady, *Goethe – Leben und Werk* (Düsseldorf and Zurich, 1999), 706–10.

Chapter 7

1. 'Seit vielen Jahren ist ein so starker Zudrang von Virtuosen nach Hamburg; es werden so viele in den hiesigen Zeitungen angepriesen, so viele Concerte angekündigt, man lieset so viel von der Musicliebhaberey hieselbst, daß es kein Wunder wäre, wenn ganze Capellen und Opern den Wanderstab ergriffen und hieher zögen, um ein solches Publicum von Musicfreunden, zumal ein so reiches, so luxuriöses, zu unterhalten'. 'Aus einem Briefe aus Hamburg, den 10ten Februar 1784', Carl Friedrich Cramer (ed.) *Magazin der Musik*, 2(1) (1784): 2.

2. Christoph Wolff, *Johann Sebastian Bach* (Frankfurt, 2000), pp. 379–91; Tanya Kevorkian, 'Changing Times, Changing Music: "New Church" Music and Musicians in Leipzig, 1699–1750', in William Weber (ed.), *The Musician as Entrepreneur, 1700–1914* (Bloomington, 2004), pp. 61–80.

3. Johannes Forner (ed.), *Die Gewandhauskonzerte zu Leipzig. Mit einem zusammenfassenden Rückblick von den Anfängen bis 1781* (2nd edn, Leipzig, 1983), p. 19.

4. *Gewandhauskonzerte*, p. 39, fig. 22.

5. '1. Nun noch ein Wort von dem berühmten großen Concert. Dieses ist ein wahrer Beweis davon, wie wenig man in den Werken der Kunst dem Urtheile derjenigen

Leute trauen muß, die selbst keine theoretische Kenntniß der Kunst, oder auch oft nicht einmal ein feines Gefühl und glückliche Organa besitzen: überhaupt, wie wenig man dem allgemeinem Rufe trauen muß. Ein feiner und scharfsinniger französischer Schriftsteller bemerkt daher sehr richtig, wie alle in der Ferne so sehr gewünschte Vergnügungen in der Nähe unendlich verlieren.

2. Es werden in diesem Concerte Symphonien gespielt, Arien gesungen – die beste Zierde des Concerts, die Madem. Schröter ihm giebt – und auf verschiedenen Instrumenten Concerte gespielt. Wenn diese aber nun auch noch so gut gewählt und ausgeführt werden, so ist die Begleitung doch immer schlecht.

3. Die Symphonien, die oft wiederholt werden, hört man zuweilen gut ausführen. Man sieht also daraus, daß die andern Sachen auch würden besser ausgeführt werden können, wenn häufigere Proben gehalten würden, wogegen dann aber die eingebildete Vollkommenheit der Herren ein starkes Hinderniß ist.

…

7. Das ist das große Concert, bey dem unser Hiller Direktor ist. Ich wünsche diesem braven, verdienstvollen Manne ein vortheilhafteres Glück an einem Orte, wo man seine Verdienste besser erkennte und belohnte.' Quoted in Peter Schleuning, *Der Bürger erhebt sich. Geschichte der deutschen Musik im 18. Jahrhundert* (Stuttgart, 2000), pp. 79–80.

6. On Reichardt, see Walter Salmen, *Johann Friedrich Reichardt, Komponist, Schriftsteller, Kapellmeister und Verwaltungsbeamter der Goethezeit* (Hildesheim, 2002).

7. There were, however, positive voices as well. According to the contemporary Ernst Ludwig Gerber, for instance, the Große Concert gave 'the impression of the most practiced princely ensemble', Schleuning, *Der Bürger*, p. 91.

8. '2 Primi Violini, oder Vorspieler bey der 1sten und 1ten Violin.
    Quoted in Alfred Dörffel, Geschichte der Gewandhausconcerte zu Leipzig vom 25. November 1781 bis 25. November 1881 (Leipzig, 1884), p. 16.

9. 'Herren und Damen, sowohl Adeliche, graduierte, als auch honette bürgerliche Personen.' Quoted in Heinrich W. Schwab, *Konzert. Öffentliche Musikdarbietungen vom 17. bis 19. Jahrhundert* (Leipzig, 1971), p. 11.

10. 'Ohnerachtet der Catastrophe, die die Tonkunst bey uns durch die Abdankung der Hofcapelle erlitten hat, erhält sie sich doch noch immer auf eine ganz

3 Violini concertanti.	1 Violoncello rip.
1 Violoncello	2 Violoni rip.
1 Flauto - -	1 Flauto rip.
1 Oboe - -	1 Oboe rip.
8 Violini ripieni.	2 Corni rip.
2 Violi rip.	2 Fagotti rip.'

unerwartete Art, und die Liebhaberey scheint sogar dabey gewonnen zu haben. Die philarmonische Gesellschaft hat diesen Winter durch, nicht nur ihr gewöhnliches Concert zur allgemeinen Zufriedenheit fortsetzen können; sondern die Anzahl der gesellschaftlichen Mitglieder hat sich dreyfach vermehrt. Ein großer Trost ist es für die hiesigen Dilettanten, daß unser vortreflicher Geiger, Hr. Braun der jüng., wieder in würkliche Dienste des Landgrafen genommen worden ist, und wir also darauf rechnen können, wenigstens diesen Virtuosen zu behalten. … Die Musik, welche diesen Winter über aufgeführt wurde, war meist von den besten Meistern; die

Symphonien größtentheils von Haydn, oft auch von Pleyel, Ditters, Zimmermann, Rosetti, und dgl. Die Claviersachen von Mozart, Kozeluch, oder Haydn; die Arien von Sacchini, Paesiello, Naumann, Piccini und Gretry. Für den bevorstehenden Charfreitage ist das Stabat mater von Pergolesi bestimmt, welches dieses mal die beiden Fräulein d'Aubigny singen werden.' Kassel, 21 March, *Magazin der Musik*, 2(2) (1787): 1274.

11. Arnold Hauser, *Sozialgeschichte der Kunst und Literatur* (Munich, 1972). On p. 236, for example, he asserts that music became 'the property of the bourgeoisie' (*Besitz des Bürgertums*): 'not only did orchestras move from castle and palace ballrooms to concert halls crowded with the bourgeoisie, but chamber music also found a home in middle-class houses rather than aristocratic drawing-rooms' ('nicht nur die Orchester übersiedeln aus den Festsälen der Schlösser und Palais in die vom Bürgertum erfüllten Konzertsäle, auch die Kammermusik findet ihre Heimat statt in den aristokratischen Salons in den bürgerlichen Häusern'). The classic study of this topic is Leo Balet and E. Gerhard, *Die Verbürgerlichung der deutschen Kunst, Literatur und Musik im 18. Jahrhundert*, ed. Gert Mattenklott (Frankfurt, 1973).

12. 'Violine: Se. Exz. Baron von Venningen, Baron v. Dalberg [der Domherr, Bruder des Intendanten], Baron v. Gemmingen, Herr v. Hetzendorff, Herr Goes und Hofkammerregistrator Heckmann, Konzertmeister Fränzl als Kapellmeister und dessen Sohn Ferdinand Fränzl. Bratsche: Herr Goetz, der Musikstecher und Musikverleger [Johann Michael Götz, der eine ausgedehnte Verlagstätigkeit entwickelte]. Horn: Herr Ziwny. Violoncello: Regierungsrat v. Weiler, Hofkammersekretär Heckmann, Hofkammerkanzlist Baumann. Kontrabaß: Sekretär im Medizinalkollegium Weber. Flöte: Baron v. Gaugreben, Kapitän von Penzel [Benzel-Sternau], Abbé von Stengel [Franz Joseph von Stengel, Coadjutor von Freising, Probst von St. Andreas in Köln], Sartori [der Theaterkassier].' Quoted in Schleuning, *Der Bürger*, p. 93.

13. 'Bei Weinhändler und Kaufmann Wilhelmi findet ein Konzert statt, dessen Orchester "aus lauter Liebhabern" besteht: Solche waren im letzten Winter bey der Violine: Hr. Kaufmann Brunstein; Hr. Candidat Quistorp; Hr. Candidat Fischer, der jüngere; Bey der zweyten Violine: Hr. Kaufmann Biel; Hr. Wilcken, Hr. Rehfeld, beide Studiosi. Bey der Bratsche: Hr. Advocat Brunstein; Hr. Magister Finelius. Beym Flügel: Hr. Director Rehfeld; Hr. Doctor von Aeminga; Hr. Advocat Graue. Beym Violoncell: Hr. Fechtmeister Willich; Hr. Candidat Fischer, der ältere. Beym Contrabaß: Hr. Hube. Bey der Flöte: Hr. Professor Otto; Hr. Registrator Dittmer; Hr. Secretair Rehfeld; Hr. Advocat Odenbrecht, der jüngere.' Greifswald, 12 May, *Magazin der Musik*, 2(2) (1786): 965–6.

14. Andreas Schulz, 'Der Künstler im Bürger. Dilettanten im 19. Jahrhundert', in Dieter Hein and Andreas Schulz (eds), *Bürgerkultur im 19. Jahrhundert* (Munich, 1996), pp. 34–52, here pp. 36–7.

15. Dörffel, *Geschichte der Gewandhausconcerte zu Leipzig*, pp. 15–18.

16. A new overview of the London concert market is provided by Simon McVeigh, 'The Musician as Concert-Promoter in London, 1780–1850', in Hans Erich Bödeker, Patrice Veit and Michael Werner (eds), *Mutations de la vie musicale en Europe de 1780 à 1914* (Paris, 2002), pp. 71–89.

17. 'Alle Virtuosen, die hieher kommen, denken, man wird sie mit offenen Armen aufnehmen, gleich Concerte und was noch besser ist, Geld und Geschenke für sie bereit haben, und sie mit Beyfall und Belohnung überhäuft von hier reisen lassen.

So lassen es die posaunenden Zeitungsartikel erwarten, und vor allem dem ist gerade das Gegentheil! Musicgönner giebts hier keinen einzigen; Beschützer der schönen Künste keinen einzigen; Liebhaber der Music genug, aber gerade eben nicht unter dem reichen Theile der Einwohner. Kaufleute haben mehr zu thun, als brodlose Künste zu erwärmen. Gelehrte leben meistens selbst von der Ehre ihrer Kunst. Damen singen und spielen zum Theil ganz artig (einige sehr gut) aber bis zur Beschützerinn erhebt sich keine, und wenige würdens können, wenn sie wollten. Es sind einige Concerte hier, aber nicht öffentliche, nicht von solcher Bedeutung, wie in Berlin, Leipzig oder zu Wien; auch erhalten sie sich mühsam durch Subscription, die nie so hoch steigt, daß nur mittelmäßige Sängerinnen oder Sänger dabey gehalten werden können. Die besten und frequentesten Concerte hatte ehemals der große Bach, und nach ihm Hr. M. Ebeling in der Handlungsacademie, aber diese sind aufgegeben worden, indem man es nachtheilig für das Institut auslegte, daß es seine Eleves in feiner Gesellschaft und mit guter Music alle Wochen ein paar Stunden unterhielt. Bach giebt sich zur Ruhe, und führt längst keine Musiken mehr im Concertsaale auf. Dazu kommt, daß im Sommer alles was beau monde heißt, auf den Gärten lebt, im Winter aber der Clubs, Assemblées, Lotteries, Piqueniques, Bälle und Schmausereyen so viele und festgesezte sind, daß ein Concert nur mit unsäglicher Mühe einige freye Stunden ausfindig macht, wo es sich einschleichen kann. Am Sonntage dürfen keine seyn; das ist wider die Orthodoxie. Drey, vier Tage sind Posttage, wo kein Kaufmann, Commis oder Handlungsbedienter jemals Zeit hat an Concerte zu denken. Die übrigen Tage sind Comödien; also bleibt nur der Sonnabendabend, wo alles sich von großen Schmausen, Spielverlusten und Geschäften erholt, und zu neuen vorbereitet. Was ist da großes für die arme Music zu hoffen?' 'Aus einem Briefe aus Hamburg, den 10ten Februar 1784', *Magazin der Musik*, 2 (1) (1784): 2ff.

18.

'Montags	Adolf Freiherr v. Knigges (oberster hannoverscher Verwaltungsbeamter) Gesellschaftstheater
Dienstags	Hesses (Handlungsgehilfe) Liebhaberkonzert auf der Domschule
Mittwochs	Dr. Schuttes (Rechtsanwalt) Privatkonzert, alternierend mit Dr. Müllers (Lehrer am Lycaeum, Gründer des Privat-Erziehungsinstituts) Übungs- bzw. Familienkonzert
Donnertags	-
Freitags	Öffentliches Winterkonzert im Börsensaal
Samstags	Alternierende Hauskonzerte bei Knigge und Dr. Iken (Sekretär) sowie sog. Insurgentenkonzerte der (singenden) musikausübenden ‚Frauenzimmer'
Sonntags	Musik in den Gottesdiensten'.

Klaus Blum, *Musikfreunde und Musici. Musikleben in Bremen seit der Aufklärung* (Tutzing, 1975), p. 44.

19. Ingeborg Allihn, 'Organisatoren und Formen der Organisation des Musiklebens in Berlin im ausgehenden 18. Jahrhundert', in Hans-Erich Bödeker, Patrice Veit and Michael Werner (eds), *Le concert et son public. Mutations de la vie musicale en Europe de 1780 à 1914 (France, Allemagne, Angleterre)* (Paris, 2002), pp. 159–73.

20. 'Die Tonkunst wirkt hier täglich das Wunder, dass man sonst nur der Liebe zuschrieb: Sie macht alle Stände gleich. Adeliche und Bürgerliche, Fürsten und ihre Vasallen, Vorgesetzte und ihre Untergebenen, sitzen an einem Pulte beysammen, und vergessen über der Harmonie der Töne die Disharmonie ihres Standes. Dem ausübenden Musiker öffnen sich alle Paläste und alle Börsen, und der Komponist von einiger Bedeutung wird mit all der Auszeichnung behandelt, die er sich nur immer wünschen kann, was bey manchem dieser Herren sehr viel sagen will.' *Vaterländische Blätter für den österreichischen Kaiserstaat* (1808): 39. English translation in Mary Sue Morrow, *Concert Life in Haydn's Vienna: Aspects of a Developing Musical and Social Institution* (Stuyvesant, NY, 1989), pp. 22–3.

21. Morrow, *Concert Life*, pp. 49–64.

22. Axel Beer, *Musik zwischen Komponist, Verlag und Publikum. Die Rahmenbedingungen des Musikschaffens in Deutschland im ersten Drittel des 19. Jahrhunderts* (Tutzing, 2000), pp. 47–50.

23. Wolff, *Johann Sebastian Bach*, p. 450. For an overview of musicians who dealt in sheet music, see Klaus Hortschansky, 'The Musician as Music Dealer in the Second Half of the Eighteenth Century', in Walter Salmen (ed.), *The Social Status of the Professional Musician from the Middle Ages to the Nineteenth Century* (New York, 1983), pp. 189–218.

24. Schleuning, *Der Bürger*, pp. 394–401. For more detail, see the same author's *Die Freie Fantasie. Ein Beitrag zur Erforschung der klassischen Klaviermusik* (Göppingen, 1973), pp. 234–70. Below are numbers for the six C.P.E. Bach collections, each with an edition size of 1,000.

No.	Year	Subscribers/connoisseurs
1	1779	519
2	1780	330
3	1781	307
4	1783	388
5	1785	308
6	1787	288

25. 'Da ich zu meiner Unterhaltung viel Werth auf neue Guitarremusicalien setze, wobey ich weniger den Gesang als besonders Clavier auch wohl mit Gesang auch mehrere Streichinstrumente z. B. Violine, Viola, Cello, auch Flöte schätze, und von d. H. Breitk & Härtel, zeither meinen Wünschen gemas nicht genügsam versorgt worden bin, so wende ich mich an Sie, mit der Anfrage, ob Sie so gefellig seyn und … von Zeit zu Zeit solche Sachen zur Auswahl an mich übersenden wollen?' Quoted in Beer, *Musik*, p. 251.

26. 'jene Gegenden und Kanäle zu bemerken, wo Ihre Lieder am besten zu verbreiten und zu debitiren sind … .' Ibid., p. 252.

27. 'Haydn, Mozart, Hoffmeister, Kreutzer, Frenzl, Gyrowetz etc. … so wohl für Clavier mit und ohne begleitung, auf die Violin, Flauten, Guitar, und so auch für weitere Instrumente … .' Ibid., p. 255.

28. 'Ein Wort zu seiner Zeit über das Modeinstrument der Ghitarre', *Journal des Luxus und der Moden* (August 1803): 429–33.

29. Cf. 'Ueber die neueste Favorit=Musik in großen Concerten, sonderlich in Rücksicht auf Damen=Gunst, in Clavier=Liebhaberey', *Journal des Luxus und der Moden* (June 1788): 230–35.

30. 'nicht alles, was im südlichen Deutschland gefällt, … auch das Glück hatte, im Nördlichen zu gefallen.' Beer, *Musik*, p. 259.

31. Ibid., pp. 262–3.

32. 'Leipziger musicalische Zeitung schon seit einer langen Reihe von Jahren die Beurtheilung, ja selbst die Anzeigung der Beethoven'schen Werke versäumt.' *Journal für Literatur, Kunst, Luxus und Mode* (28 August 1823): 635.

33. 'So hat die Neigung für Spohr, Weber, Onslow, Ries, Field sogar für Beethoven abgenommen und Rossini, Hummel, Mayseder, Moscheles, C. Czerny sind jetzt die Tonhelden des Tages in Wien.' Beer, *Musik*, p. 268.

34. 'für Musik-Liebhaber immer mehr und mehr.' Ibid., p. 272.

35. Ibid., pp. 273–9.

36. Mary Sue Morrow, *German Music Criticism in the Late Eighteenth Century: Aesthetic Issues in Instrumental Music* (Cambridge, 1997), pp. 31–5.

37. 'Warum liefert uns doch Herr Breitkopf nicht lauter solche Werke rechtschaffner geschickter Deutschen, und will der Welt lieber die Mißgeburten seichter Italiäner aufdringen'. *Bibliothek der schönen Wissenschaften*, 4(2) (1762): 822; quoted in Morrow, *German Music*, p. 177.

38. 'wenn er den Italienern einen guten Gesang ablernet, ohne den all Musik nichts werth ist und welchen wir noch in einigen seiner Ausarbeitungen vermissen … so wird seine Reise für ihn und die Musik vortheilhaft seyn.' *Hamburgischer Correspondent*, 102 (26 June 1773), quoted in Morrow, *German Music*, pp. 177–8.

39. 'sehr wenige Italiäner wird man finden, die so reich an ernsthaften, edlen Gedanke wären, und ihre Stücke so gut bearbeiten.' Translation in Morrow, *German Music*, p. 49.

40. 'Auch itzo, da er nun Italien gesehen hat, erkennen wir immer noch an ihm einen von den Deutschen, die sich zwar in alle musikalischen Trachten, wie man sie nur verlangt, einkleiden, aber doch nicht alles Gründliche in ihrem Wissen verleugnen können.' *Allgemeine Deutsche Bibliothek*, 8(1) (1768): 272–3, quoted in Morrow, *German Music*, p. 181.

41. '[Die Sonaten] sind nicht so gebunden und fugenartig, wie die vortrefflichen Trios des seel. Kapellmeister Grauns; sie sind aber auch nicht so einfach und leer wie die meisten italiänischen Trios.' Translation in Morrow, *German Music*, p. 52.

42. John Deatheridge, 'The Invention of German Music, c. 1800', in Tim Blanning and Hagen Schulze (eds), *Unity and Diversity in European Culture c. 1800* (Oxford, 2006), pp. 35–60, here pp. 41–6.

43. 'Scheint aus den Gegenden des Rheins, oder dem südlichern Deutschland zu kommen; und das ist leider genug gesagt. Alle das dortherige Geklimper kennt man den Augenblick an den einförmigen Figuren, den alltäglichen Modulationen, abgedroschnen Harfenbässen, beständigem Auf= und Herunterrennen der diatonischen Scala, und solchen Kunststücklein … .' Translation in Morrow, *German Music*, p. 55.

44. 'daß man in Greifswalde die alte Musik über alles schätzte. Graun, Hasse, die Bachs, die Bendas, Quantz und mehrere dieser Art waren dort gänge und gebe; hingegen Symphonien von Vanhall oder sonst etwas, worin das letzte Stück einem

Rondo nur ähnlich sahe, fand man ungenießbar.' Quoted in Schleuning, *Der Bürger*, p. 232.

45. 'Wenn wir auch nur einen Haydn und einen C. Ph. E. Bach hätten, so könnten wir Deutsche schon kühn behaupten, daß wir eine eigne Manier haben und unsre Instrumentalmusik die interessanteste von allen ist.' English translation in Morrow, *German Music*, p. 60.

46. 'Kurz, es ist nichts an diesen Concerten vergessen, was Kennern so wohl als Liebhabern zu einem edlen Vergnügen, und einer angenehmen Unterhaltung gereichen, und dabey ihren Geschmack bey anständiger Richtigkeit erhalten, vor Fallen in die Sümpfe der musikalischen Trivialität bewahren, im Gegentheile vielmehr ihn noch verfeinern kann.' *Berlinische Nachrichten*, 29 (9 March 1773): 144; quoted in Morrow, *German Music*, p. 182.

47. 'Für Liebhaber sind diese Stücke recht gut, für Kenner aber möchten sie wohl nicht befriedigend seyn. Mehrere neuere Componisten haben sich, seit Bach seine Sonaten für Kenner und Liebhaber herausgegeben hat, der ähnlichen Aufschrift: für Kenner bedient, ohne vielleicht zu bedenken oder einzusehen, daß Bach etwas damit sagen wollte, was er nur leisten konnte, was folglich ein anderer, der den Kennern nicht eben solche ausgesuchte musikalische Seltenheiten liefern kann, eigentlich nicht nachsagen muß.' Johann Nicolaus Forkel, *Musikalischer Almanach*, 4 (1789): 36.

48. Johann Nicolaus Forkel, *Über die Theorie der Musik, insofern sie Liebhabern und Kennern nothwendig und nützlich ist* (Göttingen, 1777), pp. 32, 39; quoted in Schleuning, *Der Bürger*, p. 131. On the notion of linking the cultivation of connoisseurs with selling strategies, see David Gramit, 'Selling the Serious: The Commodification of Music and Resistance to it in Germany, circa 1800', in W. Weber (ed.), *The Musician as Entrepreneur, 1700–1914: Managers, Charlatans, and Idealists* (Bloomington, 2004), pp. 81–101.

49. Hans Adolf Freiherr von Eschstruth, *Musikalische Bibliothek* (2 vols, 1784–85; reprint Hildesheim and New York, 1977).

50. 'Ueber Mode in Musik, und die neuesten Favorit-Stücke in einzelnen teutschen Provinzen'; 'Ueber die neueste Favorit-Musik in großen Concerten, sonderlich in Rücksicht auf Damen-Gunst, in Clavier-Liebhaberey', *Journal des Luxus und der Moden* (September 1787): 307–10.

51. Beer, *Musik*, pp. 126–9.

52. '1) Clavier- und Fortepianomusik
Bihler. Variations p. Clav. Oboe et Bass. Op. IV., Offenbach, bey Andree 3 fl.
Hoffmann, Marsch aus der Zauberflöte mit Variationen. Op. II., Ebendas. 30 fl.
C. H. Kunze, VI Anglaises et VI Allemandes p. Clav. 4me Cahier, Heilbronn, bey Ammon. 30 kr.
Beczwarzowsky. Concert en Rondeau Op. II. Offenbach, bey Andree. 2 fl.
Förster. Quartett. P. Clav. Viol. Alt. et. Bass. Op. VIII Livr. 1 Ebendas. 1 fl 45 krz.
…
B. de Dalberg. Sonate a 4 mains, in C dur. Ebendas. 1 fl 30 kr.
Kuhn. Petites pieces. Op. VIII. Ebendas. 1 fl 30 kr.
Kyrmayr. VI Airs varies. Mannheim, bey Götz; jede zu 20 kr. nehmlich No 7. Der Vogelfänger bin ich etc. No. 8. Menuet aus Don Juan. No. 9. Du feines Täubchen. No 10. Bey Männern welche Liebe fühlen. No 11. Seyd uns zum zweyten Mal willkommen. No 12. Dort vergiß etc. aus Figaro.

2) Violin-Musik

P. Wranizky. VI Quart. à 2 Viol. Alt et Bass. Op. XXX. Offenbach, bey Andree. 6 fl.

Gyrowez. III Quartett. Op XIX. Ebendas. 2 fl 45.

Luchesi. VI Duos. à 2 Vio. Augsburg, bey Gombart. 3 fl 30 kr.

Distler. VI Quartett. à Viol. Alt. et. Bass. Op. II. Ebendas. 5 fl. 30 kr.

…

4) Flöten-Musik

Monzani. VI Trios. à 2 Flutes et Bass. Augsburg, bey Gombart.

Ditters. Hieronymus Knicker für 2 Flüten und Baß. Arrangiert von Ehrenfried. Maynz, bey Schott. 3 fl.

…

6) Sinfonien

P. Winter. Sinf. In D. Livr. 1. Offenbach, bey Andree. 2 fl.'

It is interesting to note that Bertuch mixed these advertisements with reports and in some cases with reviews as well, thereby underlining his mercantile intentions. See the nicely observed account by Ulfhardt Stoewer in his 'Der "Kulturunternehmer" Friedrich Justin Bertuch im Spiegel seines "Journals des Luxus und der Moden"' (dissertation as part of the state secondary school teachers' examination, University of Greifswald, 2001), pp. 61–2.

53. Cf. Chapter 2 above.

54. Josef Mančal, 'Zu Musik und Aspekten des Musikmarkts des 18. Jahrhunderts', in Sabine Doering-Manteuffel, Josef Mančal and Wolfgang Wüst (eds), *Pressewesen der Aufklärung. Periodische Schriften im Alten Reich* (Berlin, 2001), pp. 412–15.

55. 'Durch ein besonderes Circulare haben sich bereits von hoher Noblesse und andern angesehenen Musikliebhabern, eine Anzahl zu dem in den Sommermonaten Mai, Juni, Juli, August veranstalteten Konzerten in dem von Stahlischen Garten, zwischem dem rothen und gegginger Thor, wo schon ehemals dergleichen gehalten worden, und vor einem Anwetter in Zimmern und Saal geschüzet sein kann, schriftlich zu Aboniren die Gnade und Gute gehabt; weil aber solches Vorhaben mehr andern unbekannten Liebhabern nicht wissend wäre, so habe die Ehre solches hiemit zu benachrichtigen, daß das Abonement für 17 Konzerten mit Einschluß der eigenen Hausfamilien fl. 5 kostet, wozu die Entree Billet bei unten benannten am Judenberg Lit. E. Nro. 303. gegen baaren Erlag zu bekommen sind, die nicht abonirte Personen bezahlen jedesmal beim Eintritt extra 36 kr. Das erste Konzert ist Mittwoch den 6ten Mai Abends um 5 Uhr, und wird damit an diesem Tag alle 17 Wochen continuirt.' ('Through a separate circular, members of the high nobility and other respected connoisseurs of music have been so good and gracious as to subscribe in writing to a number of concerts to be held in the summer months of May, June, July and August at von Stahl's garden between the Red Gate and the Gögging Gate – where such events have taken place in the past – and in case of inclement weather in the shelter of rooms and halls. Because, however, other, unknown connoisseurs have not yet been apprised of this undertaking, I have the honour to inform them hereby that a subscription for seventeen concerts, including admission for members of their households, costs 5 guilders. The tickets may be purchased for cash at the below-mentioned [address] Judenberg Lit. E. no. 303. Persons without subscription pay 36 kr. for each concert. The first concert will be on Wednesday 6 May at five o'clock in the evening, and will

continue on that same day for seventeen weeks.') Augsburg, 4 May 1789, Gottfried Valentin (AIZ 19/1789); and 'Liebhabern der Musik dienet zur Nachricht, daß von nächstem Mittwoch den 12. Okt. an; alle 14. Tag am Mittwoch Abends um 6 Uhr ein vollstimmiges Konzert im Gasthaus bei Hr. Aibel gehalten werden wird, wozu man sich à 4 fl. überhaupts aboniret, oder auch beim Eingang 30 kr. bezahlen kann.' ('Music lovers are hereby notified that from next Wednesday, the 12th of Oct., a full-toned concert will be given at six o'clock in the evening every other Wednesday at Herr Aibel's inn, to which one may subscribe for 4 guilders, or pay 30 kr. at the door.') Gottfried Valentin, Municipal Trumpeter (AIZ 40/1791). Quoted in Mančal, 'Musikmarkt', p. 430.

56. Eschstruth, *Musicalische Bibliothek*, 1(1) (1784): 152. The original quotation comes from a review of Klopstock's 'Morgengesang am Schöpfungsfeste', set to music by C.P.E. Bach in Hamburg. The complete quotation is as follows: 'Wer ein solches Werk unsrer beiden ersten Classiker der Dichtkunst und Tonkunst angekündigt findet, one auf di Ere unter den Beförderern desselben zu stehen eifrigst Anspruch zu machen, der rüme sich nicht Kenner oder Libhaber zu seyn.' ('Anyone who sees an announcement of such a work by our two foremost classics in poetry and music and is not eager to claim the honour of being among its promoters cannot claim to be a connoisseur or an amateur.')

Chapter 8

1. 'Außer dem Dichternamen Schiller bewirkte bei uns noch derjenige von Goethe und Lessing unfehlbar ein leeres Haus.' *Friedrich Ludwig Schmidt, Denkwürdigkeiten des Schauspielers, Schauspieldichters und Schauspieldirectors Friedrich Ludwig Schmidt (1772–1841)*, compiled and edited by Hermann Uhde using drafts left by the author (2nd edn, 2 vols, Stuttgart, 1878), vol. 2, p. 365; quoted in Ute Daniel, *Hoftheater. Zur Geschichte des Theaters und der Höfe im 18. und 19. Jahrhundert* (Stuttgart, 1995), p. 146.

2. The recognition that such an interpretation provides only an inadequate description of the development of the theatre inspired a conference organized by the German Society for the Study of the Eighteenth Century as well as a collection of essays. See Erika Fischer-Lichte, 'Zur Einleitung', in Erika Fischer-Lichte and Jörg Schönert (eds), *Theater im Kulturwandel des 18. Jahrhunderts. Inszenierung und Wahrnehmung von Körper – Musik – Sprache* (Göttingen, 1999), pp. 11–20.

3. Manfred Brauneck, *Die Welt als Bühne. Geschichte des europäischen Theaters*, vol. 2 (Stuttgart, 1996), pp. 707–18.

4. Brauneck, *Welt als Bühne*, p. 737.

5. Daniel, *Hoftheater*, p. 188.

6. Minutes of the committee meeting of 2 April 1784, quoted in Daniel, *Hoftheater*, p. 196. At this meeting, Dalberg commented as follows on Iffland's masterpiece *Verbrechen aus Ehrsucht*, 'This play does great honour to its author and our stage. As a play, it is a grand and genuine fresco painting; splendidly chosen situations, noble simplicity of plan, truth in language and expression; pure morality, far removed from local allusions, satires and bitter criticism. A most excellent drama! Were all the foremost duties of Man to be portrayed individually on the stage from this viewpoint, and in such lively pictures, the stage could become a true school of manners, and the theatre for which such plays are written on this model

would usher in a new epoch.' ('Dieses Stück macht seinem Verfasser und unsrer Bühne viel Ehre. Als Stück ist es wahre, große Freskomalerei; herrlich gewählte Situationen; edle Simplicität im Plan; Wahrheit in Sprache und Ausdruck: reine Moral, fern von Lokal-Anspielungen, Satyre und bitterer Kritik. Ein fürtreffliches Schauspiel! Würden alle die vorzüglichen Pflichten dem Menschen unter diesem Gesichtspunkt, und mit so lebhaften Bildern einzeln auf der Bühne dargestellt werden, so konnte die Bühne wahre Schule der Sitten werden; und das Theater, für welches solche Stücke nach diesem Pan geschrieben wären, würde eine neue Epoche machen.')

7. In all, 237 French (59.8%), 121 German (30.6%), 17 English (4.3%) and 21 other plays (5.3%) were staged at the *Nationaltheater* between 1767 and 1769. Figures compiled by Roland Krebs, *L'Idée de 'Théâtre National' dans L'Allemagne des Lumières. Théorie et Réalisations* (Wiesbaden, 1985), pp. 634–5; Herbert Eichhorn, *Konrad Ernst Ackermann. Ein deutscher Theaterprinzipal. Ein Beitrag zur Theatergeschichte im deutschen Sprachraum* (Emsdetten, 1965). For a list of the authors whose works Ackermann presented on stage with the performance figures for 1754–71, see pp. 263–74.

8. On Hamburg more generally, see Eichhorn, *Ackermann*; and Paul Möhring, *Von Ackermann bis Ziegel. Theater in Hamburg* (Hamburg, 1970). Where they exist, here and below, I have supplied the titles of published English translations of plays and operas.

9. 'welches jedermann dreimal in der Woche unentgeltlich besuchen darf'. Quoted in Karl Otto Conrady, *Goethe: Leben und Werk* (Düsseldorf and Zurich, 1999), p. 339.

10. Heide Eilert, 'Bertuch und das zeitgenössische Theater', in Gerhard R. Kaiser and Siegfried Seifert (eds), *Friedrich Justin Bertuch (1747–1822). Verleger, Schriftsteller und Unternehmer im klassischen Weimar* (Tübingen, 2000), pp. 113–31.

11. Karl Siegmund von Seckendorff wrote the music for both plays. See Jörg Krämer, *Deutschsprachiges Musiktheater im späten 18. Jahrhundert. Typologie, Dramaturgie und Anthropologie einer populären Gattung* (Tübingen, 1998), pp. 522–37.

12. Conrady, *Goethe*, pp. 369–76, 550–58; see also Jutta Linder, *Ästhetische Erziehung: Goethe und das Weimarer Hoftheater* (Bonn, 1991); Ulrike Müller-Harang, *Das Weimarer Theater zur Zeit Goethes* (Weimar, 1991).

13. Ibid., pp. 21–43.

14. Linder, *Ästhetische Erziehung*, pp. 101–17. On this self-dramatization, see Georg Schmidt, 'Das Jahr 1783: Goethe, Herder und die Zukunft Weimars', in Marcus Ventzke (ed.), *Hofkultur und aufklärerische Reformen in Thüringen. Die Bedeutung des Hofes im späten 18. Jahrhundert* (Cologne, Weimar and Vienna, 2002), pp. 138–68.

15. 'Ein wahrhaft imponierender Mozart-Zyklus noch zu Lebzeiten des Komponisten und kurz nach seinem Tode!' Conrady, *Goethe*, p. 735.

16. Müller-Harang, *Weimarer Theater*, pp. 32–8.

17. Volkmar Braunbehrens, *Salieri. Ein Musiker im Schatten Mozarts? Eine Biographie* (Munich, 1989), Chapters 4 and 5.

18. Brauneck, *Welt als Bühne*, pp. 883–99; Franz Hadamowsky, *Die Josefinische Theaterreform und das Spieljahr 1776/77 des Burgtheaters. Eine Dokumentation* (Vienna, 1978), and *Wiener Theatergeschichte. Von den Anfängen bis zum Ende des Ersten Weltkriegs* (Vienna, 1988); Krämer, *Deutschsprachiges Musiktheater*, pp. 396–464.

19. Reinhart Meyer, *Das deutsche Trauerspiel des 18. Jahrhunderts. Eine Bibliographie* (Munich, 1977), pp. 20–24.

20. 'das ungereimteste Werck, so der menschliche Verstand jemahls erfunden.' Johann Christoph Gottsched, *Versuch einer Critischen Dichtkunst vor die Deutschen: darinnen erstlich die allgemeinen Regeln der Poesie, hernach alle besondere Gattungen der Gedichte abgehandelt und mit Exempeln erläutert werden, überall aber gezeiget wird, daß das inner Wesen der Poesie in einer Nachahmung der Natur besteht* (Leipzig, 1730), p. 604, quoted in Gloria Flaherty, *Opera in the Development of German Critical Thought* (Princeton, 1978), p. 95.

21. Cf. Erika Fischer-Lichte, 'Der Körper als Zeichen', in Erika Fischer-Lichte and Jörg Schönert (eds), *Theater im Kulturwandel des 18. Jahrhunderts: Inszenierung und Wahrnehmung von Körper – Musik – Sprach* (Göttingen, 1999), pp. 53–68, and 'Entwicklung einer neuen Schauspielkunst', in Wolfgang F. Bender (ed.), *Schauspielkunst im 18. Jahrhundert* (Stuttgart, 1992), pp. 51–70.

22. Armas Sten Fühler, 'Das Schauspielrepertoire des Mannheimer Hof- und Nationaltheaters im Geschmackswandel des 18. und 19. Jahrhunderts (1779–1870)' (PhD dissertation, University of Heidelberg, 1935), pp. 68–9.

23. *Rheinische Musen* 3 (9) (1795): 108ff.

24. Reinhart Meyer, 'Der Anteil des Singspiels und der Oper am Repertoire der deutschen Bühnen in der zweiten Hälfte des 18. Jahrhunderts', in *Das deutsche Singspiel im 18. Jahrhundert* (Heidelberg, 1981), pp. 27–76.

25. *Journal des Luxus und der Moden* (January 1790): 47–55; (March 1790): 141–56; (February 1794): 72–8.

26. 'Durch die Erscheinung der Operette "die Entführung aus dem Serail" und d.m. fing das Publikum sowohl hier als auch anderwärts an, seine bisheriges Vergnügen an dem Schauspiel zu theilen, und die Operetten, welche bisher nur als Nebenwerk betrieben worden, mussten nun zur Abwechslung, und um sowohl dem Wunsche des Publikums Genüge zu leisten, als der Theatercasse bessere Einnahmen zu verschaffen, von allen Theaterdirectionen mit dem Schauspiele gleichgesetzt werden.' Quoted in Daniel, *Hoftheater*, p. 243.

27. Hartmut Runge, *Dessauer Theaterbilder. Zur 200-jährigen Geschichte des Theaters in Dessau* (Dessau, 1994), pp. 122ff.

28. Lutz Winkler, 'Musiktheater in der 2. Hälfte des 18. Jahrhunderts in Stralsund und Greifswald' in Ekkard Ochs, Nico Schüler and Lutz Winkler (eds), *Musica Baltica. Interregionale musikalische Beziehungen im Ostseeraum* (Frankfurt, Berlin and Berne, 1997), pp. 212–15, here pp. 221–2.

29. Krämer, *Deutschsprachiges Musiktheater*, pp. 859–68.

30. Ibid., pp. 113–18.

31. 'Welch ein Abstand von dem Studenten, der nach sorgfältiger Vorbereitung durch wiederholtes Lesen einer klassischen Dichtung mit dem Buche in der Hand der Darstellung im Parterre folgt, bis zu dem Vornehmen, der nach einem glänzenden Diner gähnend in der Loge des 1. Ranges verdaut; von dem Handwerker, der Sonntags seine Familie mit den Ersparnissen der Woche auf die Galerie führt, bis zu dem Musikkenner, der, den Klavierauszug in der Hand, die Leistung des Orchesters und der Sänger beurtheilt. Die höchste geistige Bildung neben der rohesten Vergnügungssucht, der Glanz und die Behaglichkeit der bevorrechteten Stände neben dem Mangel und der niedrigen Neigung!' *Allgemeines Theater-Lexikon oder Encyklopädie alles Wissenswerthen für Bühnenkünstler, Dilettanten und Theaterfreunde*, ed. Robert Blum, Karl Herloßsohn and Herrmann Marggraff (Altenburg and Leipzig, 1839), quoted in Sybille Maurer-Schmoock, *Deutsches Theater im 18. Jahrhundert* (Tübingen, 1982), pp. 119–20.

32. 'Montags ist Ball, – Freitags Concert, – Dienstags, Donnerstags und Sonnabends ist Comedie.' Dagmar von Gersdorff, *Goethes Mutter. Eine Biographie* (Frankfurt and Leipzig, 2001), p. 312.

33. Anne-Charlott Trepp, *Sanfte Männlichkeit und selbständige Weiblichkeit. Frauen und Männer im Hamburger Bürgertum zwischen 1770 und 1840* (Göttingen, 1996), pp. 394–6.

34. An example is Goethe's and his companion Christiane's stay in Leipzig from 10–14 May 1800, when they indulged in luxury shopping and cultural consumption in equal measure. Sigrid Damm, *Christiane und Goethe: Eine Recherche* (Frankfurt, 2001), p. 258.

35. Maurer-Schmoock, *Deutsches Theater*, pp. 75–86.

36. Daniel, *Hoftheater*, pp. 240–41.

37. Jörg Krämer, 'Auge und Ohr. Rezeptionsweisen im deutschen Musiktheater des späten 18. Jahrhunderts', in Fischer-Lichte and Schönert (eds), *Theater im Kulturwandel*, pp. 109–32, here pp. 121–9.

38. Krämer, *Musiktheater*, pp. 11–113, Quotation on p. 113.

39. Daniel, *Hoftheater*, p. 237.

40. *Journal des Luxus und der Moden* (March 1786): 121–2.

41. *Journal des Luxus und der Moden* (January 1790): 53.

42. 'Die Indianer in England haben hier ziemliches Glück gemacht. Sie wurden so oft und schnell Nacheinander auf vieles Begehren gegeben, dass man jetzt mit dem Bootsknechte Jack vor Anker zu liegen, und davon auszuruhen scheint. Madam Unzelmann spielte die Rolle der Burley mit solcher Naivetät und Liebenswürdigkeit, dass man bloß darüber den Fehler der Unwahrscheinlichkeit oder vielmehr der moralischen Unmöglichkeit einer so weitgehenden Ignoranz vergessen konnte. Herr Fleck als Kaberdar erschien ganz in seinem Fache, und wer es vorher nicht wußte was er in Indien war, dem gab sein Ton, sein Auge, sein Alles deutlich genug zu verstehen, daß er – ein Nabob war. … – Als Musaffery, der treue Anhänger der Religion seiner Väter, bey den zu Ende vorkommenden wunderbaren Entwicklungen des Schicksals, allemal in ein Dankerfülltes und wirklich charackteristisches: o Brama! Brama sey gelobt! ausbrach, lachte man. Wohl gemerkt; man lachte! Ein neuer Beweiß der Wahrheit, daß Teutschland noch kein National-Parterre habe, an welches man über guten Geschmack, feines und richtiges Urtheil appelliren könnte.' Ibid., p. 55.

43. 'Die Indianer in England … ausserordentlich; besonders durch das unnachahmliche Spiel der Mamsell Witthoft als Indianerin.' *Journal des Luxus und der Moden* (March 1790): 147.

44. 'Am 3ten Jänner trat Mad. Beck nach ihrer Niederkunft zum erstenmale wieder auf, als Therese in Felix; man empfing sie – wie gewöhnlich; und rufte heraus! Nach Brauch und Sitte.' Ibid., pp. 146–7.

45. Ibid., p. 143.

46. Peter Schmitt, *Schauspieler und Theaterbetrieb. Studien zur Sozialgeschichte des Schauspielerstandes im deutschsprachigen Raum 1700–1900* (Tübingen, 1990), pp. 190–94.

47. Gersdorff, *Goethes Mutter*, pp. 283–310.

48. Ruth B. Emde, *Schauspielerinnen im Europa des 18. Jahrhunderts. Ihr Leben, ihre Schriften und ihr Publikum* (Amsterdam and Atlanta, 1997), pp. 268–300.

49. Barbara Becker-Cantarino, *Der lange Weg zur Mündigkeit. Frau und Literatur (1500–1800)* (Stuttgart, 1987), pp. 333–9. See also the autobiography, *Die Erinnerungen der*

Karoline Jagemann nebst zahlreichen unveröffentlichten Dokumenten aus der Goethezeit, ed. Eduard v. Bamberg (Dresden, 1926).

Chapter 9

1. 'Um diese Zeit kam auch ein Englisch Mann in Hamburg [an] und fing an Thee wie auch Coffee zu schenken, diesem folgte ein Holländer: daraus denn das Thee und Coffee trinken sehr gemein geworden, das jedermann, der es nur bezahlen können, es zu trinken angefangen und nunmehr eine Veranlassung worden ist vieler Zusammenkünfte.' Quoted in Wolfgang Jünger, *Herr Ober, ein' Kaffee! Illustrierte Kulturgeschichte des Kaffeehauses* (Munich, 1955), p. 32.
2. Jürgen Schneider, 'Die neuen Getränke: Schokolade, Kaffee und Tee (16.–18. Jahrhundert)', in Simonetta Cavaciocchi (ed.), *Prodotti e tecniche d'oltremare nelle economie europee secc. XIII–XVIII* (Prato, 1998), pp. 541–90, here p. 556.
3. Ulla Heise, *Kaffee und Kaffeehaus. Eine Kulturgeschichte* (Leipzig, 1987), p. 131.
4. John Brewer, *The Pleasures of the Imagination: English Culture in the Eighteenth Century* (New York, 1997), pp. 33–4.
5. Brewer, *Pleasures*, pp. 34–40.
6. Robert Riemer, 'Exotische Genußmittel: Kaffee, Tabak, Tee, Zucker. Mit Schwerpunkt beim Kaffee und seiner Sozialgeschichte in Form der Kaffeehäuser – von ihrem Aufkommen bis in die Mitte des 19. Jahrhunderts' (seminar paper, University of Greifswald, 1999), p. 32; Roman Sandgruber, *Die Anfänge der Konsumgesellschaft. Konsumgüterverbrauch, Lebensstandard und Alltagskultur in Österreich im 18. und 19. Jahrhundert* (Vienna, 1982), pp. 1934.
7. 'Man darf zu allen Zeiten des Tages in die Kaffeehäuser und im Sommer in die Kaffeegärten gehen, so findet man beständig eine Menge Menschen, die sich mit nichts beschäftigen.' In 1804, Ernst Moritz Arndt complained in a similar vein that 'in den Wiener Kaffeehäusern zwar immer Gesellschaft, aber nur selten Unterhaltung'. Quoted in Riemer, 'Exotische Genussmittel', p. 34.
8. Jürgen Habermas, *The Structural Transformation of the Public Sphere: An Inquiry into a Category of Bourgeois Society*, trans. Thomas Burger (Cambridge, MA, 1991). For sociability and social life in the coffee houses, see James V.H. Melton, *The Rise of the Public in Enlightenment Europe* (Cambridge, 2001), pp. 240–51, and Brian Cowan, *The Social Life of Coffee: The Emergence of the British Coffeehouse* (New Haven and London, 2005).
9. Friedrich Nicolai, *Beschreibung einer Reise durch Deutschland und die Schweiz im Jahre 1781* (12 vols, Berlin, 1783–96), here vol. 5, p. 236; quoted in Sandgruber, *Konsumgesellschaft*, p. 195.
10. Cornelius Bontekoe, 'Drei neue curieuse Tractätgen von dem Brand Cafe, chinesischen The und der Chocolata', in his *Kurze Abhandlung von dem menschlichen Leben, Gesundheit, Krankheit und Tod* (Rudolstadt, 1692).
11. Heise, *Kaffee*, p. 333.
12. Johannes Forner (ed.), *Die Gewandhauskonzerte zu Leipzig. Mit einem zusammenfassenden Rückblick von den Anfängen bis 1781* (2nd edn, Leipzig, 1983), pp. 18–19.
13. Wolfgang Nahrstedt, *Die Entstehung der Freizeit. Dargestellt am Beispiel Hamburgs. Ein Beitrag zur Strukturgeschichte und zur strukturgeschichtlichen Grundlegung der Freizeitpädagogik* (Bielefeld, 1998), pp. 177–8.

14. Gisela Jaacks, 'Landhausleben', in *Gärten, Landhäuser und Villen des hamburgischen Bürgertums. Kunst, Kultur und gesellschaftliches Leben in vier Jahrhunderten* (Hamburg, 1975), pp. 45–52, here p. 46.

15. Anne-Charlott Trepp, *Sanfte Männlichkeit und selbständige Weiblichkeit. Frauen und Männer im Hamburger Bürgertum zwischen 1770 und 1840* (Göttingen, 1996), pp. 226–31.

16. 'dass der Thee so beliebt ist, dass ohne diesen kein Hamburger leben kann'. Quoted in Eckart Klessmann, *Geschichte der Stadt Hamburg* (Hamburg, 1981), p. 297.

17. Schneider, 'Die neuen Getränke', pp. 564–5.

18. John E. Wills, 'European Consumption and Asian Production in the Seventeenth and Eighteenth Centuries', in John Brewer and Roy Porter (eds), *Consumption and the World of Goods* (London, 1993), pp. 141–2, 144.

19. Stephanus Blancardus, *Haustus polychresti: Oder Zuverlässige Gedancken vom Theé, Coffeé, Chocolate, u. Taback, mit welchen der grosse Nutze dieser ausländischen Wahren so wol in gesunden als krancken Tagen gründlich und umständlich gelehret wird* (Hamburg, 1705).

20. Günter Wiegelmann, *Alltags- und Festspeisen. Wandel und gegenwärtige Stellung* (Marburg, 1967), pp. 171ff.

21. Quoted in Sandgruber, *Konsumgesellschaft*, p. 196.

22. 'For a decade now the drinking of coffee, which is so popular in the northern regions of Germany, has penetrated even to the valleys of Berchtesgaden, and the rotund local woman perhaps finds her coffee with thick cream still more delicious than the slim lady of Berlin.' ('Seit einem Jahrzehnte ist der Gebrauch des in den nördlichen Gegenden von Deutschland so beliebten Kaffees auch in die Thäler von Berchtesgaden gedrungen, und die dickbauchige Berchtesgadenerin findet den Kaffee mit ihrer fetten Sahne vielleicht noch kostbarer als die schlanke Berliner Dame.') Johann Peter Willebrandt, *Historische Berichte und praktische Anmerkungen auf Reisen in Deutschland, in die Niederlande, in Frankreich, England, Dänemark, Böhmen und Ungarn* (3rd edn, Hamburg, 1761), p. 306.

23. 'Thee wird sehr wenig … getrunken. Welchen man bekommt, ist mit Citronen-Scalen und Caneel verdorben und wird aus Caffee-Schalen eingeschenkt.' 'Die Frauenzimmer vom höheren Stand nehmen noch immer den kaffee und die Schokolade ganz ausnehmend in Schutz. Die ausländischen Theesorten wollen ihnen gar nicht, und die inländischen nur als Arzney behagen.' *Neueste Gemälde von Wien* (Hamburg, 1797), p. 167, quoted in Sandgruber, *Konsumgesellschaft*, pp. 195–6.

24. Annerose Menninger, *Genuss im kulturellen Wandel. Tabak, Kaffee, Tee und Schokolade in Europa (16.-19. Jahrhundert)* (Stuttgart, 2004), pp. 355–63.

25. I thank Frank Schulenburg for providing me with the data. Cf. *Statistik des Hamburger seewärtigen Einfuhrhandels im 18. Jahrhundert. Nach den Admiralitäts- und Convoygeld-Einnahmebüchern*, ed. Jürgen Schneider, Otto-Ernst Krawehl and Markus A. Denzel (St Katharinen, 2001), pp. 391–6, 541–2.

26. Hans-Jürgen Gerhard and Karl Heinrich Kaufhold, *Preise im vor- und frühindustriellen Deutschland*, vol. 2: *Nahrungsmittel, Getränke, Gewürze, Rohstoffe und Gewerbeprodukte* (Stuttgart, 2001), pp. 112–13, 126–7.

27. Hans-Jürgen Gerhard, 'Entwicklungen auf europäischen Kaffeemärkten 1735–1810. Eine preishistorische Studie zur Geschichte eines Welthandelsgutes', in Rainer Gömmel and Markus A. Denzel (eds), *Weltwirtschaft und Wirtschaftsordnung (Festschrift Jürgen Schneider)* (Stuttgart, 2002), pp. 151–68.

28. Hans-Jürgen Gerhard, *Diensteinkommen der Göttinger Officianten 1750–1850* (Göttingen, 1978), pp. 156–83. John Brewer, 'Was können wir aus der Geschichte der frühen

Neuzeit für die moderne Konsumgeschichte lernen?', in Hannes Siegrist, Hartmut Kaelble and Jürgen Kocka (eds), *Europäische Konsumgeschichte. Zur Gesellschafts- und Kulturgeschichte des Konsums (18. bis 20. Jahrhundert)* (Frankfurt and New York, 1997), pp. 51–74, here pp. 63–4.

29. Compare the literature in Chapter 4 above. Jörg Driesner, 'Materielle Kultur in Greifswald im 17. und 18. Jahrhundert' (MA thesis, University of Greifswald, 2002), and Driesner, 'Frühmoderne Alltagswelten im Ostseeraum: Materielle Kultur in Stralsund, Kopenhagen und Riga – Drei Regionen im Vergleich' (PhD dissertation, University of Greifswald, 2006); Corina Heß, 'Die materielle Wohnkultur Danzigs des 17. und 18. Jahrhunderts im Spiegel von Nachlassinventaren' (PhD dissertation, University of Greifswald, 2005), and *Danziger Wohnkultur in der Frühen Neuzeit* (Münster, 2007).

30. 'ein beutel mit türckischen bohnen, während der fürstliche Hofgerichtsassessor Conring 1695 auf seinem Gut Groß Twülpstedt bereits (u. a.) ein zinnern theetopf, … ein cofféetopf, eine théebüchse …, zwey alte hamburg. Theenäpgens, ein ehrnen theetopf [sowie] ein klein theetisch mit zwey schachteln.' Ruth-Elisabeth Mohrmann, *Alltagswelt im Land Braunschweig: Städtische und ländliche Wohnkultur vom 16. bis zum frühen 20. Jahrhundert* (Münster, 1990), p. 562.

31. 'an silber – eine coffeekanne, eine milchkanne, ein theekännichen, eine zuckerschachtel, eine theebüchße, eine zuckerbüchße, 11 stück théelöffel, 1 coffeetopf; an meßing – 1 theemachine, 1 theetopf mit einer machine zum spiritus, an zinn – 1 choccoladentopf, 1 klein theetopf, an blech – 1 kl. theebüchse, 2 theedosen, 1 dose mit thee; an porcellain – 5 ½ paar weißblaue in golde echte tassen, 1 dergleichen kumpe, 1 zuckerkumpe mit einen deckel, 6 paar kleine bunte tassen, 1 theetopf, 1 weiß unechter milchtopf, 1 zuckerdose mit deinen deckel, 1 choccoladenbecher, 6 braune coffeetassen, 2 choccoladenbecher, 1 theetopf von terra sigillata, 1 papieren beutel darin coffeebohnen.' Mohrmann, *Alltagswelt*, p. 562.

32. 'ein coffee- und thee-service von dresdner porcellain als: eine koffee-kanne mit unterschüssel, eine milchkanne, eine theetopf, ein spühlkumpen, eine zuckedose, ein dutzend coffee-schaalen, ½ dutzend thee-schaalen, ½ dutzend chocoladen-tassen – 15 rtl 14 gr, ein kleines thee-service von gleichen porcellain; ein theetopf mit unterschaale, eine milchkanne mit dito, ein spühlkumpen, 5 paar theeschaalen – 2 rtl, ein dutzend savanische koffee-schaalen – 1 rtl 10 gr, ein kleiner kumpen mit teller von savanischen porcellain – 9 gr, fünf köpfgen blaue ostindische theeschalen, ein blaue ostinidische zuckerdose – 9 gr 6 dn, fünf dito unterschaalen, ein schälgen von dito porcellain – 2 gr 6 dn, ein theetopf mit beschlag von ostindischen porcellan – 9 gr 6 dn, ein dito von terra sigillata – 2 gr, eine kaffeekanne, ein theetopf, eine zuckerdose, eine theebüchse, ein spühlkumpen, vier unterschaalen, zwey köpfgen, von blau und weißen dresdner porcellain, fast durchgängig sehr schadhaft – 12 gr.' Mohrmann, *Alltagswelt*, p. 564.

33. '6. paar braune Caffee geschirr …, 1. braun thee potgen, noch 1. dreßdner thee potgen und 2. paar dito kopgen und tassen …, 4. leinene Caffee tücher …, 1. Messingerne Caffee kanne, 1. dito choclad kanne …, 1. Caffeetisch mit Wachstuch …, 1. dito [Messing] Caffee Kessel …, 3. große und Kleine dito [Kupfer] thee Kessel, 1. dito choclade Kanne.' ICC Frankfurt 756.

34. '1. Thée Keßel mit Kohlpfanne, 2. Thée potgen, 2. kleine ditto …, 2. Kupferne Théekeßel, 1. Caffée Keßelgen …, 2. messingene Caffée Keßel …, 1. ditto Thée

Machine ..., 2. alte Theé Tische ..., 1. Caffée Keßel mit hölzern Griff ..., 1. ditto Thée Machine, 1. ditto Caffée Kann mit Kranen, 1. ditto Caffée[kann] ..., 1. Théepotgen mit hölzern Grif [Silber] ..., 5. Thée Kännger [Silber], 1. Caffeebret [Silber] ..., 2. Théeflaschen ..., 9. blau und weis leinene Caffée Tücher ..., 3. kleine cottunene Caffée Tücher ..., 1. gelbe Caffée Kanne [Porzellan] ..., 1. ditto Théepot ..., 6. detti Chocolade Becher, 6. paar detti Thée Tassen, 1. ditto Thée Flasche ..., 6. paar braune Caffée Schaalen, inwendig mit roth und blauen Blumen, 8. Caffée Schaalen und 5. Kopfgern mit blauen Blumen, 4. Schaalen und 5 Kopfgern mit grün und rothen Blumen, 6. Kopfern und 6. braune Caffée Schaalen ..., 6. blau und weise Chocolade Becher, 12. Schaalen und 12. Kopfern weis mit färbiger Blumen ..., 2. detti Thée Potgen ..., 6 paar grau und blaue Théeschaalen ..., 1. Thée Potgen mit Unterschaale ..., 2. laquirte Caffée Tisch., 1. Caffée Tisch mit Wachstuch ..., 1. damast gebildet Caffée Tuch ..., 2. Caffée Tisch mit Wachstuch ..., 1. zinnen Théebrett ..., 3. laquirte Cafféebretter, 1. nusbaumenes ditto ..., 5. Theekannen ..., 2. Cafféekeßel ..., 3. Cafféekannen ..., 1. messingern Theekeßel.' ICC Frankfurt 37.

35. '1. Caffe Tisch mit Wachstuch ..., 1. kupferne Theekanne ..., 1. Cafféekanne mit Kranen [Zinn] ..., 2. Caffee Kannen [Zinn] ..., 1. Thee Potgen [Zinn], 1. kleines ditto ..., 1. Caffeé Kann [Kupfer] ..., 1. Caffeé Keßel [Messing] ..., 12. Chocolade Schalen in 1. Körbgen ..., 1. meßingene Caffe Kanne ..., 1. Caffeé Kanne [Zinn], 1. Thee =kannen [Zinn].' ICC Frankfurt 453.

36. 'Ein Thée=Brett [Silber], Fünf Thée=löffel ..., Zwey Thée-Keßel und 1. do=deckel [Kupfer] ..., Ein Thee-Pott mit Spriet-Lampe [Kupfer] ..., Eine Coffée-Kanne, mit drey Hähne [Messing], Eine do mit einem Hahn, Ein Thée-Keßel, mit Spriet-Lampe [Messing] ..., Ein Coffée=Brenner, mit Fuß [Eisen] ..., Eine Coffée=Kanne [Blech] ..., Ein roth mit Gold laquirter Thée-Tisch ..., Ein kleiner Thée-Tisch, mit Wachstuch beschlagen ..., Sieben paar bunte porcellaine Thée-Taßen, Sechs paar dito Coffée-Taßen, Ein Thée-Topf [Porzellan] ..., Eine Thée-Dose [Porzellan] ..., Zwey metallen Thée-Löffel ..., Ein hölzern Thée-bock ..., Eine alte Thée-Kiste ..., Ein feuern Coffee-Stuhl ..., Etliche kleine alte Thée-Kisten'. StA Hamburg, Erbschaftsamt, D 71.

37. Driesner, 'Materielle Kultur in Greifswald', pp. 18, 73.

38. Driesner, 'Frühmoderne Alltagswelten im Ostseeraum', p. 132, and Stadtarchiv Hansestadt Stralsund (StA HST), Rep. 3, 'Das Gerichtswesen der Stadt Stralsund', no. 5384 (Inventory of Diedrich Meyers Weyland, 1738).

39. Ruth-Elisabeth Mohrmann, 'Leben und Wohnen in der alten Stadt – Osnabrück im hansestädtischen Vergleich', *Hansische Geschichtsblätter*, 106 (1988): 109–26, here pp. 124–5.

40. 'VI. Ueber den modernen Luxus des Thee=Trinkens', *Journal des Luxus und der Moden*, 3 (August 1788): 336f.

41. 'Das jetzt so sehr beliebte Thee=Trinken ist ein schädlicher Luxus, der wie andern Bequemlichkeiten und Genußen aus England zu uns herübergeschlichen, und beynahe schon, sonderlich in der höheren Claße der schönen Welt, allgemein eingeführt ist. Man besucht sich einander gegen Abend zum Thee; es ist den Damen so angenehm sich richtig um 6 Uhr einander beym Thee=Tische zu finden, sich traulich herum zu setzen, zu plaudern und zu scherzen. Dieß ist Englische Sitte, nun leider schon nach Teutschland verpflanzt. England ist das erste Land in der Welt daß jährlich eine ungeheure Menge, und gewiß mehr als China selbst,

Thee verbraucht, weil fast jedermann täglich in England Thee trinckt, und zwar
ohne daß man eben so auffallend verwüstende Folgen für die Gesundheit davon
bemerkte, als in andern Ländern. Allein in England wird das Thee=Trinken für die
Gesundheit dadurch etwas weniger nachtheilig, weil man dort sehr spät zu Mittag,
und Abends oft gar nicht ißt, und viele starcke Speißen und Getränke genießt,
die durch den Thee verdünnt und gemildert werden. Dazu kommt auch die viele
und starke Bewegung, welche sich der Engländer giebt; und daß in England faßt
gar kein Caffee getrunken wird. Lauter Umstände die bey uns, und sonderlich bey
unseren Damen nicht so sind. Unsere vornehmere schöne Welt führt meistens ein
sitzendes, ruhiges, ja ich darf beynahe sagen träges Leben, trinckt weniger starcke
Weine und Biere, aber dafür auch zweymal des Tags Caffee, ist zwar weichere aber
dafür auch weit fetter bereitete Speißen und Backwerk als die Engländer; lauter
Umstände die für sie den nun noch dazu kommenden täglichen Gebrauch des
Thees nachtheilig machen müßen.' … 'So gern wir auch zugeben daß der sparsame
Gebrauch des Thees, als ein hautöffnendes und Transpiration beförderndes Mittel
allerdings wohlthätig sey, und der Thee=Tisch etwas zu den Annehmlichkeiten
des Lebens beytragen könne, so sehr sind wir doch mit dem Herrn Verfaßer des
vorstehenden Aufsatzes sowohl darinn einverstanden daß der übertriebene und
tägliche Genuß des Thees bey unserer übrigen Lebens=Art schädlich sey; als auch,
daß wir diesen Luxus hauptsächlich von England gelernt haben. Dieß beweißt der
ganze geschmackvolle Apparat eines Englischen Thee=Tisches, und die schöne
Form und Materie eines Engl. Thee=Zeugs … .' 'VII. Tisch= und Trink=Geschirr.
Englisches Thee=Zeug', *Journal des Luxus und der Moden* (August 1788):
340–41. Bertuch continues his advertisement by describing the new products and
explaining that 'We offer one of the same in the newest taste in Plate 24; not,
to be sure, because it is new and unfamiliar to our readers, but rather because it
belongs to the plan of our Journal (as a chronicle and repertorium of the luxury
and fashions of our age) and to its completeness. Fig. 1 is an Engl. tea urn of
brown polished copper with silver or silver-plated ornaments; and Fig. 6 is the
tap belonging to it, which is shown separately for the sake of clarity. The English
generally keep the water inside hot by means of a red-hot steel cylinder, which
is however rather laborious, and yet not effective. Our court coppersmith Herr
Pflug in Jena, whose skill we have lauded on many occasions, produces such tea
urns whose beauty of form, colour and polish is in every way the equal of the
English models, with a little coal-pan inside, which is far more convenient and
efficacious. Figs. 2, 3 and 4 show an English teapot, cream jug and sugar basin, in
black so-called basalt ware, painted in blue and white in the Etrurian taste from
Wedgwood's renowned Etruria works. Fig. 5 shows an English finely polished glass
tea bottle, of which one usually has two, for Hyson and Bohea tea, in a finely
worked box. Take a tastefully made table, decorated in bronze, and a lacquered and
finely painted platter, and one has all the makings of a modern English tea table.'
('Wir liefern hier eins dergl. vom neuesten Geschmacke auf Taf. 24; zwar nicht als
etwas unsern Lesern Neues und Unbekanntes, sondern vielmehr weil es zum Plane
unsers Journals (als Chronick und Repertorium des Luxus und der Moden unserer
Zeit) und zur Vollständigkeit deselben gehört. Fig. 1 ist eine engl. Thee=Maschiene
von braunen Glanz=Kupfer mit silbernen oder plattirten Verzierungen; und Fig. 6
ist der dazugehörige Hahn, welcher der Deutlichkeit wegen besonders gezeichnet
ist. Die Engländer erhalten das Waßer darinnen gewöhnlich mit einem glühenden

Stahle heiß, welches aber etwas mühsam ist, und doch die gehörige Würckung nicht thut. Unser Hr. Hofkupferschmied Pflug in Jena, deßen Geschicklichkeit wir schon mehrmals hier gerühmt haben, verfertigt dergl. Thee=Maschienen die an schöner Form Farbe und Politur den Englischen vollkommen gleichen, mit einer drinn angebrachten Kohlen=Pfanne; welches weit bequemer und würcksamer ist. Fig 2, 3, 4, ist eine Engl. Theekanne, Milchtopf, und Zuckerdose, von schwarzer sogenannter Basalt=Waare, blau und weiß in Hetrurischem Geschmacke gemahlt, aus Wedgwoods berühmter Hetruria=Fabrick. Fig. 5 ist eine Englische schöngeschliffene gläserne Thee=Flasche, dergleichen man gewöhlich zwey, zu Heysang und Bohea=Thee, in einem schön gearbeiteten Kästgen hat. Nimmt man nun noch dazu einen geschmackvoll gearbeiteten Tisch, mit Bronze decorirt, und einem lackirten und schön gemählten Blatte, so hat man den ganzen Apparat eines modernen Engl. Thee=Tisches ziemlich vollständig.')

42. 'wider das zu weit gehende Thee- und Coffee-Trinken, der gemeinen Bürger, Handwerker, Tagelöhner und Tagelöhnerinnen, Gesinde, auch Bauern, Cossäthen, Einlieger, Müller und dergleichen … .' Schneider, 'Die neuen Getränke', p. 563; Menninger, *Genuss*, pp. 384–90.

43. 'manchen neuen Aufwand veranlaßt, nähmlich: 1. den Ankauf des Porzellanes. … Man muß, die Mode befiehlt es, nicht allein zum eigenen täglichen Gebrauch, sondern auch für Fremde besondere Tassen haben. … 2. Die auch ganz neue Vermehrung des Hausrathes durch das übrige Kaffeegeschirr. Man hat jetzt Brenner, Mühlen, Töpfe, Kannen und mehrere Kleinigkeiten nöthig, die unsere Vorfahren nicht brauchten. … 3. Die Anlegung der Besuchszimmer, die unstreitig in den meisten Häusern ihren Ursprung dem Kaffe zu danken haben, da alle alte Leute wissen, daß sie zu Anfange dieses Jahrhundertes noch in den wenigsten Häusern vorhanden waren, weil man sie durchaus nicht eher brauchte, als bis es anfing zur guten Lebensart zu gehören, daß wenigstens die Hausfrau Kaffebesuch annahm. … 4. Die Ausgabe endlich für den Kaffe und dessen Zubehör selbst … die Nahrung vom Bierbrauen [fiel] an den meisten Orten so …, wie der Gebrauch des Kaffees gestiegen ist … .' Johann Georg Krünitz, *Oeconomische Encyclopädie*, vol. 32 (Berlin, 1784), pp. 195–9.

44. Peter Albrecht, 'Es geht doch nicht an, dass all und jeder Kaffee trinkt! Kaffeeverbote in der Frühen Neuzeit', in Eva Dietrich and Roman Rossfeld (eds), *Am Limit: Kaffeegenuss als Grenzerfahrung* (Zurich, 2002), pp. 22–35.

45. Menninger, *Genuss*, pp. 338–45.

Conclusion

1. Martina Kessel, *Langeweile. Zum Umgang mit Zeit und Gefühlen in Deutschland vom späten 18. bis zum frühen 20. Jahrhundert* (Göttingen, 2001), p. 40.

2. Thomas Nipperdey, *Deutsche Geschichte 1800–1866. Bürgerwelt und starker Staat* (Munich, 1983), pp. 539–42.

3. Karin A. Wurst, 'The Self-Fashioning of the Bourgeoisie in Late-Eighteenth-Century German Culture: Bertuch's *Journal des Luxus und der Moden*', *Germanic Review* 72(3) (1997): 170–82.

4. *Journal des Luxus und der Moden* (May, 1798): 279, Astrid Ackermann, *Paris, London und die europäische Provinz: Die frühen Modejournale 1770–1830* (Frankfurt, 2005), p. 396.

5. Maxine Berg, *Luxury and Pleasure in Eighteenth-Century Britain* (Oxford, 2005), pp. 195–6.

6. Lothar Gall, "'… Ich wünschte ein Bürger zu sein". Zum Selbstverständnis des deutschen Bürgertums im 19. Jahrhundert', *Historische Zeitschrift* 245 (1987): 601–23.

7. Hans-Ulrich Wehler, *Deutsche Gesellschaftsgeschichte*, vol. 1: *1700–1815*, (Munich, 1987), pp. 202–10. See also the introduction by Dieter Hein and Andreas Schulz (eds), in *Bürgerkultur im 19. Jahrhundert. Bildung, Kunst und Lebenswelt* (Munich, 1996), pp. 9–16.

8. Benedict Anderson, *Imagined Communities: Reflections on the Origin and Spread of Nationalism* (London, 1983). Bernhard Giesen (ed.), *Nationale und kulturelle Identität. Studien zur Entwicklung des kollektiven Bewußtseins in der Neuzeit* (Frankfurt, 1991). Martin Krieger, 'Patriotismus-Diskurs und die Konstruktion kollektiver Identitäten in Hamburg in der ersten Hälfte des 18. Jahrhunderts' (Habilitation thesis, University of Greifswald, 2001).

9. Ute Daniel, 'Vom fürstlichen Gast zum Konsumenten: Das Hoftheaterpublikum in Deutschland vom 18. zum 19. Jahrhundert', in Hans-Erich Bödecker, Patrice Veit and Michael Werner (eds), *Le concert et son public. Mutations de la vie musicale en Europe de 1780 à 1914 (France, Allemagne, Angleterre)* (Paris, 2002), pp. 349–82, here p. 355.

10. *Journal des Luxus und der Moden* (January 1786): 16.

11. *Charis. Ein Magazin für das Neueste in Kunst, Geschmack und Mode, Lebensgenuß und Lebensglück* (1805): 341–2. Quoted in Ackermann, Paris, London, p. 110.

12. Friedrich Schiller to the Inspector of the Gallery of Antiquities in Dresden Wilhelm Gottlieb Becker, 10 October 1802, in *Schillers Werke. Nationalausgabe*, ed. Stefan Ormanns, vol. 31 (Weimar, 1985), pp. 164–5, here p. 165.

Select Bibliography and Archival Sources

Abbt, Thomas, *Vom Verdienste* (Frankfurt and Leipzig, 1783).

Ackermann, Astrid, 'Eine nationale Aufgabe – Mode und Kommerz', in Andreas Klinger and Gonthier-Louis Fink (eds), *Identitäten. Erfahrungen und Fiktionen um 1800* (Frankfurt, 2003), pp. 232–7.

Ackermann, Astrid, *Paris, London und die europäische Provinz. Die frühen europäischen Modejournale (1770–1830)* (Frankfurt, 2005).

Adelung, Johann Christoph, *Grammatisch-kritisches Wörterbuch der Hochdeutschen Mundart, mit beständiger Vergleichung der übrigen Mundarten, besonders aber der Oberdeutschen* (2nd edn, vol. 3, Leipzig, 1798).

Albrecht, Peter, 'Es geht doch nicht an, dass all und jeder Kaffee trinkt! Kaffeeverbote in der Frühen Neuzeit', in Eva Dietrich and Roman Rossfeld (eds), *Am Limit. Kaffeegenuss als Grenzerfahrung* (Zurich, 2002), pp. 22–35.

Allgemeine Deutsche Bibliothek (Berlin and Stettin, 1765–1806).

Allgemeine Musikalische Zeitung (Leipzig, 1798–1848).

Allgemeines Theater-Lexikon oder Encyklopädie alles Wissenswerthen für Bühnenkünstler, Dilettanten und Theaterfreunde, ed. Robert Blum, Karl Herloßsohn and Herrmann Marggraff (Altenburg and Leipzig, 1839).

Allihn, Ingeborg, 'Organisatoren und Formen der Organisation des Musiklebens in Berlin im ausgehenden 18. Jahrhundert', in Hans-Erich Bödeker, Patrice Veit and Michael Werner (eds), *Le concert et son public. Mutations de la vie musicale en Europe de 1780 à 1914 (France, Allemagne, Angleterre)* (Paris, 2002), pp. 159–73.

Anderson, Benedict, *Imagined Communities: Reflections on the Origin and Spread of Nationalism* (London, 1983).

Badstübner-Gröger, Sybille, 'Einige Bemerkungen zur geschmacksbildenen Rolle der Berliner Akademie-Ausstellungen im späten 18. Jahrhundert', in Michael North (ed.), *Kunstsammeln und Geschmack im 18. Jahrhundert* (Berlin, 2002), pp. 195–215.

Baillie, Granville Hugh, *Watchmakers and Clockmakers of the World* (3rd edn, London, 1951, reprint London, 1972).

Balet, Leo and Gerhard, E., *Die Verbürgerlichung der deutschen Kunst, Literatur und Musik im 18. Jahrhundert*, ed. Gert Mattenklott (Frankfurt, 1973).

Bartell, Edmund, *Über die malerische Anlage und Verbesserung kleiner geschmackvoller Landhäuser oder sogenannter englischer Cottages* (Weimar, 1805).

Batsch, August, *Botanik für Frauenzimmer und Pflanzenliebhaber, welche keine Gelehrten sind* (Weimar, 1795).

Bauche, Ulrich, 'Von bürgerlicher Gartenkunst', in *Gärten, Landhäuser und Villen des hamburgischen Bürgertums* (1975), pp. 19–25.

Bausinger, Herman, Beyrer, Klaus and Korff, Gottfried (eds), *Reisekultur. Von der Pilgerfahrt zum modernen Tourismus* (Munich, 1991).

Becker-Cantarino, Barbara, *Der lange Weg zur Mündigkeit. Frau und Literatur (1500–1800)* (Stuttgart, 1987).

Beckmann, Johann, *Literatur der älteren Reisebeschreibungen. Nachrichten von ihren Verfassern, von ihrem Inhalte, von ihren Ausgaben* (2 vols, Göttingen, 1807–10).

Beer, Axel, *Musik zwischen Komponist, Verlag und Publikum. Die Rahmenbedingungen des Musikschaffens in Deutschland im ersten Drittel des 19. Jahrhunderts* (Tutzing, 2000).

Behringer, Wolfgang, *Im Zeichen des Merkur: Reichspost und Kommunikationsrevolution in der Frühen Neuzeit* (Gottingen, 2003).

Berckenmeyer, Paul Ludolf, *Vermehrter Curieuser Antiquarius, Das ist: Allerhand auserlesene Geographische und Historische Merckwürdigkeiten / So in denen Europæischen Ländern zu finden; Aus Berühmter Männer Reisen zusammengetragen / und mit einem zweyfachen Register versehen* (Hamburg, 1711).

Berg, Maxine, 'French Fancy and Cool Britannia. The Fashion Markets of Early Modern Europe', in Simonetta Cavaciocchi (ed.), *Fiere e mercati nella integrazione delle economie Europe secc. XIII–XVIII* (Prato, 2001), pp. 519–56.

Berg, Maxine, *Luxury and Pleasure in Eighteenth-Century Britain* (Oxford, 2005).

Berg, Maxine and Clifford, Helen (eds), *Consumers and Luxury: Consumer Culture in Europe 1650–1850* (Manchester, 1999).

Berg, Maxine and Eger, Elizabeth (eds), *Luxury in the Eighteenth Century: Debates, Desires and Delectable Goods* (London, 2003).

Berger, Joachim, 'Geselligkeit, Mäzenatentum und Kunstliebhaberei am "Musenhof" Anna Amalias – Neue Ergebnisse, neue Fragen', in Joachim Berger (ed.), *Der Musenhof Anna Amalias. Geselligkeit, Mäzenatentum und Kunstliebhaberei im klassischen Weimar* (Cologne, Weimar and Vienna, 2001), pp. 1–17.

Berger, Theodor, *Vor-Urtheile der Deutschen bey Antretung ihrer Reisen in auswärtige Lande, u. bes. nach Franckreich, nebst Anhang von Deutschlands Macht gegen angräntzende Königreiche u. Länder* (Frankfurt, 1734).

Berlinische Nachrichten, 29 (9 March 1773).

Bermingham, Ann and Brewer, John (eds), *The Consumption of Culture 1600–1800. Image, Object, Text* (London and New York, 1995).

Beyrer, Klaus, 'Des Reisebeschreibers "Kutsche". Aufklärerisches Bewußtsein im Postreiseverkehr des 18. Jahrhunderts', in Wolfgang Griep and Hans-Wolf Jäger (eds), *Reisen im 18. Jahrhundert. Neue Untersuchungen* (Heidelberg, 1986), pp. 50–90.

Beyrer, Klaus (ed.), *Zeit der Postkutschen. Drei Jahrhunderte Reisen 1600–1900* (Karlsruhe, 1992).

Bibliothek der schönen Wissenschaften und der freyen Künste (Leipzig, 1757–65).

Black, Jeremy, *France and the Grand Tour* (Basingstoke, 2003).

Black, Jeremy, *Italy and the Grand Tour* (New Haven and London, 2003).

Blancardus, Stephanus, *Haustus polychresti: Oder Zuverlässige Gedancken vom Theé, Coffeé, Chocolate, u. Taback, mit welchen der grosse Nutze dieser ausländischen Wahren so wol in gesunden als krancken Tagen gründlich und umständlich gelehret wird* (Hamburg, 1705).

Blanning, Tim C.W., *The Culture of Power and the Power of Culture: Old Regime Europe 1660–1789* (Oxford, 2002).

Blum, Klaus, *Musikfreunde und Musici. Musikleben in Bremen seit der Aufklärung* (Tutzing, 1975).

Bödeker, Hans Erich, 'Reisen: Bedeutung und Funktion für die deutsche Aufklärungsgesellschaft', in Wolfgang Griep and Hans-Wolf Jäger (eds), *Reisen im 18. Jahrhundert. Neue Untersuchungen* (Heidelberg, 1986), pp. 91–110.

Bok, Marten Jan, *Vraag en aanbod op de Nederlandse kunstmarkt, 1580–1700* (Utrecht, 1994).

Bonfait, Oliver, 'Les collections de parlementaires parisiens de XVIIIe siècle', *Revue de l'art*, 73 (1986): 28–42.

Böning, Holger, *Das Intelligenzblatt. Dokumentation zu einer literarisch-publizistischen Gattung der deutschen Aufklärung* (Bremen, 1991).

Böning, Holger, 'Aufklärung und Presse im 18. Jahrhundert', in Hans-Wolf Jäger (ed.), *'Öffentlichkeit' im 18. Jahrhundert* (Göttingen, 1997), pp. 151–63.

Böning, Holger, 'Das Intelligenzblatt', in Ernst Tischer, Wilhelm Haefs and York-Gothart Mix (eds), *Von Almanach bis Zeitung. Ein Handbuch der Medien in Deutschland 1700–1800* (Munich, 1999), pp. 89–104.

Bontekoe, Cornelius, 'Drei neue curieuse Tractätgen von dem Brand Cafe, chinesischen The und der Chocolata', in *Kurze Abhandlung von dem menschlichen Leben, Gesundheit, Krankheit und Tod* (Rudolstadt, 1692).

Boyle, Nicholas, *Goethe. Der Dichter in seiner Zeit*, vol. 1: *1749–1790* (Munich, 1999).

Braunbehrens, Volkmar, *Salieri. Ein Musiker im Schatten Mozarts? Eine Biographie* (Munich, 1989).

Braunbehrens, Volkmar, *Mozart in Wien* (5th edn, Munich and Zurich, 1997).

Brauneck, Manfred, *Die Welt als Bühne. Geschichte des europäischen Theaters*, vol. 2 (Stuttgart, 1996).

Brewer, John, '"The most polite age and the most vicious". Attitudes towards Culture as a Commodity, 1660–1800', in Ann Bermingham and John Brewer (eds), *The Consumption of Culture 1600–1800. Image, Object, Text* (London and New York, 1995), pp. 341–61.

Brewer, John, 'Was können wir aus der Geschichte der frühen Neuzeit für die moderne Konsumgeschichte lernen?', in Hannes Siegrist, Hartmut Kaelble and Jürgen Kocka (eds), *Europäische Konsumgeschichte. Zur Gesellschafts- und Kulturgeschichte des Konsums (18. bis 20. Jahrhundert)* (Frankfurt and New York, 1997), pp. 51–74.

Brewer, John, *The Pleasures of the Imagination: English Culture in the Eighteenth Century* (London, 1997).

Brewer, John and Porter, Roy (eds), *Consumption and the World of Goods* (London, 1993).

Brewer, John and Trentmann, Frank (eds), *Consuming Cultures, Global Perspectives: Historical Trajectories, Transnational Exchanges* (Oxford and New York, 2006).

Bringemeier, Martha, 'Wandel der Mode im Zeitalter der Aufklärung', *Rheinisch-Westfälische Zeitschrift für Volkskunde*, 13 (1966): 5–59.

Brockes, Barthold Heinrich, *Irdisches Vergnügen in Gott bestehend in verschiedenen aus der Natur und Sitten=Lehre hergenommenen Gedichten, nebst einem Anhange etlicher hieher gehörigen Uebersetzungen von des Hrn. de La Motte Französis. Fabeln mit Genehmhaltung des Herrn Verfassers nebst einer Vorrede herausgegeben von C. F. Weichmann* (Hamburg, 1721).

Busch-Salmen, Gabriele, Salmen, Walter and Michel, Christoph, *Der Weimarer Musenhof. Dichtung, Musik und Tanz, Gartenkunst, Geselligkeit, Malerei* (Stuttgart and Weimar, 1998).

Butret, C. de, *Gründlicher Unterricht vom Schnitte der Fruchtbäume und anderen Verrichtungen, die Bezug auf ihre Pflege haben*, trans. J.V. Sikler (Weimar, 1797).

Buttlar, Adrian von, *Der Landschaftsgarten* (Munich, 1980).

Caspar Wolf (1735–1783). Landschaft im Vorfeld der Romantik, exhibition catalogue (Basel, 1980).

Caspar Wolf. Ein Panorama der Schweizer Alpen (Aarau, 2001).

Catalogue d'un fameux Cabinet de tableaux des meilleurs maîtres, recueilli, avec beaucoup de choix et d'exactitude pendant plusieurs années et délaisse par feu monsieur le baron de Haeckel dont la vente se fera publiquement a Francfort sur le Mein, dans un terme qu'on annoncera par les Gazettes (Frankfurt, 1762). Städelsches Kunstinstitut, Frankfurt.

Catalogue d'un recueil d'un grand Seigneur de plusieurs superbes tableaux des plus Peintres, Italiens, François, Flamands, Hollandais & Allemands, qui ont été amenés des Pays-Bas ici à Francfort sur le Mayn avec beaucoup d'autres pièces précieuses en yvoire, en porcelaine & en ambre, de même que six pièces de paisages à la mosaïque avec des pierres orientales (Frankfurt, 1765), pp. 15, 35. Bibliothèque d'Art et d'Archéologie de l'Université, Paris.

Catalogus einer Sammlung auserlesener Kunst-Mahlereyen, welche am Donnerstage, den 31 Julii, vormittags um 10 Uhr, im Dennerischen Hause am Gaensemarkt oeffentlich an die Meistbietende verkauft werden sollen (Hamburg, 1749). Landeshauptarchiv Schwerin.

Catalogus einer schönen Sammlung auserlesener Cabinet=Mahlereyen und Portraits, welche in einem bekannten Sterbehause in der Neustädter Fuhlentwiete, an der Ecke der Neustraße, den 12ten April 1775 an die Meistbietenden verkauft werden sollen (Hamburg, 1775). Hamburger Kunsthalle, Hamburg.

Catalogus eines vortrefflichen Sammlung Cabinet=Mahlereyen, welche vor funfzig und mehreren Jahren mit vielem Gusto und Kenntniß gesammelt worden und sich unter dem Nachlaß des seel. Herrn Joachim Hinrich Thielcke befinden, in dessen Sterbehause auf den großen Bleichen selbige auch den 18 Merz, 1782, und folgende Tage durch Mackler

Peter Texier an den Meistbiethenden, gegen baare Bezahlung, grob Courant, öffentlich verkauft werden sollen (Hamburg, 1782). Hamburger Kunsthalle, Hamburg.

Charis. Ein Magazin für das Neueste in Kunst, Geschmack und Mode, Lebensgenuß und Lebensglück (Leipzig, 1802–04).

Chartier, Roger, *The Cultural Uses of Print in Early Modern France*, trans. Lydia G. Cochrane (Princeton, 1987).

Chartier, Roger, *Lesewelten. Buch und Lektüre in der Frühen Neuzeit* (Frankfurt and New York, 1990).

Cilleßen, Wolfgang, 'Modezeitschriften', in Ernst Fischer, Wilhelm Haefs and York-Gothart Mix (eds), *Von Almanach bis Zeitung. Ein Handbuch der Medien in Deutschland 1700–1800* (Munich, 1999), pp. 207–24.

Clodius, Christian August, *Neue vermischte Schriften*, vol. 3: *Dinokrates* (Leipzig, 1780).

Clunas, Craig, *Superfluous Things: Material Culture and Social Status in Early Modern China* (Chicago, 1991).

Cohen, Lizabeth, *A Consumer's Republic: The Politics of Mass Consumption in Postwar America* (New York, 2003).

Conrady, Karl Otto, *Goethe. Leben und Werk* (Düsseldorf and Zurich, 1999).

Cowan, Brian, 'Areas of Connoisseurship: Auctioning Art in Later Stuart England', in Michael North and David Ormrod (eds), *Art Markets in Europe, 1400–1800* (Aldershot, 1998), pp. 153–66.

Cowan, Brian, *The Social Life of Coffee: The Emergence of the British Coffeehouse* (New Haven and London, 2005).

Cramer, Carl Friedrich, *Magazin der Musik* (Hamburg, 1784–87).

Cremer, Claudia Susannah, 'Hagedorns Geschmack. Studien zur Kunst-kennerschaft in Deutschland im 18. Jahrhundert' (PhD dissertation, University of Bonn, 1989).

Crow, Thomas, *Painters and Public Life in Eighteenth-Century Paris* (New Haven and London, 1985).

Damm, Sigrid, *Christiane und Goethe. Eine Recherche* (Frankfurt, 2001).

Daniel, Ute, *Hoftheater. Zur Geschichte des Theaters und der Höfe im 18. und 19. Jahrhundert* (Stuttgart, 1995).

Daniel, Ute, 'Höfe und Aufklärung in Deutschland – Plädoyer für eine Begegnung der dritten Art', in Marcus Ventzke (ed.), *Hofkultur und aufklärerische Reformen in Thüringen. Die Bedeutung des Hofes im späten 18. Jahrhundert* (Cologne, Weimar and Vienna, 2002), pp. 11–31.

Daniel, Ute, 'How Bourgeois was the Public Sphere of the Eighteenth Century? or: Why it is Important to Historicize "Strukturwandel der Öffentlichkeit"', *Das Achtzehnte Jahrhundert* 26 (2002): 9–17.

Daniel, Ute, 'Vom fürstlichen Gast zum Konsumenten: Das Hoftheaterpublikum in Deutschland vom 18. zum 19. Jahrhundert', in Hans-Erich Bödeker, Patrice Veit and Michael Werner (eds), *Le concert et son public. Mutations de la vie musicale en Europe de 1780 à 1914 (France, Allemagne, Angleterre)* (Paris, 2002), pp. 349–82.

Dann, Otto, 'Die Lesegesellschaften und die Herausbildung einer modernen bürgerlichen Gesellschaft in Europa', in Otto Dann (ed.), *Lesegesellschaften und bürgerliche Emanzipation – Ein europäischer Vergleich* (Munich, 1981), pp. 9–28.

Dann, Otto (ed.), *Lesegesellschaften und bürgerliche Emanzipation – Ein europäischer Vergleich* (Munich, 1981).

Dann, Otto, 'Eine höfische Gesellschaft als Lesegesellschaft', in Hans-Erich Bödeker (ed.), *Lesekulturen im 18. Jahrhundert* (Hamburg, 1992), pp. 43–57.

Danreitter, Frantz Antoni, *Die Gärtnerey, so wohl in ihrer Theorie oder Betrachtung als Praxi oder Übung: allwo von denen schönen Gärten, welche man nur insgemein die Lust- und Zierd-Gärten zu nennen pflegt …* (Augsburg, 1731).

Daunton, Martin and Hilton, Matthew (eds), *The Politics of Consumption: Material Culture and Citizenship in Europe and America* (Oxford, 2001).

Deatheridge, John, 'The Invention of German Music, c. 1800', in Tim Blanning and Hagen Schulze (eds), *Unity and Diversity in European Culture c. 1800* (Oxford, 2006), pp. 35–60.

De la Motte Fouqué, Caroline, *Geschichte der Moden 1785–1829* (reprint Hanau, 1988).

Der geheime Ausrufer 11 (1808).

Der Teutsche Merkur (Weimar, 1773–89).

Descamps, Jean Baptiste, *La vie des peintres flamands, allemands et hollandois: avec des portraits gravés en taille-douce, une indication de leurs principaux ouvrages, [et] des réflexions sur leurs differentes manieres* (4 vols, Paris, 1753–63).

Die Erinnerungen der Karoline Jagemann nebst zahlreichen unveröffentlichten Dokumenten aus der Goethezeit, ed. Eduard v. Bamberg (Dresden, 1926).

Doering-Manteuffel, Sabine, Mančal, Josef and Wüst, Wolfgang (eds), *Pressewesen der Aufklärung. Periodische Schriften im Alten Reich* (Berlin, 2001).

Dörffel, Alfred, *Geschichte der Gewandhausconcerte zu Leipzig vom 25. November 1781 bis 25. November 1881* (Leipzig, 1884).

Driesner, Jörg, 'Materielle Kultur in Greifswald im 17. und 18. Jahrhundert' (MA thesis, University of Greifswald, 2002).

Driesner, Jörg, 'Frühmoderne Alltagswelten im Ostseeraum: Materielle Kultur in Stralsund, Kopenhagen und Riga – Drei Regionen im Vergleich' (PhD dissertation, University of Greifswald, 2006).

Eckhart, Edith, 'Die Verlassenschaften von Gobelsburg und Hadersdorf am Kamp als Quelle für die Kultur von Bürgern und Inwohnern im 18. Jahrhundert' (PhD dissertation, University of Vienna, 1977).

Ehret, Gloria, *Deutsche Möbel des 18. Jahrhunderts. Barock – Rokoko – Klassizismus* (Munich, 1986).

Eichhorn, Herbert, *Konrad Ernst Ackermann. Ein deutscher Theaterprinzipal. Ein Beitrag zur Theatergeschichte im deutschen Sprachraum* (Emsdetten, 1965).

Eilert, Heide, 'Bertuch und das zeitgenössische Theater', in Gerhard R. Kaiser and Siegfried Seifert (eds), *Friedrich Justin Bertuch (1747–1822). Verleger, Schriftsteller und Unternehmer im klassischen Weimar* (Tübingen, 2000), pp. 113–31.

Elias, Norbert, *Über den Prozeß der Zivilisation*, vol. 1, (2nd edn, Berne and Munich, 1969).

Elkar, Rainer S., '"Reisenbildet". Überlegungen zur Sozial- und Bildungsgeschichte des Reisens während des 18. und 19. Jahrhunderts', in B.I. Krasnobaev, Gert Robel and Herbert Zeman (eds), *Reisen und Reisebeschreibungen im 18. und 19. Jahrhundert als Quellen der Kulturbeziehungsforschung* (Essen, 1987), pp. 51–82.

Emde, Ruth B., *Schauspielerinnen im Europa des 18. Jahrhunderts. Ihr Leben, ihre Schriften und ihr Publikum* (Amsterdam and Atlanta, 1997).

Emmerich, Angelika and Schroeder, Susanne, 'Weimarer historische Interieurs. Zum Ameublement im "Journal des Luxus und der Moden"', in Gerhard R. Kaiser and Siegfried Seifert (eds), *Friedrich Justin Bertuch (1747–1822), Verleger, Schriftsteller und Unternehmer im klassischen Weimar* (Tübingen, 2000), pp. 501–18.

Engel, Helmut, *Villen und Landhäuser* (Berlin, 2001).

Engelsing, Rolf, 'Die Perioden der Lesegeschichte in der Neuzeit. Das statistische Ausmaß und die soziokulturelle Bedeutung der Lektüre', *Archiv für Geschichte des Buchwesens*, 10 (1970): cols 945–1002.

Engelsing, Rolf, *Analphabetentum und Lektüre. Zur Sozialgeschichte des Lesens in Deutschland zwischen feudaler und industrieller Gesellschaft* (Stuttgart, 1973).

Engelsing, Rolf, *Der Bürger als Leser. Lesegeschichte in Deutschland 1500–1800* (Stuttgart, 1974).

Erhart, Walter, 'Beziehungsexperimente: Goethes "Werther" und Wielands "Musarion"', *Deutsche Vierteljahrschrift für Literaturwissenschaft und Geistesgeschichte*, 2 (1992): 333–60.

Eschstruth, Hans Adolf Freiherr von, *Musikalische Bibliothek* (2 vols, 1784–85; reprint Hildesheim and New York, 1977).

Faessler, Peter, 'Reiseziel Schweiz: Freiheit zwischen Idylle und "großer" Natur', in Herman Bausinger, Klaus Beyrer and Gottfried Korff (eds), *Reisekultur. Von der Pilgerfahrt zum modernen Tourismus* (Munich, 1991), pp. 243–8.

Faulstich, Werner, *Die bürgerliche Mediengesellschaft (1700–1830)* (Göttingen, 2002).

Fischer, Ernst, 'Clodius, Christian August', in Walther Killy (ed.), *Literaturlexikon. Autoren und Werke deutscher Sprache* (2 vols, Gütersloh and Munich, 1989), pp. 431–2.

Fischer-Lichte, Erika, 'Entwicklung einer neuen Schauspielkunst', in Wolfgang F. Bender (ed.), *Schauspielkunst im 18. Jahrhundert* (Stuttgart, 1992), pp. 51–70.

Fischer-Lichte, Erika, 'Der Körper als Zeichen', in Erika Fischer-Lichte and Jörg Schönert (eds), *Theater im Kulturwandel des 18. Jahrhunderts: Inszenierung und Wahrnehmung von Körper – Musik – Sprache* (Göttingen, 1999), pp. 53–68.

Fischer-Lichte, Erika, 'Zur Einleitung', in Erika Fischer-Lichte and Jörg Schönert (eds), *Theater im Kulturwandel des 18. Jahrhunderts. Inszenierung und Wahrnehmung von Körper – Musik – Sprache* (Göttingen, 1999), pp. 11–20.

Flaherty, Gloria, *Opera in the Development of German Critical Thought* (Princeton, 1978).

Flik, Reiner, 'Statt Hofpoet Kulturunternehmer. Der Werdegang Friedrich Justin Bertuchs (1747–1822) und sein Beitrag zur Weimarer Klassik', in Marcus Ventzke (ed.), *Hofkultur und aufklärerische Reformen in Thüringen. Die Bedeutung des Hofes im späten 18. Jahrhundert* (Cologne, Weimar and Vienna, 2002), pp. 197–222.

Flik, Reiner, 'Das Journal des Luxus und der Moden: Produktion, Vertrieb, Geschäftsergebnisse und Leserkreis', in Klaus Manger and Gerhard R. Kaiser (eds), *Das Journal des Luxus und der Moden. Kultur um 1800* (Heidelberg, 2004).

Folter, Roland, *Deutsche Dichter- und Germanistenbibliotheken. Eine kritische Bibliographie ihrer Kataloge* (Stuttgart, 1975).

Forkel, Johann Nicolaus, *Über die Theorie der Musik, insofern sie Liebhabern und Kennern nothwendig und nützlich ist* (Göttingen, 1777).

Forkel, Johann Nicolaus (ed.), *Musikalischer Almanach* (Leipzig, 1782–89).

Forner, Johannes (ed.), *Die Gewandhauskonzerte zu Leipzig. Mit einem zusammenfassenden Rückblick von den Anfängen bis 1781* (2nd edn, Leipzig, 1983).

François, Etienne, 'Buch, Konfession und städtische Gesellschaft im 18. Jahrhundert. Das Beispiel Speyer', in *Mentalitäten und Lebensverhältnisse. Beispiele aus der Sozialgeschichte der Neuzeit. Rudolf Vierhaus zum 60. Geburtstag* (Göttingen, 1982), pp. 34–91.

Frank, Christoph, 'Die Gemäldesammlungen Gotzkowsky, Eimbke und Stein: Zur Berliner Sammlungsgeschichte während des Siebenjährigen Krieges', in Michael North (ed.), *Kunstsammeln und Geschmack im 18. Jahrhundert* (Berlin, 2002), pp. 117–94.

Frankfurter Modespiegel, exhibition catalogue, Historical Museum of Frankfurt am Main, with an introduction by Bernward Deneke (Frankfurt, 1962).

Friedhoff, Jens, '"Magnificence" und "Utilité". Bauen und Wohnen 1600–1800', in Ulf Dirlmeier (ed.), *Geschichte des Wohnens*, vol. 2: *500–1800: Hausen, Wohnen, Residieren* (Stuttgart, 1998), pp. 503–815.

Fühler, Armas Sten, 'Das Schauspielrepertoire des Mannheimer Hof- und Nationaltheaters im Geschmackswandel des 18. und 19. Jahrhunderts (1779–1870)' (PhD dissertation, University of Heidelberg, 1935).

Furttenbach, Joseph, *Architectura civilis* (Ulm, 1628).

Furttenbach, Joseph, *Architectura universalis* (Ulm, 1635).

Furttenbach, Joseph, *Architectura recreationis* (Ulm, 1640).

Furttenbach, Joseph, *Architectura private* (Ulm, 1641).

Füssel, Stephan, *Georg Joachim Göschen. Ein Verleger der Spätaufklärung und der deutschen Klassik*, vol. 1: *Studien zur Verlagsgeschichte und zur Verlegertypologie der Goethe-Zeit* (Berlin and New York, 1999).

Gabrielsson, Peter, 'Zur Entwicklung des bürgerlichen Garten- und Landhausbesitzes bis zum Beginn des 19. Jahrhunderts', in *Gärten, Landhäuser und Villen des hamburgischen Bürgertums: Kunst, Kultur und gesellschaftliches Leben in vier Jahrhunderten* (Hamburg, 1975), pp. 11–18.

Gall, Lothar, "'… Ich wünschte ein Bürger zu sein'". Zum Selbstverständnis des deutschen Bürgertums im 19. Jahrhundert', *Historische Zeitschrift*, 245 (1987): 601–23.

Garten und Wildnis. Landschaft im 18. Jahrhundert, ed. Hansjörg and Ulf Küster (Munich, 1997).

Gerhard, Hans-Jürgen, *Diensteinkommen der Göttinger Officianten 1750–1850* (Göttingen, 1978).

Gerhard, Hans-Jürgen and Kaufhold, Karl Heinrich, *Preise im vor- und frühindustriellen Deutschland*, vol. 2: *Nahrungsmittel, Getränke, Gewürze, Rohstoffe und Gewerbeprodukte* (Stuttgart, 2001).

Gerhard, Hans-Jürgen, 'Entwicklungen auf europäischen Kaffeemärkten 1735–1810. Eine preishistorische Studie zur Geschichte eines Welthandelsgutes', in Rainer Gömmel and Markus A. Denzel (eds), *Weltwirtschaft und Wirtschaftsordnung (Festschrift Jürgen Schneider)* (Stuttgart, 2002), pp. 151–68.

Gersdorff, Dagmar von, *Goethes Mutter. Eine Biographie* (Frankfurt and Leipzig, 2001).

Gierl, Irmgard, 'Die Einrichtung der Weilheimer Bürgerhäuser von 1650–1724', *Bayerisches Jahrbuch für Volkskunde* (1969): 120–4.

Giesen, Bernhard (ed.), *Nationale und kulturelle Identität. Studien zur Entwicklung des kollektiven Bewußtseins in der Neuzeit* (Frankfurt, 1991).

Gläntzer, Volker, 'Nord-Süd-Unterschiede städtischen Wohnens um 1800 im Spiegel der zeitgenössischen Literatur', in Günter Wiegelmann (ed.), *Nord-Süd-Unterschiede in der städtischen und ländlichen Kultur Mitteleuropas* (Münster, 1985), pp. 73–88.

Goethe, Johann Wolfgang von, 'Der deutsche Gil Blas', in Johann Christoph Sachse, *Der deutsche Gil Blas* (Munich, 1964), pp. 5–6.

Goethe, Johann Wolfgang von, *Briefe an Auguste Gräfin zu Stolberg*, ed. Jürgen Behrens (Frankfurt, 1982).

Goethe, Johann Wolfgang von, *From My Life: Poetry and Truth*, vol. I, trans. R.R. Heitner, *Goethe's Collected Works*, vol. 4 (New York, 1987).

Goldfriedrich, Johann, *Geschichte des deutschen Buchhandels*, vol. 2 (Leipzig, 1908).

Gottsched, Johann Christoph, *Versuch einer Critischen Dichtkunst vor die Deutschen: darinnen erstlich die allgemeinen Regeln der Poesie, hernach alle besondern Gattungen der Gedichte abgehandelt und mit Exempeln erläutert werden, überall aber gezeiget wird, daß das inner Wesen der Poesie in einer Nachahmung der Natur besteht* (Leipzig, 1730).

Graf, Martina, *Buch- und Lesekultur in der Residenzstadt Braunschweig zur Zeit der Spätaufklärung unter Herzog Karl Wilhelm Ferdinand (1770–1806)* (Frankfurt, 1994).

Gramit, David, 'Selling the Serious: The Commodification of Music and Resistance to it in Germany, circa 1800', in W. Weber (ed.), *The Musician as Entrepreneur, 1700–1914: Managers, Charlatans, and Idealists* (Bloomington, Indiana, 2004), pp. 81–101.

Grazia, Victoria de and Furlough, Ellen (eds), *The Sex of Things: Gender and Consumption in Historical Perspective* (Berkeley, CA, 1996).

Griep, Wolfgang and Jäger, Hans-Wolf (eds), *Reisen im 18. Jahrhundert. Neue Untersuchungen* (Heidelberg, 1986).

Grimm, Jacob and Wilhelm, *Deutsches Wörterbuch*, 33 vols (Munich, 1991).

Grosser, Thomas, 'Tour de France – Frankreich als Ziel deutscher Reisender', in Herman Bausinger, Klaus Beyrer and Gottfried Korff (eds), *Reisekultur. Von der Pilgerfahrt zum modernen Tourismus* (Munich, 1991), pp. 229–35.

Grosser, Thomas, 'Der mediengeschichtliche Funktionswandel der Reiseliteratur in den Berichten deutscher Reisender aus dem Frankreich des 18. Jahrhunderts', in Hans-Wolf Jäger (ed.), *Europäisches Reisen im Zeitalter der Aufklärung* (Heidelberg, 1992), pp. 275–310.

Haase, Carl, 'Der Bildungshorizont der norddeutschen Kleinstadt am Ende des 18. Jahrhunderts. Zwei Bücherverzeichnisse der Lesegesellschaften in Wunstorf aus dem Jahre 1794', in Otto Brunner, Hermann Kellenbenz, Erich Maschke and Wolfgang Zorn (eds), *Festschrift Hermann Aubin zum 80. Geburtstag* (2 vols, Wiesbaden, 1965), pp. 518–25.

Haase, Carl, 'Die Buchbestände einiger Lesegesellschaften im Elbe-Weser-Winkel im Jahre 1794', *Stader Jahrbuch* (1977): 56–80.

Habermas, Jürgen, *The Structural Transformation of the Public Sphere: An Inquiry into a Category of Bourgeois Society*, trans. Thomas Burger (Cambridge, MA, 1991).

Hadamowsky, Franz, *Die Josefinische Theaterreform und das Spieljahr 1776/77 des Burgtheaters. Eine Dokumentation* (Vienna, 1978).

Hadamowsky, Franz, *Wiener Theatergeschichte. Von den Anfängen bis zum Ende des Ersten Weltkriegs* (Vienna, 1988).

Hamburgische neue Zeitung (1767–1826).

Hamburgischer Correspondent (1731–1881).

Hardenberg, Karl August von, *Tagebücher und autobiographische Aufzeichungen*, ed. Thomas Stamm-Kuhlmann (Munich, 2000).

Hartmann, Peter Claus, *Kulturgeschichte des Heiligen Römischen Reiches 1648 bis 1806. Verfassung, Religion und Kultur* (Vienna, Cologne and Graz, 2001).

Haupt, Heinz-Gerhard, *Konsum und Handel: Europa im 19. und 20. Jahrhundert* (Göttingen, 2003).

Hauser, Arnold, *Sozialgeschichte der Kunst und Literatur* (Munich, 1972).

Hedinger, Bärbel, *C.F. Hansen in Hamburg, Altona und den Elbvororten. Ein dänischer Architekt des Klassizismus* (Munich and Berlin, 2000).

Hein, Dieter and Schulz, Andreas (eds), *Bürgerkultur im 19. Jahrhundert. Bildung, Kunst und Lebenswelt* (Munich, 1996), pp. 9–16.

Heise, Ulla, *Kaffee und Kaffeehaus. Eine Kulturgeschichte* (Leipzig, 1987).

Helvetien und Deutschland. Kulturelle Beziehungen zwischen der Schweiz und Deutschland in der Zeit von 1770–1830, ed. Hellmut Thomke, Martin Bircher and Wolfgang Proß (Amsterdam and Atlanta, 1994).

Hennebo, Dieter and Hoffmann, Alfred, *Geschichte der deutschen Gartenkunst* (3 vols, Hamburg, 1962–65).

Heß, Corina, 'Die materielle Wohnkultur Danzigs des 17. und 18. Jahrhunderts im Spiegel von Nachlassinventaren' (PhD dissertation, University of Greifswald, 2005).

Heß, Corina, *Danziger Wohnkultur in der Frühen Neuzeit* (Münster, 2007).

Hirsch, Erhard, 'Hortus Oeconomicus: Nutzen, Schönheit, Bildung. Das Dessau-Wörlitzer Gartenreich als Landschaftsgestaltung der europäischen Aufklärung', in Heinke Wunderlich (ed.), *'Landschaft' und Landschaften im achtzehnten Jahrhundert* (Heidelberg, 1995), pp. 179–207.

Hirschfeld, Christian Cay Lorenz, *Theorie der Gartenkunst* (5 vols, Leipzig, 1779–85).

Höher, Peter, 'Konstanz und Wandel in Wohnausstattung und Hauswirtschaft (1630–1899). Das Beispiel Nürtingen am Neckar', in Günter Wiegelmann (ed.), *Wandel der Alltagskultur seit dem Mittelalter* (Münster, 1987), pp. 309–31.

Hollmer, Heide, '"Ohne Künstler kann man nicht leben weder in Süden noch Norden" – Herzogin Anna Amalias Kunstwahrnehmung und Kunstförderung während der Italienreise (1788–1790)', in Joachim Berger (ed.), *Der Musenhof Anna Amalias. Geselligkeit, Mäzenatentum und Kunstliebhaberei im klassischen Weimar* (Cologne, Weimar and Vienna, 2001), pp. 107–24.

Holst, Niels von, 'Beiträge zur Geschichte des Sammlertums und des Kunsthandels in Hamburg von 1700 bis 1840', *Zeitschrift des Vereins für hamburgische Geschichte*, 38 (1939): 253–88.

Hortschansky, Klaus, 'The Musician as Music Dealer in the Second Half of the Eighteenth Century', in Walter Salmen (ed.), *The Social Status of the Professional Musician from the Middle Ages to the Nineteenth Century* (New York, 1983), pp. 189–218.

Hundert Jahre Staatliches Museum Schwerin 1882–1982. Holländische und flämische Malerei des 17. Jahrhunderts (Schwerin, 1982).

Hüsgen, Heinrich Sebastian, *Verrätherische Briefe von Historie und Kunst* (Frankfurt, 1776).

Hüsgen, Heinrich Sebastian, *Nachrichten von Frankfurter Künstlern und Kunst-Sachen enthaltend das Leben und die Werke aller hiesigen Mahler* (Frankfurt, 1780).

Institut für Stadtgeschichte, Frankfurt am Main, records of the Imperial Chamber Court (ICC Frankfurt) 37, 453, 455, 578, 756, 802, 902, 1302.

In Rembrandts Manier. Kopie, Nachahmung und Aneignung in den graphischen Künsten des 18. Jahrhunderts, exhibition catalogue (Bremen and Lübeck, 1986–87).

Inventar der Akten des Reichskammergerichts 1495–1806. Frankfurter Bestand, ed. Inge Kaltwasser (Frankfurt, 2000).

Jaacks, Gisela, 'Landhausleben', in *Gärten, Landhäuser und Villen des hamburgischen Bürgertums. Kunst, Kultur und gesellschaftliches Leben in vier Jahrhunderten* (Hamburg, 1975), pp. 45–52.

Jaacks, Gisela, 'Modechronik, Modekritik oder Modediktat?, Zu Funktion, Thematik und Berichtstil früher deutscher Modejournale am Beispiel des "Journal des Luxus und der Moden"', *Waffen- und Kostümkunde*, 24 (1982): 58–61.

Jardine, Lisa, *Worldly Goods: A New History of the Renaissance* (London, 1996).

Jaumann, Herbert, 'Emanzipation als Positionsverlust. Ein sozialgeschichtlicher Versuch über die Situation des Autors im 18. Jahrhundert', *Zeitschrift für Literaturwissenschaft und Linguistik*, 11 (1981): 46–72.

Jentzsch, Rudolf, *Der deutsch-lateinische Büchermarkt nach den Leipziger Ostermeß-Katalogen von 1740, 1770 und 1800 in seiner Gliederung und Wandlung* (Leipzig, 1912).

Journal des Luxus und der Moden (Weimar, 1786–1813).

Journal für Literatur, Kunst, Luxus und Mode (Weimar, 1815–37).

Jünger, Wolfgang, *Herr Ober, ein' Kaffee! Illustrierte Kulturgeschichte des Kaffeehauses* (Munich, 1955).

Kaiser, Gerhard R. and Seifert, Siegfried (eds), *Friedrich Justin Bertuch (1747–1822). Verleger, Schriftsteller und Unternehmer im klassischen Weimar* (Tübingen, 2000).

Kant, Immanuel, *Anthropology from a Pragmatic Point of View*, ed. Robert B. Louden (Cambridge, 2006).

Kehn, Wolfgang, 'Ästhetische Landschaftserfahrung und Landschaftsgestaltung in der Spätaufklärung: Der Beitrag von Christian Cay Lorenz Hirschfelds Gartentheorie', in Heinke Wunderlich (ed.), *'Landschaft' und Landschaften im achtzehnten Jahrhundert* (Heidelberg, 1995), pp. 1–23.

Kemper, Hans-Georg, Ketelsen, Uwe-K. and Zelle, Carsten (eds), *Barthold Heinrich Brockes (1680–1747) im Spiegel seiner Bibliothek und Bildergalerie* (2 vols, Wiesbaden, 1998).

Kennedy, Rachel, 'Fashion Magazines', in Michael Snodin and John Styles (eds), *Design and the Decorative Arts: Georgian Britain 1714–1838* (London, 2004), pp. 92–3.

Kessel, Martina, *Langeweile. Zum Umgang mit Zeit und Gefühlen in Deutschland vom späten 18. bis zum frühen 20. Jahrhundert* (Göttingen, 2001).

Ketelsen, Thomas, 'Barthold Heinrich Brockes "irdisches Vergnügen" in Gemälden und Zeichnungen. Ein Beitrag zum Sammlungs- und Auktionswesen im frühen 18. Jahrhundert', *Das Achtzehnte Jahrhundert*, 21 (1997): 153–77.

Ketelsen, Thomas, 'Art Auctions in Germany during the Eighteenth Century', in Michael North and David Ormrod (eds), *Art Markets in Europe 1500–1800* (Aldershot, 1998), pp. 143–52.

Ketelsen, Thomas and Stockhausen, Tilmann von, *Verzeichnis der verkauften Gemälde im deutschsprachigen Raum vor 1800*, vol. 1: *A–Hi* (Munich, 2002).

Kevorkian, Tanya, 'Changing Times, Changing Music: "New Church" Music and Musicians in Leipzig, 1699–1750', in William Weber (ed.), *The Musician as Entrepreneur, 1700–1914* (Bloomington, IN, 2004), pp. 61–80.

Kiesel, Helmuth and Münch, Paul, *Gesellschaft und Literatur im 18. Jahrhundert. Voraussetzungen und Entstehung des literarischen Marktes in Deutschland* (Munich, 1977).

Kleinert, Annemarie, *Die frühen Modejournale in Frankreich. Studien zur Literatur der Mode von den Anfängen bis 1848* (Berlin, 1980).

Kleinert, Annemarie, *Le 'Journal des Dames et des Modes' ou la conquête de l'Europe féminine (1797–1839)* (Stuttgart, 2001).

Kleinert, Annemarie and Wagner, Gretel, 'Mode und Politik. Die Vermarktung der französischen Revolution in Frankreich und Deutschland (1789–1793)', *Waffen- und Kostümkunde*, 1 (1959), pp. 24–38.

Klessmann, Eckart, *Geschichte der Stadt Hamburg* (Hamburg, 1981).

Koch, Hugo, *Sächsische Gartenkunst* (Berlin, 1910, reprint Beucha, 1999).

Koch-Mertens, Wiebke, *Der Mensch und seine Kleider*, vol. 1: *Die Kulturgeschichte der Mode bis 1900* (Düsseldorf, 2000).

König-von Dach, Charlotte, *Johann Ludwig Aberli, 1723–1786* (Berne, 1987).

Köhler, Johann David, *Anweisung zur Reiseklugheit für junge Gelehrte, um Bibliotheken, Münzkabinette, Antiquitätenzimmer, Bildergalerien, Naturalienkabinette und Kunstkammern mit Nutzen zu besehen*, ed. Johann Friedrich August Kinderling (2 vols, Magdeburg, 1788).

Kölsch, Gerhard, 'Die Gemäldesammlung der Prinzessin Henriette Amalie von Anhalt-Dessau sowie ihre weitern Sammlungen im Überblick', in Manfred Großkinsky and Norbert Michels (eds), *Die verstoßene Prinzessin. Kunst, Karriere und Vermächtnis der Henriette Amalie von Anhalt-Dessau* (Frankfurt, 2002), pp. 71–90.

Kopitzsch, Franklin, *Grundzüge einer Sozialgeschichte der Aufklärung in Hamburg und Altona* (2nd edn, Hamburg, 1990).

Korff, Gottfried, 'Museumsreisen', in Herman Bausinger, Klaus Beyrer and Gottfried Korff (eds), *Reisekultur. Von der Pilgerfahrt zum modernen Tourismus* (Munich, 1991), pp. 311–19.

Korthals-Altes, Everard, 'The Art Tour of Friedrich of Mecklenburg-Schwerin', *Simiolus*, 31(3) (2004–05): 216–50.

Krämer, Jörg, *Deutschsprachiges Musiktheater im späten 18. Jahrhundert. Typologie, Dramaturgie und Anthropologie einer populären Gattung* (Tübingen, 1998).

Krämer, Jörg, 'Auge und Ohr. Rezeptionsweisen im deutschen Musiktheater des späten 18. Jahrhunderts'', in Erika Fischer-Lichte and Jörg Schönert (eds), *Theater im Kulturwandel des 18. Jahrhunderts. Inszenierung und Wahrnehmung von Körper – Musik – Sprache* (Göttingen, 1999), pp. 109–32.

Krasnobaev, B.I., Robel, Gert and Zeman, Herbert (eds), *Reisen und Reisebeschreibungen im 18. und 19. Jahrhundert als Quellen der Kulturbeziehungsforschung* (Essen, 1987).

Krebs, Roland, *L'Idée de 'Théâtre National' dans L'Allemagne des Lumières. Théorie et Réalisations* (Wiesbaden, 1985).

Krieger, Martin, '"Ein scharfsinniger Gelehrter, und dabey ein redlicher Mann ..." – Zur Biographie Johann Georg Keyßlers, Privatgelehrter und Erzieher bei den Grafen Bernstorff (1689–1743)', *Zeitschrift der Gesellschaft für Schleswig-Holsteinische Geschichte*, 125 (2000): 63–89.

Krieger, Martin, 'Patriotismus-Diskurs und die Konstruktion kollektiver Identitäten in Hamburg in der ersten Hälfte des 18. Jahrhunderts' (Habilitation thesis, University of Greifswald, 2001).

Kripsin, Stefanie, *'bei seinem Vergnügen in müßigen Stunden unterhalten seyn'. Lesegesellschaften in Detmold um 1800* (Bielefeld, 1999).

Krünitz, Johann Georg, *Oeconomische Encyclopädie* (Berlin, 1779).

Kuczynski, Ingrid, 'Ins gelobte Land der Freiheit und des Wohlstands: Reisen nach England', in Herman Bausinger, Klaus Beyrer and Gottfried Korff (eds), *Reisekultur. Von der Pilgerfahrt zum modernen Tourismus* (Munich, 1991), pp. 237–43.

Kuhles, Doris, 'Das "Journal des Luxus und der Moden" (1786–1827). Zur Entstehung seines inhaltlichen Profils und seiner journalistischen Struktur', in Gerhard R. Kaiser and Siegfried Seifert (eds), *Friedrich Justin Bertuch (1747–1822). Verleger, Schriftsteller und Unternehmer im klassischen Weimar* (Tübingen, 2000), pp. 489–99.

Kuhles, Doris, *Journal des Luxus und der Moden 1786–1827. Analytische Bibliographie mit sämtlichen 517 schwarzweißen und 976 farbigen Abbildungen der Originalzeitschrift* (Munich, 2003).

Kutter, Uli, *Reisen – Reisehandbücher – Wissenschaft: Materialien zur Reisekultur im 18. Jahrhundert* (Neuried, 1996).

Laird, Mark, *The Formal Garden: Traditions of Art and Nature* (London, 1992).

Lauts, Jan, *Karoline Luise von Baden. Ein Lebensbild aus der Zeit der Aufklärung* (Karlsruhe, 1980, 2nd edn, 1990).

Lehmann, Peter Ambrosius, *Die vornehmsten Europäischen Reisen* (Hamburg, 1729).

Leisewitz, Johann Anton, *Johann Anton Leisewitzens Tagebücher*, ed. Heinrich Mack and Johannes Lochner (2 vols, Weimar, 1920).

Linder, Jutta, *Ästhetische Erziehung: Goethe und das Weimarer Hoftheater* (Bonn, 1991).

Lippincott, Louise, *Selling Art in Georgian London: The Rise of Arthur Pond* (New Haven and London, 1983).

Luther, Edith, *Johann Friedrich Frauenholz (1758–1822). Kunsthändler und Verleger in Nürnburg* (Nuremberg, 1988).

Magazin der Musik, ed. Carl Friedrich Cramer (Hamburg, 1783–86).

Mai, Ekkehard (ed.), *'Vom Adel der Malerei'. Holland um 1700* (Cologne, 2006).

Mančal, Josef, 'Zu Musik und Aspekten des Musikmarkts des 18. Jahrhunderts', in Sabine Doering-Manteuffel, Josef Mančal and Wolfgang Wüst (eds), *Pressewesen der Aufklärung. Periodische Schriften im Alten Reich* (Berlin, 2001), pp. 412–15.

Martens, Wolfgang, *Die Botschaft der Tugend. Die Aufklärung im Spiegel der deutschen Moralischen Wochenschriften* (Stuttgart, 1968).

Mathieu, Kai and Fischer, Manfred F., 'Baukunst und Architekten', in *Gärten, Landhäuser und Villen des hamburgischen Bürgertums. Kunst, Kultur und gesellschaftliches Leben in vier Jahrhunderten* (Hamburg, 1975), pp. 26–44.

Maurer, Michael (ed.), *Ich bin mehr Herz als Kopf. Sophie von La Roche. Ein Lebensbild in Briefen* (Leipzig and Weimar, 1985).

Maurer, Michael, *Aufklärung und Anglophilie in Deutschland* (Göttingen, 1987).

Maurer, Michael, 'Italienreisen – Kunst und Konfession', in Herman Bausinger, Klaus Beyrer and Gottfried Korff (eds), *Reisekultur. Von der Pilgerfahrt zum modernen Tourismus* (Munich, 1991), pp. 221–9.

Maurer-Schmoock, Sybille, *Deutsches Theater im 18. Jahrhundert* (Tübingen, 1982).

Mayer, Johann Prokop, *Pomona Franconia: Description des arbres fruitiers les plus connus et les plus éstimés en Europe, qui se cultivent maintenent au Jardin de La Cour de Wurzbourg*, vol. 1 (Nuremberg, 1776).

McKendrick, Neil, Brewer, John and Plumb, J.H., *The Birth of a Consumer Society: The Commercialization of Eighteenth-Century England* (London, 1982).

McClellan, A., 'Watteau's Dealer: Gersaint and the Marketing of Art in Eighteenth-Century Paris', *Art Bulletin,* 78 (1996): 439–53.

McVeigh, Simon, 'The Musician as Concert-Promoter in London, 1780–1850', in Hans Erich Bödeker, Patrice Veit and Michael Werner (eds), *Mutations de la vie musicale en Europe de 1780 à 1914* (Paris, 2002), pp. 71–89.

Medick, Hans, 'Ein Volk "mit" Büchern. Buchbesitz und Buchkultur auf dem Lande am Ende der Frühen Neuzeit: Laichingen 1748–1820', in Hans-Erich Bödeker (ed.), *Lesekulturen im 18. Jahrhundert* (Hamburg, 1992), pp. 59–94.

Meier, Albert, 'Als Moralist durch Italien. Johann Caspar Goethes "Viaggio per l'Italia fatto nel anno MDCCXL"', in Hans-Wolf Jäger (ed.), *Europäisches Reisen im Zeitalter der Aufklärung* (Heidelberg, 1992), pp. 71–85.

Meier, Albert, 'Textsorten-Dialektik. Überlegungen zur Gattungsgeschichte des Reiseberichts im späten 18. Jahrhundert', in Michael Maurer (ed.), *Neue Impulse der Reiseforschung* (Berlin, 1999), pp. 237–45.

Meiners, Uwe, 'Zur Wohnkultur der münsterschen Bevölkerung in der zweiten Hälfte des 18. Jahrhundert. Eine Fallstudie anhand von Nachlaßverzeichnissen', *Rheinisch-westfälische Zeitschrift für Volkskunde*, 25 (1979–80): pp. 80–103.

Meiners, Uwe, 'Wohnkultur in süddeutschen Kleinstädten vom 17. bis zum 19. Jahrhundert. Soziale Unterschiede und Wertstrukturen', in Günter Wiegelmann (ed.), *Nord-Süd-Unterschiede in der städtischen und ländlichen Kultur Mitteleuropas* (Münster, 1985), pp. 157–222.

Meiners, Uwe, 'Stufen des Wandels. Aspekte der Periodisierung der bürgerlichen und bäuerlichen Kultur im Münsterland (1500–1800)', in Günter Wiegelmann (ed.), *Wandel der Alltagskultur seit dem Mittelalter. Phasen – Epochen – Zäsuren* (Münster, 1987), pp. 275–308.

Melton, James V.H., *The Rise of the Public in Enlightenment Europe* (Cambridge, 2001).

Menninger, Annerose, *Genuss im kulturellen Wandel. Tabak, Kaffee, Tee und Schokolade in Europa (16.–19. Jahrhundert)* (Stuttgart, 2004).

Merck, E., *Johann Heinrich Merck (1741–1791). Ein Leben für Freiheit und Toleranz – Zeitdokumente* (Darmstadt, 1991).

Meyer, Friedrich Johann Lorenz, *Skizzen zu einem Gemälde von Hamburg* (Hamburg, 1802).

Meyer, Reinhart, *Das deutsche Trauerspiel des 18. Jahrhunderts. Eine Bibliographie* (Munich, 1977).

Meyer, Reinhart, 'Der Anteil des Singspiels und der Oper am Repertoire der deutschen Bühnen in der zweiten Hälfte des 18. Jahrhunderts', in *Das deutsche Singspiel im 18. Jahrhundert* (Heidelberg, 1981), pp. 27–76.

Michel, Patrick, 'Quelques aspects du marché de l'art à Paris dans la 2e moitié du XVIIIe siècle: collectionneurs, ventes publiques et marchands', in Michael North (ed.), *Kunstsammeln und Geschmack im 18. Jahrhundert* (Berlin, 2002), pp. 25–46.

Michelletti, Michele (ed.), *Political Virtue and Shopping: Individuals, Consumerism, and Collective Action* (Basingstoke, 2003).

Möhring, Paul, *Von Ackermann bis Ziegel. Theater in Hamburg* (Hamburg, 1970).

Mohrmann, Ruth-Elisabeth, 'Städtische Wohnkultur in Norddeutschland vom 17. bis zum 19. Jahrhundert (aufgrund von Inventaren)', in Günter Wiegelmann (ed.), *Nord-Süd-Unterschiede in der städtischen und ländlichen Kultur Mitteleuropas* (Münster, 1985), pp. 89–155.

Mohrmann, Ruth-Elisabeth, 'Leben und Wohnen in der alten Stadt – Osnabrück im hansestädtischen Vergleich', *Hansische Geschichtsblätter*, 106 (1988): 109–26.

Mohrmann, Ruth-Elisabeth, *Alltagswelt im Land Braunschweig: Städtische und ländliche Wohnkultur vom 16. bis zum frühen 20. Jahrhundert* (2 vols, Münster, 1990).

Möller, Horst, *Aufklärung in Preußen. Der Verleger, Publizist und Geschichtsschreiber Friedrich Nicolai* (Berlin, 1974).

Montias, John Michael, 'Cost and Value in Seventeenth-Century Dutch Art', *Art History*, 10 (1987): pp. 455–66.

Montias, John Michael, 'Estimates of the Number of Dutch Master-Painters, their Earnings and their Output in 1650', *Leidschrift*, 6(3) (1990): 59–74.

Morrow, Mary Sue, *Concert Life in Haydn's Vienna: Aspects of a Developing Musical and Social Institution* (Stuyvesant, NY, 1989).

Morrow, Mary Sue, *German Music Criticism in the Late Eighteenth Century: Aesthetic Issues in Instrumental Music* (Cambridge, 1997).

Mosser, Monique and Teyssot, Georges, *Die Gartenkunst des Abendlandes. Von der Renaissance bis zur Gegenwart* (Stuttgart, 1993).

Mount, H.T., 'The Reception of Dutch Genre Painting in England, 1695–1829' (PhD dissertation, Cambridge University, 1991).

Müller, Ulrich, 'Friedrich Justin Bertuch und die landschaftliche Gartenkunst', in Gerhard R. Kaiser and Siegfried Seifert (eds), *Friedrich Justin Bertuch (1747–1822). Verleger, Schriftsteller und Unternehmer im klassischen Weimar* (Tübingen, 2000), pp. 607–27.

Müller, Winfried, *Die Aufklärung* (Munich, 2002).

Müller-Harang, Ulrike, *Das Weimarer Theater zur Zeit Goethes* (Weimar, 1991).

Musikalisches Kunstmagazin (Berlin, 1782–91).

Nahrstedt, Wolfgang, *Die Entstehung der Freizeit. Dargestellt am Beispiel Hamburgs. Ein Beitrag zur Strukturgeschichte und zur strukturgeschichtlichen Grundlegung der Freizeitpädagogik* (Bielefeld, 1998).

Nehring, Dorothee, 'Die Gartenentwürfe Joseph Furttenbachs d. Ä.', in Monique Mosser and Georges Teyssot (eds), *Die Gartenkunst des Abendlandes. Von der Renaissance bis zur Gegenwart* (Stuttgart, 1993), pp. 156–8.

Neue Bibliothek der wichtigsten Reisebeschreibungen, ed. Friedrich Justin Bertuch, (65 vols, Weimar, 1815–32).

Neueste Gemälde von Wien (Hamburg, 1797).

Neumann, Hildegard, *Der Bücherbesitz der Tübinger Bürger von 1750–1850* (Munich, 1978).

Nicolai, Friedrich, *Beschreibung der Königlichen Residenzstädte Berlin und Potsdam* (Berlin, 1769; reprint Hildesheim, Zurich and New York, 1988).

Nicolai, Friedrich, *Das Leben und die Meinungen des Herrn Magister Sebaldus Nothanker,* vol. 1 (Berlin and Stettin, 1774).

Nicolai, Friedrich, *Beschreibung einer Reise durch Deutschland und die Schweiz im Jahre 1781. Nebst Bemerkungen über Gelehrsamkeit, Industrie, Religion und Sitten* (12 vols, Berlin, 1783–96).

Nicolai, Friedrich, *Beschreibung der Königlichen Residenzstädte Berlin und Potsdam, aller daselbst befindlicher Merkwürdigkeiten, und der umliegenden Gegend* (3 vols, Berlin, 1786).

Niebuhr, Carsten, *Reisebeschreibung nach Arabien und andern umliegenden Ländern* (2 vols, Copenhagen, 1774, 1778).

Niedermeier, Michael, 'Germanen in den Gärten. "Altdeutsche Heldengräber", "gotische" Denkmäler und die patriotische Gedächtniskultur', in Jost Hermand and Michael Niedermeier, *Revolutio germanica. Die Sehnsucht nach der 'alten Freiheit' der Germanen 1750–1820* (Frankfurt, 2002), pp. 21–116.

Nipperdey, Thomas, *Deutsche Geschichte 1800–1866. Bürgerwelt und starker Staat* (Munich, 1983).

North, Gottfried, 'Eine Revolution im Reiseverkehr – Die Schnellpost', in Herman Bausinger, Klaus Beyrer and Gottfried Korff (eds), *Reisekultur. Von der Pilgerfahrt zum modernen Tourismus* (Munich, 1991), pp. 291–7.

North, Michael, *Art and Commerce in the Dutch Golden Age* (London and New Haven, 1997).

North, Michael, *Kommunikation, Handel, Geld und Banken in der Frühen Neuzeit,* Enzyklopädie Deutscher Geschichte, vol. 59 (Munich, 2000).

North, Michael, *Das Goldene Zeitalter. Kunst und Kommerz in der niederländischen Malerei des 17. Jahrhunderts* (Cologne, Weimar and Vienna, 2001).

North, Michael, 'Kunstsammeln in Hamburg im 18. Jahrhundert', in Olaf Matthes and Arne Steinert (eds) *Museum – Musen – Meer. Jörgen Bracker zum 65. Geburtstag* (Hamburg, 2001), pp. 53–65.

North, Michael (ed.), *Kunstsammeln und Geschmack im 18. Jahrhundert* (Berlin, 2002).

North, Michael, 'Kunstsammeln und Geschmack im ausgehenden 18. Jahrhundert: Frankfurt und Hamburg im Vergleich', in Michael North (ed.), *Kunstsammeln und Geschmack im 18. Jahrhundert* (Berlin, 2002), pp. 85–103

North, Michael, 'The Hamburg Art Market and Influences on Northern and Central Europe', *Scandinavian Journal of History*, 28 (2003): 253–61.

North, Michael, *Genuss und Glück des Lebens: Kulturkonsum im Zeitalter der Aufklärung* (Cologne, Weimar and Vienna, 2003).

North, Michael, 'Art Markets', in J. Mokyr (ed.), *The Oxford Encyclopaedia of Economic History*, vol. 1 (Oxford, 2003), pp. 167–74.

North, Michael, 'Die niederländische Republik im 18. Jahrhundert', in Ekkehard Mai, Sander Paarlberg and Gregor J.M. Weber (eds), *Vom Adel der Malerei. Holland um 1700* (Cologne, 2006), pp. 87–98.

North, Michael, 'Auctions and the Emergence of an Art Market in Eighteenth-Century Germany', in Neil De Marchi and Hans J. Van Miegroet (eds), *Mapping Markets for Paintings in Europe, 1450–1750* (Turnhout, 2006), pp. 285–304.

North, Michael, 'Cultural Relations between the Netherlands and the Baltic Region', in Jan Harasimowicz, Piotr Oszczanowski and Marcin Wisłocki (eds), *On the Opposite Sides of the Baltic Sea. Relations between Scandinavian and Central European Countries 2* (Wrocław, 2006), pp. 341–6.

North, Michael, 'Republican Art? Dutch and Swiss Art and Art Production Compared', in André Holenstein, Thomas Maissen and Maarten Prak (eds), *The Republican Alternative. The Netherlands and Switzerland Compared* (Amsterdam, 2008), pp. 193–210.

North, Michael and Ormrod, David (eds), *Markets for Art, 1400–1800* (Aldershot, 1998).

Ormrod, David, 'Dealers, Collectors and Connoisseurship in Seventeenth & Eighteenth-Century London 1660–1760', in Michael North (ed.), *Kunstsammeln und Geschmack im 18. Jahrhundert* (Berlin, 2002), pp. 15–23.

Panke-Kochinke, Birgit, *Göttinger Professorenfamilien. Strukturmerkmale weiblichen Lebenszusammenhangs im 18. und 19. Jahrhundert* (Pfaffenweiler, 1993).

Paul, Jean, 'Brief und bevorstehender Lebenslauf. Konjektural-Biographie, sechste poetische Epistel', in Jean Paul, *Werke*, ed. Norbert Miller, vol. 4 (Munich, 1962).

Pomeranz, Kenneth, *The Great Divergence: China, Europe and the Making of the Modern World Economy* (Princeton, 2000).

Pomian, Krzysztof, *Collectors and Curiosities. Paris and Venice, 1500–1800* (Cambridge, 1990).

Porter, Roy, *The Enlightenment* (2nd edn, Basingstoke, 2001).

Posselt, Franz, *Apodemik oder die Kunst zu reisen. Ein systematischer Versuch zum Gebrauch junger Reisenden aus den Gebildeten Ständen überhaupt und angehender Gelehrten und Künstler* (2 vols, Leipzig, 1795).

Prinz, Michael (ed.), *Der lange Weg in den Ueberfluss. Anfänge und Entwicklung der Konsumgesellschaft seit der Vormoderne* (Paderborn, 2003).

Pullat, Raimo, *Die Nachlassverzeichnisse der deutschen Kaufleute in Tallinn 1702–1750* (Tallinn, 1997).

Purdy, Daniel L., *The Tyranny of Elegance: Consumer Cosmopolitanism in the Era of Goethe* (Baltimore, 1998).

Raabe, Mechthild, *Leser und Lektüre im 18. Jahrhundert. Die Ausleihbücher der Herzog August Bibliothek Wolfenbüttel 1714–1799* (4 vols, Munich, London and New York, 1989).

Raeber, Willi, *Caspar Wolf 1735–1783. Sein Leben und sein Werk* (Munich, 1979).

Rapaport, Erika Diane, *Shopping for Pleasure: Women and the Making of London's West End* (Princeton, 2000).

Rauers, Friedrich, *Kulturgeschichte der Gaststätte* (2 vols, Berlin, 1942).

Rebel, Ernst, *Faksimile und Mimesis. Studien zur deutschen Reproduktionsgrafik des 18. Jahrhunderts* (Mittenwald, 1981).

Rees, Joachim, 'Vom Fürst und Bürgerfreund. Zum Funktionswandel der Prinzenreise in der zweiten Hälfte des 18. Jahrhunderts – ein Generationsvergleich aus Schwarzburg-Rudolstadt', in Marcus Ventzke (ed.), *Hofkultur und aufklärerische Reformen in Thüringen. Die Bedeutung des Hofes im späten 18. Jahrhundert* (Cologne, Weimar and Vienna, 2002), pp. 100–37.

Rees, Joachim, Siebers, Winfried and Tilgner, Hilmar, 'Reisen im Erfahrungsraum Europa. Forschungsperspektiven zur Reisetätigkeit politisch-sozialer Eliten des Alten Reiches (1750–1800)', *Das Achtzehnte Jahrhundert*, 26 (2002): 35–62.

Reichert, Johann Friedrich, *Hortus Reichertianus, oder vollständiger Catalog für Handelsgärtner und Liebhaber der Gärtnerei* (Weimar, 1804).

Reichardt, Johann Friedrich and Goethe, Johann Wolfgang von, *Briefwechsel*, ed. Volkmar Braunbehrens, Gabriele Busch-Salmen and Walter Salmen (Weimar, 2002).

Reinhardt, Helmut, 'Gartenkunst in Deutschland im 18. Jahrhundert: Klassik, Rokoko und Neoklassizismus', in Monique Mosser and Georges Teyssot (eds), *Die Gartenkunst des Abendlandes. Von der Renaissance bis zur Gegenwart* (Stuttgart, 1993), pp. 289–300.

Reipsch, Ralph-Jürgen, 'Telemanns "Bluhmen-Liebe"', in *Günter Fleischhauer zum 60. Geburtstag am 8 Juli 1988, Telemann-Beiträge: Abhandlungen und Berichte*, 2 (1989): 34–46.

Rheinische Musen (Mannheim, 1794–97).

Riemer, Robert, 'Exotische Genußmittel: Kaffee, Tabak, Tee, Zucker. Mit Schwerpunkt beim Kaffee und seiner Sozialgeschichte in Form der Kaffeehäuser – von ihrem Aufkommen bis in die Mitte des 19. Jahrhunderts' (seminar paper, University of Greifswald, 1999).

Riesbeck, Johann Kaspar, *Briefe eines reisenden Franzosen über Deutschland. An seinen Bruder in Paris*, vol. 1 (n.p. [Zurich], 1783).

Robel, Gert, 'Reisen und Kulturbeziehungen im Zeitalter der Aufklärung', in B.I. Krasnobaev, Gert Robel and Herbert Zeman (eds), *Reisen und Reisebeschreibungen im 18. und 19. Jahrhundert als Quellen der Kulturbeziehungsforschung* (Essen, 1987), pp. 9–37.

Roche, Daniel, *The Culture of Clothing. Dress and Fashion in the Ancien Regime* (Cambridge, 1994).

Rosenstrauch, Hazel, *Buchhandelsmanufaktur und Aufklärung. Die Reformen des Buchhändlers und Verlegers Ph. E. Reich (1717–1787)* (Frankfurt, 1986).

Rostow, Walt Whitman, *The Stages of Economic Growth: A Non-Communist Manifesto* (Cambridge, 1960).

Rudolphi, Johann Chr., *Nelkentheorie oder eine in systematischer Ordnung nach der Natur gemalte Nelkentabelle* (Meißen, 1787).

Runge, Hartmut, *Dessauer Theaterbilder. Zur 200-jährigen Geschichte des Theaters in Dessau* (Dessau, 1994).

Saldern, Adelheid von, 'Im Hause, zu Hause. Wohnen im Spannungsfeld von Gegebenheiten und Aneignungen', in Jürgen Reulecke (ed.), *Geschichte des Wohnens*, vol. 3: *1800–1918. Das bürgerliche Zeitalter*, (Stuttgart, 1997), pp. 145–332.

Salmen, Walter, *Johann Friedrich Reichardt, Komponist, Schriftsteller, Kapellmeister und Verwaltungsbeamter der Goethezeit* (Hildesheim, 2002).

Sandgruber, Roman, *Die Anfänge der Konsumgesellschaft. Konsumgüterverbrauch, Lebensstandard und Alltagskultur in Österreich im 18. und 19. Jahrhundert* (Vienna, 1982), pp. 193–6.

Schaller, Marie-Louise, *Annäherung an die Natur. Schweizer Kleinmeister in Bern 1750–1800* (Berne, 1990).

Scheibe, Jörg, *Der 'Patriot' (1724–1726) und sein Publikum. Untersuchungen über die Verfasserschaft und die Leserschaft einer Zeitschrift der frühen Aufklärung* (Göppingen, 1973).

Schiller, Friedrich von, *Werke. Nationalausgabe*, vol. 31, ed. Stefan Ormanns (Weimar, 1985).

Schleuning, Peter, *Die Freie Fantasie. Ein Beitrag zur Erforschung der klassischen Klaviermusik* (Göppingen, 1973).

Schleuning, Peter, *Der Bürger erhebt sich. Geschichte der deutschen Musik im 18. Jahrhundert* (Stuttgart, 2000).

Schlögl, Rudolf, 'Geschmack und Interesse. Privater Bildbesitz in rheinisch-westfälischen Städten vom 18. bis zum beginnenden 19. Jahrhundert', in Hans-Ulrich Thamer (ed.), *Bürgertum und Kunst in der Neuzeit* (Cologne, 2002), pp. 125–57.

Schloß Wilhelmshöhe Kassel. Antikensammlung, Gemäldegalerie Alte Meister, Graphische Sammlung, ed. Peter Gercke, Christiane Lukatis, Bernhard Schnackenburg et al. (Munich, London and New York, 2000).

Schlözer, August Ludwig, *Vorlesungen über Land- und Seereisen (1795/96)* (Göttingen, 1962).

Schmidt, Friedrich Ludwig, *Denkwürdigkeiten des Schauspielers, Schauspieldichters und Schauspieldirectors Friedrich Ludwig Schmidt (1772–1841)*, comp. and ed. Hermann Uhde (2nd edn, 2 vols, Stuttgart, 1878).

Schmidt, Georg, 'Das Jahr 1783: Goethe, Herder und die Zukunft Weimars', in Marcus Ventzke (ed.), *Hofkultur und aufklärerische Reformen in Thüringen. Die*

Bedeutung des Hofes im späten 18. Jahrhundert (Cologne, Weimar and Vienna, 2002), pp. 138–68.

Schmidt, Siegfried J., *Die Selbstorganisation des Sozialsystems Literatur im 18. Jahrhundert* (Frankfurt, 1989).

Schmidt, Ulrich, 'Die privaten Kunstsammlungen in Frankfurt am Main von ihren Anfängen bis zur Ausbildung der reinen Kunstsammlung' (PhD dissertation, University of Göttingen, 1960).

Schmidt-Linsenhoff, Victoria and Wettengl, Kurt, *Bürgerliche Sammlungen in Frankfurt 1700–1830* (Frankfurt, 1988).

Schmitt, Peter, *Schauspieler und Theaterbetrieb. Studien zur Sozialgeschichte des Schauspielerstandes im deutschsprachigen Raum 1700–1900* (Tübingen, 1990).

Schnabel, Johann Gottfried, *Wunderliche Fata einiger See-Fahrer, absonderlich Alberti Julii, eines gebohrnen Sachsens, und seiner auf der Insel Felsenburg errichteten in vollkommenen Stand gebrachten Colonien* (Nordhausen, 1731–43).

Schneider, Angelika, 'Friedrich Justin Bertuch – ein Beförderer der Gartenkunst', in Gerhard R. Kaiser and Siegfried Seifert (eds), *Friedrich Justin Bertuch (1747–1822). Verleger, Schriftsteller und Unternehmer im klassischen Weimar* (Tübingen, 2000), pp. 629–57.

Schneider, Jürgen, 'Die neuen Getränke: Schokolade, Kaffee und Tee (16.–18. Jahrhundert)', in Simonetta Cavaciocchi (ed.), in *Prodotti e tecniche d'oltremare nelle economie europee secc. XIII–XVIII* (Prato, 1998), pp. 541–90.

Schramm, Percy Ernst, *Neun Generationen. Dreihundert Jahre deutscher 'Kulturgeschichte' im Lichte der Schicksale einer Hamburger Bürgerfamilie (1648–1948)* (2 vols, Hamburg, 1963–64).

Schultz, Helga, 'Der Verleger Friedrich Justin Bertuch als Kaufmann und Literaturpolitiker', in Gerhard R. Kaiser and Siegfried Seifert (eds), *Friedrich Justin Bertuch (1747–1822). Verleger, Schriftsteller und Unternehmer im klassischen Weimar* (Tübingen, 2000), pp. 331–50.

Schulz, Andreas, 'Der Künstler im Bürger. Dilettanten im 19. Jahrhundert', in Dieter Hein and Andreas Schulz (eds), *Bürgerkultur im 19. Jahrhundert* (Munich, 1996), pp. 34–52.

Schulz, Friedrich, *Reise eines Liefländers von Riga nach Warschau, durch Südpreußen, über Breslau, Dresden, Karlsbad, Bayreuth, Nürnberg, Regensburg, München, Salzburg, Linz, Wien und Klagenfurt, nach Botzen in Tyrol*, vol. 1 (Berlin, 1795).

Schütz, Rosemarie, 'David Roentgen (1743–1807). Der "Königliche Kabinettmacher" aus Neuwied', in Rosemarie Schütz (ed.), *Möbel von Abraham und David Roentgen. Sammlung Kreismuseum Neuwied* (Neuwied, 1990), pp. 17–38.

Schwab, Heinrich W., *Konzert. Öffentliche Musikdarbietungen vom 17. bis 19. Jahrhundert* (Leipzig, 1971).

Schwetschke, Gustav, *Codex nundinarius Germaniae literatae bisecularis. Meß-Jahrbücher des Deutschen Buchhandels*, vol. 1: *Von dem Erscheinen des ersten Meß-Katalogs im Jahre 1564 bis zu der Gründung des ersten Buchhändlervereins im Jahre 1765* (Halle, 1850).

Seibert, Peter, *Der literarische Salon. Literatur und Geselligkeit zwischen Aufklärung und Vormärz* (Stuttgart and Weimar, 1993).

Seifert, Siegfried, '"Genie und Lumpen" – Programmatische Entwürfe Bertuchs zur Reform des deutschen Verlagsbuchhandels vor 1800. Überlegungen zu einem Forschungsansatz', in Gerhard R. Kaiser and Siegfried Seifert (eds), *Friedrich Justin Bertuch (1747–1822). Verleger, Schriftsteller und Unternehmer im klassischen Weimar* (Tübingen, 2000), pp. 291–9.

Sell, Johann Jacob, *Brief über Stettin und die umliegende Gegend auf einer Reise dahin im Sommer 1797 geschrieben* (Berlin, 1800).

Selwyn, Pamela E., *Everyday Life in the German Book Trade: Friedrich Nicolai as Bookseller and Publisher in the Age of Enlightenment 1750–1810* (University Park, PA, 2000).

Shammas, Carole, *The Pre-Industrial Consumer in England and America* (Oxford, 1990).

Siebers, Winfried, 'Bildung auf Reisen. Bemerkungen zur Peregrinatio academica, Gelehrten- und Gebildetenreise', in Michael Maurer (ed.), *Neue Impulse der Reiseforschung* (Berlin, 1999), p. 177–88.

Simanowski, Roberto, *Die Verwaltung des Abenteuers. Massenkultur um 1800 am Beispiel Christian August Vulpius* (Göttingen, 1998).

Slater, Don, *Consumer Culture and Modernity* (Cambridge, 1997).

Solkin, David H., *Painting for Money: The Visual Arts and the Public Sphere in Eighteenth-Century England* (New Haven and London, 1993).

Spohn, Thomas, 'Veränderungen der Tischsitten im Spiegel bürgerlicher Inventare des 17. und 18. Jahrhunderts', *Rheinisch-westfälische Zeitschrift für Volkskunde*, 30/31 (1954): 167–81.

Staatsarchiv Hamburg, Erbschaftsamt, D 71, D 74.

Staatsarchiv Hamburg, Reichskammergerichtsakten, O 17, S 116.

Staatsarchiv Schwerin, Hofstaatssachen – Kunstsammlungen – Angebote und Erwerbungen: 101, Gemäldehändler Morell 1745, f. 14v–15.

Stadtarchiv Hansestadt Stralsund (StA HST), Rep. 37, no. 199; Rep. 3, no. 5384; Rep. 3, no. 5468.

State Archive Latvia/Riga (StA Riga), Vogteigericht no. 1378–1–936; no. 1378–1–94.

Stagl, Justin, 'Der wohl unterwiesene Passagier. Reisekunst und Gesellschaftsbeschreibung vom 16. bis zum 18. Jahrhundert', in B.I. Krasnovaev, Gert Robel and Herbert Zeman (eds), *Reisen und Reisebeschreibungen im 18. und 19. Jahrhundert als Quellen der Kulturbeziehungsforschung* (Essen, 1987), pp. 353–84.

Stagl, Justin, *Eine Geschichte der Neugier. Die Kunst des Reisens 1550–1800* (Vienna, Cologne and Weimar, 2002).

Statistik des Hamburger seewärtigen Einfuhrhandels im 18. Jahrhundert. Nach den Admiralitäts- und Convoygeld-Einnahmebüchern, ed. Jürgen Schneider, Otto-Ernst Krawehl and Markus A. Denzel (St Katharinen, 2001).

Steiner, Walter and Kühn-Stillmark, Uta (eds), *Friedrich Justin Bertuch. Ein Leben im klassischen Weimar zwischen Kultur und Kommerz,* (Cologne, Weimar and Vienna, 2001).

Stockhausen, Tilmann von, 'Kunstauktionen im 18. Jahrhundert. Ein Überblick über das Verzeichnis der verkauften Gemälde im deutschsprachigen Raum', *Das Achtzehnte Jahrhundert,* 26 (2002): 63–78.

Stoewer, Ulfhardt, 'Der "Kulturunternehmer" Friedrich Justin Bertuch im Spiegel seines "Journals des Luxus und der Moden"' (dissertation as part of the state secondary school teachers' examination, University of Greifswald, 2001).

Stollberg-Rilinger, Barbara, *Europa im Jahrhundert der Aufklärung* (Stuttgart, 2000).

Strasser, Susan, McGovern, Charles and Judt, Mathias (eds), *European and American Consumer Societies in the Twentieth Century* (Cambridge, 1998).

Stuck, Gottlieb Heinrich, *Verzeichnis von älteren und neueren Land- und Reisebeschreibungen,* (vols. 1 and 2, Halle, 1783 and 1787, Nachtrag [addendum] to vol. 1, 1785).

Sturm, Leonhard Christoph, *Vollständige Anweisung alle Arten von Bürgerlichen Wohn-Häusern wohl anzugeben* (Augspurg, 1721), fol. B 1a, fol. C 1b.

Stürmer, Michael, *Handwerk und höfische Kultur. Europäische Möbelkunst im 18. Jahrhundert* (Munich, 1982).

Stützel-Prüsener, Marlies, 'Die deutschen Lesegesellschaften im Zeitalter der Aufklärung', in Otto Dann (ed.), *Lesegesellschaften und bürgerliche Emanzipation – Ein europäischer Vergleich* (Munich, 1981), pp. 71–86.

Sulzer, Johann Georg, *Allgemeine Theorie der schönen Künste* (2 vols, Leipzig, 1771, 1774).

Tenner, Helmut, *Mannheimer Kunstsammler und Kunsthändler bis zur Mitte des 19. Jahrhunderts* (Heidelberg, 1966).

The Lady's Magazine or Entertaining Companion for the Fair Sex (London, 1801).

Thomke, Hellmut, Bircher, Martin and Proß, Wolfgang (eds), *Helvetien und Deutschland. Kulturelle Beziehungen zwischen der Schweiz und Deutschland in der Zeit von 1770–1830* (Amsterdam and Atlanta, 1994).

Thurn, Hans Peter, *Der Kunsthändler. Wandlungen eines Berufes* (Munich, 1994).

Tischer, Ernst, Haefs, Wilhelm and Mix, York-Gothart, 'Aufklärung, Öffentlichkeit und Medienkultur in Deutschland im 18. Jahrhundert', in Ernst Tischer, Wilhelm Haefs and York-Gothart Mix (eds), *Von Almanach bis Zeitung. Ein Handbuch der Medien in Deutschland 1700–1800* (Munich, 1999), pp. 18–21.

Torras, Jaume and Yun, Bartolomé (eds), *Consumo, condiciones de vida y comercialización. Cataluña y Castilla, siglos XVII–XIX* (Valladolid, 1999).

Trachsler, Beat, '1750–1790: Ludwig Aberli und Caspar Wolf' and '1790–1810: Die Kleinmeister und ihre Welt', in *Malerische Reisen durch die schöne alte Schweiz* (Zurich, 1982), pp. 88–185.

Trentmann, Frank, 'Beyond Consumerism: New Perspectives on Consumption', *Journal of Contemporary History*, 39(3) (2004): 373–401.

Trentmann, Frank, 'The Modern Genealogy of the Consumer: Meanings, Identities and Political Synapses', in John Brewer and Frank Trentmann (eds), *Consuming Cultures. Global Perspectives: Historical Trajectories, Transnational Exchanges* (Oxford and New York, 2005), pp. 19–69.

Trentmann, Frank, 'Knowing Consumers – Histories, Identities, Practices: An Introduction', in Frank Trentmann (ed.), *Making of the Consumer: Knowledge, Power and Identity in the Modern World* (Oxford and New York, 2006), pp. 1–27.

Trentmann, Frank (ed.), *The Making of the Consumer: Knowledge, Power and Identity in the Modern World* (Oxford and New York, 2006).

Trepp, Anne-Charlott, *Sanfte Männlichkeit und selbständige Weiblichkeit. Frauen und Männer im Hamburger Bürgertum zwischen 1770 und 1840* (Göttingen, 1996).

Treue, Wilhelm, 'Zum Thema der Auslandsreisen im 17. Jahrhundert', *Archiv für Kulturgeschichte*, 35 (1953): 199–212.

Treue, Wilhelm, 'Zum Thema der Auslandsreisen im 18. und 19. Jahrhundert', *Archiv für Kulturgeschichte*, 35 (1953): 328–33.

Umbach, Maiken, *Federalism and Enlightenment in Germany 1740–1806* (London and Rio Grande, Ohio, 2000).

Unseld, Siegfried, *Goethe und seine Verleger* (Frankfurt and Leipzig, 1993).

Van der Woude, Ad and Schuurmann, Anton (eds), *A New Source for the Historical Study of Wealth, Material Culture and Agricultural Development Probate Inventories* (Utrecht, 1980).

Vaterländische Blätter für den österreichischen Kaiserstaat (Vienna, 1808).

Ventzke, Marcus (ed.), *Hofkultur und aufklärerische Reformen in Thüringen. Die Bedeutung des Hofes im späten 18. Jahrhundert* (Cologne, Weimar and Vienna, 2002).

Verzeichnis einer betraechtlichen Gemaeldesammlung von den beruehmtesten Italiaenischen, Deutschen und Niederlaendischen Meistern, welche von den Eigenthümern Kaller und Michael in dem allhiesigen Bildersaal im Creuzgange, Mittwochs den 25ten August durch die Geschwornen Herrn Ausruefer an die Meistbietende gegen baare Bezahlung im 24 fl. Fuß losgeschlagen und ueberlassen werden sollen (Frankfurt, 1790). Städelsches Kunstinstitut, Frankfurt.

Verzeichnis einer betraechtlichen Sammlung von Gemaelden der besten und beruehmesten Teutschen, Italiaenischen und Niederlaendischen Meister, nebst einem Anhang von einigen Kupferstichen. Welche die Jacob Bernusische Beneficial-Erben in ihrem Haus zum großen Saalhof allhier in Frankfurt am Mayn, gleich nach hiesiger Ostermeß, Montag den May 1781 und die folgende Tage, durch oeffentliche Versteigerung zu den Meistbietenden zu überlassen gesonnen sind (Frankfurt, 1780). Städelsches Kunstinstitut, Frankfurt.

Verzeichnis einer Sammlung von Gemaelden, Handzeichnungen, Kupferstichen, Alterthuemern, geschnittenen- und ungeschnitten Steinen, Kunstsachen von Holz und Elfenbein, nebst Kupferwerken, Buechern etc., welche der verstorbene Herr Hofrath H. G.

Huesgen hinterlassen und am 9ten May dieses Jahrs und folgende Taege, dahier oeffentlich versteigert werden sollen (Frankfurt, 1808).

Verzeichnis einer schoenen Gemaelde-Sammlung von Italienischen, hollaendischen und Deutschen Meistern, groeßtenteils in sehr saubern Raehmen, aus einer hiesigen bekannten Verlassenschaft entstehend, welche den 7ten Juny 1793 auf dem Boersen-Saal oeffentlich an den Meistbietenden verkauft werden soll, durch die Mackler: Bostelmann & Pakischefski (Hamburg, 1793), Hamburger Kunsthalle, Hamburg.

Verzeichnis einiger Schildereyen und auserlesener Zeichnungen von den beruehmtesten Meistern, so von dem seel. Herrn Raths-Herrn Brockes gesammelt worden, und allhier im April dieses Jahres oeffentlich an den Meistbietenden verkaufet werden sollen (Hamburg, 1747) Schleswig-Holsteinisches Landesarchiv, Schleswig.

*Verzeichnis von Gemaelden der beruehmtesten Niederlaendischen, Franzoesischen, Italiaenischen und Deutschen Meister, welche von den Freyherrl. Von Berberichschen Erben zu Frankfurt am Mayn in dem Senkenbergischen Stiftungs-Hause nach der naechstbevorstehenden Herbst-Messe, Montags, den 27. September und die darauf folgenden Tage, oeffentlich an den Meistbietenden gegen baare Bezahlung ueberlassen werden sollen (*Frankfurt, 1784). Städelsches Kunstinstitut, Frankfurt.

Verzeichniß der Gemälde, Handzeichnungen, Kupferstiche und Bücher, welche zur Hinterlassenschaft von Herrn Johann Valentin Prehn gehören, und zu Ende nächster Herbstmesse versteigert werden sollen (Frankfurt, 1829).

Vickery, Amanda, *The Gentleman's Daughter: Women's Lives in Georgian England* (New Haven and London, 1998).

Viehberg, Maud Antonia, 'Vom Tauschhandel zum modernen Buchmarkt. Die Etappen des deutschen Buchhandels im 18. Jahrhundert' (MA thesis, University of Greifswald, 2001).

Vries, Jan de, 'Between Purchasing Power and the World of Goods', in John Brewer and Roy Porter (eds), *Consumption and the World of Goods* (London, 1993), pp. 85–132.

Vries, Jan de, 'The Industrial Revolution and the Industrious Revolution', *The Journal of Economic History*, 54 (2) (1994): 249–70.

Weatherill, Lorna, *Consumer Behaviour and Material Culture in Britain, 1660–1760* (London and New York, 1988).

Weber, Walter, 'Von Wirtshäusern, Reisenden und Literaten. Eine kleine Chronique scandaleuse des Wirtshauslebens', in Herman Bausinger, Klaus Beyrer and Gottfried Korff (eds), *Reisekultur. Von der Pilgerfahrt zum modernen Tourismus* (Munich, 1991), pp. 82–90.

Wehler, Hans-Ulrich, *Deutsche Gesellschaftsgeschichte*, vol. 1: *1700–1815* (Munich, 1987).

Welke, Martin, 'Gemeinsame Lektüre und frühe Formen von Gruppenbildung im 17. und 18. Jahrhundert: Zeitungslesen in Deutschland', in Otto Dann (ed.), *Lesegesellschaften und bürgerliche Emanzipation – Ein europäischer Vergleich* (Munich, 1981), pp. 29–53.

Wiegelmann, Günter, *Alltags- und Festspeisen. Wandel und gegenwärtige Stellung* (Marburg, 1967).

Wiegelmann, Günter (ed.), *Nord-Süd-Unterschiede in der städtischen und ländlichen Kultur Mitteleuropas* (Münster, 1985).

Wiegelmann, Günter (ed.), *Wandel der Alltagskultur seit dem Mittelalter. Phasen – Epochen – Zäsuren* (Münster, 1987).

Wielands Briefwechsel, ed. Waltraud Hagen, vol. 7 (January 1778–June 1782), (Berlin, 1992).

Wies, Ruth, 'Das Journal des Luxus und der Moden (1786–1827), ein Spiegel kultureller Strömungen der Goethezeit' (PhD dissertation, University of Munich, 1953).

Wiesehöfer, Josef and Conermann, Stephan (eds), *Carsten Niebuhr (1733–1815) und seine Zeit*, (Stuttgart, 2002).

Wietek, Gerhard, *C. F. Hansen 1756–1845 und seine Bauten in Schleswig-Holstein* (Neumünster, 1982).

Wilhelm, Karl, *Wirtschafts- und Sozialgeschichte des Kunstauktionswesens in Deutschland vom 18. Jahrhundert bis 1945* (Munich, 1990).

Willebrandt, Johann Peter, *Historische Berichte und practische Anmerkungen auf Reisen in Deutschland, in die Niederlande, in Frankreich, England, Dännemark, Böhmen und Ungarn* (Hamburg, 1758).

Wills, John E., 'European Consumption and Asian Production in the Seventeenth and Eighteenth Centuries', in John Brewer and Roy Porter (eds), *Consumption and the World of Goods* (London, 1993), pp. 133–47.

Winckelmann, Johann Joachim, *Sendschreiben von den herculanischen Entdeckungen* (Dresden, 1762).

Winckelmann, Johann Joachim, *Anmerkungen über die Geschichte der Kunst des Alterthums* (Dresden 1767).

Winkler, Lutz, 'Musiktheater in der 2. Hälfte des 18. Jahrhunderts in Stralsund und Greifswald', in Ekkard Ochs, Nico Schüler and Lutz Winkler (eds), *Musica Baltica. Interregionale musikalische Beziehungen im Ostseeraum* (Frankfurt, Berlin and Berne, 1997), pp. 212–25.

Wittmann, Reinhard (ed.), *Bücherkataloge als buchgeschichtliche Quellen in der frühen Neuzeit* (Wiesbaden, 1984).

Wittmann, Reinhard, 'Die frühen Buchhändlerzeitschriften als Spiegel des literarischen Lebens', *Archiv für Geschichte des Buchwesens*, 13 (1973): cols 828–9.

Wittmann, Reinhard, *Geschichte des deutschen Buchhandels. Ein Überblick* (Munich, 1991).

Wittmann, Reinhard, 'Gibt es eine Leserevolution am Ende des 18. Jahrhunderts?', in Roger Chartier and Guglielmo Cavallo (eds), *Die Welt des Lesens. Von der Schriftrolle zum Bildschirm* (Frankfurt, 1999), pp. 419–54.

Wittmann, Walter, *Beruf und Buch im 18. Jahrhundert. Ein Beitrag zur Erfassung und Gliederung der Leserschaft im 18. Jahrhundert, insbesondere unter Berücksichtigung des Einflusses auf die Buchproduktion (Nachlaßinventare 1695–1705, 1746–1755 und 1795–1805)* (Hanover, 1934).

Wolbring, Barbara, 'Auch ich in Arkadien! Die bürgerliche Kunst- und Bildungsreise im 19. Jahrhundert', in Dieter Hein and Andreas Schulz (eds),

Bürgerkultur im 19. Jahrhundert. Bildung, Kunst und Lebenswelt (Munich, 1996), pp. 82–101.

Wolff, Christoph, *Johann Sebastian Bach* (Frankfurt, 2000).

Wurst, Karin A., 'The Self-Fashioning of the Bourgeoisie in Late-Eighteenth-Century German Culture: Bertuch's *Journal des Luxus und der Moden*', *Germanic Review*, 72 (3) (1997): 170–82.

Zedelmaier, Helmut, 'Lesetechniken. Die Praktiken der Lektüre in der Neuzeit', in Helmut Zedelmaier and Martin Mulsow (eds), *Die Praktiken der Gelehrsamkeit in der Frühen Neuzeit* (Tübingen, 2001), pp. 11–30.

Zedler, Johann Heinrich, *Großes Vollständiges Universal-Lexikon*, 68 vols (Leipzig and Halle, 1732–54, reprint, Graz, 1993–99).

Zelle, Carsten, 'Kunstmarkt, Kennerschaft und Geschmack. Zu Theorie und Praxis in der Zeit zwischen Barthold Heinrich Brockes und Christian Ludwig von Hagedorn', in Michael North (ed.), *Kunstsammeln und Geschmack im 18. Jahrhundert* (Berlin, 2002), pp. 217–38.

Zelle, Carsten, 'Auf dem Spielfeld der Autorschaft. Der Schriftsteller des 18. Jahrhunderts im Kräftefeld von Rhetorik, Medienentwicklung und Literatursystem', in Klaus Städtke and Ralph Kray (eds), *Spielräume des auktorialen Diskurses* (Berlin, 2003), pp. 1–37.

Index